The Price Guide to

Antique Edged Weapons

Leslie Southwick

Antique Collectors' Club

ISBN 0 902028 94 4

While every care has been exercised in the compilation of the information contained in this book, neither the author nor the Antique Collectors' Club Ltd. accept any liability for loss, damage or expense incurred by reliance placed on the information contained in this book.

British Library CIP Data
Southwick, Leslie
The price guide to antique edged weapons.
1. Arms and armour — Collectors and collecting
I. Title
739.7′2 U850

Published for the Antique Collectors' Club
by the Antique Collectors' Club Ltd.

The endpapers show the 'Battle of Waterloo' by Denis Dighton (1792-1827). Courtesy National Trust, Plas Newydd.

Printed in England by Baron Publishing, Woodbridge, Suffolk

Antique Collectors' Club

The Antique Collectors' Club was formed in 1966 and now has a five figure membership spread throughout the world. It publishes the only independently run monthly antiques magazine *Antique Collecting* which caters for those collectors who are interested in increasing their knowledge of antiques, both by increasing the members' knowledge of quality as well as in discussing the factors which influence the price that is likely to be asked. The Antique Collectors' Club pioneered the provision of information on prices for collectors and still leads in the provision of detailed articles on a variety of subjects.

It was in response to the enormous demand for information on "what to pay" that the price guide series was introduced in 1968 with the first edition of *The Price Guide to Antique Furniture* (completely revised, 1978), a book which broke new ground by illustrating the more common types of antique furniture, the sort that collectors could buy in shops and at auctions, rather than the rare museum pieces which had previously been used (and still to a large extent are used) to make up the limited amount of illustrations in books published by commercial publishers. Many other price guides have followed, all copiously illustrated, and greatly appreciated by collectors for the valuable information they contain, quite apart from prices. The Antique Collectors' Club also publishes other books on antiques, including horology and art reference works, and a full book list is available.

Club membership, which is open to all collectors, costs £9.95 per annum. Members receive free of charge *Antique Collecting,* the Club's magazine (published every month except August), which contains well-illustrated articles dealing with the practical aspects of collecting not normally dealt with by magazines. Prices, features of value, investment potential, fakes and forgeries are all given prominence in the magazine.

Among other facilities available to members are private buying and selling facilities, the longest list of "For Sales" of any antiques magazine, an annual ceramics conference and the opportunity to meet other collectors at their local antique collectors' club. There are nearly eighty in Britain and so far a dozen overseas. Members may also buy the Club's publications at special pre-publication prices.

As its motto implies, the Club is an amateur organisation designed to help collectors to get the most out of their hobby: it is informal and friendly and gives enormous enjoyment to all concerned.

For Collectors — By Collectors — About Collecting

The Antique Collectors' Club, 5 Church Street, Woodbridge, Suffolk

Price Revision List

Published annually in April
(the first list will be published in 1983)

The usefulness of a book containing prices rapidly diminishes as market values change.

In order to keep the prices in this book updated, a price revision list will be issued in April each year. This will record the major price changes in the values of the items covered under the various headings in the book.

To ensure you receive the price revision list, complete the pro forma invoice inserted in this book and send it to the address below:

ANTIQUE COLLECTORS' CLUB
5 CHURCH STREET, WOODBRIDGE, SUFFOLK

CONTENTS

LIST OF COLOUR PLATES

ACKNOWLEDGEMENTS

This book would not have been possible without the generous help of Christie's and Sotheby's and various dealer friends in supplying the bulk of the photographs. I would like to thank Peter Hawkins, William Tilley and Anthony Thompson of Christie, Manson & Woods, and David Jeffcoat of Sotheby, Parke-Bernet, London, and their offices in New York and Los Angeles. Also Peter Dale Ltd., Weller & Dufty Ltd., the Trustees of the Victoria and Albert Museum, the Trustees of the Wallace Collection, the Director of the National Army Museum, London, and the Director of the National Maritime Museum, Greenwich.

I would especially like to thank the following who allowed objects in their care to be used or who allowed me to draw on their wide knowledge of arms and armour in order to improve this work: A.V.B. Norman, Master of the Tower Armouries, John Wallace, Derek Spalding, Howard Ricketts, Robert Hales, Michael C. German and Dr. J.F. Hayward. Finally, I would like to thank Ian Campbell, who kindly read the text in manuscript and made many useful suggestions.

PREFACE

This book is intended to be a guide to the pricing of swords, daggers and staff weapons, and to provide a useful illustrational reference to the many types of edged weapons in use from the medieval period to the early twentieth century. It is not meant to be a history, nor does it claim to be comprehensive. The select bibliography provides a list of works, specialising in various aspects of the history of edged weapons; also included is an illustrated section on terminology, as well as a glossary. It is hoped these will be of use and interest both to the student and to the collector.

Most of the examples in this book fall within the price range of £50-£1,000. However, in order to compare and contrast the quality and value of individual items, some of the finest extant pieces have been included as well as some very plain examples.

What gives an object its value? First demand. Certain weapons hold or increase their value simply because collectors want to buy them. Rapiers are a good example. They are the most popular European edged weapons and, although many appear on the market, value continually increases. When fine examples appear, competition increases and prices rise considerably. The second factor affecting value is rarity. Rare objects are bound to command higher prices.

Quality and condition are, however, the most important factors. A rapier with a silvered or chiselled hilt or retaining an original blued finish will of course fetch a higher price than a worn example retaining none of its original finish. Condition is particularly important when comparing regulation arms or the many different types of eastern sword which appear each year. There are many to choose from because many were made; therefore buy the one in the best condition.

The fairest way of assessing the value of an antique is by competitive bidding at auction. Auction houses are the market place and those who bid (the dealers and the experienced collectors) know why they are bidding, know the market value of an object and bring a great deal of experience to bear on their choice of purchase. Thus, if you are unsure about what you want to buy, ask the advice of a reputable dealer. The object may cost you a little more, but you will have a dealer's reputation and guarantee to support you.

The book has been divided into three main sections, and each section sub-divided, either into a named group of weapons or into a recognisable typological grouping. I hope this will give the reader easy access to the type of weapon he wants to find. Combination weapons have been included under their main sections rather than grouped separately. The sub-section termed 'Eastern swords and open-hilted swords' includes the various types of eastern sword and swords which do not fit easily into other categories. They are predominantly swords with simple guards or cross-hilted, curve-bladed weapons, as opposed to the cross-hilted medieval sword.

The descriptions have been kept to a minimum and the illustrations allowed to speak for themselves. In the cases of weapons which I have not been able to examine personally, I have used auction and dealers' catalogues for length (where known), inscriptions or maker's marks or signatures.

TERMINOLOGY

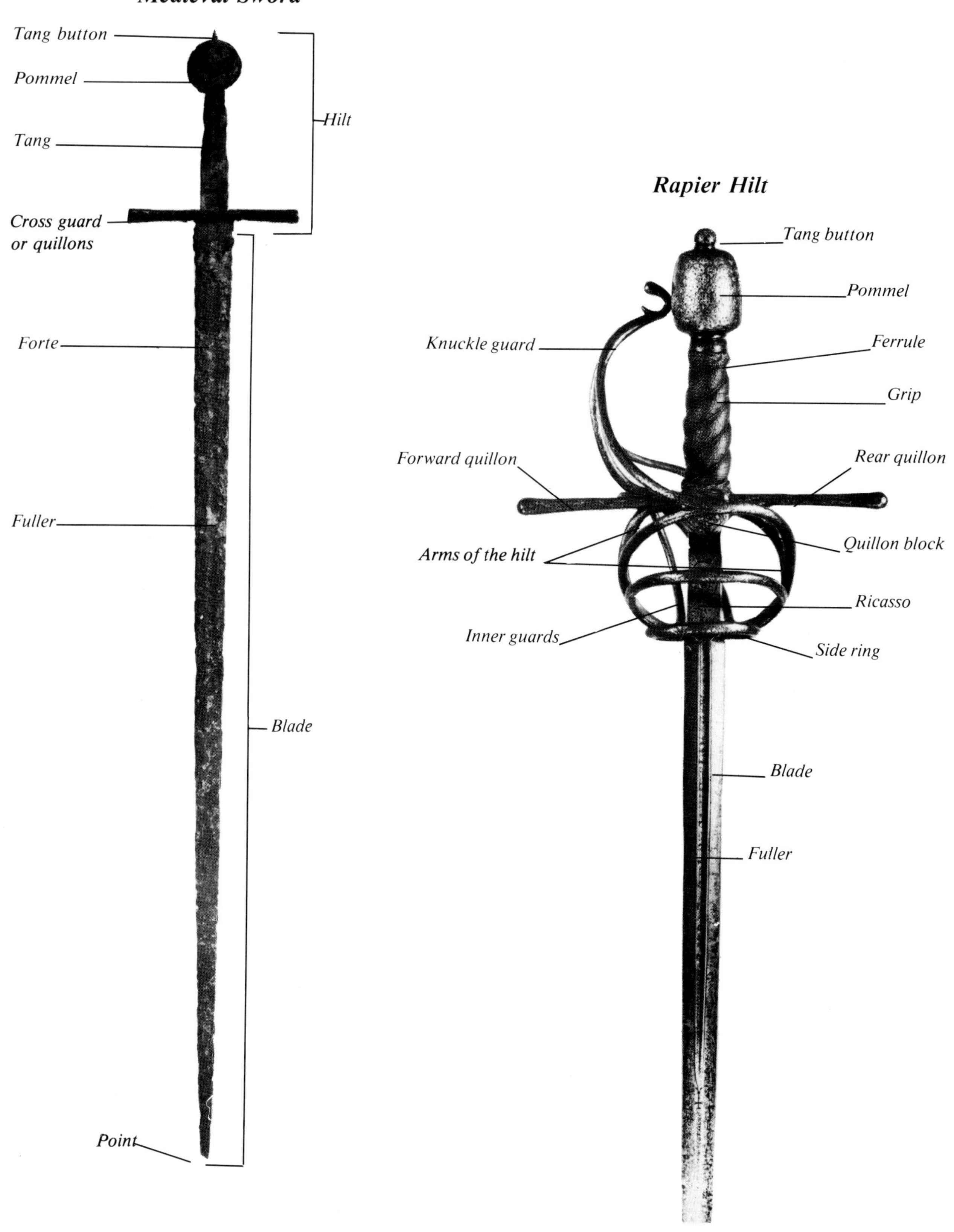

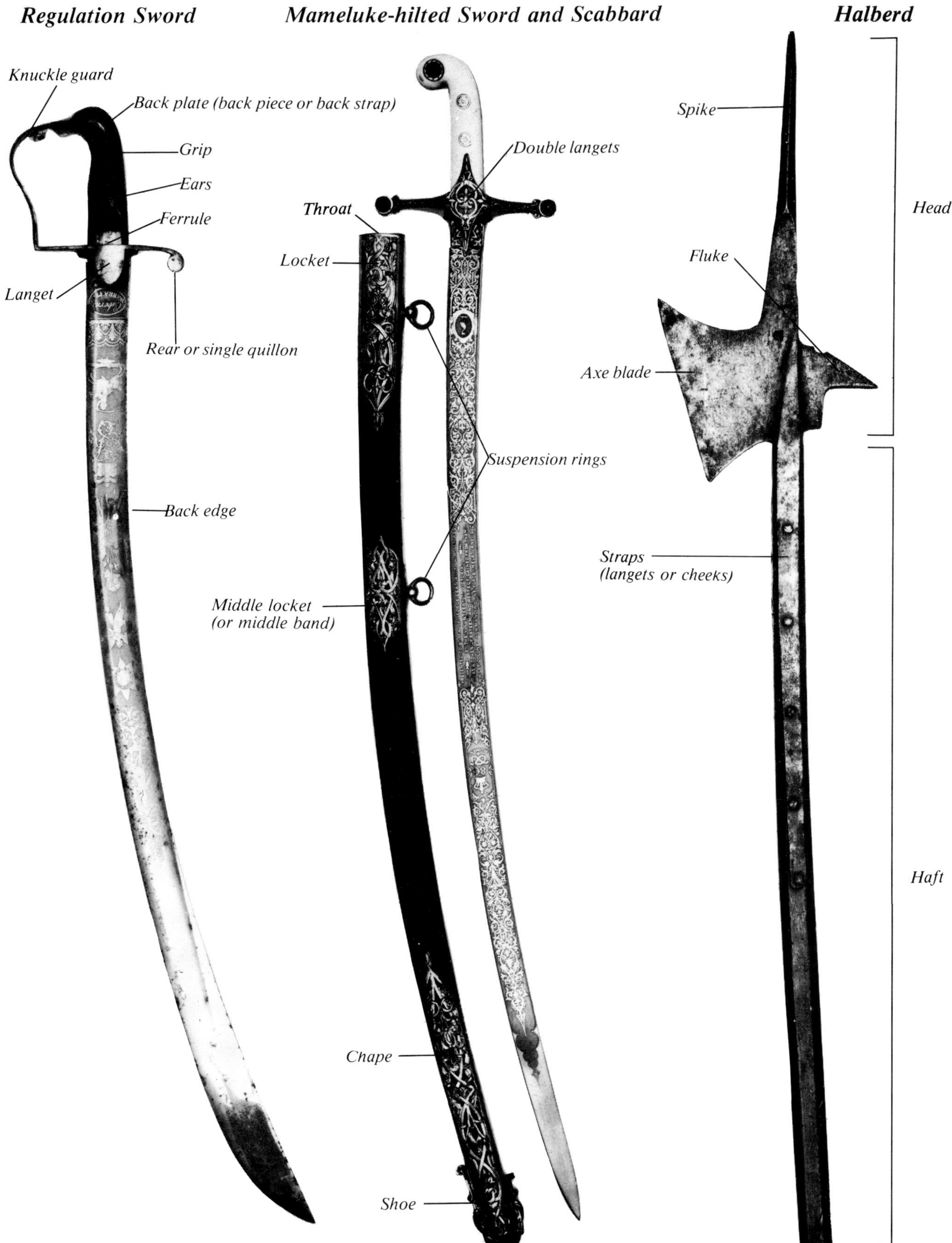
Regulation Sword
Mameluke-hilted Sword and Scabbard
Halberd
Knuckle guard
Back plate (back piece or back strap)
Grip
Ears
Ferrule
Langet
Rear or single quillon
Back edge
Double langets
Throat
Locket
Suspension rings
Middle locket
(or middle band)
Chape
Shoe
Spike
Head
Fluke
Axe blade
Straps
(langets or cheeks)
Haft

1. SWORDS

Cross-hilted swords and early hilt development

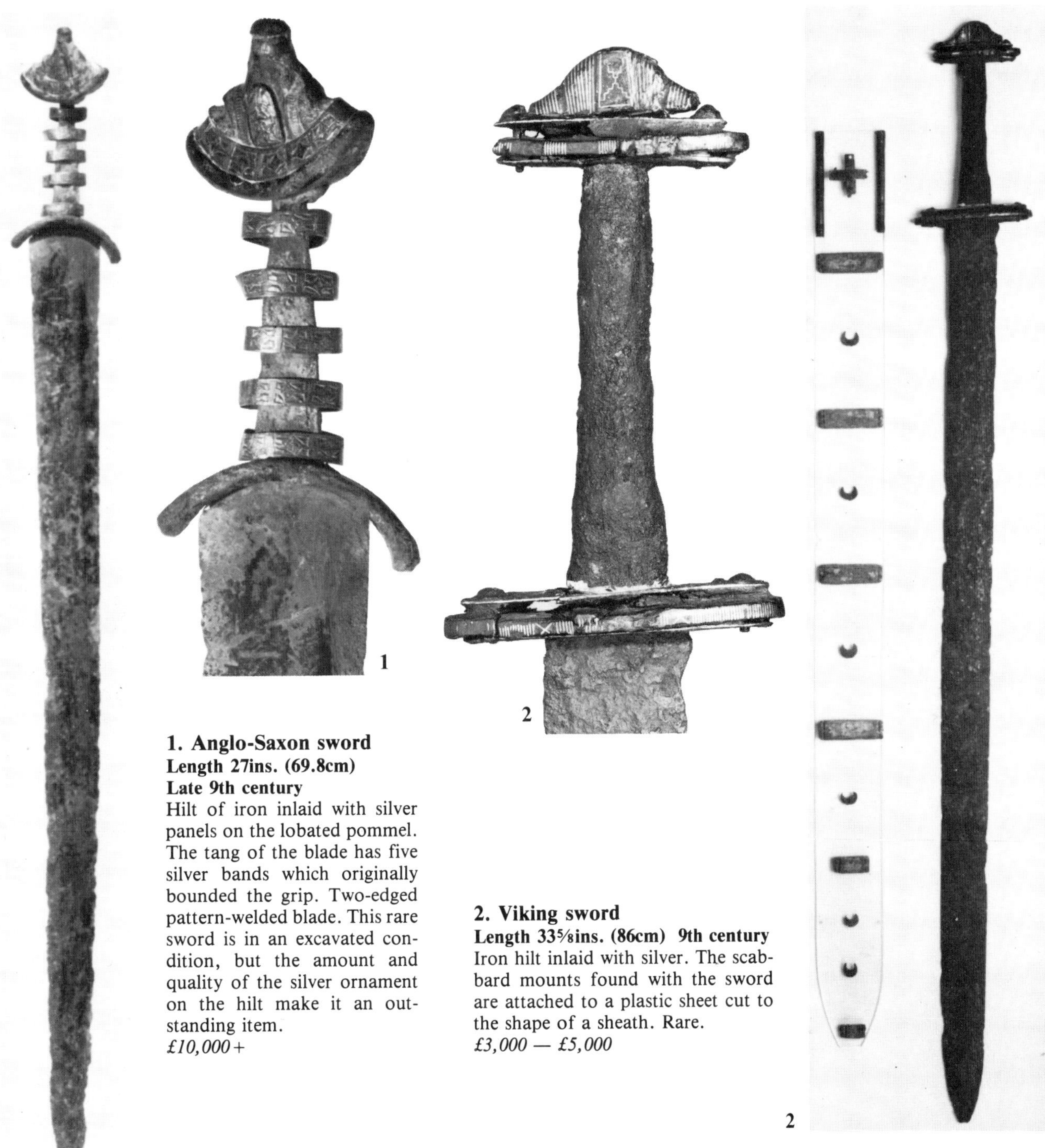

1. Anglo-Saxon sword
Length 27ins. (69.8cm)
Late 9th century
Hilt of iron inlaid with silver panels on the lobated pommel. The tang of the blade has five silver bands which originally bounded the grip. Two-edged pattern-welded blade. This rare sword is in an excavated condition, but the amount and quality of the silver ornament on the hilt make it an outstanding item.
£10,000+

2. Viking sword
Length 33⅝ins. (86cm) 9th century
Iron hilt inlaid with silver. The scabbard mounts found with the sword are attached to a plastic sheet cut to the shape of a sheath. Rare.
£3,000 — £5,000

Photographs: Christie's

3. Viking sword

Blade 30¼ins. (76.5cm) 9th/10th century

Iron hilt decorated with brass inlay on the pommel. The pattern-welded two-edged blade has a figure-of-eight mark on the forte.

£1,500 — £3,000

5

6

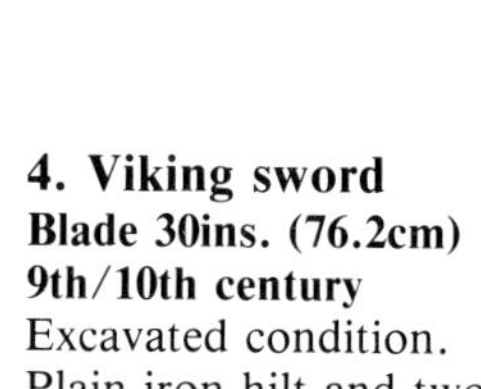

4. Viking sword

Blade 30ins. (76.2cm)
9th/10th century

Excavated condition. Plain iron hilt and two-edged blade badly corroded, especially on the edges.

£800 — £1,200

5. Knightly sword

Blade 30½ins. (77.5cm)
Late 12th century

Excavated condition. Iron hilt. The corroded blade has a full-length fuller.

£1,000 — £1,500

3

6. Unusual medieval sword

Length 36ins. (91.4cm) Second half 13th century

Iron hilt with horn-like quillons turned down towards the blade, and similar design inverted on the pommel. Excavated condition. Now in the Tower of London Armouries (IX-1107).

£800 — £1,500

Photographs:
3-5 Christie's;
6 Sotheby's

4

7. Medieval knightly sword

Blade 30½ins. (77.5cm) About 1300
Iron hilt with straight quillons of rounded section and flat-sided 'wheel' pommel. Tapered blade with wide fuller. A beautifully proportioned sword of classic form.
£3,000

8. Knightly sword

Blade 27½ins. (70cm)
About 1300
Similar to 7 but with horizontal quillons widening at the tips, and with brass 'wheel' pommel. Good quality.
£1,000 — £1,500

9. Knightly sword

Blade 31ins. (78.7cm)
Early 14th century
A well-proportioned sword; the blade with three fullers on each side.
£2,000 — £3,000

10. Unusual medieval sword

Blade 34ins. (86.3cm)
14th century
Excavated condition. Most medieval swords of this form have two-edged blades. This example has, on one side, a flattened blunted edge for two-thirds of its length.
£500 — £600

7

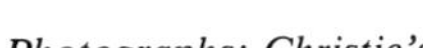

Photographs: Christie's

8 9 10

11

11. Knightly sword
Length 31½ins. (80cm) About 1300-1325
Iron hilt with slightly arched quillons and wheel pommel with a coat of arms set within a recess. The pommels on swords 9 and 15 were probably also inlaid with a similar device. Rare.
£3,000 — £4,000

Photographs: Christie's

12

12. Medieval boy's sword
Blade 17⅜ins. (44.2cm), length overall 21⅞ins. (55.2cm) First half 14th century
Iron hilt retaining the wooden core of the grip. Rare. See also 19.
£800 — £1,500

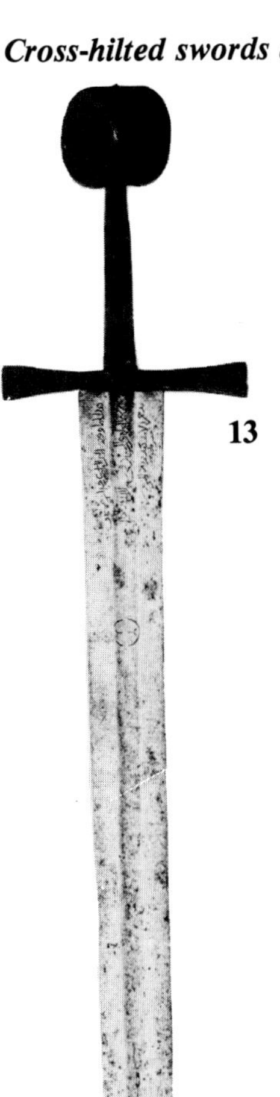

13

14. Italian sword
Length 40ins. (101.6cm) About 1400-1420
Blade with twig mark on each side and with Arabic inscription recording its presentation to a Turkish arsenal, probably that at Alexandria. Swords with similar inscriptions are believed to have been captured by Sultan Barsbay when he raided Cyprus in 1426 (see also 38). Rare and of fine quality. Good condition. Grip missing.
£2,000 — £4,000

15. Knightly sword
Blade 31¼ins. (79.4cm) Early 15th century
Wheel pommel with protruding sides recessed for a coat of arms (see 11). Good quality. Excavated condition.
£2,000 — £4,000

16

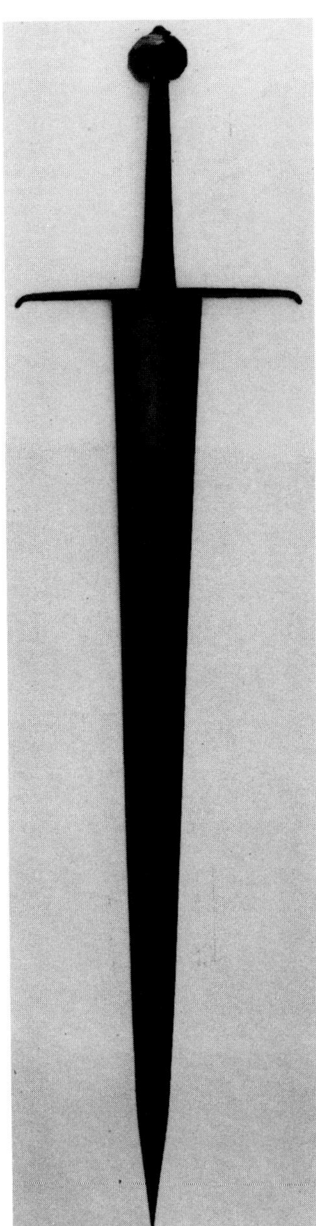

14

15

13. European knightly sword
Length 35½ins. (90.2cm) 14th century
Two-edged blade with Arabic inscription stating its presentation by his Excellency Nasir ad-Din Muhammed Ibn Hamud, to commemorate exploits performed during a holy campaign. Bladesmith's marks, an S and cross encircled. An elegant sword of fine quality. Grip missing.
£5,000 — £6,000

16. Knightly sword
About 1420-1450
Similar to the fighting sword in Westminster Abbey believed to have belonged to Henry V (1413-22). Excavated condition.
£1,200 — £2,000

Photographs: 13, 14 and 16 Sotheby's; 15 Christie's

18. Rare English two-hand sword
Blade 44¼ins. (112.4cm) Late 15th century
In excavated condition. One of only a small number known to exist (see Oakeshott, 1980, p. 146).
£1,200 — £1,800

19. Medieval boy's sword
Blade 24¾ins. (62.8cm) First half 15th century
Rare. Reasonable condition.
£600 — £800

20. Knightly sword
Blade 37ins. (94cm) Mid-15th century
In excavated condition. Similar to 19 but with a fish-tail pommel. The grip retains fragments of wood and cloth.
£1,500 — £2,000

17

18

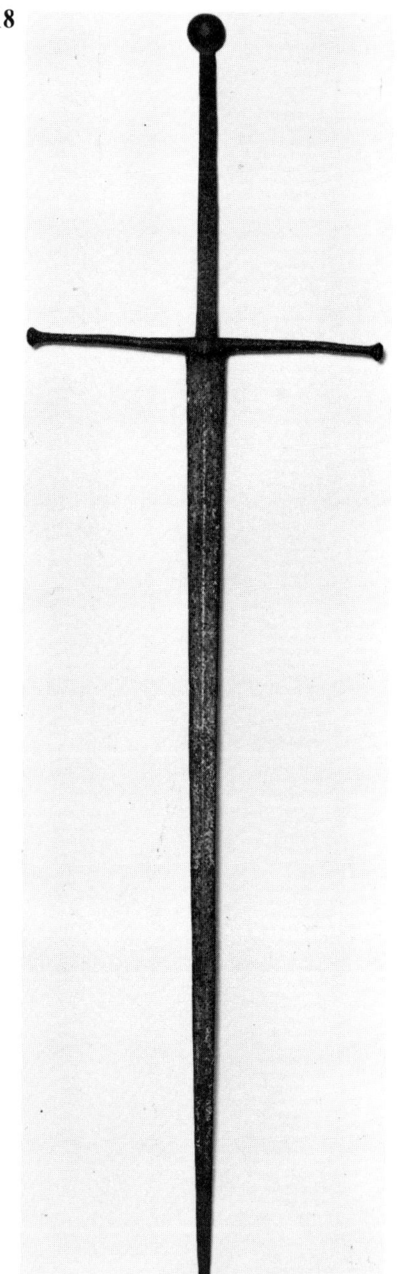

19

20

17. German hand-and-a-half sword
Length 46ins. (116.8cm)
15th century
Blade with brass bladesmith's mark (an arrow). A sword of good form, but pitted and worn. The leather covering on the shouldered grip has been restored.
£1,000 — £1,800

Photographs: 17 Sotheby's; 18-20 Christie's

21

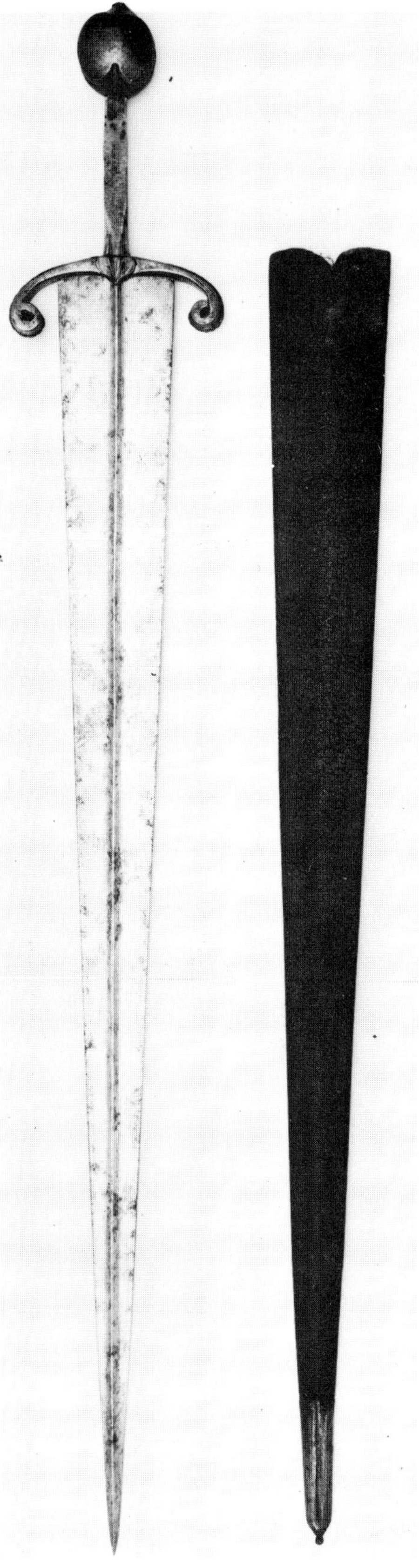

22

21. Medieval knightly sword, possibly Flemish
About 1450
Hilt of gilded iron (worn) with distinctive fish-tail pommel and quillon finials of similar design. Grip replaced. Fine quality and very good condition.
£5,000+

22. Italian knightly sword
Length 37½ins. (95.2cm) About 1500
Hilt of steel; strongly tapered two-edged blade with prominent central ridge on each side. Original leather-covered scabbard with steel chape. A fine quality sword in very good condition. Only the grip is missing.
£6,000 — £10,000

Photographs: 21 Peter Dale Ltd.; 22 Sotheby's

24. German boar-hunting sword

Length 47½ins. (120.6cm) About 1500

Cross-hilt of steel with two-hand leather-covered grip. The long robust blade of rectangular section sharpened on both edges only at the final third. The blade is also pierced for a stopping lug to prevent an enraged animal from impaling itself and possibly reaching the huntsman. Rare, good condition.

£1,500 — £2,500

25. Italian hand-and-a-half sword

Blade 41½ins. (105.4cm) First half 16th century

Blade with long fullered ricasso. Probably Venetian. Grip replaced. Rare. Very good condition.

£1,500 — £2,000

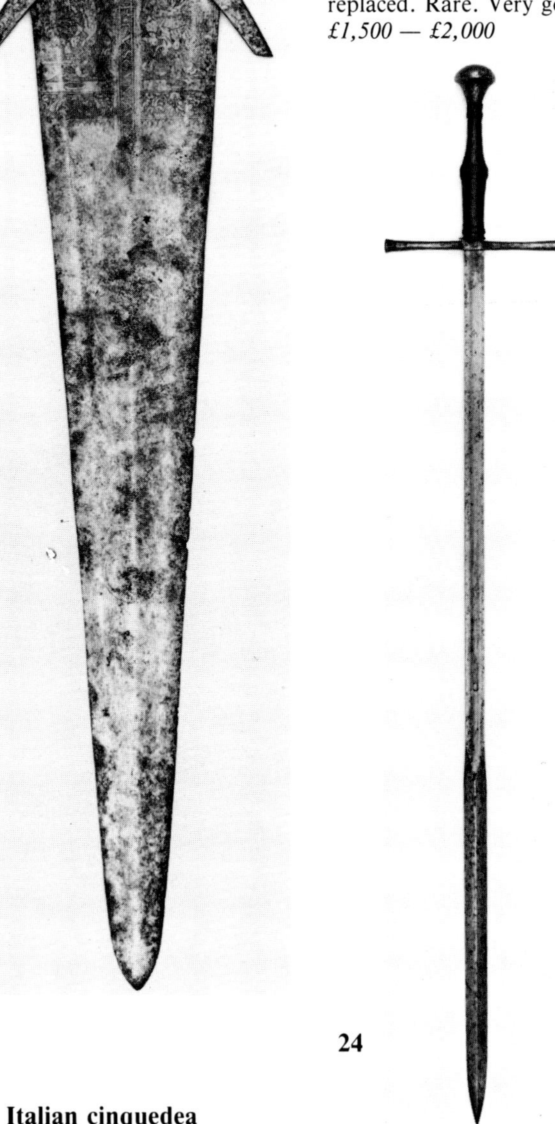

23

24

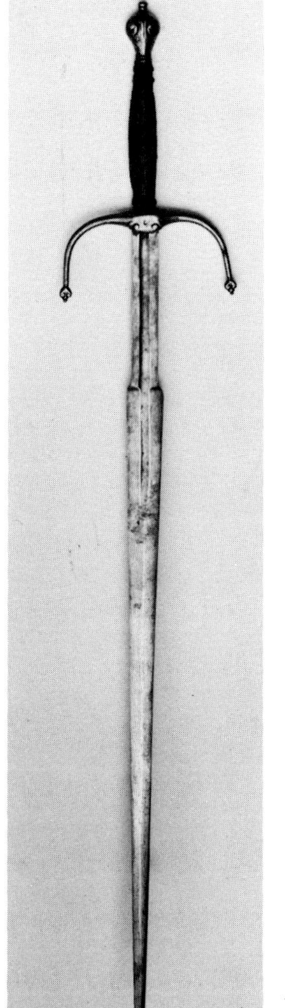

25

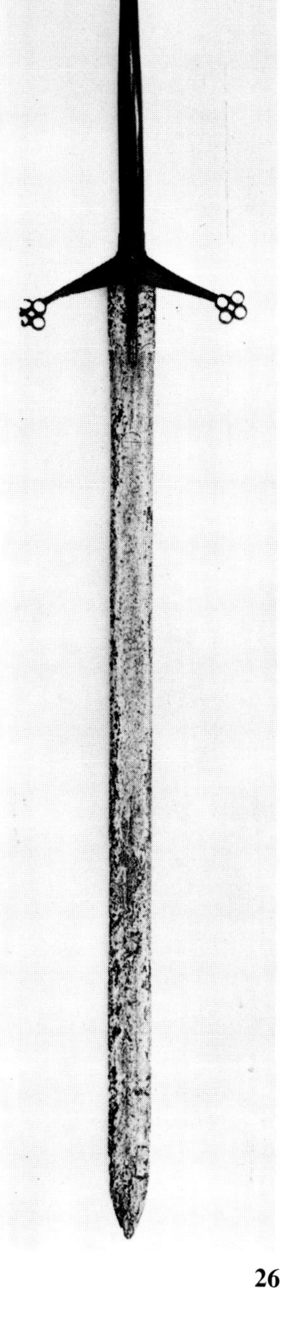

26

23. Italian cinquedea

Length 28ins. (71.2cm) About 1500

Hilt of gilded iron with horn plaque grips and gilt-metal mounts. Tapered panelled blade etched with inscriptions and classical scenes. Genuine cinquedeas are very rare. This example has lost much of the etched decoration on the blade.

£5,000 — £6,000

26. Highland claymore

Length 58⅞ins. (149.5cm) 16th century

Two-hand hilt of characteristic form. Broad double-edged blade (pitted) with orb and sceptre mark. Rare. Good condition. Tower of London Armouries (IX-912).

£3,000 — £5,000

Photographs: 23 and 24 Sotheby's; 25 Christie's; 26 Crown Copyright

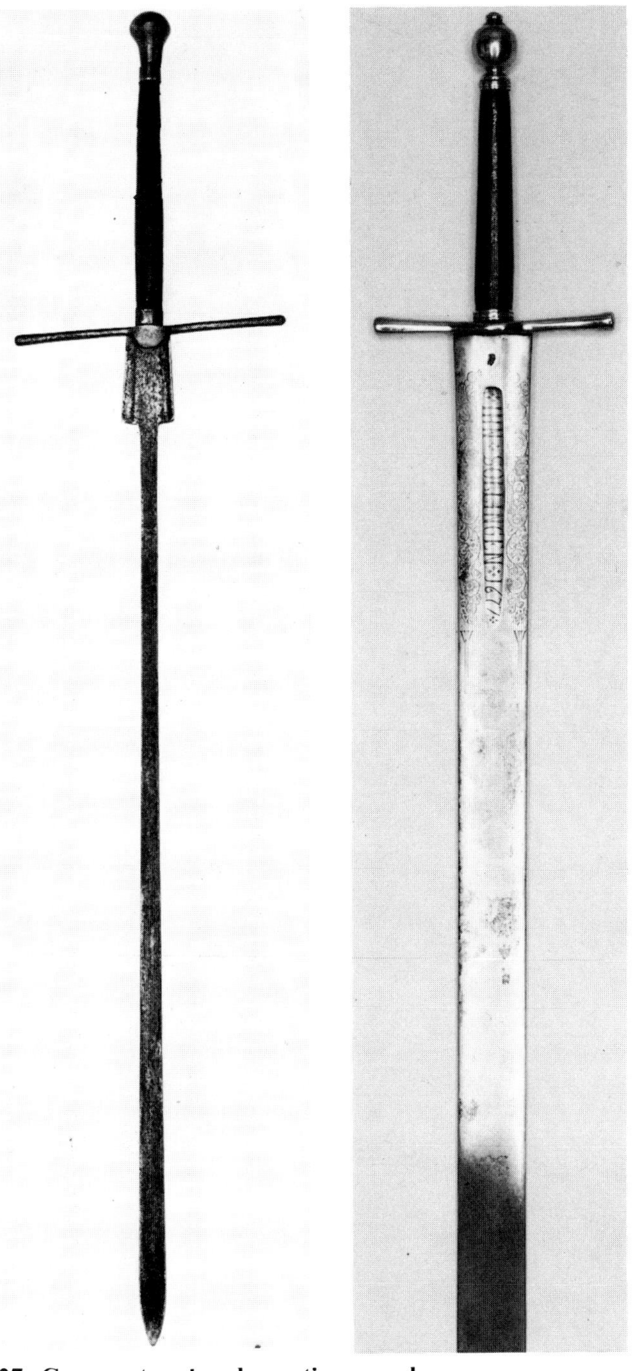

27 28

29. German executioner's sword
Blade 33¼ins. (84.5cm) Dated 1714
Gilded cruciform hilt with the initials 'JHG' and the date 1714 on the quillon block. Etched blade inscribed with the motto 'HUT DICH, THU KEIN BÖSES NICHT, SO KOMMST DU NICH INS GERICHT' (Be careful, do no ill, and you will not come to Judgement). Reputedly used by the Thüringen executioner Balthasar Glaser. Very good quality and condition.
£1,200 — £2,000

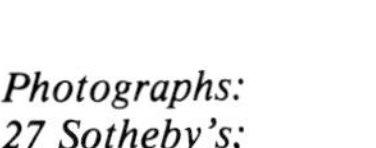

29

Photographs:
27 Sotheby's;
28 and 29 Christie's

27. German two-hand practice sword
Length 53⅜ins. (135cm) First half 16th century
Long blade tapering towards the forte and widening to form two shoulders to prevent a sliding blade reaching the hand. Rare and unusual. Very good condition.
£1,000 — £1,800

28. German executioner's sword
Blade 32⅝ins. (83cm) Dated 1677
Brass hilt with leather-covered two-hand grip. Etched broad blade inscribed 'IHN SOLINGEN, 1677', and struck with the king's head mark of the Wundes family. Very good quality and condition.
£1,000 — £1,800

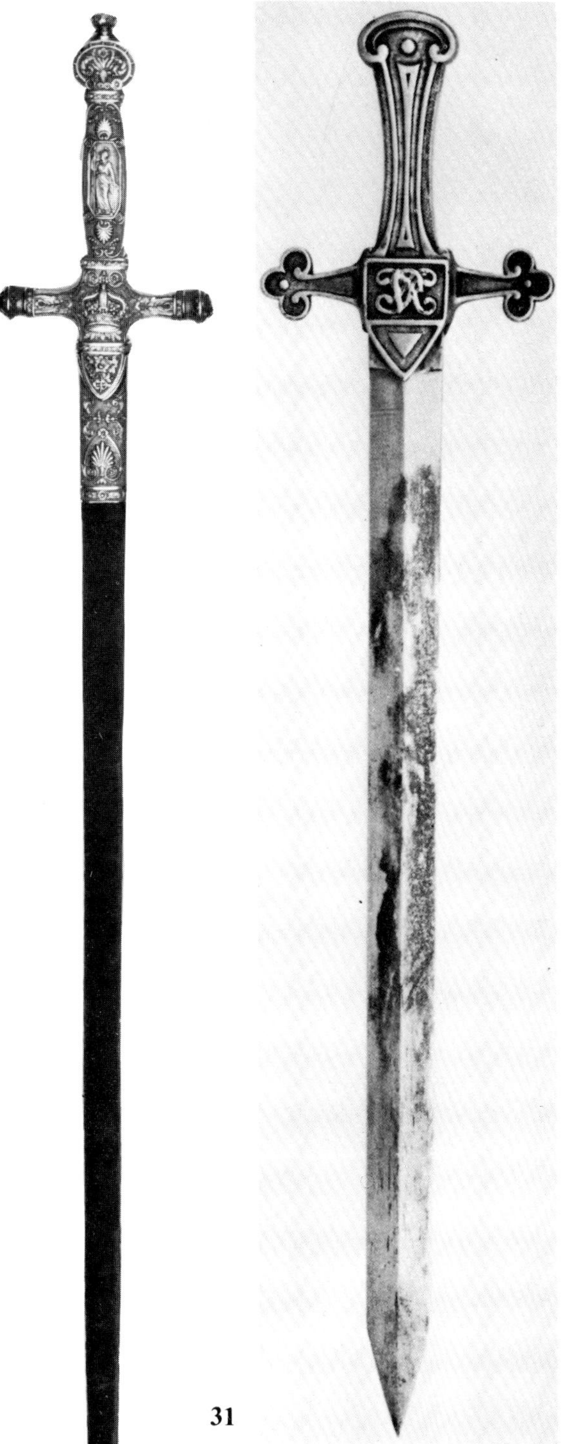

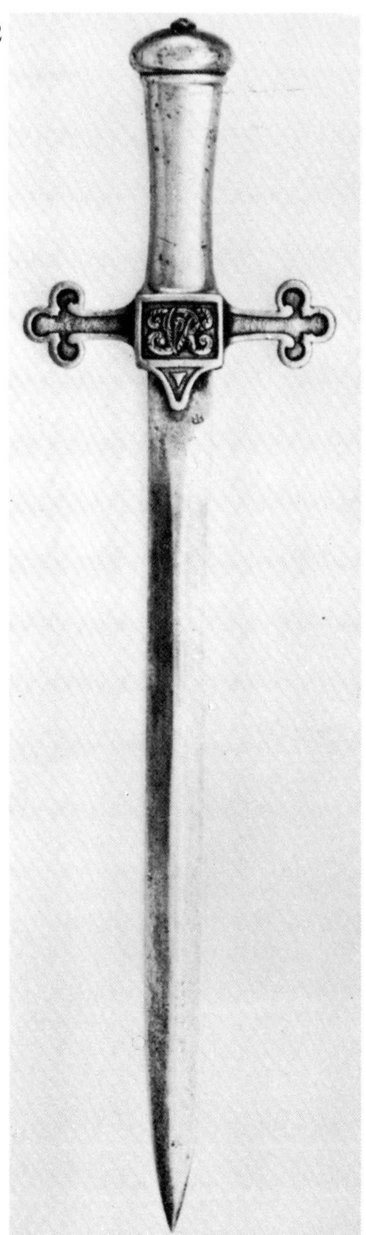

32

32. British drummer's sword (Mark II)
Blade 13⅛ins. (33.2cm)
1895-1901
Brass hilt with Victorian cypher. This sword pattern was introduced in 1895. As with the Mark I (see 31), swords with cast iron hilts were issued to buglers. Reasonable condition.
£40 — £50

31

31. British drummer's sword (Mark I)
Blade 19ins. (48.2cm) Second half 19th century
Brass cruciform hilt with Victorian cypher. This pattern of sword was adopted in 1856. Buglers' swords of the same design had hilts of cast iron. Regulation issue. Reasonable condition.
£40 — £50

30

30. 1st Duke of Cambridge's robe sword
About 1820
The sword, with gilt-metal hilt and scabbard mounts, was copied from a sword (now in the Wellington Museum, London) made for Napoleon I by the French Silversmith Blennais, and was worn by the Duke of Cambridge at the coronation of George IV. Fine condition.
£1,500

Photographs: 30 Peter Dale Ltd.; 31 and 32 private collection

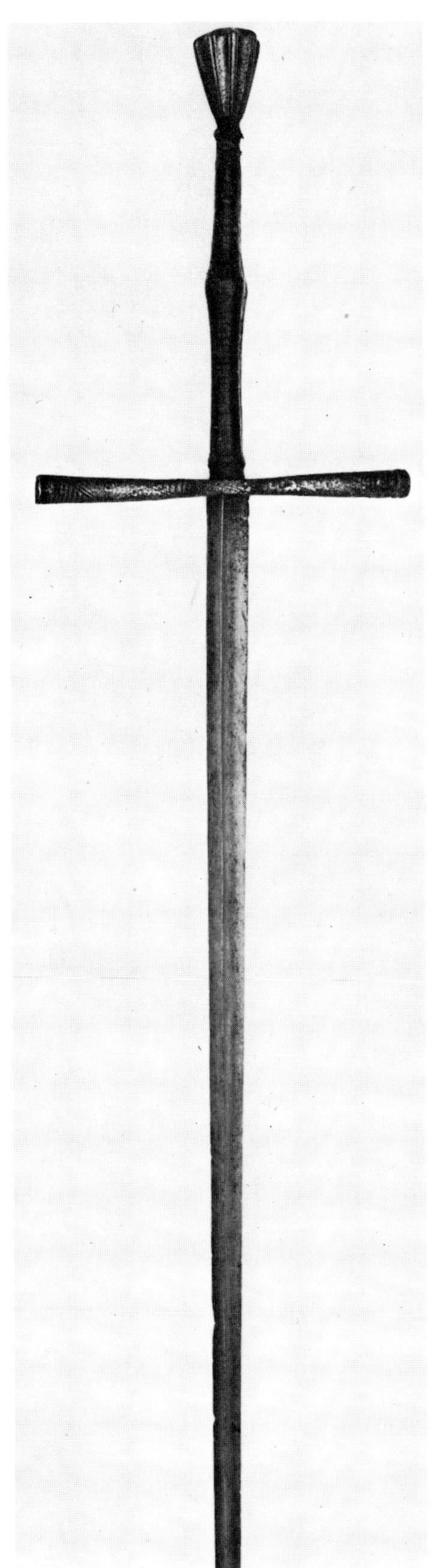
33

33. German two-hand tuck
Length 55ins. (139.7cm)
About 1500
Engraved steel hilt with horizontally recurved quillons and leather-covered grip. The stout blade of hollow triangular section. Rare. Very good condition.
£4,000 — £5,000

34. Venetian sword
Length 45ins. (114.3cm)
Late 15th century
Steel hilt with horizontally recurved quillons and shield-shaped pommel. Grip missing. An example of the type of sword carried by the *schiavoni,* Dalmatian troops serving the Republic of Venice. Such swords seem to have been called 'schiavonas' in the 15th and 16th centuries (Blair, 1962, p. 10) but today the term is applied to the distinctive basket-hilted sword (see 415-418). Rare, good condition.
£1,500 — £2,500

35. Venetian hand-and-a-half sword

Blade 33¼ins. (85.7cm)
Late 15th century
Rare, condition reasonable, grip replaced. Compare 34.
£800 — £1,000

Photographs: 33 and 34 Sotheby's; 35 Christie's

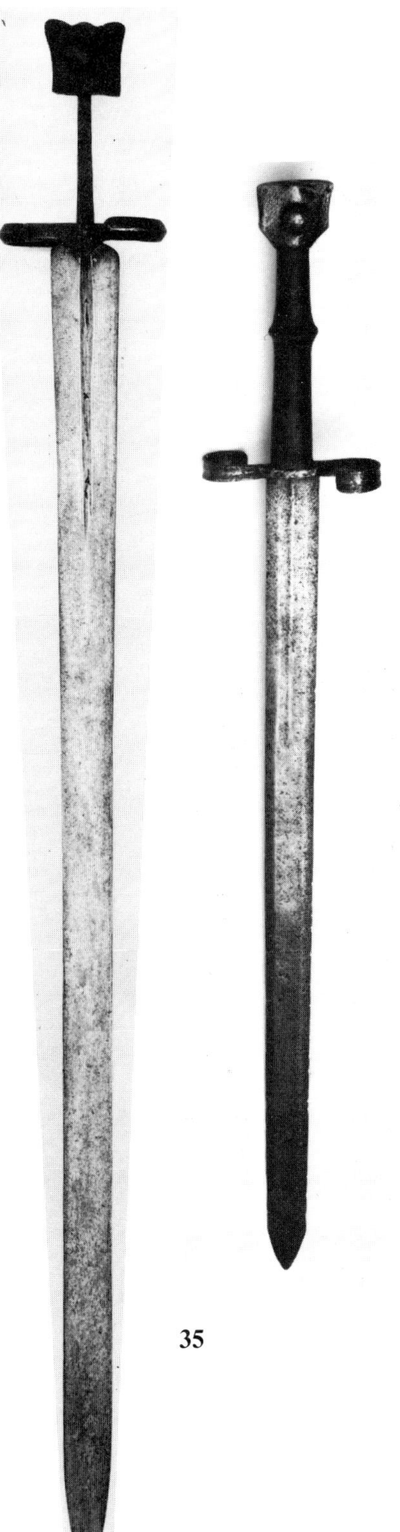
35

34

36. German Landsknecht sword

Length 33⅛ins. (84.2cm) About 1510

Steel hilt with recurved quillons. Two-edged blade. The leather-covered wooden scabbard is fitted with compartments for the knife and bodkins. Rare and fine. The metal parts a little worn. Tower of London Armouries (Sir James Mann Bequest).

£4,000+

37. German tuck

Length 48¾ins. (123.8cm) About 1550

Steel hilt with a guard formed of two side loops. Robust blade of hollow ground diamond section struck with the orb mark. Rare, excellent condition.

£3,000 — £4,000

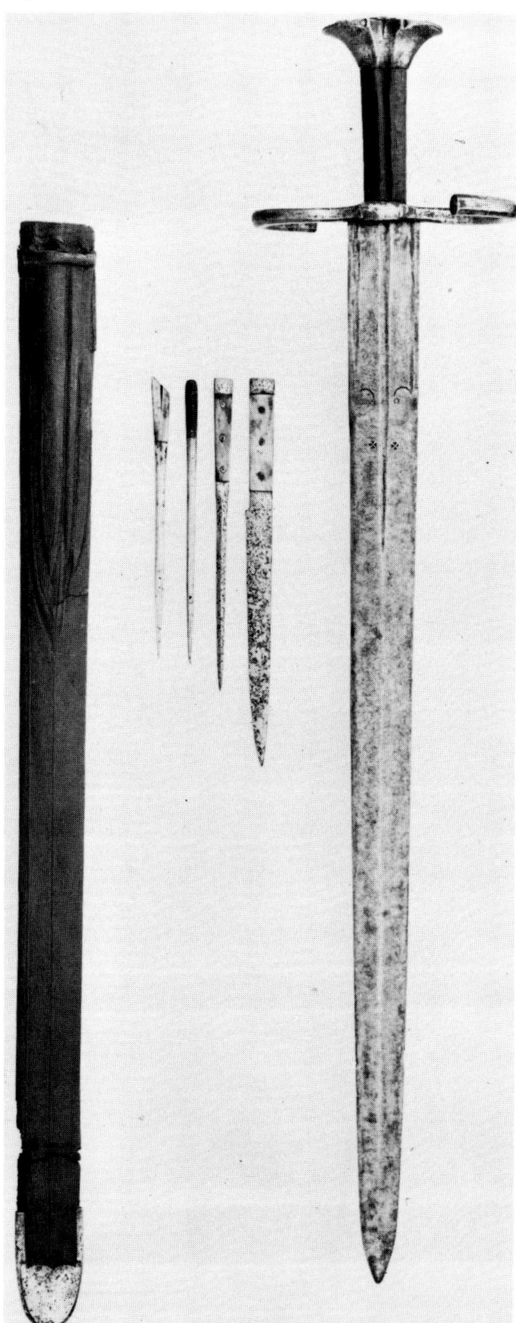

36

37

38

38. Medieval sword with finger guard

Length 42⅞ins. (108.5cm) About 1400-1425

The two-edged blade with Naskhi inscription on the ricasso recording its presentation to the Turkish arsenal at Alexandria in A.H. 836 (A.D. 1432). Like 14, this sword was possibly captured during Sultan Barsbay's raid on Cyprus in 1426. Rare, grip missing.

£7,000 — £10,000

Photographs: 36 Crown Copyright; 37 and 38 Sotheby's

41. Venetian sword
1470s
Steel hilt with wooden grip. The single-edged blade, with side lug, struck with a bladesmith's mark (a crown). Rare, reasonable condition.
£1,000 — £1,500

42. Italian falchion
Length 32¼ins. (82cm) Early 17th century
Hilt of steel. The single-edged curved blade with clipped point stamped 'CAINO'. Good condition.
£600 — £700

Photographs: 39 and 41 Christie's; 40 Crown Copyright; 42 Sotheby's

39

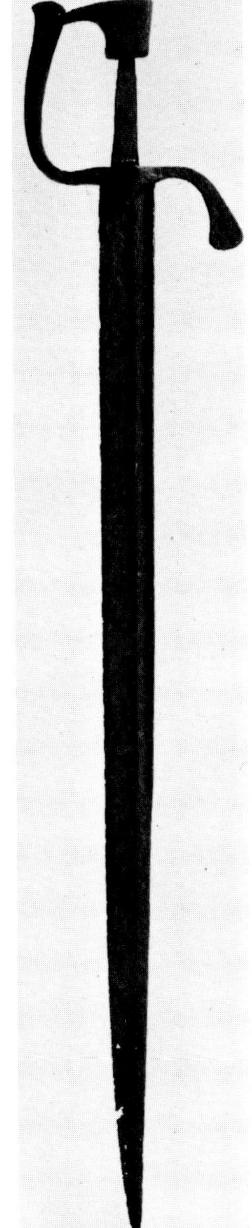

40

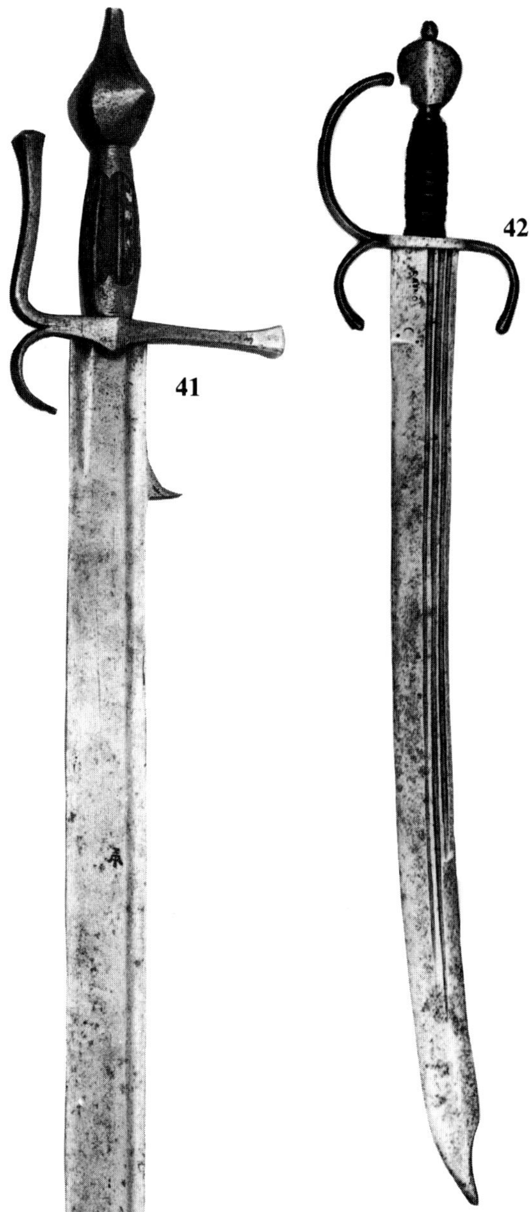

39. The Wakefield sword
Length 33¼ins. (84.5cm) About 1450
An English bowman's sword with blackened iron hilt retaining fragments of the original grip. The two-edged blade with short fuller stamped with a maker's mark (a star above three pellets in a shield). The sword was reputedly found at the site of the Battle of Wakefield (1460). Excavated condition. Very rare.
£800 — £1,200

40. Short sword, possibly English
Length 31⅝ins. (80.4cm) About 1450
Fullered blade, single-edged for two-thirds of its length. The similarity of form to 39 suggests that they are contemporary and possibly of the same nationality. Rare. Excavated condition. Tower of London Armouries (IX-144).
£800 — £1,000

43

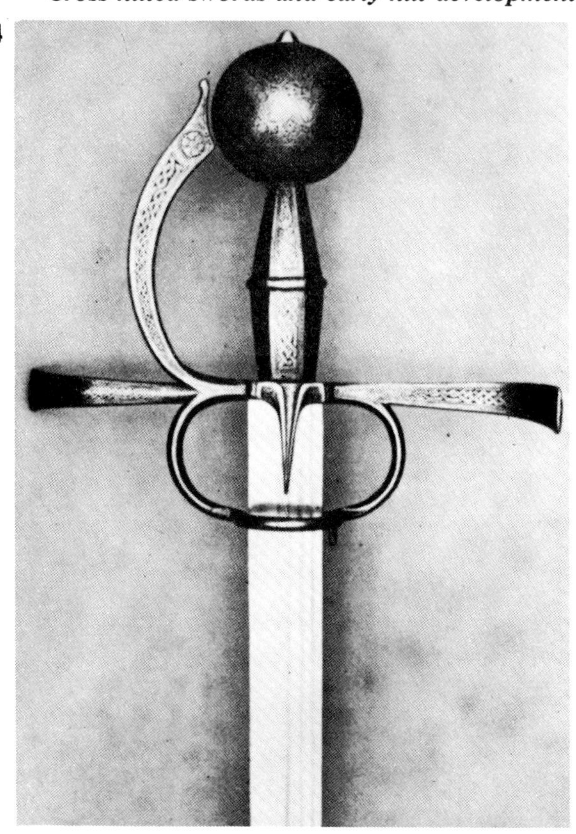

44

Photographs: 43 Christie's; 45 Howard Ricketts Ltd.

45

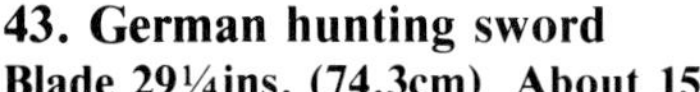

43. German hunting sword
Blade 29¼ins. (74.3cm) About 1510

Iron hilt with straight quillons fitted with a rectangular fluted plate guard curved towards the hand. Buck-horn grips. Quite a rare sword but worn and pitted especially on the blade. Now in the Tower of London Armouries (IX-1328).
£1,500 — £2,000

44. Venetian sword
About 1495

Hilt of steel finely engraved with Saracenic ornament against a silvered ground. Fullered single-edged blade. Fine quality and condition. Metropolitan Museum of Art, New York (14.25.1169).
£5,000+

45. Spanish sword
Blade 36¼ins. (92cm) 1520s

Two-edged blade struck with a mark (a stag in a circle). Grip rebound after manufacture. This sword, lighter than the medieval knightly sword, may be a rare example of an *espado ropera* (robe or costume sword) thought to be the prototype of the rapier. Fine condition.
£5,000 — £10,000

46 47 48

Photographs: 46 and 48 Sotheby's; 47 Christie's; 49 Peter Dale Ltd.

49. German hand-and-a-half sword
Second quarter 16th century
Steel hilt with side ring, arms and counter guards chiselled with cabled decoration. Two-edged blade struck with a bladesmith's mark in the fuller. Fine quality, good condition.
£2,000 — £3,000

49

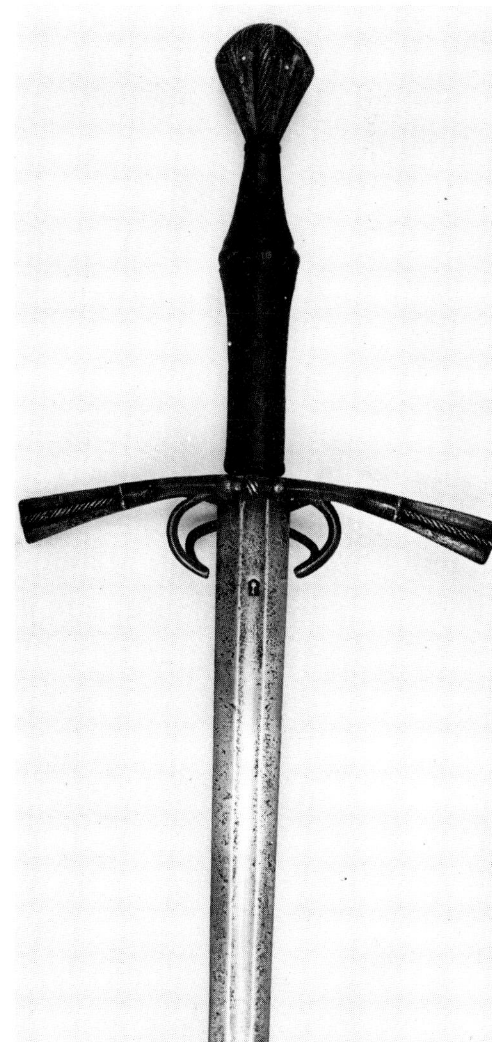

46. Italian sword
Length 40½ins. (103cm) 1520s
Hilt of steel with two curved arms below the quillons ending in two lugs or pegs. A rare sword in rather poor condition.
£500 — £800

47. German hand-and-a-half sword
Blade 35ins. (89cm) About 1530
Steel hilt with side ring and inner guard. Original three stage leather-covered grip. Blade struck with half-moon marks. Good condition.
£1,200 — £1,500

48. German hand-and-a-half sword
About 1525
Engraved steel hilt with side ring and single arm beneath the forward quillon, continuing diagonally across the back of the blade to form the inner guard. Good condition.
£1,200 — £1,800

50

50. Swiss or German hand-and-a-half sword

Blade 42½ins. (108cm) About 1530

Steel hilt with side ring and inner guard. Blade with maker's mark (a crowned 'B' reversed). Good condition.

£2,000 — £3,000

51. German two-hand sword

Length 61ins. (155 cm) First half 16th century

Hilt of steel with side rings on each side; the leather-covered grip bound with wire. Blade of hexagonal section struck with bladesmith's mark (a cross) at the forte. Very good quality, fine condition.

£2,000 — £3,000

52. German two-hand processional sword

Blade 54¼ins. (137.7cm) About 1580

Hilt of blackened steel with side rings at the front and back. The blade with long ricasso lined with wooden slats and overlaid with leather. A distinctive sword in fine condition.

£2,000 — £3,000

53. German two-hand processional sword

Blade 54½ins. (138.5cm) About 1580

Similar to 52 but with double side rings linked by the arms of the hilt and with stopping lugs on the ricasso. Very good condition.

£2,000 — £3,000

Photographs: 50, 52 and 53 Christie's; 51 Sotheby's

51

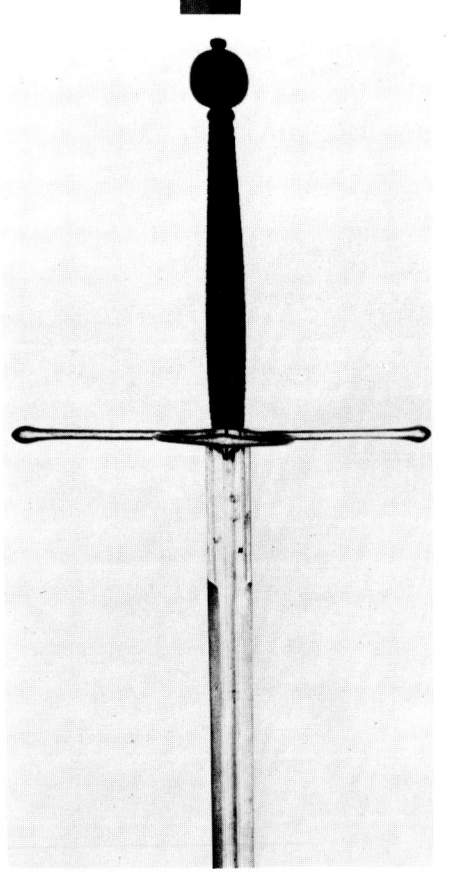

53

52

54

54. Saxon riding tuck
Blade 53ins. (134.6cm) About 1570
Blackened steel hilt fitted with an in-filled side ring, single arm and thumb guard. Robust blade of hollowed triangular section. The pierced holes on the quillons and side ring were for attaching decorative silver panels similar to those on 55. Good condition.
£4,000 — £4,500

55. Saxon rapier
Length 47ins. (119.5cm) About 1590
Hilt of blackened steel mounted with engraved silver sheet and with a silver wire-bound grip. Contemporary but associated scabbard with silver locket *en suite* with the sword hilt, designed to slot into the socket covering the ricasso to prevent rain ruining the blade. Fine quality, excellent condition.
£15,000+

56. Saxon silver-mounted rapier
Length 48ins. (122cm) About 1590
Blackened iron hilt almost entirely encased in silver sheet decorated with birds, hares and hounds amongst foliage. Silver wire-bound grip. A sword of high quality in excellent condition.
£15,000+

55

56

Photographs: 54 Christie's; 55 and 56 Sotheby's

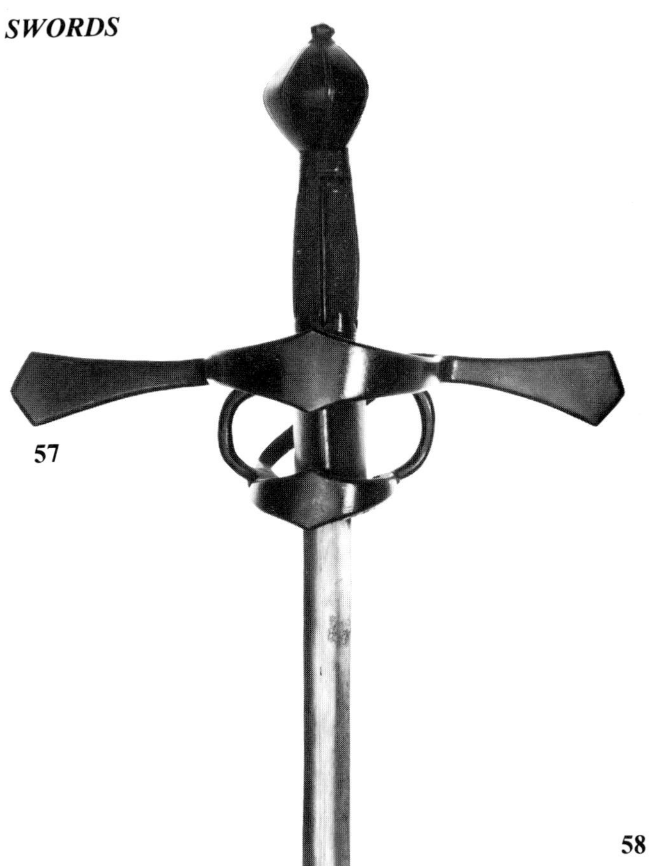

57

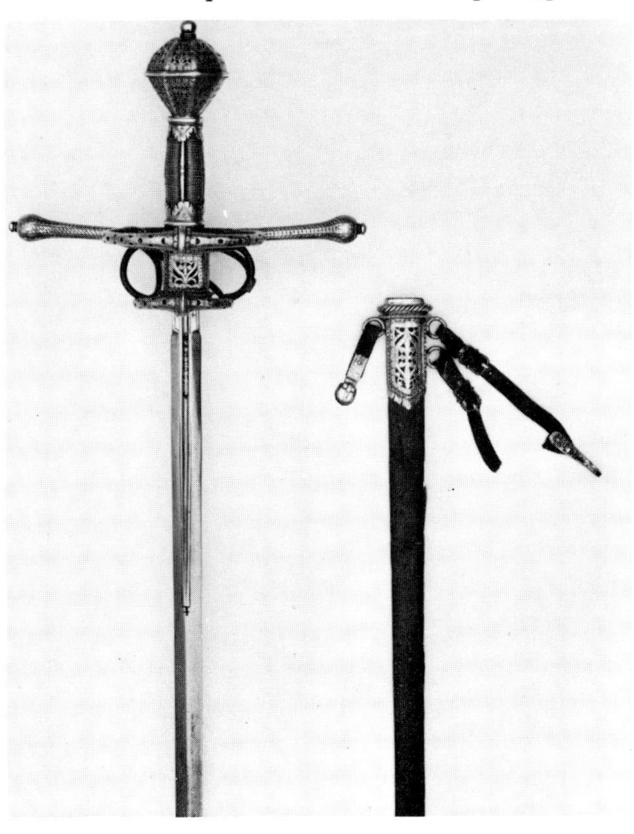

58

59

57. Saxon duelling tuck
Blade 42ins. (106.8cm) About 1570
Hilt of blackened iron with double side rings, arms and diagonal inner guard. Fish-skin covered grip. A quality sword in fine condition.
£5,000 — £6,000

58. Saxon silver-mounted rapier
Length 49ins. (124.5cm) About 1580
Blackened steel hilt encased (except for the counter guards) with engraved and pierced silver sheet. Blade stamped 'ANDREA FERARO' in the fuller, and struck on the silver locket with the Dresden town mark and maker's mark of Wolf Paller of Dresden (d.1583). Very fine quality and condition.
£20,000+

59. Saxon sword-rapier
Length 44½ins. (113cm) About 1590
Silver-mounted blackened steel hilt, the silver wire-bound grip with silver ferrules. Fine quality, excellent condition.
£15,000+

Photographs: 57 Christie's; 58 Sotheby's; 59 Howard Ricketts Ltd.

Colour Plate 1. *Saxon royal rapier, signed Israel Scheuch, dated 1606. For details see nos. 72 and 73.*
Sotheby's

60

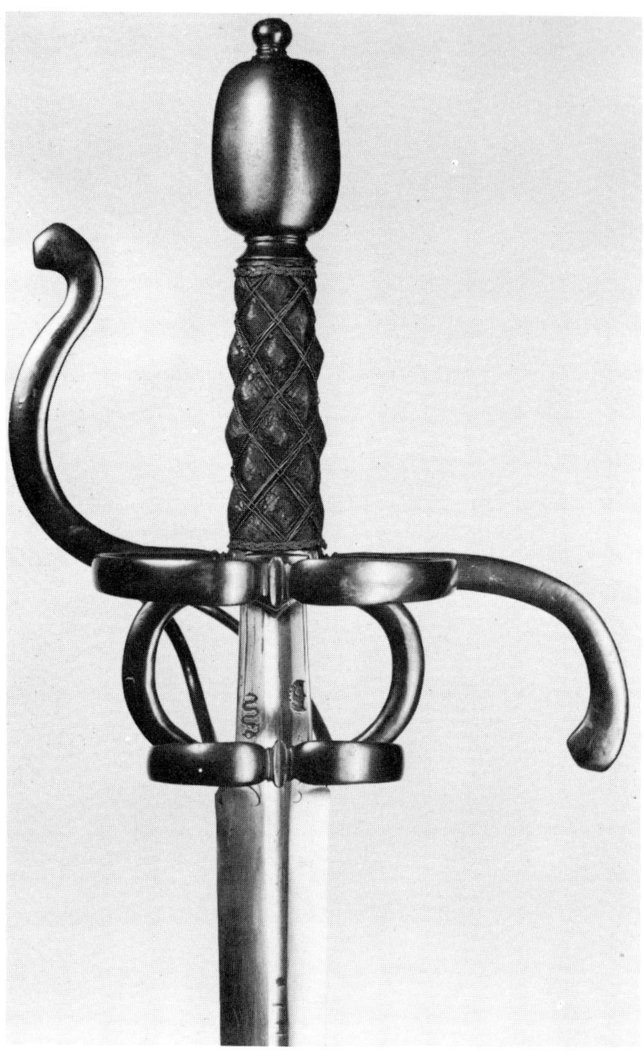

60. Saxon musketeer's rapier
About 1600-1610
Hilt of blued steel stamped with the mark of Anton Scheuch of Dresden. Blade struck on the ricasso with the half moon and serpent marks, probably of a Milanese bladesmith. Comparatively simple in form but of fine quality. Victoria and Albert Museum (M50-1947).
£5,000 — £8,000

Photograph: 61 Christie's

61

61. North European rapier
Blade 38ins. (96.5cm) About 1600-1610
Hilt with two side rings, the lower filled with a pierced plate, and with a steel plate guard on the inside. Good quality, but worn and pitted on the blade and pommel.
£500 — £800

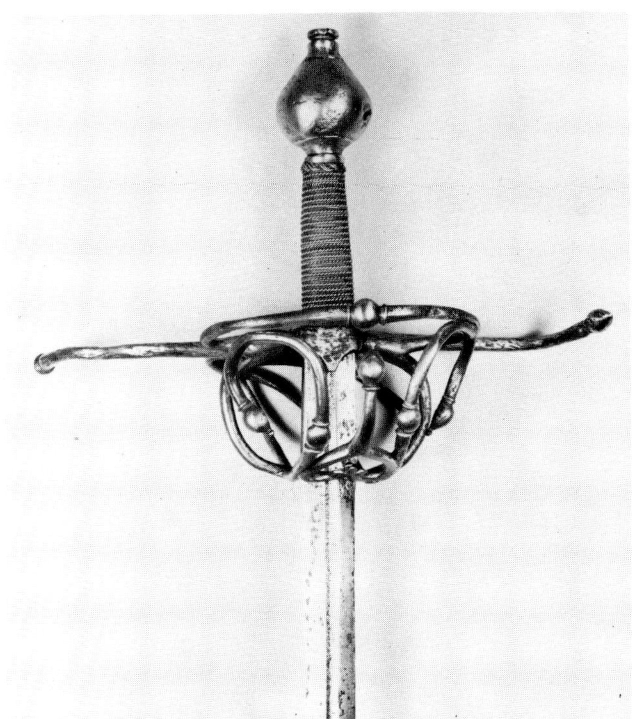

62

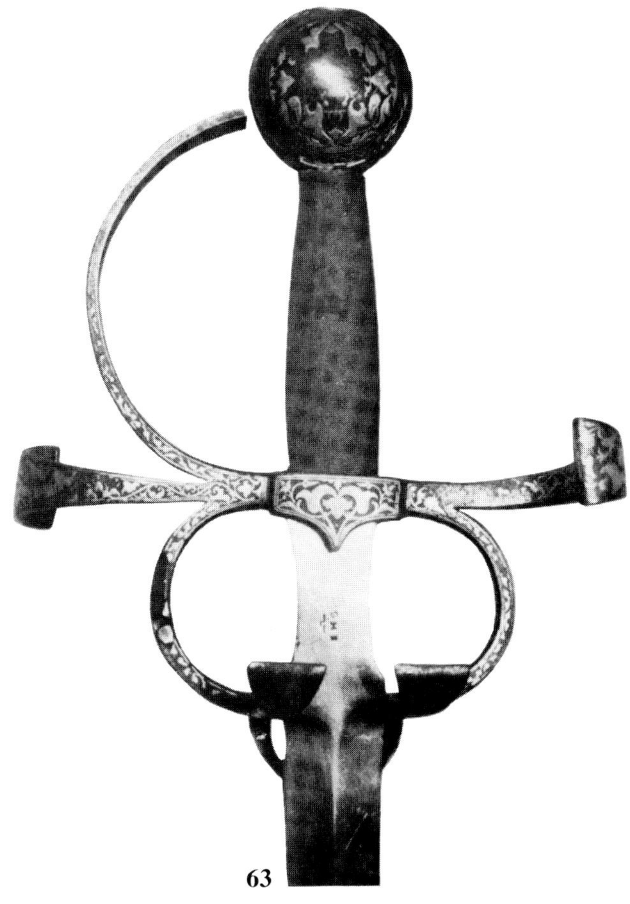

63

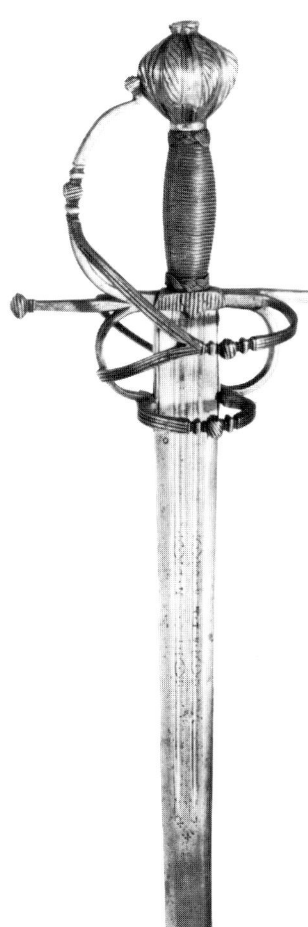

64

62. Rapier, possibly north European
1570s
Cup-like guard formed of scrolled bars, retaining some original gilt finish. Rather worn overall. Grip replaced.
£400 — £600

63. Spanish rapier
Length 32¾ins. (83cm) 1530s
Hilt of steel damascened in gold. Blade stamped 'MATEO' and with the sacred monogram 'IHS'. The sword is traditionally believed to have belonged to Francisco Pizarro (d. 1541), the conqueror of Peru. Fine quality. Royal Armoury, Madrid (G35).
£4,000+

64. Swept-hilt rapier
Blade 37½ins. (94.4cm) Second quarter 16th century
Blade associated. A rare sword in reasonable condition.
£600 — £800

Photographs: 62 Peter Dale Ltd.; 64 Christie's

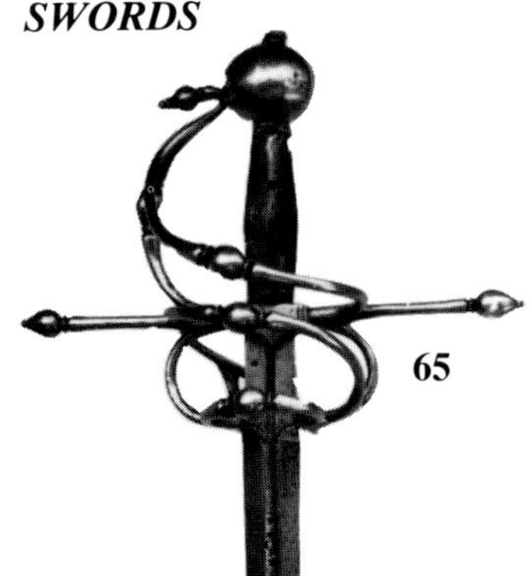

65

65. Italian swept-hilt rapier
About 1570
Grip binding missing. Good quality and condition.
£600 — £1,000

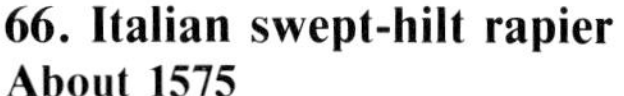

66. Italian swept-hilt rapier
About 1575
Steel guard formed of sweeping bifurcating bars; short wire-bound grip and associated quillons. Blade inscribed 'IN SOLINGEN'. Very good quality and condition. Tower of London Armouries (IX-112).
£1,000 — £2,000

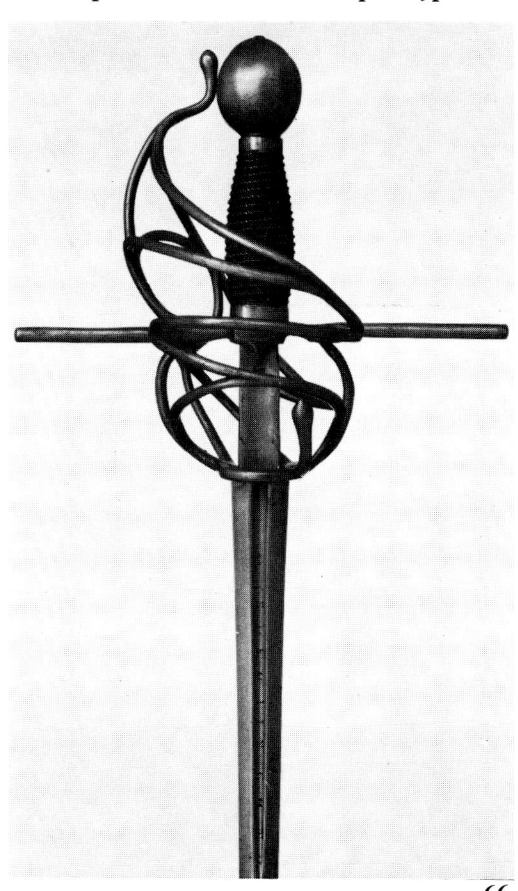

66

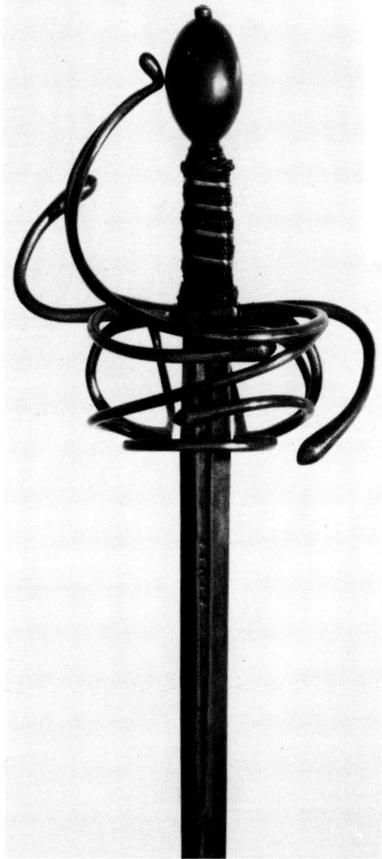

67

67. North European rapier
Blade 41½ins. (105.5cm) About 1580
Hilt with sweeping bars swelling at the tips; grip bound with wire and copper strip. Narrow blade struck in the fuller with sacred monogram 'IHS'. Good quality and condition.
£600 — £1,000

Photographs: 65 Sotheby's; 66 Crown Copyright; 67 Christie's.

68

69

68. Saxon swept-hilt rapier
Blade 40½ins. (102.5cm) About 1580-1590
Hilt of silvered steel with ι side ring filled with a pierced plate and a silver wire-bound grip. Blade stamped in the fullers 'VALENCIA ME FECIT', and etched with devices of the Spanish monarchs Ferdinand and Isabella, and spurious Arabic lettering. Very fine quality and condition.
£8,000 — £10,000

69. Saxon sword-rapier
Blade 38¼ins. (97.2cm) About 1590-1610
Silver-plated swept hilt, with copper wire-bound grip, and blade of diamond section. Fine quality and condition. The plating a little worn.
£4,000 — £6,000

Photographs: Christie's

70

71

70. Saxon rapier and dagger
Sword length 48ins. (122cm) Dagger 19½ins. (49cm)
About 1590-1610

Rapier and companion left-hand dagger. Hilts of blued steel each with a side ring filled with a pierced plate. Sword blade inscribed 'IS TOLETTO' and stamped on the ricasso with a mark (a man holding a staff), probably that of Johannes Hoppe. Of the type carried by the bodyguard of the Electors of Saxony. Fine quality, excellent condition.
£12,000 — £15,000

71. German swept-hilt riding sword
Blade 34ins. (86.3cm) About 1600

Broad tapered blade struck on the ricasso with the mark of Wolfgang Stantler of Munich ('S' over 'T' below a crown). Of the type carried by the Town or Ducal Guard of Munich. Very good quality and condition.
£3,000 — £5,000

Photographs: 70 Sotheby's; 71 Christie's

72. Saxon royal rapier
Length 48½ins. (123cm) Dated 1606
Cast and chiselled swept hilt of gilt bronze set with pearls, cabochon and crystal. Pierced Spanish blade struck with the Toledo mark and half-moon marks and inscribed 'JUAN MARTINEZ EN TOLEDO, ESPADERO DE RE' (swordsmith of the king) and 'IN TE DOMINE' (In thee, O Lord, we trust).

Made for either the Elector Christian II of Saxony or his brother Duke Johann George. It is one of only two rapiers known for certain to have been made by the Dresden swordcutler Israel Scheuch, and signed by him. The whereabouts of the second sword, formerly at Dresden, is not known (see 'Highly Important Arms from the Saxon Royal Collections', Sotheby & Co. cat., 23 March 1970, lot 34).

A sword of the highest quality in fine condition. In 1970 it sold for £21,000 and would probably be worth three times that amount today. Now in the Metropolitan Museum of Art, New York (1970-77). Also shown in Colour Plate 1.

73. Saxon royal rapier
The back of 72. One of the inner guards is missing. The dark space on the rear arm (left) is where the third bar should spring from to join the other two.

72

73

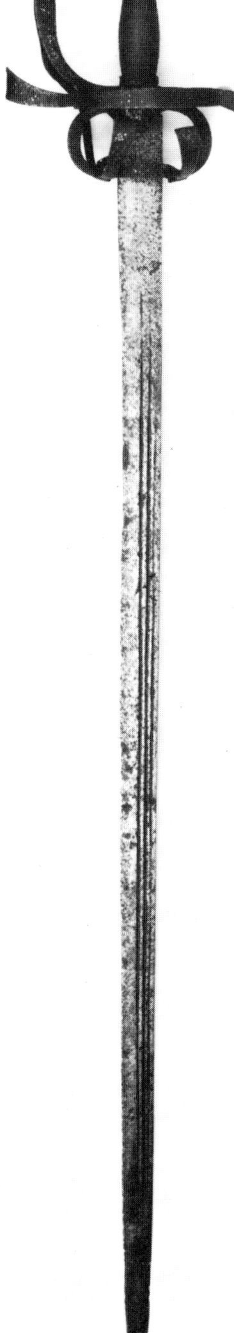
74

74. English swept-hilt riding sword
Length 40ins. (101.6cm) Early 17th century
Gold damascened hilt and single-edged fullered blade. A rare sword, originally of fine quality, but now in poor condition. Much of the original gold inlay has worn away and the blade has become pitted. Grip rebound.
£1,000

Photographs: Sotheby's

75

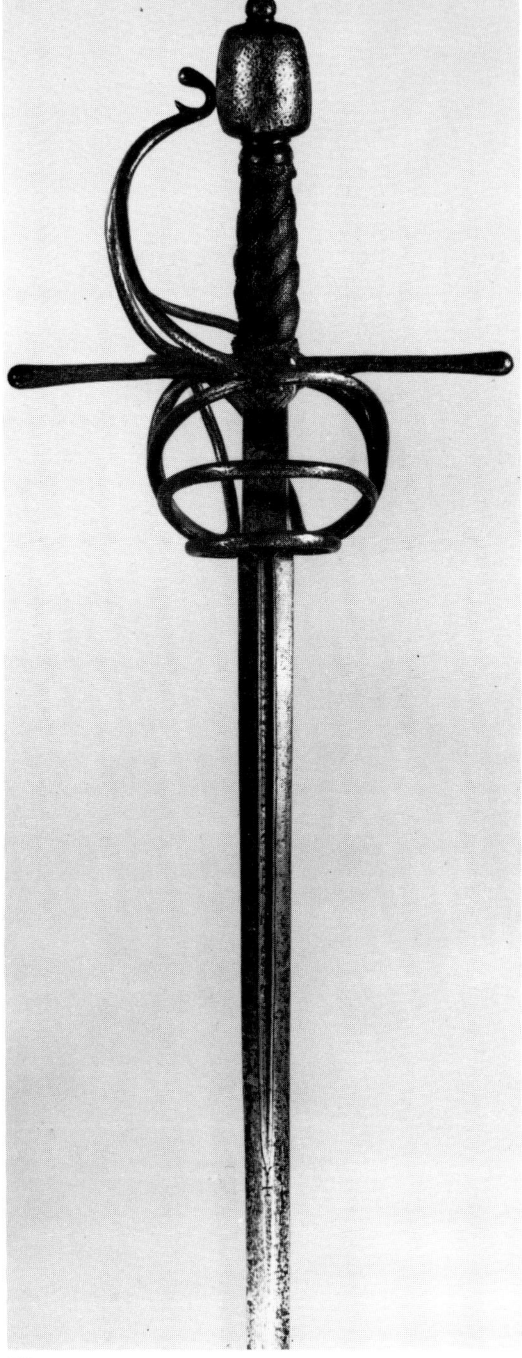

76

75. Swept-hilt rapier
Blade 43ins. (109cm) About 1600
Hilt of chiselled steel embellished with silver pellets and retaining traces of gold decoration. Blade stamped in the fuller with the sacred monogram 'IHS'. A fine and attractive sword in very good condition.
£4,000 — £6,000

76. Italian swept-hilt rapier
Blade 43½ins. (110.5cm) About 1620-1630
Hilt with punched foliate design heightened with silver dots. Blade of diamond section stamped 'SANDRI SCACHI' on the ricasso and 'MONTE IN TOLEDO' in the fuller. Fine quality but worn.
£1,500 — £2,000

Photographs: Christie's

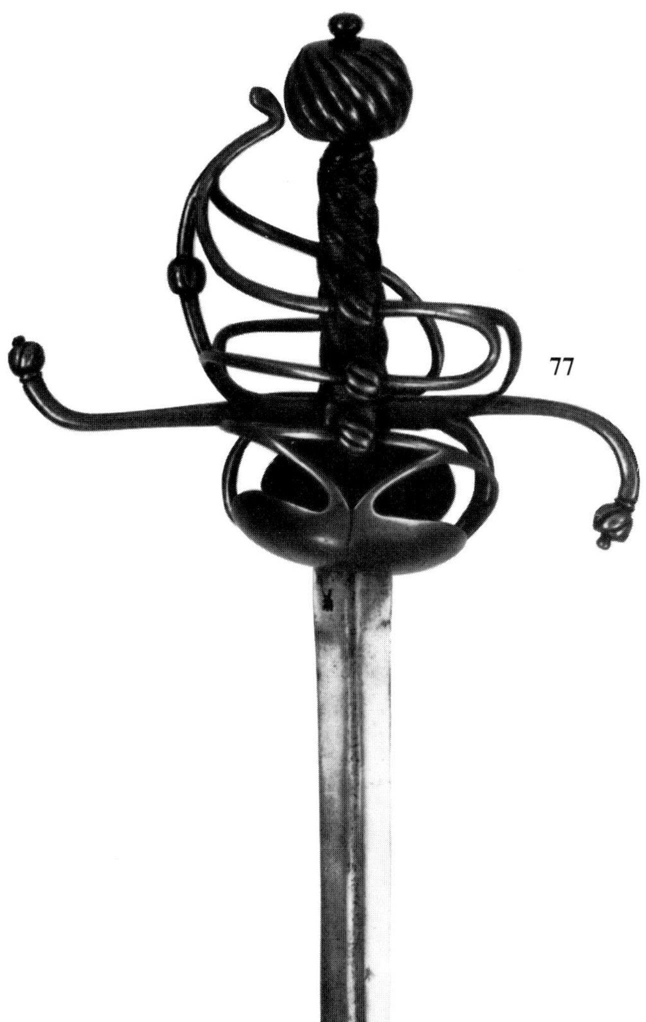

77

77. North European sword-rapier
Blade 36ins. (91.5cm) Late 16th/early 17th century
Swept hilt of steel fitted with plate guards. The two-edged fullered blade with maker's mark (a crowned pair of pincers). The form of the hilt is rare, see Norman, p. 149, hilt 76. Fine condition.
£3,000 — £5,000

78

Photographs: Christie's

78. North European Pappenheimer hilted rapier
Blade 47½ins. (120.6cm) About 1630
Gilded swept hilt of characteristic form with pierced plate guards below the hand. Associated horn grip. The blade stamped on the ricasso with bladesmith's mark ('SS' beneath a crown). Fine quality, good condition. Gilding worn.
£4,000 — £5,000

79

79. German rapier
Length 52½ins. (133.3cm)
Second quarter 17th century
Russet steel hilt of Pappenheimer type. Blade of diamond section with leaf-shaped point signed 'CLEMENS DINGER ME FECIT SOLINGEN'. A solid but attractive sword in excellent condition.
£4,000 — £5,000

80. North European rapier
Blade 41ins. (104cm) 1630s
Gilded hilt of variant Pappenheimer form with two side rings (front and back) linked to each other by scrolled bars, the lower ring filled with a plate decorated with a crowned double-headed eagle. Fine quality, good condition. Gilding worn, pommel associated.
£2,500 — £3,500

81. North European rapier
Blade 44½ins. (113cm) 1630s
Pappenheimer-type hilt of silvered steel with silver wire-bound grip. Blade stamped in the fuller 'FRANCISCO RUIZ IN TOLEDO'. Fine quality. One quillon replaced and tip of blade missing.
£3,000 — £4,000

Photographs: 79 Sotheby's; 80 and 81 Christie's

80

81

82

82. North European rapier
Second quarter 17th century
The steel hilt is missing the plate guards which probably filled the middle side rings. Good quality and condition.
£800 — £1,200

Photographs: 82 Peter Dale Ltd.; 83 and 84 Christie's

84. Swept-hilt rapier
Length 44ins. (112cm) 1630s
Silver inlaid hilt decorated with silver studs on the oval plaques. Fine quality and condition.
£3,000 — £5,000

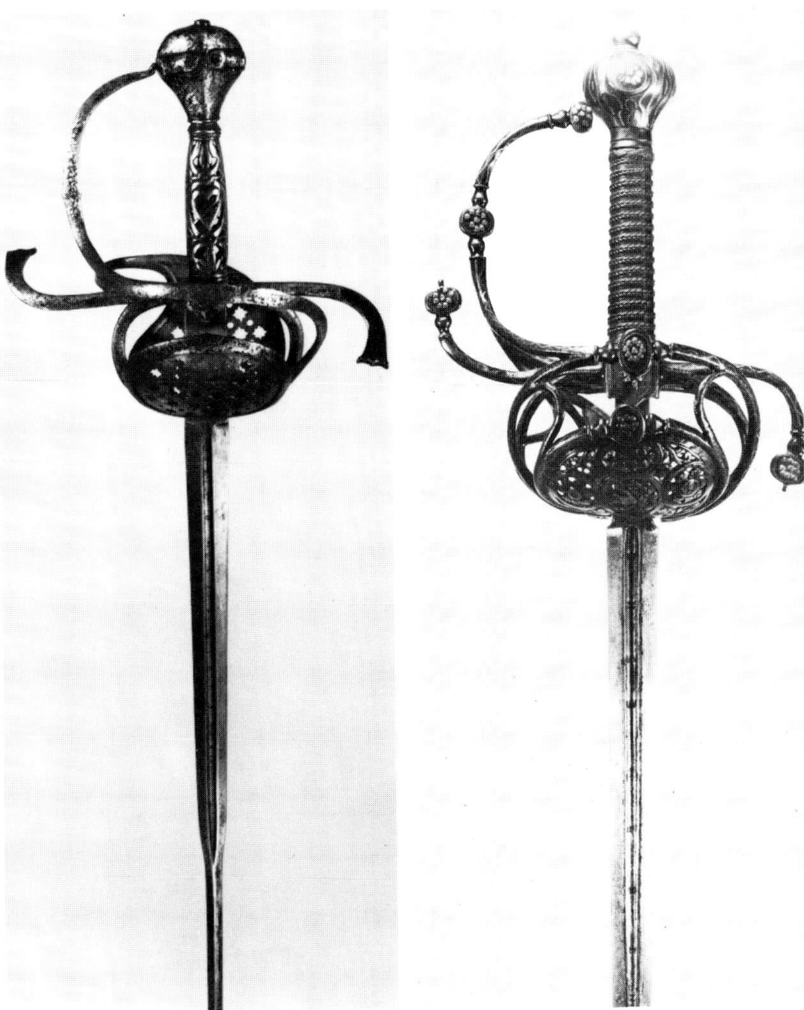

83 84

83. North European rapier
Blade 38ins. (96.5cm) 1630s
All-steel hilt of variant Pappenheimer type with single filled ring and loop guard at the front, and inner guard shaped like an inverted comma. The Spanish blade stamped 'TOMAS AIALA EN TOLEDO'. Good condition.
£2,000 — £3,000

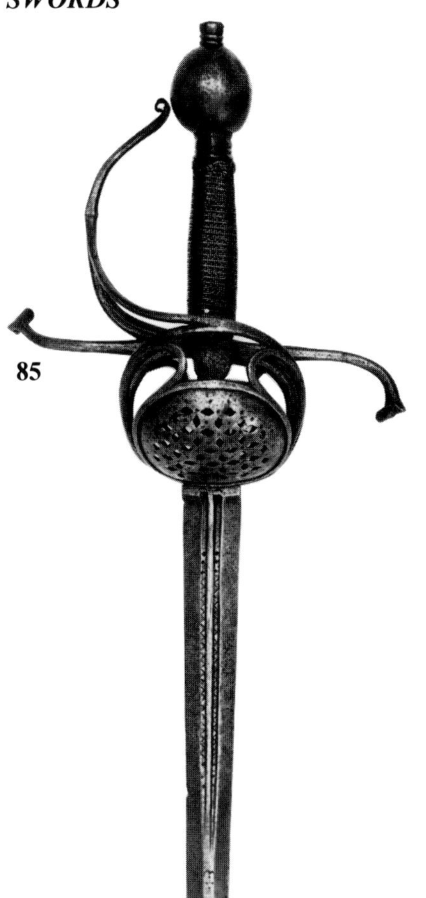

Photographs: Sotheby's

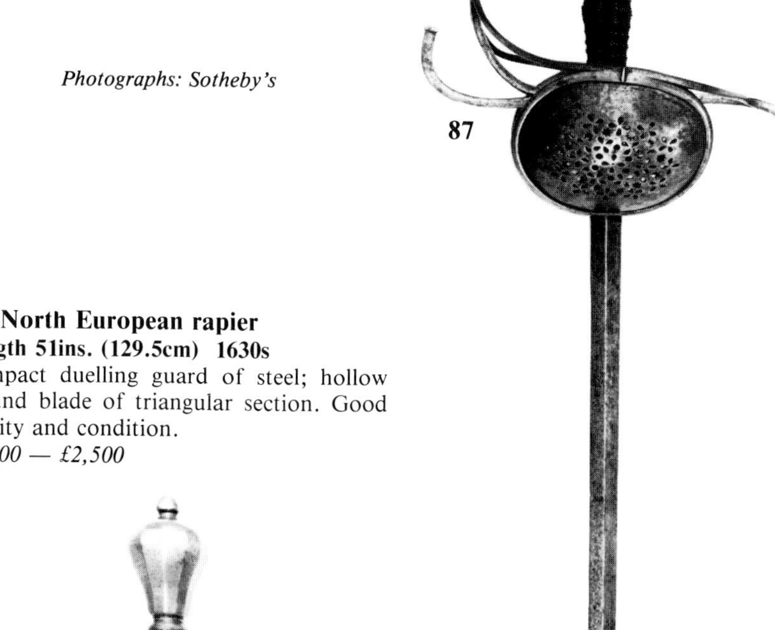

86. North European rapier
Length 51ins. (129.5cm) 1630s
Compact duelling guard of steel; hollow ground blade of triangular section. Good quality and condition.
£1,500 — £2,500

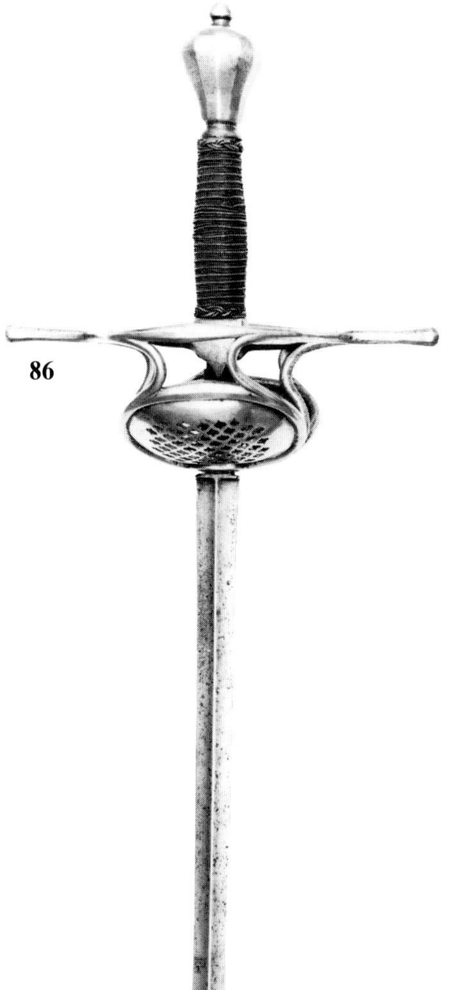

85. Italian rapier
Length 49ins. (124.5cm) 1630s
Robust swept hilt of steel with associated pommel. Reasonable to good condition.
£1,000 — £1,500

87. North European rapier
Length 47½ins. (120.5cm) 1630s
Swept hilt with single side ring (front and back) filled with a pierced plate. Blade stamped on the ricasso 'ANTONIO PICININO'. Good quality and condition.
£1,000 — £1,500

88

88. German rapier

Length 49ins. (124.5cm) Second quarter 17th century
Hilt with chiselled steel plate guards and associated pommel. Blade inscribed in copper 'CIVITAS SERVAL' (City of Serval). Good condition.
£800 — £1,200

Photographs: 88 and 89 Sotheby's; 90 Christie's

89 90

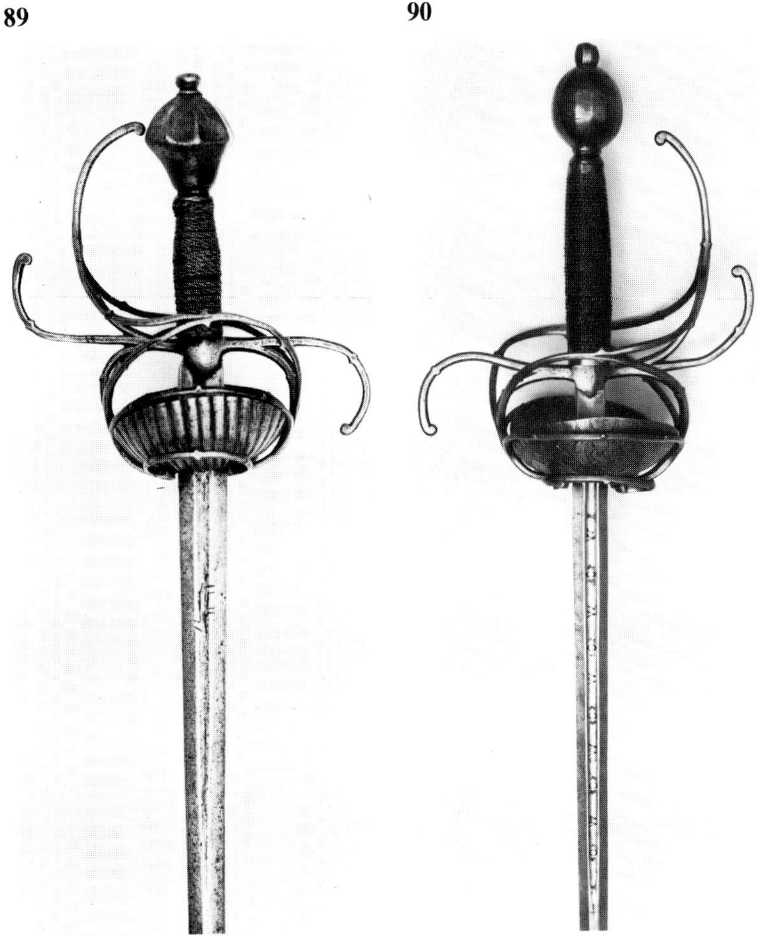

89. Italian rapier

Length 48¾ins. (123.8cm) 1640s
Swept steel hilt with loose fitting fluted plate guards. Blade with running wolf mark. Good quality and reasonable condition.
£600 — £800

90. Southern European rapier

Blade 46¾ins. (118.7cm) About 1640-1650
Hilt with rebound grip and later plate guards. Good quality, fair condition.
£800 — £1,000

91

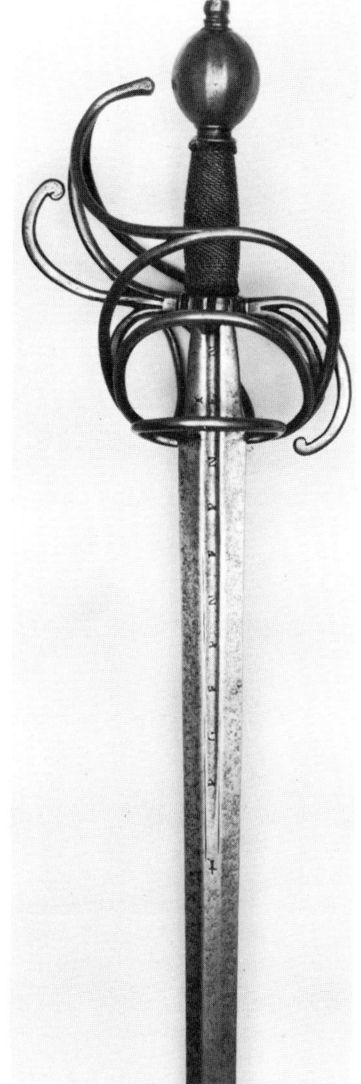

92. Spanish or Italian rapier
About 1640
Blackened steel hilt with four side rings at the front and back, the lower filled with a pierced plate. The blade stamped 'TOMASO AYALA' and struck with half-moon marks on the ricasso. Very good quality and condition.
£2,000

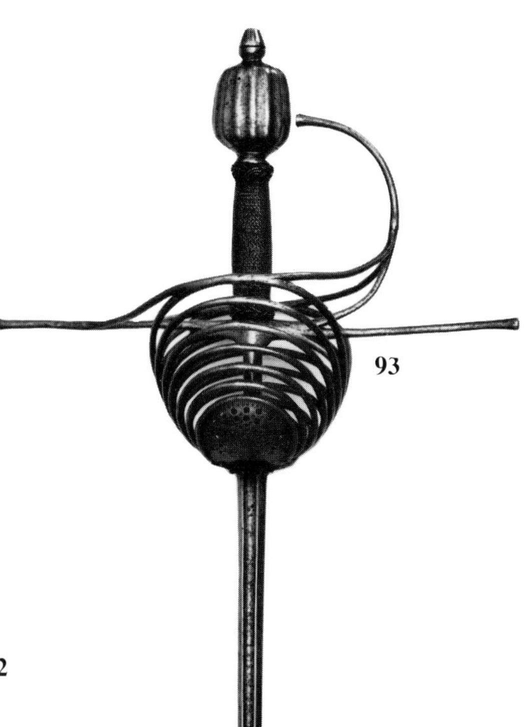

93

92

91. North European rapier
Blade 43½ins. (110.5cm) About 1640-1650
Of robust form, but now without the steel plates below the hand, compare 89 and 90. Good condition.
£800 — £1,200

Photographs: 91 Christie's; 92 Peter Dale Ltd.; 93 Sotheby's

93. Spanish or Italian seven-ringed rapier
Length 53ins. (134.6cm) Second quarter 17th century
Very good quality, reasonable condition.
£2,000

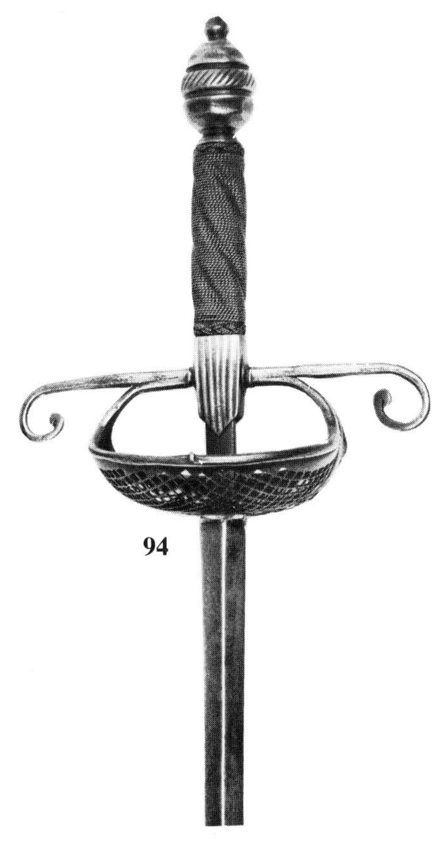

94

94. Duelling rapier, probably English
1630s
Hilt with pierced shallow bowl guard linked by arms to the quillons. Pommel associated. Good quality and condition.
£600 — £800

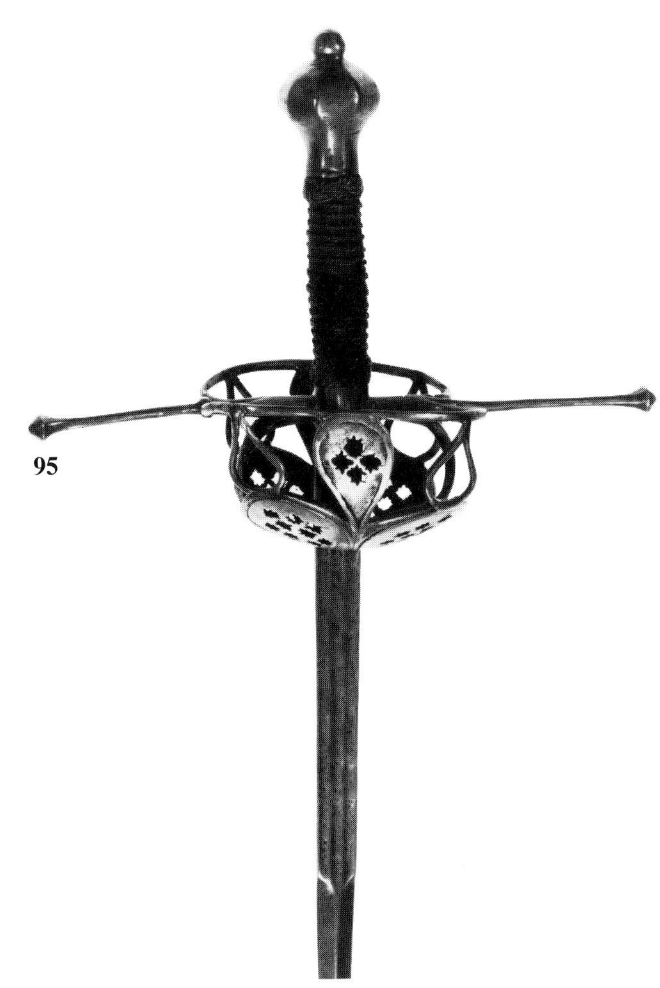

95

95. Duelling rapier
Blade 41½ins. (105.5cm) About 1630-1640
Hilt with guard formed of slender bars filled with pierced plates. Pommel associated. Good quality and condition.
£600 — £800

96

Photographs: 94 Peter Dale Ltd.; 95 Christie's; 96 Crown Copyright

96. English swept-hilt rapier
Blade 37¾ins. (97.5cm) About 1635
Gold damascened hilt with spiral guard at the front and rear. Fine quality, good condition. Blade pitted, gold inlay rubbed, and grip replaced. Tower of London Armouries (IX-1329).
£1,000 — £1,500

97. English rapier
Blade 41ins. (104.1cm) 1630s
Silver encrusted hilt. Blade signed 'JACOP BRACH'. A fine, distinctly English, sword in good condition. Wooden grip replaced.
£2,000

Photographs: 97 Christie's; 98 Crown Copyright; 99 Peter Dale Ltd.

99. English rapier
1630s
Silver damascened hilt; blade inscribed 'SAHAGAM'. Fine quality, good condition. Hilt and blade with some wear.
£1,500

98

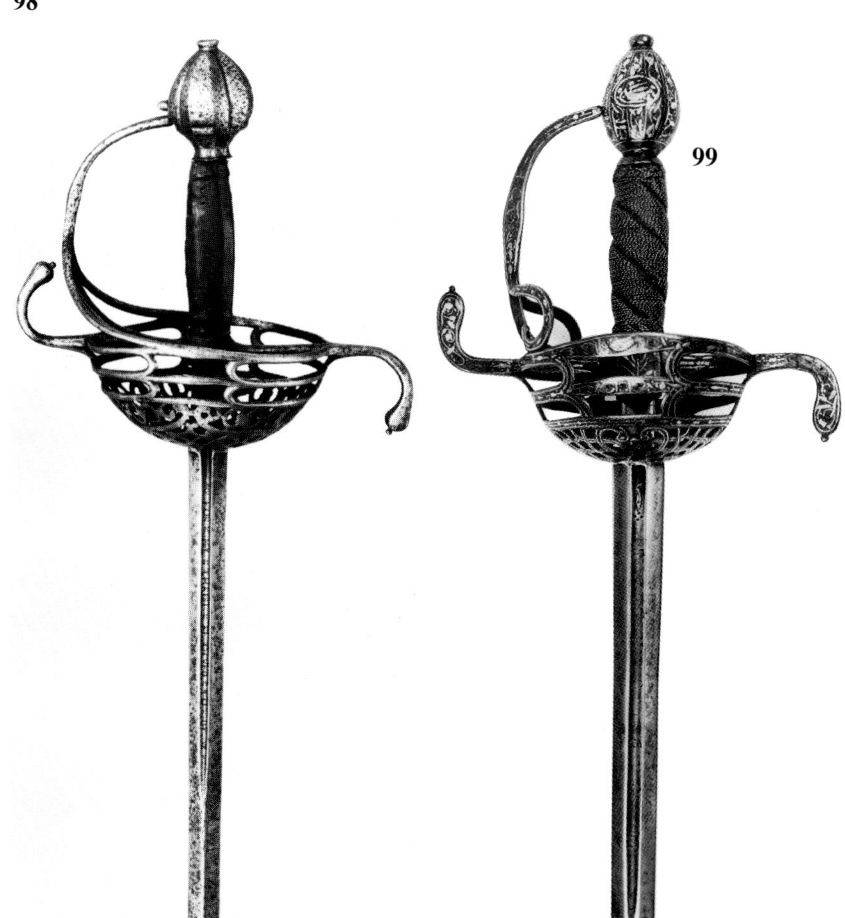

99

97

98. English rapier
About 1625-1640
Steel hilt. Blade of narrow diamond section inscribed with the motto 'FOR MY CHRIST RESOLVED TO DY, WHO HAVES ME LET HIM WARE ME'. Good quality. Worn overall, the grip without its wire binding. Tower of London Armouries (IX-1380).
£600 — £800

100

101

101. English rapier
100 restored and carefully cleaned; the grip with new wire binding.
£700 — £800

Photographs: 100 Sotheby's; 101 Peter Dale Ltd.; 102 Crown Copyright.

102. English rapier
Length 46½ins. (118.1cm) About 1640
Steel hilt, formerly gilt, chiselled with portrait heads thought to portray Charles I (executed 1649) and his Queen, Henrietta Maria. Blade stamped 'VICENCIO GIMAN'. Very fine quality. Compare the quality of the chiselling on this hilt with 101. Tower of London Armouries (IX-883).
£2,000

102

100. English rapier
Length 44⅜ins. (112.7cm) 1640s
Gilded iron hilt chiselled with fruit, satyrs and swags. Blade stamped 'CLEMENS MEIGENN'. Fine quality but in rather poor condition. Grip binding missing (see 101).
£350 — £450

103

105. English rapier
About 1640-1645
Russet iron hilt chiselled with baskets of fruit, scrolls and winged cherubs' heads. Pierced blade signed 'CLEMENS POTER'. Fine quality, very good condition.
£1,500

103. English rapier
About 1630-1650
Brass hilt retaining traces of original silver coating. Fine quality but worn overall. Tower of London Armouries (IX-1011).
£800 — £1,200

Photographs: 103 Crown Copyright; 104 Christie's; 105 Peter Dale Ltd.

104. English rapier
Blade 36½ins. (92.7cm) 1630-1650
Chiselled iron hilt similar to 103 but with two quillons. Blade stamped 'IANIES WIRSBERG'. Originally of fine quality, reasonable condition. Grip rebound.
£800 — £1,200

104 105

106

106. English rapier
Length 43½ins. (110.5cm) About 1640-1645
Hilt similar in form to 105 but chiselled with cavalry combat scenes, trophies and portrait medallions. Blade stamped 'DE FRANCISCO RUIS EN TOLEDO'. Very fine quality and condition. Grip binding missing. Tower of London Armouries (IX-986).
£2,000

107

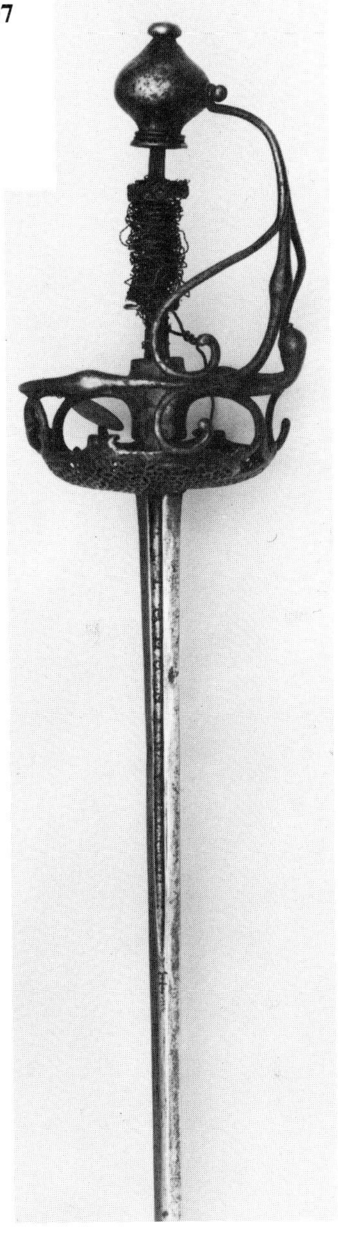

107. Rapier, possibly English
Blade 41¾ins. (106cm) 1650s
Blade signed 'CLEMENS IHN SOLINGEN'. Worn overall and in need of restoration (see 108).
£300 — £400

108. Rapier, possibly English
107 cleaned, and fitted with a new grip binding.
£500 — £600

108

Photographs: 106 Crown Copyright; 107 Christie's; 108 Sotheby's

***Colour Plate 2.** American War of Independence sword of honour, Paris, 1779. For details see no. 193.*
Sotheby, Parke-Bernet, NY

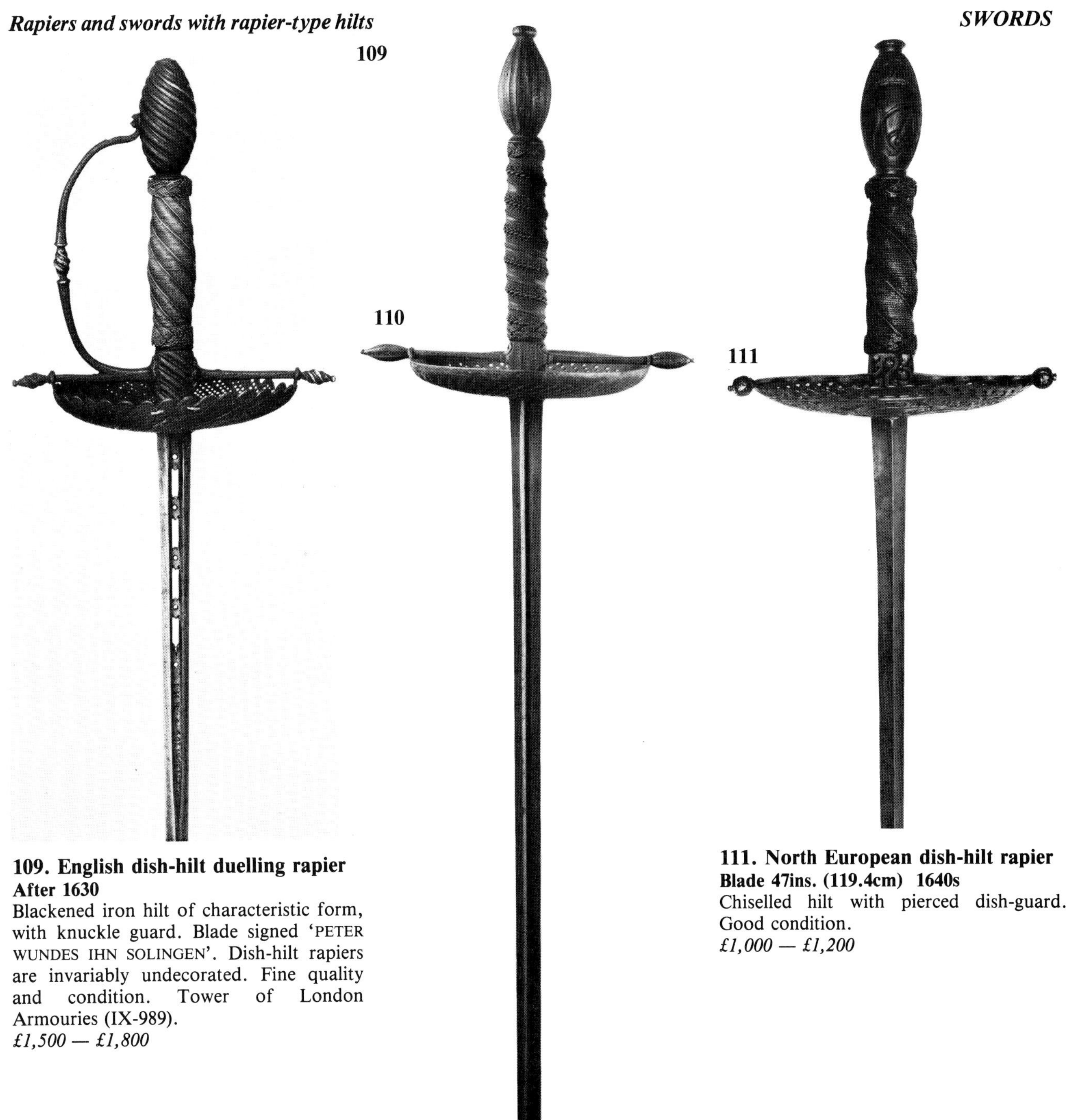

109. English dish-hilt duelling rapier
After 1630
Blackened iron hilt of characteristic form, with knuckle guard. Blade signed 'PETER WUNDES IHN SOLINGEN'. Dish-hilt rapiers are invariably undecorated. Fine quality and condition. Tower of London Armouries (IX-989).
£1,500 — £1,800

111. North European dish-hilt rapier
Blade 47ins. (119.4cm) 1640s
Chiselled hilt with pierced dish-guard. Good condition.
£1,000 — £1,200

110. German dish-hilt duelling rapier
Length 52ins. (132cm) About 1650
Hilt of russet steel. A fine sword in excellent condition.
£1,200 — £1,800

Photographs: 109 Crown Copyright; 110 Sotheby's; 111 Christie's

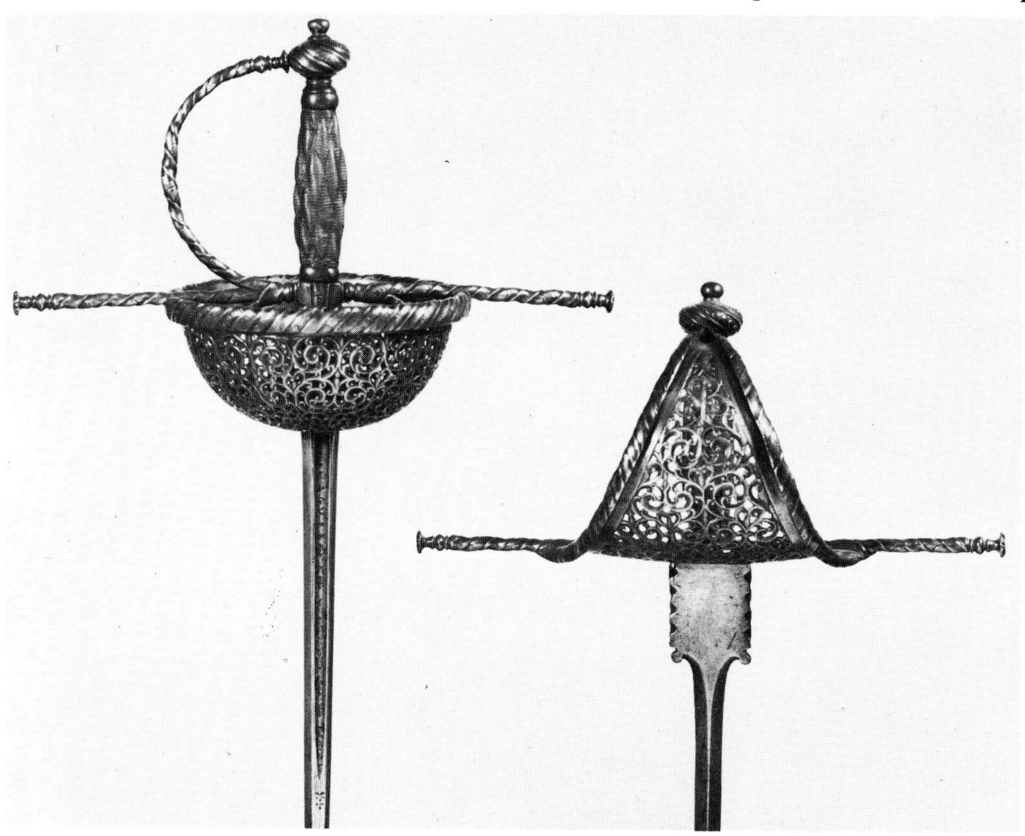

112

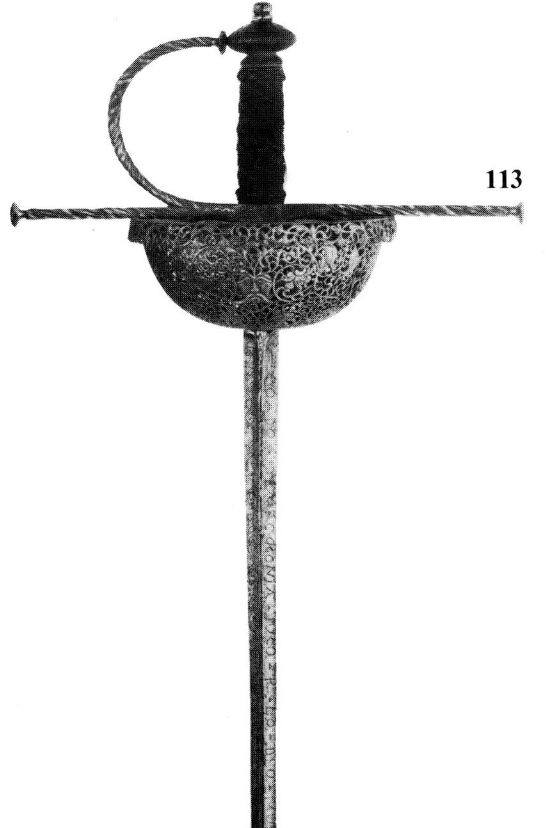

113

112. Spanish or Neapolitan cup-hilt rapier and dagger
Sword blade 39½ins. (100cm), dagger blade 19½ins. (49.5cm)
Third quarter 17th century
Companion left-hand dagger. The cup and triangular guard have turned rims (*rompepuntas*), and are finely chiselled and pierced with foliate scrolls. The sword blade is signed 'HORTUNA AGUIRE EN TOLEDO'. Fine quality and condition.
£6,000 — £10,000

113. Neapolitan cup-hilt rapier
Length 51¼ins. (130cm) Third quarter 17th century
The cup guard chiselled with masks and scrolled foliage and signed 'LAURENTIUS PALUMBO DE NEAPOLI FECIT' (Laurentius Palumbo of Naples made this). Fine quality, very good condition.
£1,500 — £2,000

Photographs: 112 Christie's; 113 Sotheby's

114

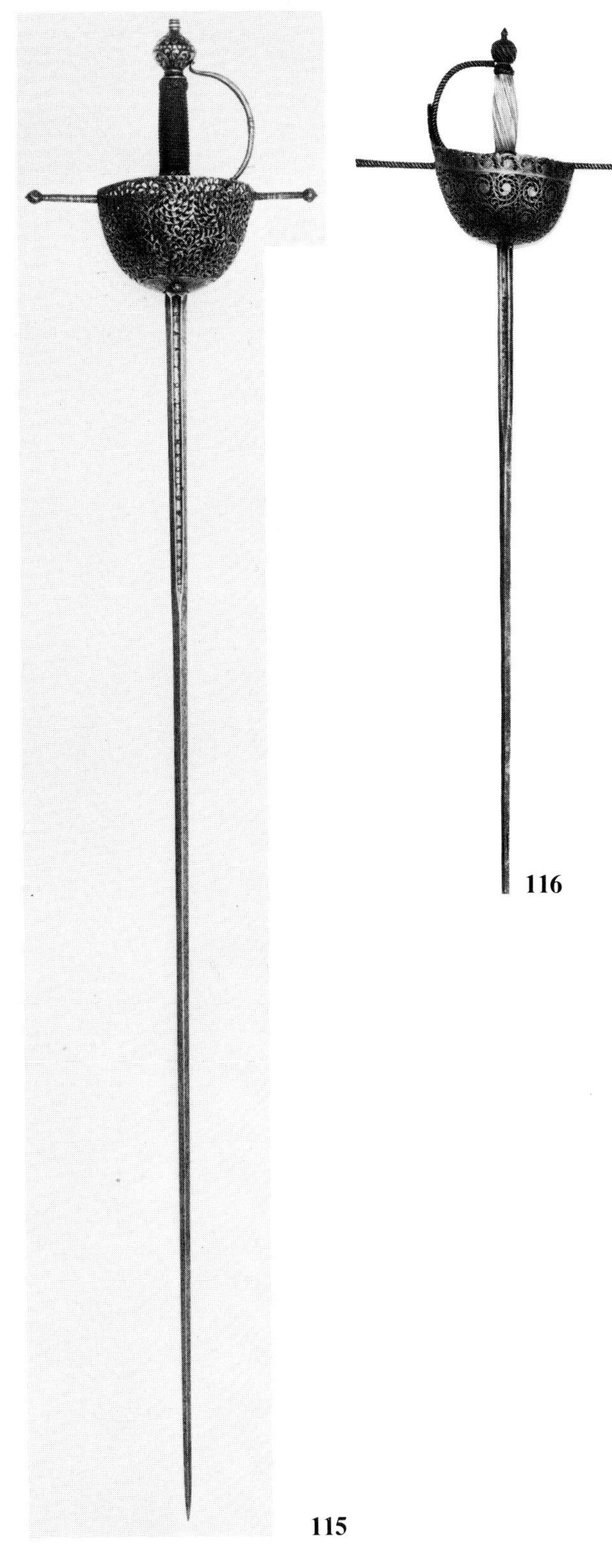
116

115

114. Spanish cup-hilt rapier
Blade 43½ins. (110.5cm) Third quarter 17th century
The steel hilt with chiselled and pierced cup and pommel, and wire-bound grip secured by vertical copper straps and brass ferrules. The blade inscribed in Portuguese 'ENRIKE COL ESPADEIRO DEL REY EM ALEMANHA' (Henry, at the Royal swordsmiths, in Germany). Very good quality, good condition.
£1,500 — £2,000

115. Sicilian rapier
Length 45ins. (114.5cm) Second half 17th century
The steel hilt with deep cup guard, chiselled and pierced. Pommel associated. The long blade of diamond section signed in the fuller 'BARTOLOMEO LOPRESTI, FABRICA DI PALERMO' (Bartolomeo Lopresti at the workshop in Palermo). Rare and of fine quality, good condition.
£1,500 — £2,500

116. Italian rapier
Length 51½ins. (130.8cm) Second half 17th century
The deep cup curves upwards to join the knuckle guard on the forward side. Writhen ivory grip and associated pommel. A quality sword in reasonable condition.
£1,200 — £1,800

Photographs: 114 Christie's; 115 and 116 Sotheby's

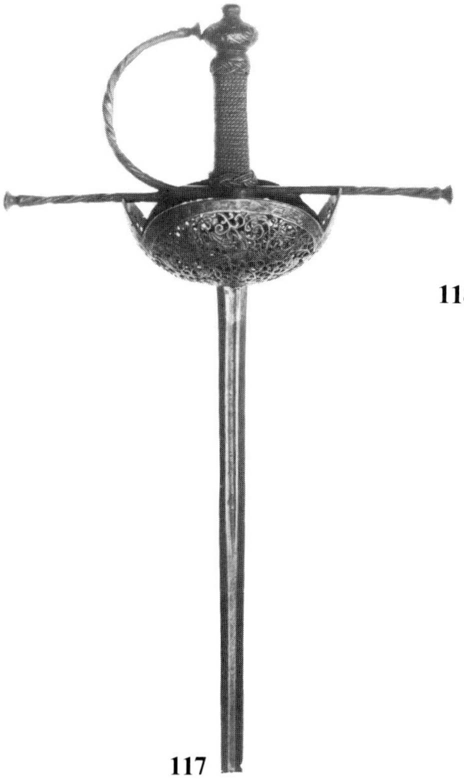

117. Brescian cup-hilt rapier
Blade 41ins. (104cm) Third quarter 17th century
The steel hilt chiselled and pierced with birds among foliage on the cup. Blade stamped 'LUIGI SAHAGUM'. Fine quality, very good condition.
£2,000 — £2,500

118

117

118. Brescian cup-hilt rapier
Detail of the cup of 117.

119. Brescian cup-hilt rapier
Inside of the cup of 117 showing the dust guard *(guardapolvo)* pierced and chiselled *en suite* with the hilt.

119

Photographs: Christie's

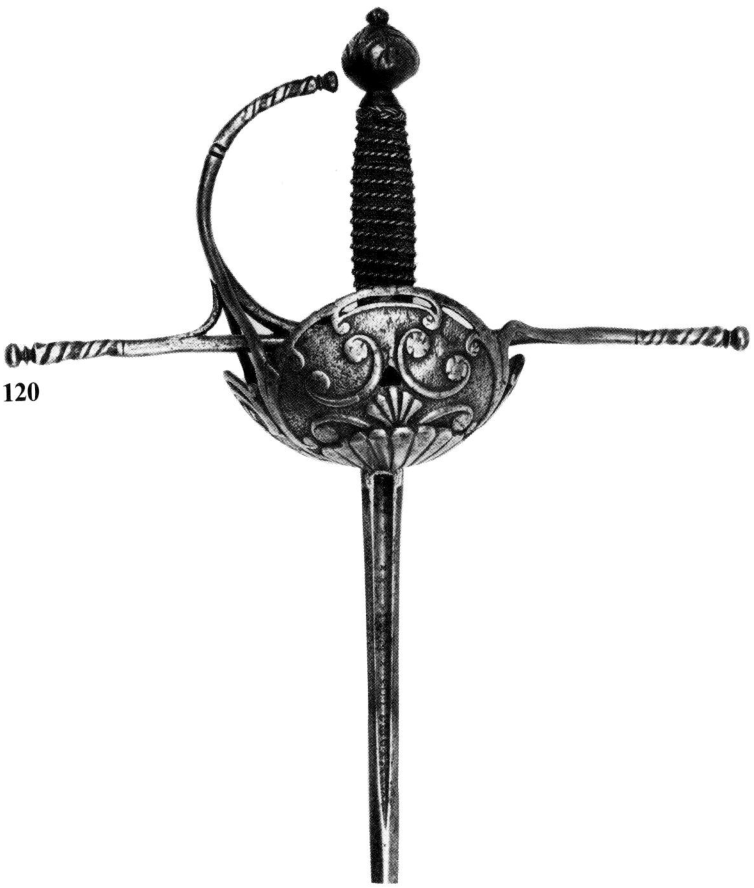

122

120

121

120. Spanish or Neapolitan cup-hilt rapier
Second half 17th century
The steel hilt boldly embossed with scallop shell motifs and scrolls on the cup. Blade stamped 'IHN SOLINGEN'. Good quality, worn overall.
£600 — £800

121. Spanish or Neapolitan rapier
Length 45ins. (114cm) Second half 17th century
The cup guard formed of two plates embossed with cavalry combats and linked to each other by steel loops. The blade of hexagonal section signed 'FRANCISCO RUIZ'. Good quality and condition.
£600 — £800

122. North Italian rapier
Length 43ins. (109.2cm) Second half 17th century
The hilt constructed in a similar way to 121; pommel associated. Good quality, reasonable condition.
£500 — £800

Photographs: 120 Peter Dale Ltd.; 121 Sotheby's; 122 Christie's

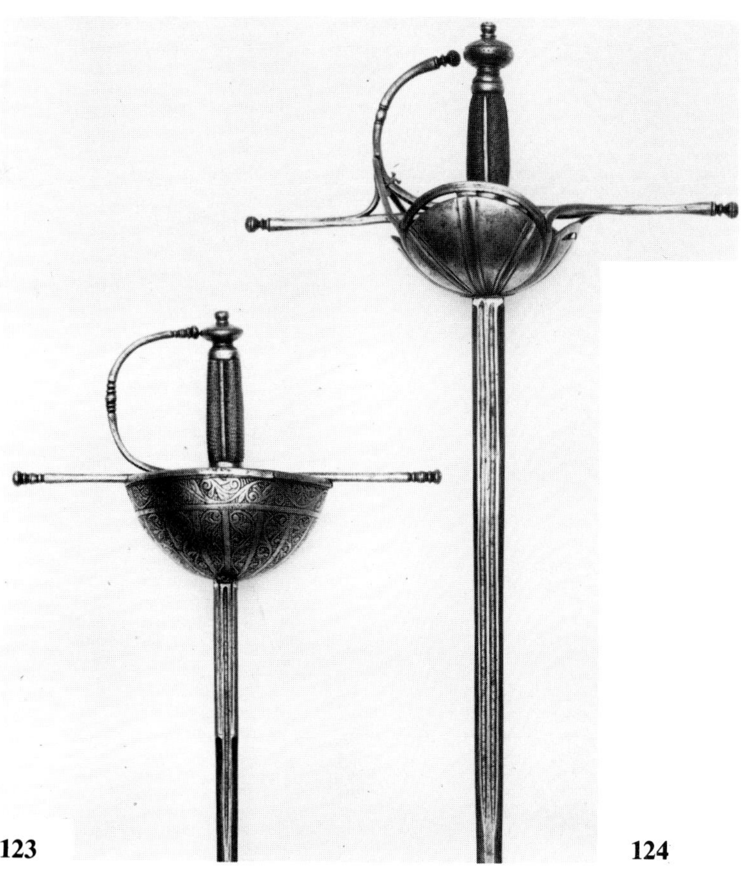

123 124

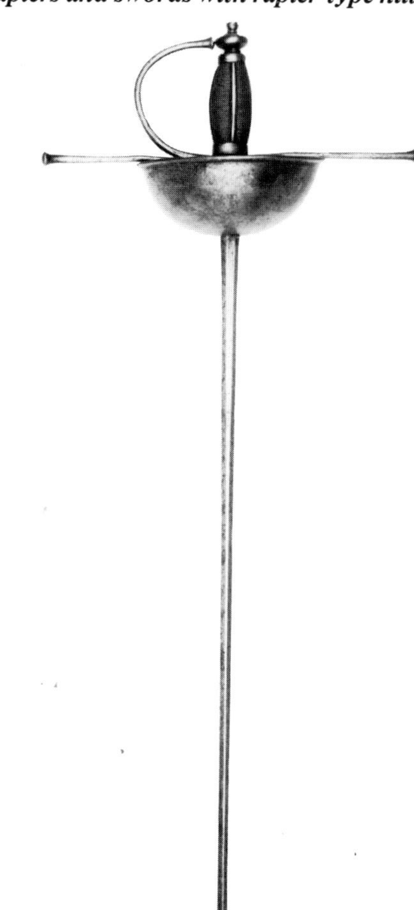

125

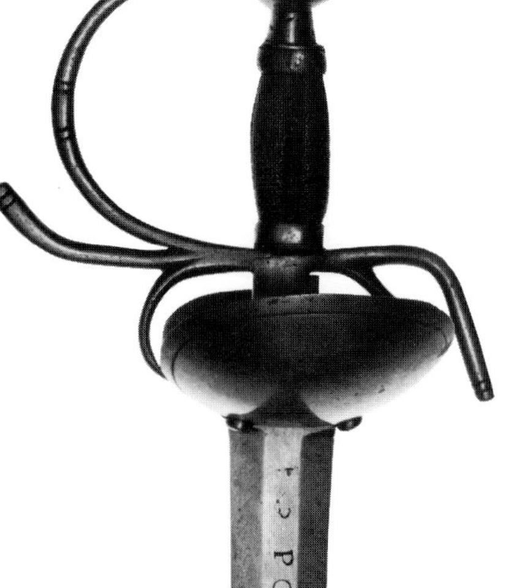

126

Photographs: 123-125 Sotheby's; 126 Christie's

123. Spanish cup-hilt rapier
Length 43ins. (109.2cm) About 1675 or later
The hilt with etched cup and fitted with an earlier blade signed 'PEDRO LORACO ME FECIT SOLINGEN ANNO 1617' (Pedro Loraco made me in Solingen, 1617). Good quality and condition.
£800 — £1,200

124. Spanish cup-hilt rapier
Length 45½ins. (115.5cm) About 1675 or later
Good quality and condition.
£800 — £1,200

125. Spanish cup-hilt rapier
Length 46ins. (117cm) About 1675 or later
The steel hilt has a plain bowl guard. The narrow blade is inscribed with brass lettering 'SOLINGEN, QUE ES EN ALEMANIA' (Solingen, which is in Germany). A light and attractive sword in good condition.
£350 — £450

126. Spanish 'bilbo'-hilted guardsman's sword
Blade 39ins. (99cm) Dated 1771
Robust hilt of steel with wire-bound grip. The two-edged blade inscribed 'POR EL REY CARLOS III' (For King Carlos III). Regulation issue, good condition.
£120 — £180

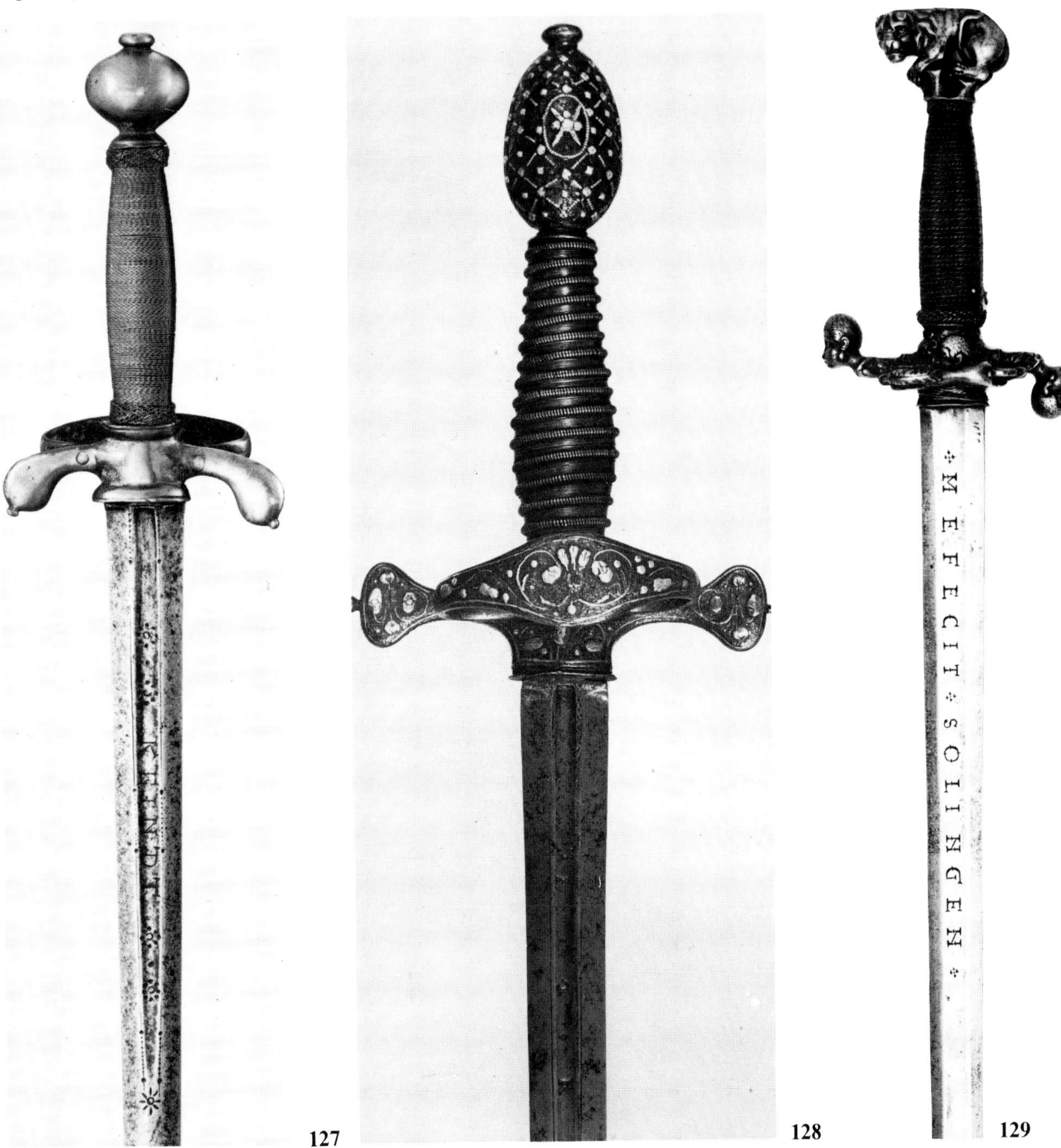

127 128 129

127. English light rapier
About 1650
The hilt of brass with side ring filled with a steel plate. Blade signed in the fullers 'IOHANNES KEINDT'. Good quality and condition. Tower of London Armouries (IX-1374).
£300 — £600

128. North European light rapier
Blade 38¾ins. (97cm) 1650s
Silver encrusted hilt with side ring and associated pommel of earlier date (about 1610). Blade stamped 'ANDREA FERARA'. Fine quality, good condition.
£300 — £600

129. Dutch sword
Length 40¼ins. (102.2cm) Mid-17th century
The chiselled steel hilt, with side ring, is decorated with blackamoor-head quillons and a pommel in the form of a squatting lion. Blade inscribed 'MEVES BERNS ME FECIT SOLINGEN'. Fine quality, good condition.
£1,500+

Photographs: 127 Crown Copyright; 128 Sotheby, Parke-Bernet, LA; 129 Sotheby's

130. Light rapier, probably Italian
Third quarter 17th century
Steel hilt chiselled with winged cherubs' heads and fitted with a side ring filled with a plate.
£600

131. Light rapier, probably German
Third quarter 17th century
Blackened iron hilt chiselled with similar features to 129.
£1,000+

132. Light rapier, probably North Italian (Brescian)
Third quarter 17th century
Chiselled steel hilt. Blade inscribed 'EN TOLEDO'.
£600 — £800

Photographs: 130-132 Peter Dale Ltd.

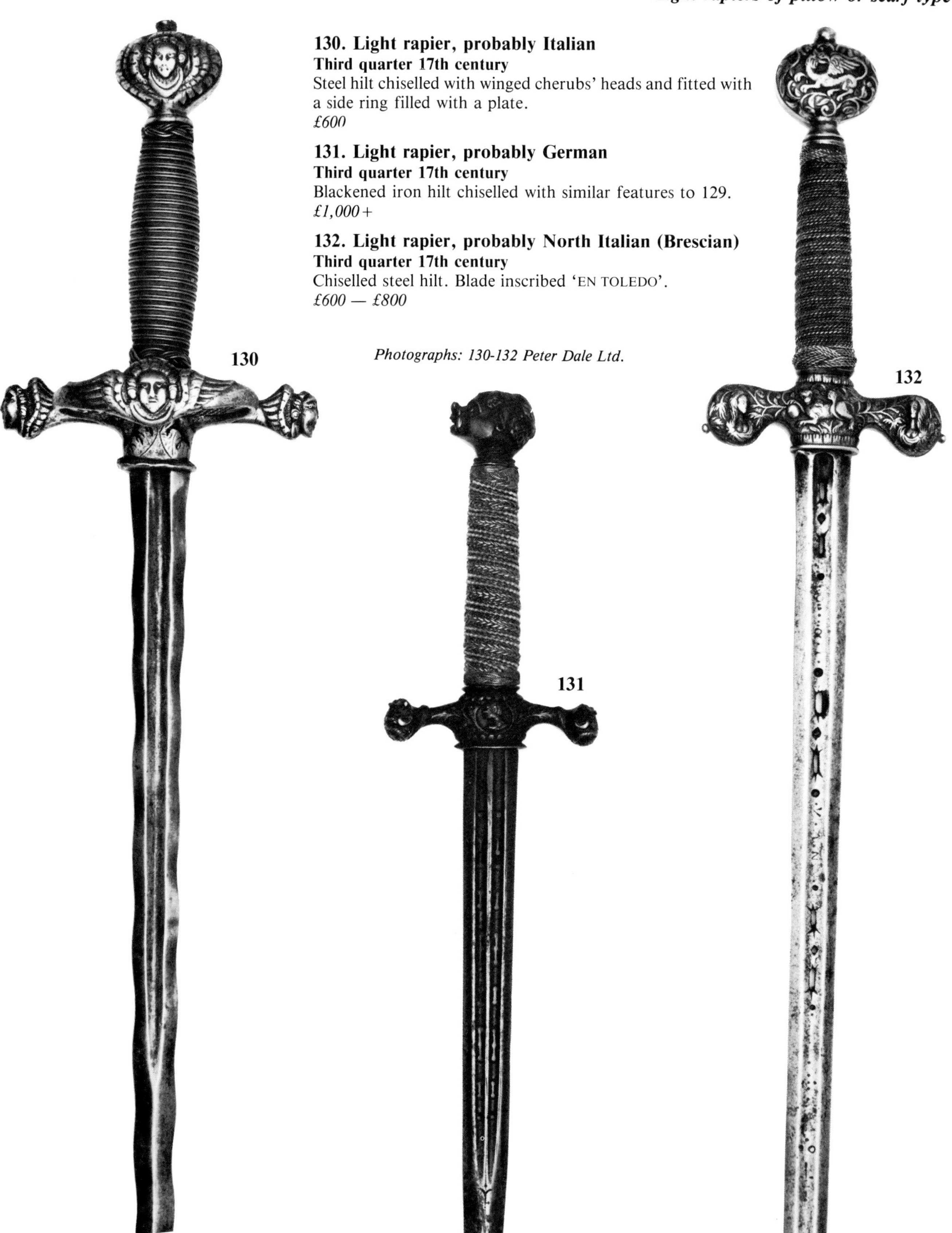

130

131

132

133

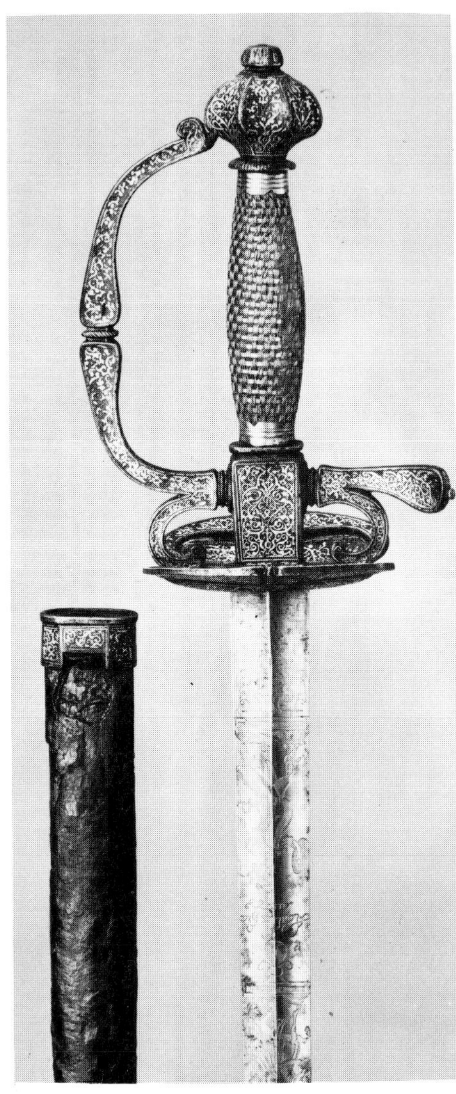

134

135

133. French small-sword
Dated 1651
The russet steel hilt damascened in gold. Etched and gilt blade of incurved triangular section. A very fine quality sword, traditionally believed to have belonged to the parliamentarian commander Major General Charles Worsley (d. 1656). Tower of London Armouries (IX-1428).
£2,000+

134. English small-sword
Length 41ins. (104.1cm) About 1650
The hilt of blackened iron encrusted with silver. Fine quality; some wear on the etched blade. Tower of London Armouries (IX-997).
£1,000 — £1,500

135. North European small-sword
About 1660
The iron hilt heavily encrusted with silver. Fine quality, very good condition. Grip binding missing. Wrangel Armoury, Skokloster (7240).
£800 — £1,200

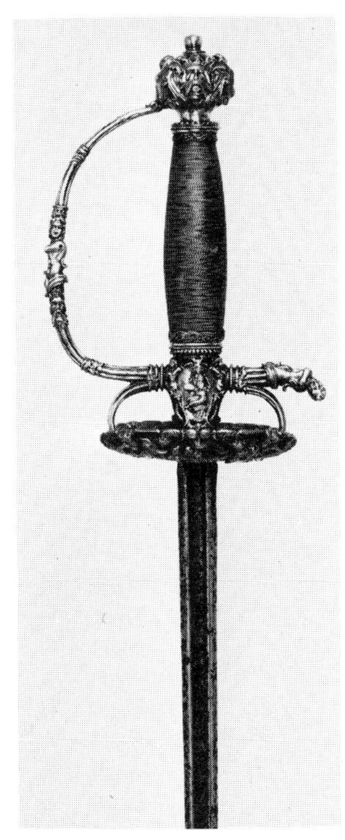

136

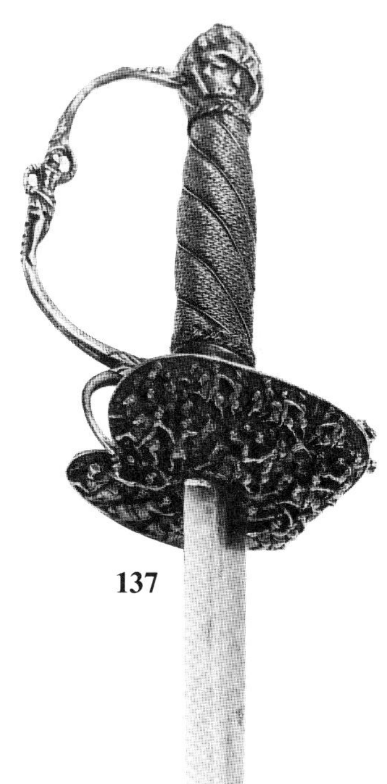

137

136. Small-sword, probably Dutch
About 1650-1660
A very fine quality sword with chiselled steel hilt. Blade worn. Victoria and Albert Museum (61.1947).
£2,000

137. Dutch small-sword
About 1660
The steel hilt chiselled with a spirited equestrian battle scene on the shell-guards. Fine quality, good condition.
£800 — £1,200

Photographs:
133 and 134 Crown Copyright;
137 Peter Dale Ltd.

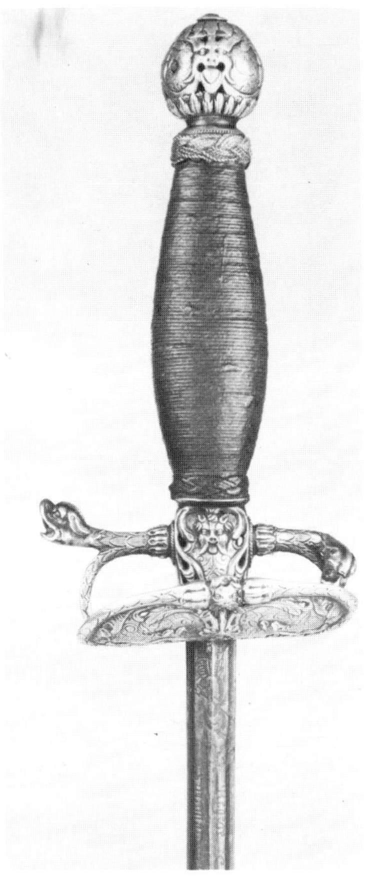

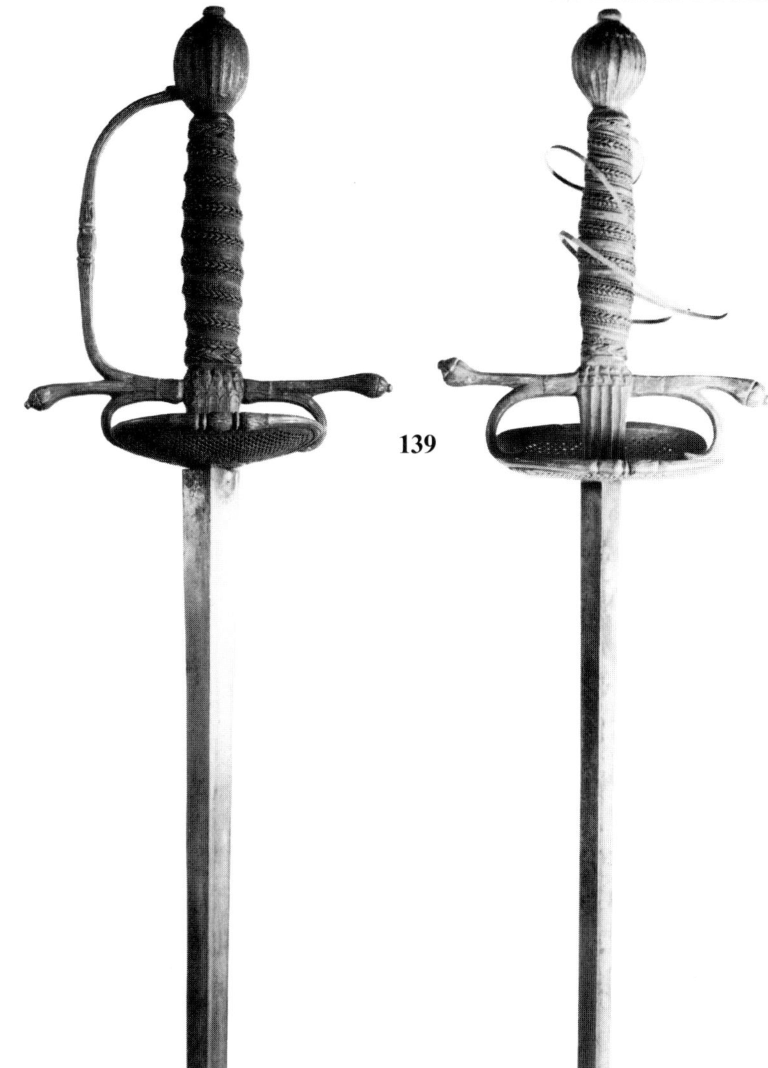

139

138

140

138. English silver-hilted small-sword
Blade 29ins. (73.6cm) London, 1673-1674
A rare example of early date decorated with grotesques and stamped with an unidentified maker's mark 'D.D.' Etched blade. Good condition. One quillon bent.
£1,000

139. German duelling swords
Left: Length 44ins. (111.8cm) About 1675
Right: Length 46¾ins. (118.8cm) About 1675
The left-hand example has a russet steel hilt with long quillons and pierced shell guards. Complete with scabbard (not shown). Plain, but of very good quality and condition. The right-hand example is similar but without a knuckle guard. Fine condition. The steel ribbon binding on the grip is loose but can be repaired easily.
Left: £1,000 — £1,500
Right: £800 — £1,200

140. Silver-hilted small-sword, probably Dutch
Blade 32ins. (81.3cm) Last quarter 17th century
Cast and chased hilt fitted with a grip of later date (about 1810). Fine quality, good condition. The etched blade is later.
£600 — £800

Photographs: 138 and 140 Christie's; 139 Sotheby's

141

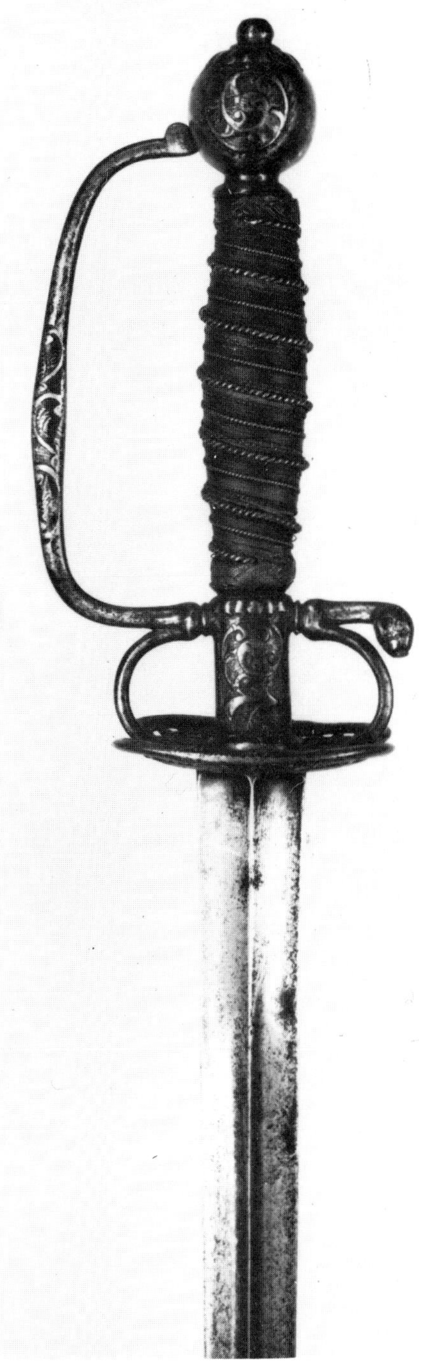

142

143

141. English or Dutch small-sword
Blade 36ins. (91.5cm) About 1690
Brass hilt formerly gilt; the blade with pronounced rib. Fine quality. Good condition but the quillon is bent.
£600

142. English small-sword
Blade 38½ins. (90.2cm) About 1690
Silver encrusted iron hilt with re-bound grip. Originally of fine quality, but now worn overall.
£500 — £600

143. English or Dutch small-sword
Blade 32ins. (81.1cm) About 1690
The hilt of chiselled steel with pierced shell guards and silver wire-bound grip. Fine quality, good condition.
£500 — £600

Photographs: Christie's

144

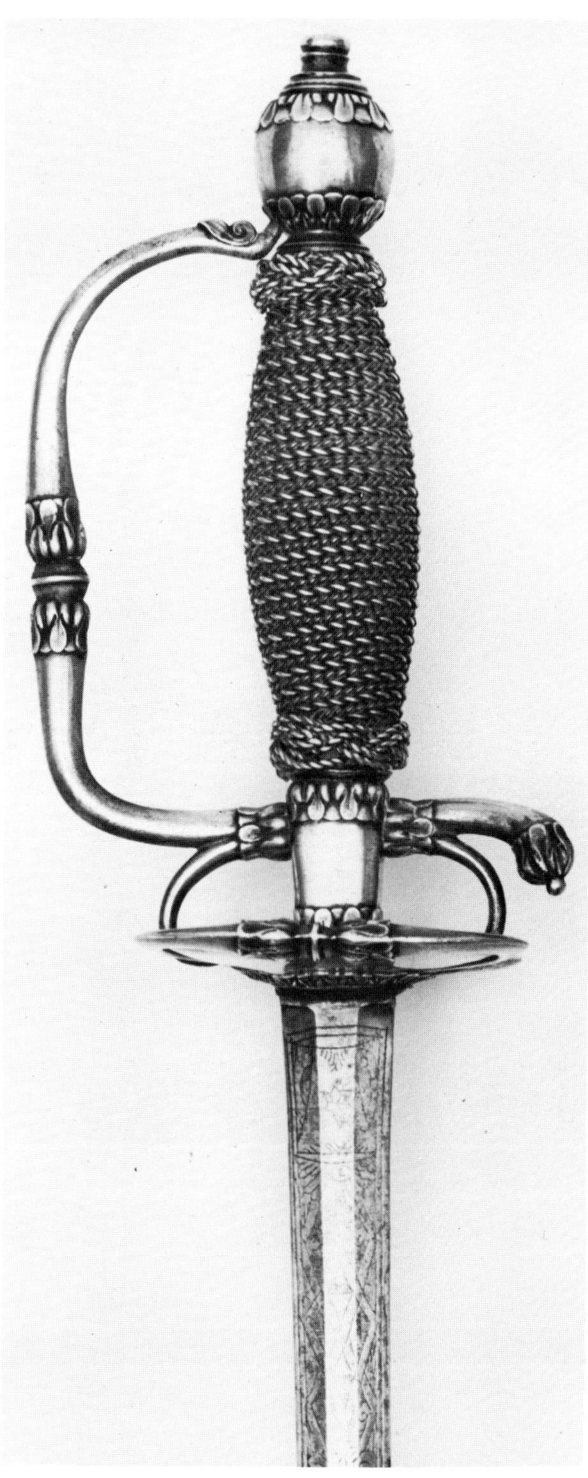

145

144. Dutch silver-hilted small-sword of English type
Late 17th century
A sword of robust form cast with acanthus ornament on the silver hilt. Etched blade of hexagonal section. Fine quality, very good condition.
£500 — £600

145. English silver-hilted small-sword
London, 1696-1697
Cast and chased hilt struck on the shell guards with London hallmarks and with an unidentified maker's mark ('RF' conjoined in a shield). Fine quality and condition.
£500 — £800

Photographs: Peter Dale Ltd.

146

148

147. North European small-sword
About 1700
Finely chiselled steel hilt pierced on the sleeve covering the ricasso. The narrow blade signed in the fuller 'ANTONIO RUIS'. Very fine quality and condition. Victoria and Albert Museum (M.71-1947).
£2,000

146. Small-sword, probably Dutch
Blade 32½ins. (87cm) About 1700
The steel hilt with longitudinal grooved decoration and replaced grip. The etched slender blade with fuller. Good quality and condition.
£400 — £600

148. Dutch small-sword
Blade 29¾ins. (75.5cm) About 1700
The hilt of blackened iron cut with flutes and chequering. The etched blade of incurved triangular section is heavily pitted. Good quality and condition.
£400 — £500

147

Photographs: Christie's

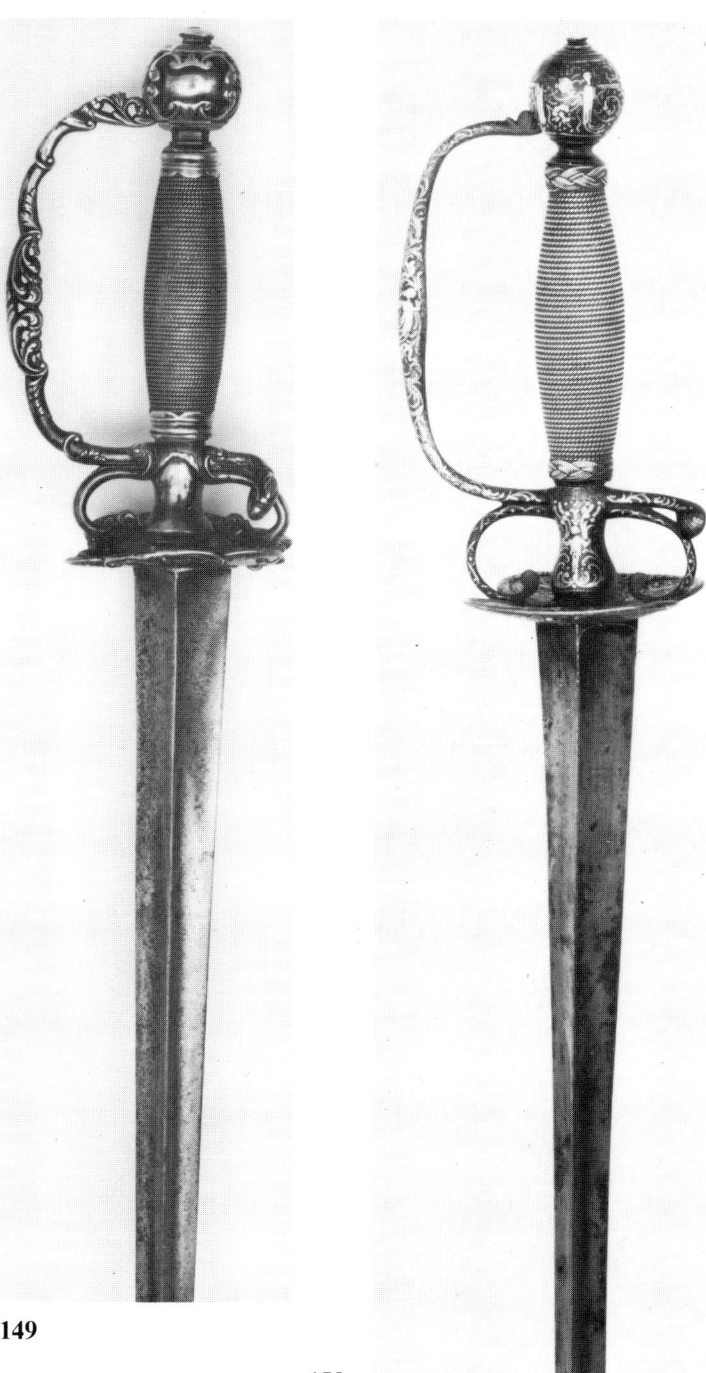

149

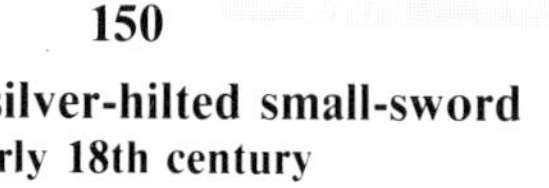

150

151

149. Dutch or English silver-hilted small-sword
Blade 29½ins. (75cm) Early 18th century
The hilt struck with an unknown maker's mark, 'D.H'. Fine quality, good condition. The shell guard is slightly buckled and the quillon bent.
£400 — £600

150. French small-sword
Blade 30ins. (76.2cm) Early 18th century
An attractively proportioned sword with gold damascened hilt and silver wire-bound grip. Good condition.
£400 — £500

151. French small-sword
Blade 31ins. (80cm) Early 18th century
The iron hilt encrusted with gold trophies of arms and foliage. The dark patches on the blade are the result of cleaning away rust. Fine quality, good condition.
£500 — £600

Photographs: Christie's

153

Photographs: 152 Peter Dale Ltd.; 153 and 154 Christie's

152

152. German silver-hilted small-sword
Augsburg, early 18th century
The hilt is fitted with a faceted bloodstone grip. The etched and gilt blade is of oval section. Fine quality and condition, but the gilding on the blade is worn.
£500 — £700

153. English silver-hilted small-sword
30¼ins. (76.8cm) London, 1717-1718
The cast and chased silver hilt is rather worn and the silver wire-binding on the grip is loose. Originally of fine quality. Good condition.
£400 — £600

154. English silver-hilted small-sword
Blade 31ins. (78.7cm) London, 1721-1722
A plain but elegant sword struck with an unidentified maker's mark ('WM' in monogram). The etched colichemarde blade worn. Very good condition.
£400

154

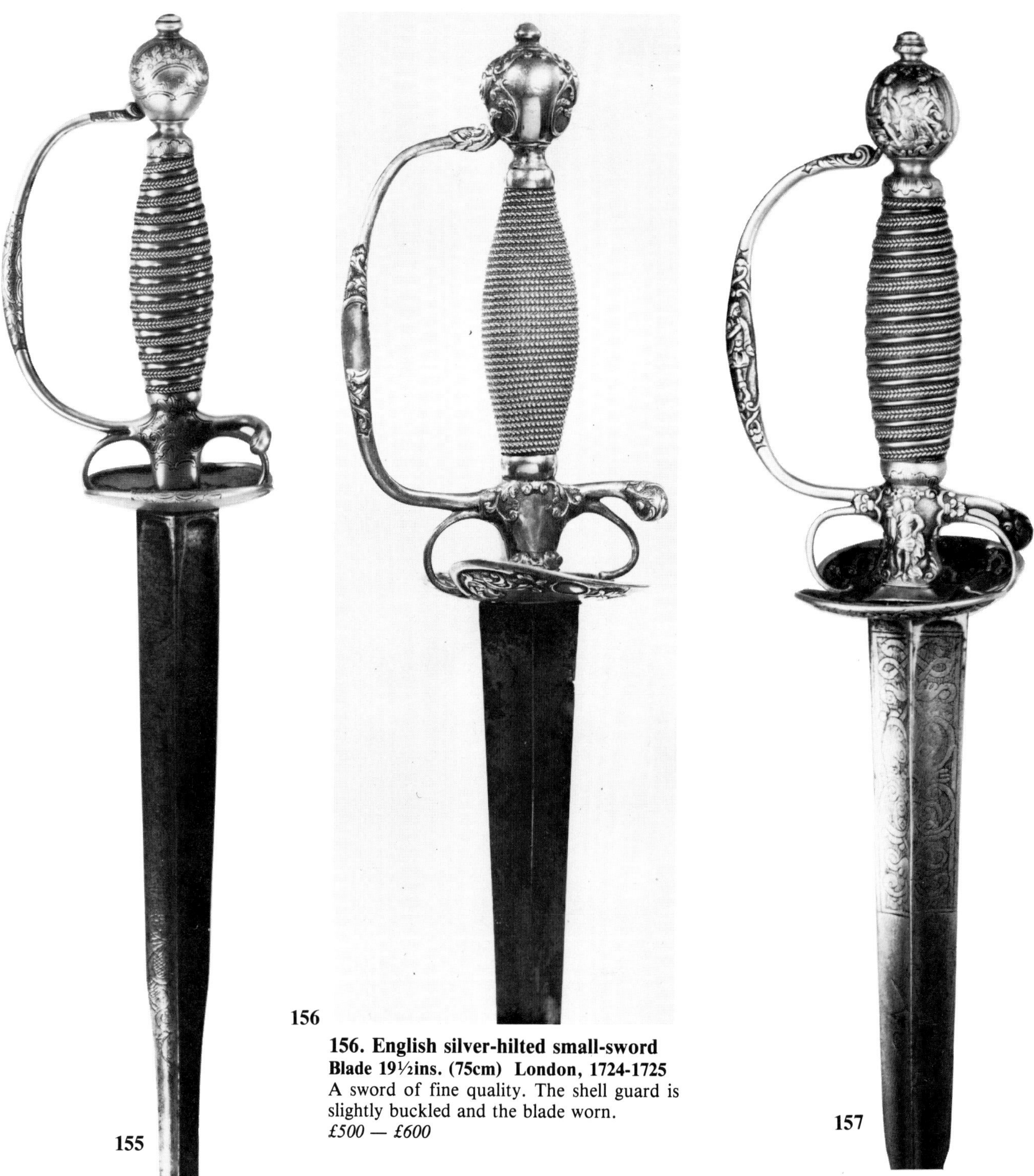

155 156 157

156. English silver-hilted small-sword
Blade 19½ins. (75cm) London, 1724-1725
A sword of fine quality. The shell guard is slightly buckled and the blade worn.
£500 — £600

155. English silver-hilted small-sword
Blade 32½ins. (82.5cm) London, 1723-1724
The hilt engraved with later rococo ornament and struck with an unidentified maker's mark (apparently 'MW'). Etched colichemarde blade. Fine quality, very good condition.
£500 — £600

157. English silver-hilted small-sword
Blade 33¼ins. (82cm) London, 1724-1725
Hilt cast and chased with mythological figures and scrolls. Etched colichemarde blade. Fine quality, very good condition.
£500 — £600

Photographs: Christie's

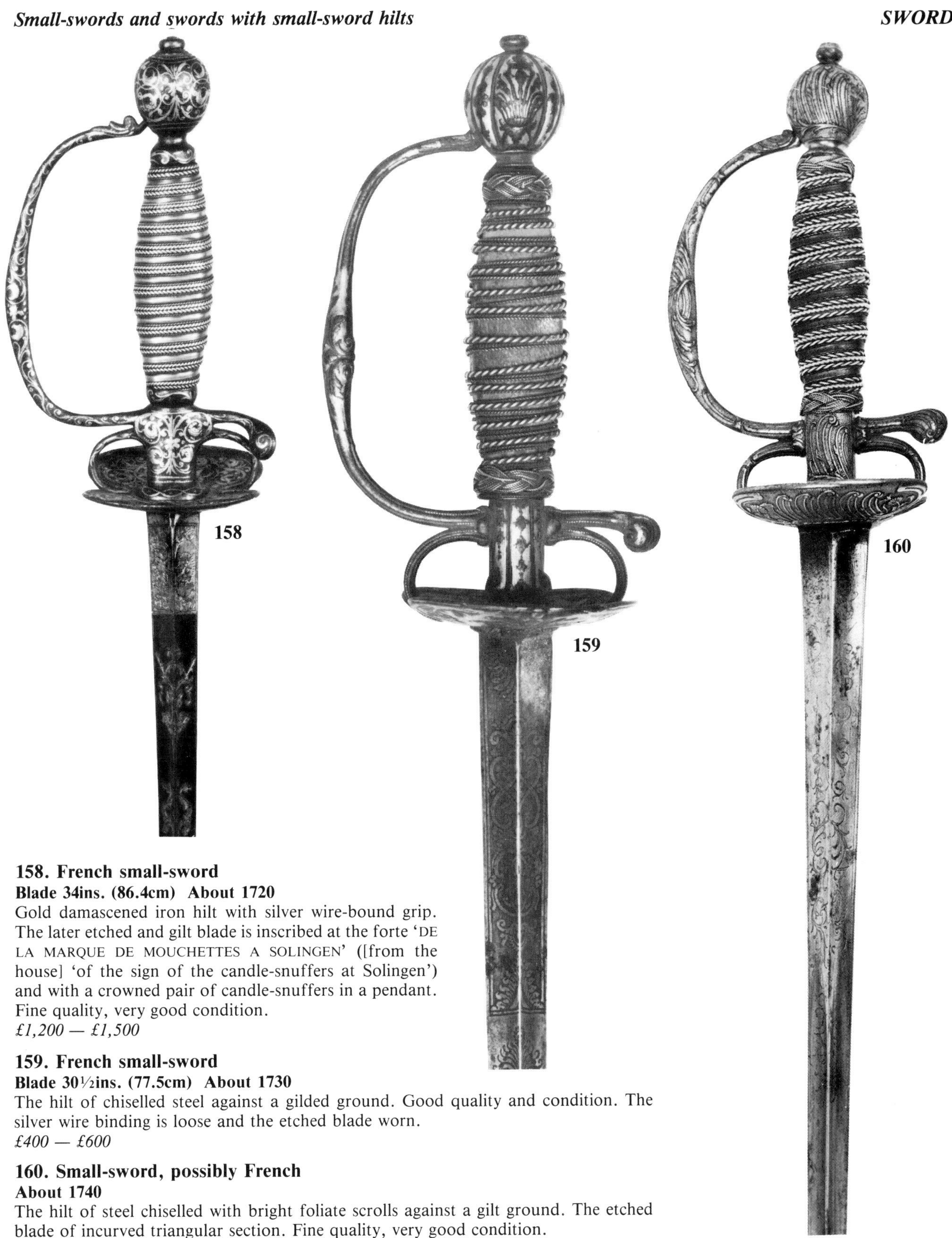

158. French small-sword
Blade 34ins. (86.4cm) About 1720
Gold damascened iron hilt with silver wire-bound grip. The later etched and gilt blade is inscribed at the forte 'DE LA MARQUE DE MOUCHETTES A SOLINGEN' ([from the house] 'of the sign of the candle-snuffers at Solingen') and with a crowned pair of candle-snuffers in a pendant. Fine quality, very good condition.
£1,200 — £1,500

159. French small-sword
Blade 30½ins. (77.5cm) About 1730
The hilt of chiselled steel against a gilded ground. Good quality and condition. The silver wire binding is loose and the etched blade worn.
£400 — £600

160. Small-sword, possibly French
About 1740
The hilt of steel chiselled with bright foliate scrolls against a gilt ground. The etched blade of incurved triangular section. Fine quality, very good condition.
£1,000

Photographs: 158-159 Christie's; 160 Peter Dale Ltd.

162. English silver-hilted small-sword
Blade 32ins. (81.2cm) London, 1741-1742
The hilt cast and chased with classical figures and lions' heads, and struck with an unidentified maker's mark, 'MC' in script with a pellet between. The etched and gilt blade with the royal coat of arms and inscribed 'VIVAT GEORGE KONIG VON ENGELANDT.' Fine quality. Blade worn.
£500 — £600

163. English silver-hilted small-sword
Blade 30¾ins. (78cm) London, 1744-1745
Rococo decorated hilt struck with an unidentified maker's mark, 'PM'. Fine quality, very good condition.
£400 — £500

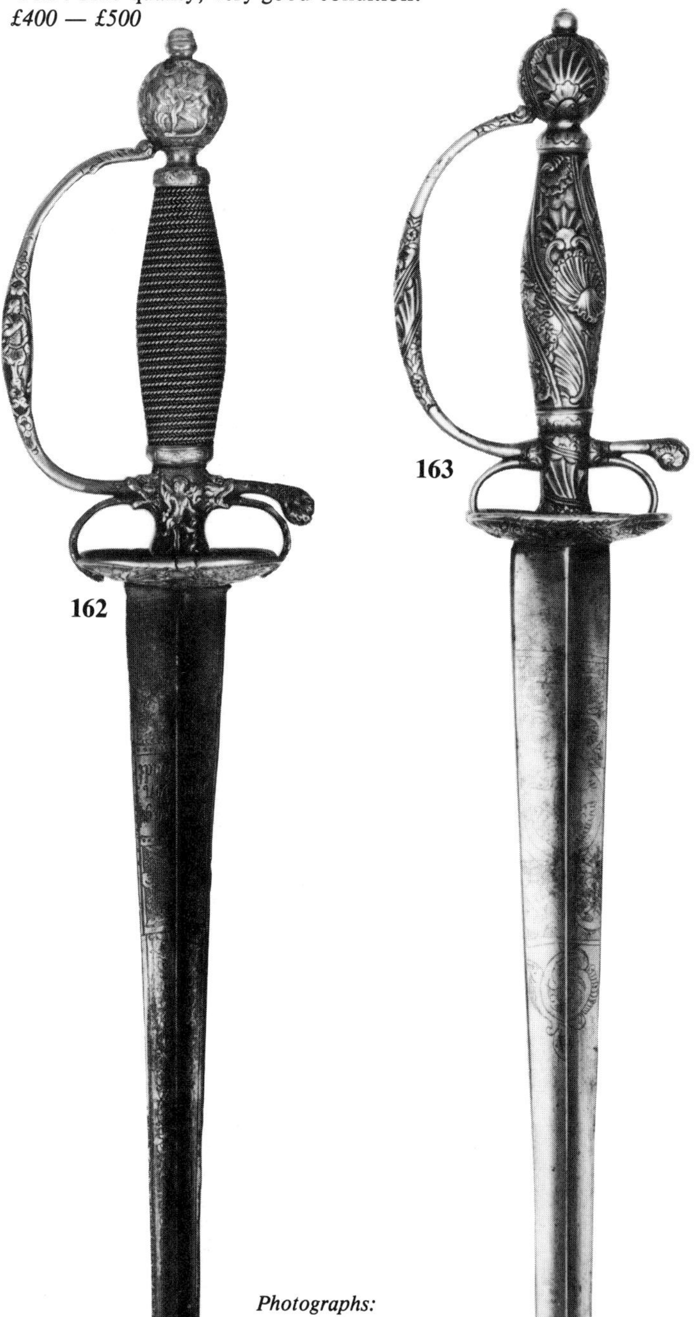

161. French small-sword
Length 34¼ins. (87cm) About 1740-1750
The steel hilt chiselled with trophies of arms and foliage against a gilt ground and with silver wire-bound grip. Original scabbard with locket decorated *en suite* with the hilt. A very attractive sword, of fine quality, in very good condition.
£500 — £600

Photographs:
161 and 164 Sotheby's;
162-163 Christie's

164. English silver-hilted small-sword
Length 39ins. (99cm) London, 1744-1745
The silver hilt, made by John Carmen, pierced and decorated with musical trophies and foliage. Fine quality, good condition, the colichemarde blade repaired.
£400 — £500

165

168

166. English silver-hilted small-sword
Blade 31¼ins. (79.4cm) About 1745-1750
Similar to 165 but with indistinct hallmarks. Very good condition. The etched blade has small patches of wear.
£300 — £400

167. English silver-hilted small sword
Blade 28½ins. (72.5cm) About 1745-1750
The hilt cast and chased with classical figures in relief against a punched ground. Plain blade. Fine quality, good condition.
£500 — £600

166

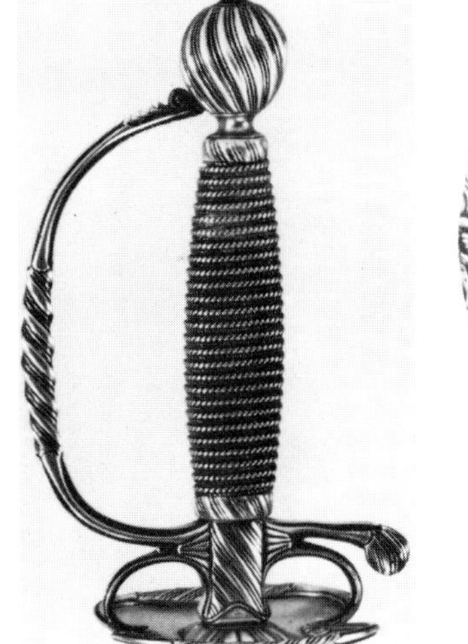

167

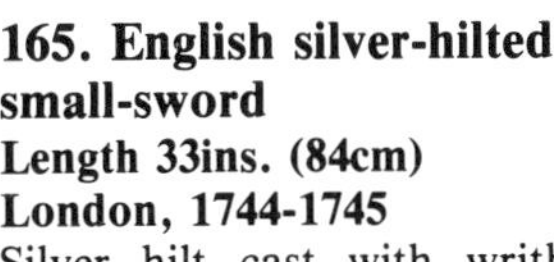

165. English silver-hilted small-sword
Length 33ins. (84cm)
London, 1744-1745
Silver hilt cast with writhen fluting and with a silver wire and ribbon bound grip. Etched colichemarde blade. Fine quality and very good condition. The front shell guard is slightly buckled.
£500 — £600

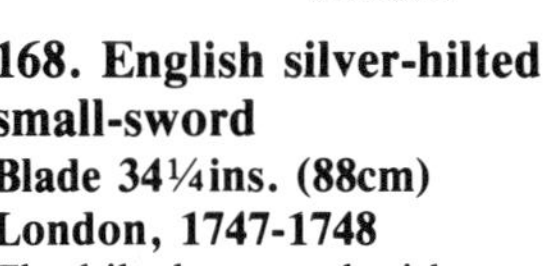

168. English silver-hilted small-sword
Blade 34¼ins. (88cm)
London, 1747-1748
The hilt decorated with rococo ornament and embellished with gilt. The collar beneath the pommel inscribed 'NORTHESK' (for Admiral George, the sixth Earl of Northesk). The name of the original owner adds value to the sword. Fine quality and very good condition. The etching on the blade worn.
£600 — £900

Photographs: Christie's

169

169. English silver-hilted small-sword
London, 1747-1748
A sword of fine quality in very good condition. Plain blade of triangular section.
£500 — £600

170. Japanese small-sword in the European style
First half 18th century
The hilt of *shakudo* (black alloy of copper and gold) made for export to Europe probably at the Dutch East India Company's factory at Deshima, Japan (Norman, 347). The etched blade inscribed 'RIEN NE M'ARETTE' (Nothing stops me). Quite a rare sword of fine quality in very good condition.
£600 — £800

170

171

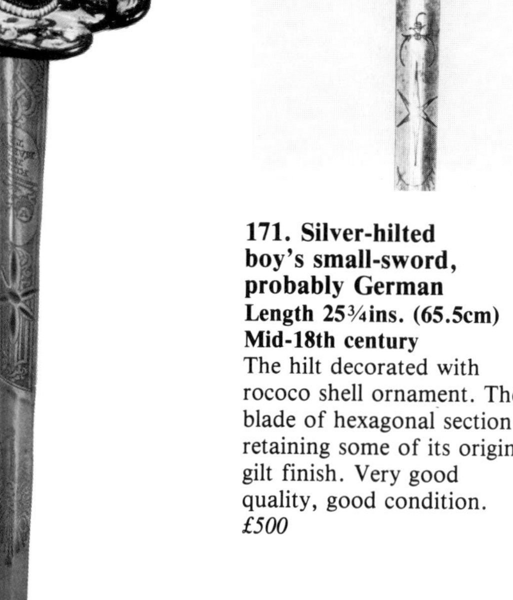

171. Silver-hilted boy's small-sword, probably German
Length 25¾ins. (65.5cm)
Mid-18th century
The hilt decorated with rococo shell ornament. The blade of hexagonal section retaining some of its original gilt finish. Very good quality, good condition.
£500

172

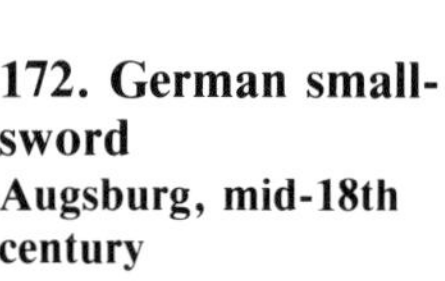

172. German small-sword
Augsburg, mid-18th century
The gilt copper hilt, with loop guard, fitted with a white Meissen porcelain grip painted with flowers. A delicate attractive sword of fine quality.
£1,000

Photographs: 169, 170 and 172 Peter Dale Ltd.; 171 Sotheby's

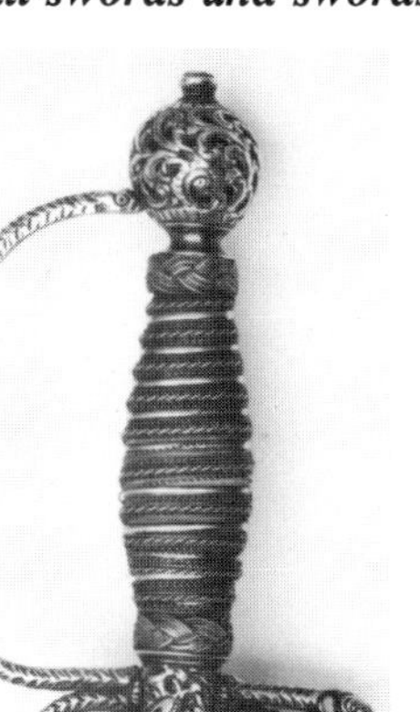

173 **176**

173. Dutch silver-hilted small-sword
Blade 33ins. (84cm) Amsterdam, about 1750
The etched colichemarde blade signed 'JACOBUS COENRAADTS & ZOON M. SWAARTVEGER TOT AMSTERDAM'. Good condition.
£400 — £600

174

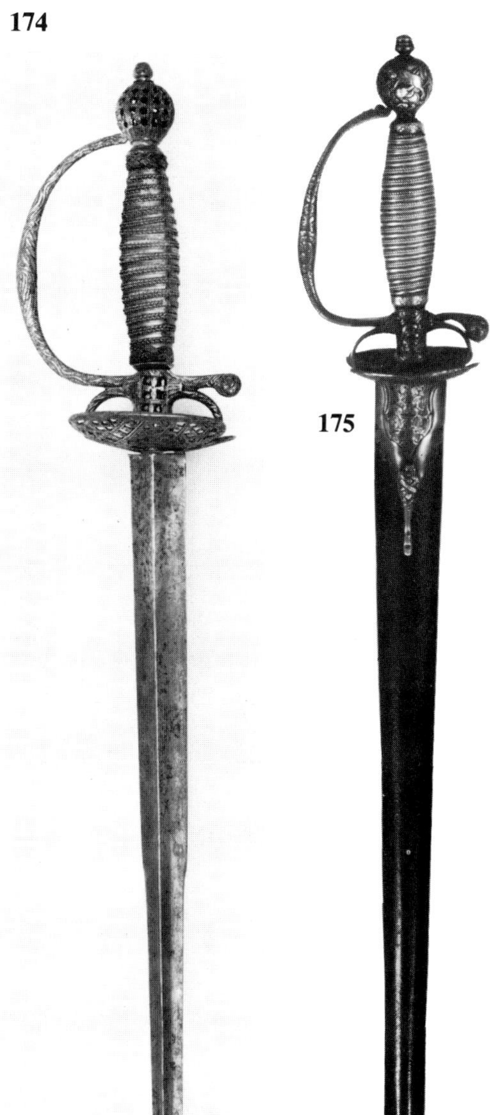

175

174. German small-sword
Length 39ins. (99cm)
Mid-18th century
The steel hilt with pierced guard and pommel. Etched colichemarde blade. Good quality, very good condition.
£200 — £300

175. English silver-hilted small-sword
Blade 32ins. (81.2cm) London, 1751-1752
The hilt with maker's mark 'JC', probably for John Carmen. Mounted by Langford, Serjeants Inn, Fleet St. Very good quality and condition.
£500 — £700

176. French small-sword
Blade 30¾ins. (78cm) About 1750-1760
The hilt of chiselled steel against a gilt ground and with silver-wire grip binding. The locket inscribed 'BOUGUES FOURBISSEUR DU ROY DES MOUSQUETAIRES' (Bougues royal supplier to the musketeers). Good condition.
£600 — £800

Photographs: 173, 175 and 176 Christie's; 174 Sotheby's

177 179

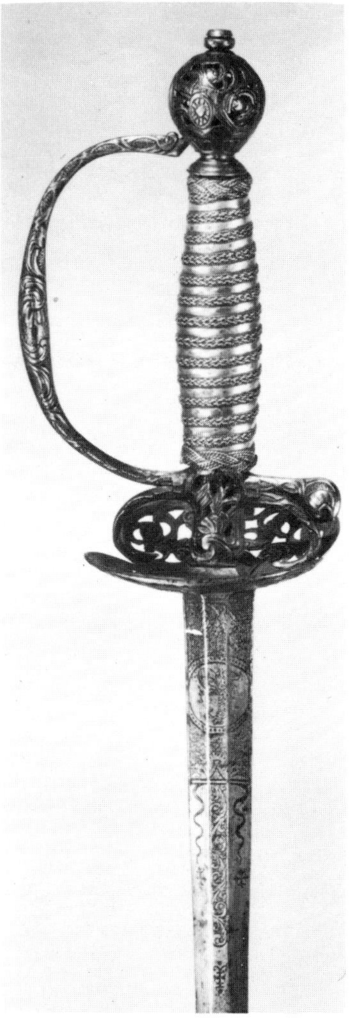

179. English silver-hilted small-sword
Length 38½ins. (97.8cm)
London, 1759-1760
Made by John Radbone. The silver hilt with small arms, double quillons and oval guard. Copper wire-bound grip. Good condition.
£300 — £500

178

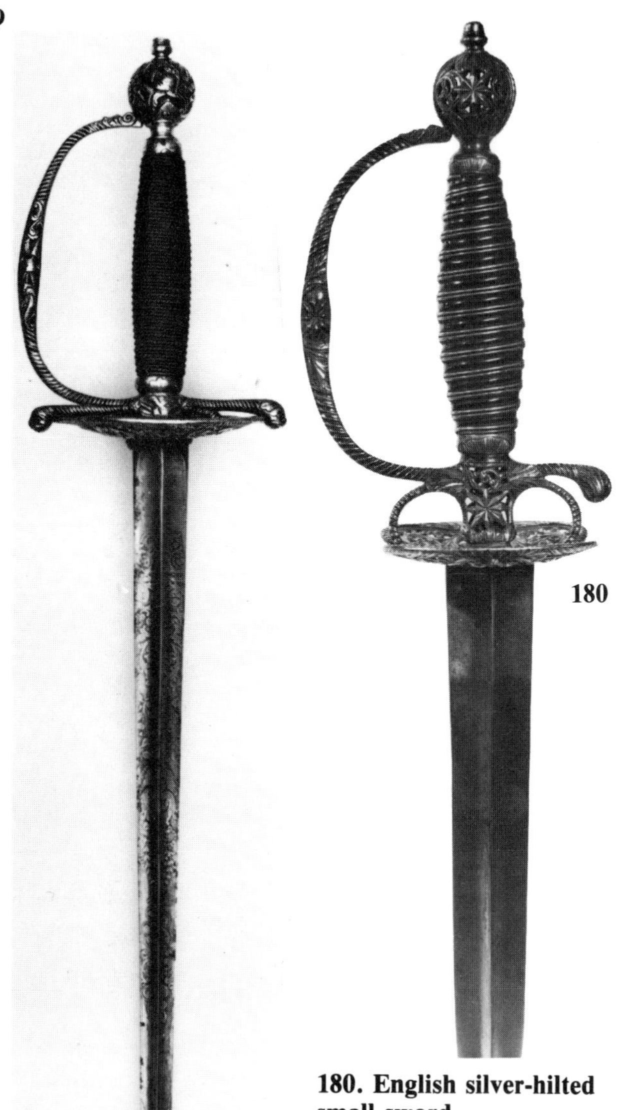

180

177. Small-sword of provincial French type
Blade 31ins. (78.8cm)
About 1750-1760
Pierced steel hilt with silver wire-bound grip. The etched blade of flattened hexagonal section. Good quality and condition.
£300 — £400

180. English silver-hilted small-sword
Blade 32ins. (81.3cm)
London, 1760-1761
Cast and pierced hilt with unidentified maker's mark of 'IB' with a pellet between. Plain colichemarde blade. Very good quality and condition.
£400 — £500

178. English silver-hilted small-sword
Length 34ins. (86.3cm)
London, 1757-1758
The hilt stamped with an unidentified maker's mark 'TB'. The etched colichemarde blade worn and pitted. Originally of fine quality. Good condition.
£300 — £500

Photographs:
177 and 180 Christie's;
178 and 179 Sotheby's

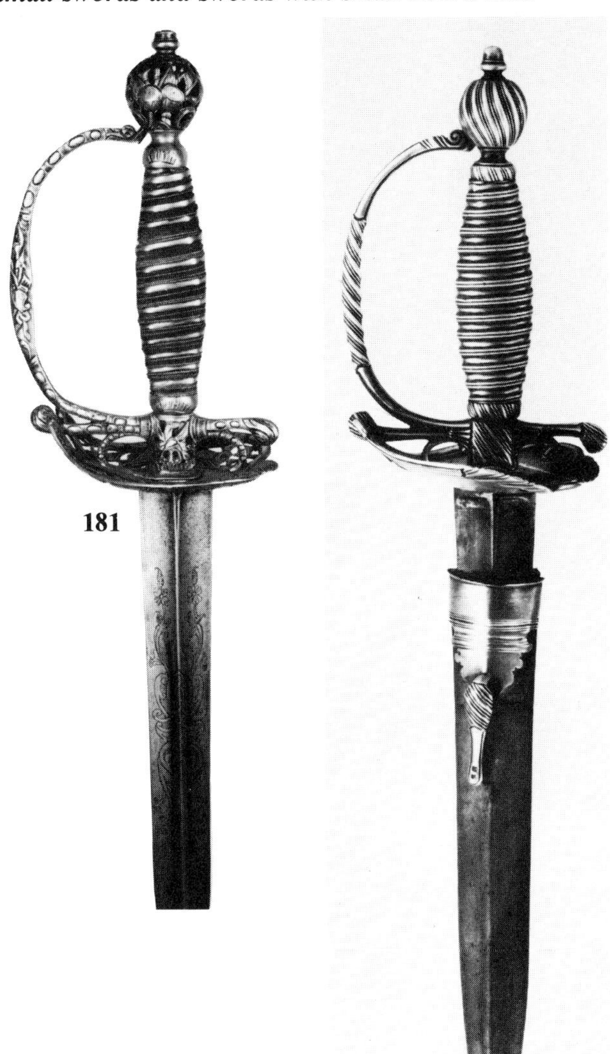
181
182

181. English silver-hilted small-sword with boat-shell guard
Blade 33ins. (83.8cm) London, 1760/1761
Cast and chased silver hilt with silver wire-bound grip. Etched colichemarde blade. Very good quality, the blade a little worn.
£500 — £600

182. English silver-hilted small-sword with boat-shell guard
Blade 34ins. (86.3cm) London, 1761-1762
The hilt similar in design to 181 but cast with writhen fluting and struck with maker's mark of 'WK' and a pellet between. The wood lined vellum-covered scabbard inscribed on the silver locket with the name of the assembler and retailer 'CULLUM, CHARING CROSS'. A familiar design of sword in very good condition.
£600

183 184

183. North Indian small-sword of English form
Blade 33ins. (83.8cm) Third quarter 18th century
Gold damascened hilt made for export to Europe. The replaced vellum-covered scabbard with locket decorated *en suite* with the hilt. A very attractive sword of very fine quality.
£800+

184. Dress sword for officers of British Heavy Cavalry Regiments, 1796 pattern
Blade 32¾ins. (83.2cm)
Gilt-brass hilt with silver wire-bound grip. Single-edged spadroon blade. The steel scabbard is associated. It should be one of black leather with gilt-brass mounts. A common sword in good condition.
£150 — £250

Photographs: Christie's

185

186

185. Continental silver-hilted small-sword
Blade 32ins. (81.2cm) About 1765
The hilt pierced and decorated with trelliswork and scrolls, and with silver wire and ribbon-bound grip. Very good quality and condition.
£200 — £300

186. Small-sword, probably French
Third quarter 18th century
Steel hilt finely pierced and chiselled with foliate scrolls and musical trophies. The etched blade of incurved triangular section. Fine quality, very good condition. The decoration on the blade worn.
£600+

187

188

187. Silver-hilted small-sword, probably Dutch
Blade 31ins. (78.7cm) Third quarter 18th century
The hilt cast and chased with rococo ornament of griffins surrounded by columns and shells. Complete with ostrich-skin and silver-mounted scabbard (not shown). Very good quality and condition.
£300 — £400

188. French small-sword
Length 42ins. (106.8cm) Third quarter 18th century
The hilt of blued steel chiselled and embellished with silver fluting, flowers and rosettes. The grip bound with silver wire and blued steel strip. Blade inscribed 'BIESSARD FILS MARCHAND, RUE DE LA MADELAINE A BRUXELLES'. A striking sword of high quality.
£500 — £600

Photographs: 185 Christie's;
186 and 188 Peter Dale Ltd.;
187 Sotheby, Parke-Bernet, LA

189

189. French small-sword
Third quarter 18th century
Steel hilt finely chiselled with flowers within cartouches against gilt grounds. The fish-skin covered scabbard with mounts decorated *en suite* with the hilt. Very fine quality and condition.
£1,000

190

190. English silver-hilted small-sword
Blade 33ins. (83.8cm)
London, 1767-1768
The hilt struck with a maker's mark 'IB', probably for John Bennett. Mounted by Marr & Third, Arundel St., Strand. Complete with silver-mounted scabbard (not shown). Fine quality, very good condition.
£500 — £600

Photographs: 189 Peter Dale Ltd.; 190, 191 and 192 Christie's

191

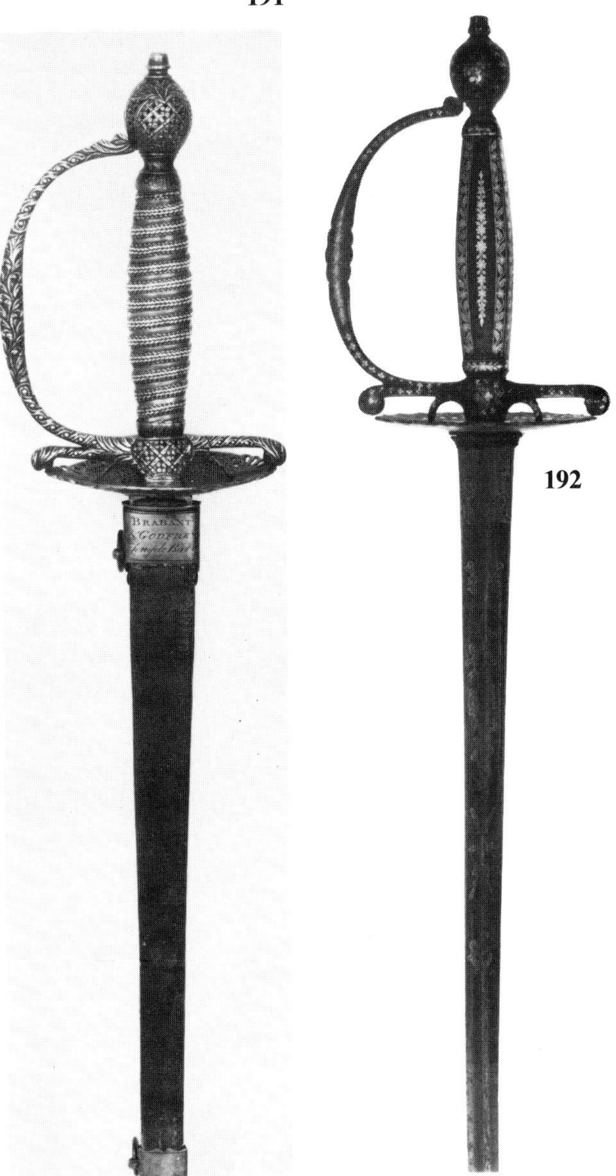

192

191. English small-sword
Blade 32½ins. (82.5cm) About 1775
The steel hilt, similar in design to 190, with silver wire and silver ribbon-bound grip. The steel-mounted scabbard inscribed on the locket 'BRABANT & GODFREY, TEMPLE BAR'. Fine quality, very good condition.
£400 — £500

192. North Indian small-sword
Blade 33¼ins. (84.5cm) About 1775
Gold damascened blued steel hilt, designed in the English fashion, and made for sale in Europe. The etched blued and gilt blade of incurved triangular section. Rare, fine quality, a little rubbed overall.
£300 — £400

193. American War of Independence sword of honour
Length 38½ins. (97.8cm) Paris, 1779
Presented by the Continental Congress to General Marie Joseph Paul Lafayette (1757-1834). The gold hilt is inscribed on the knuckle guard 'FROM THE CONTINENTAL CONGRESS TO THE MARQUIS DE LAFAYETTE, 1779.' The blade is associated. It is from another presentation sword given to Lafayette by the National Guard of Paris in 1791 and is inscribed 'REVEIL DE LA LIBERTE' (The awakening of Liberty). A sword of historical importance and of the finest quality. In 1976 it sold for £85,295 ($145,000) and would doubtless exceed that figure today. Also shown in Colour Plate 2.

193

194

195. English silver-hilted small-sword
Blade 32ins. (81.3cm)
London, 1778-1779
The hilt cast and chased to simulate brilliants, and struck with an unidentified maker's mark 'NW' with a pellet between (? Nicholas Winkins). Very good quality and condition.
£400

195

196

194. French small-sword
Blade 33¼ins. (84.5cm) About 1775-1780
The hilt of steel beautifully chiselled with soldiers and military scenes against a partly gilt ground. The grip bound with silver wire and strip. The etched, blued and gilded blade inscribed 'JE SUIS FERME COMME UNE ROCHE POUR LE SALUT DE MA PATRIE' (I am as steady as a rock for the safety of my country). Very fine quality and condition.
£2,000 — £2,500

196. English silver-gilt hilted small-sword
London, 1783-1784
Made by William Kinman. A sword of fine quality. The grip binding is loose and the etching on the blade worn. Victoria and Albert Museum (M.956-1928).
£600

Photographs: 193 Sotheby, Parke-Bernet, NY; 194 and 195 Christie's

197 198 199

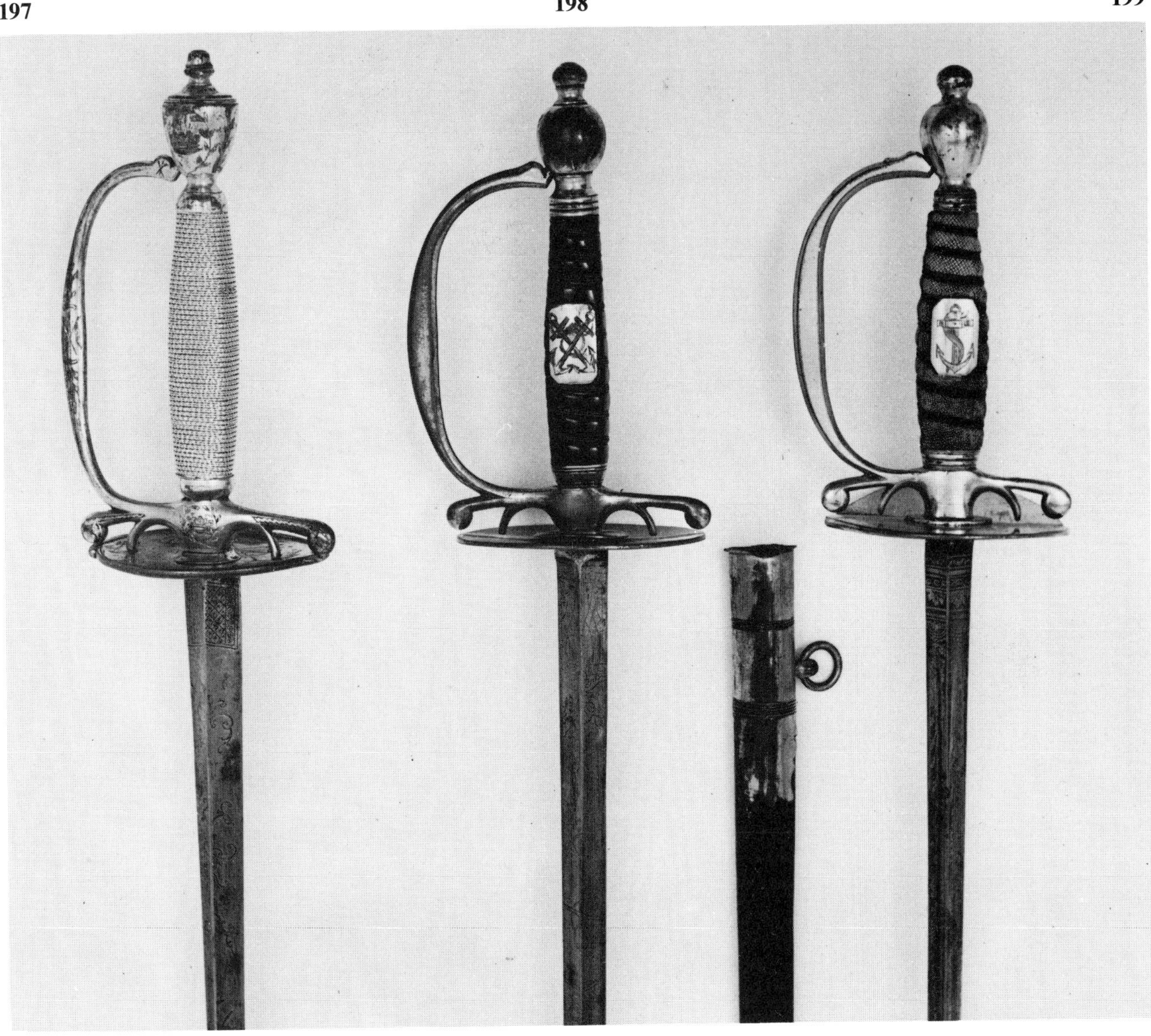

197. British naval officer's small-sword
Blade 31¼ins. (79.4cm) About 1780
Hilt of gilt-brass engraved with the naval coronet on the pommel and quillon block, and with trophies of arms on the oval guard. Silver wire-bound grip. Good quality and condition.
£150 — £200

198. British naval small-sword for a purser
Blade 31¼ins. (79.4cm) 1825-1832
Gilt-brass hilt engraved on the cartouche with the crossed foul anchor badge. Good condition.
£100 — £200

199. British naval small-sword for a surgeon
Blade 31¼ins. (79.4cm) 1825-1832
Hilt of gilt-brass with fish-skin covered grip. The cartouche engraved with a snake entwining an anchor. Gilt-brass mounted leather-covered scabbard. Good condition.
£100 — £200

Photographs: Peter Dale Ltd.

203

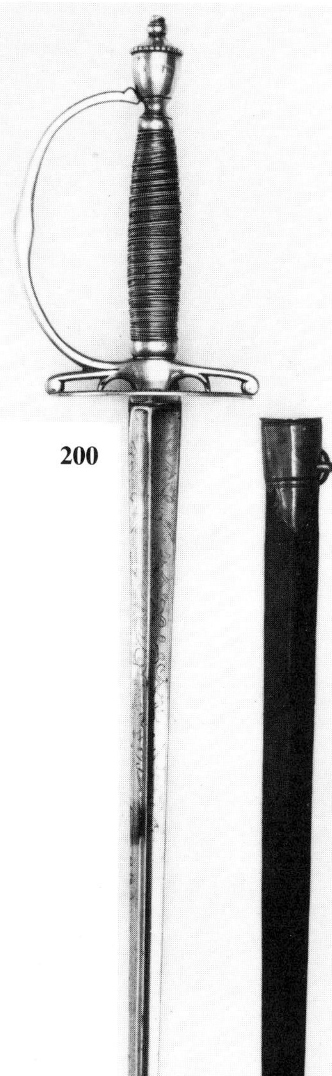

200

201. Small-sword with loop guard, possibly English

Blade 32½ins. (82.5cm) About 1780

Steel hilt chiselled and pierced with overlapping scale motifs and embellished with gold. The vellum-covered scabbard with steel mounts is inscribed on the locket 'BLAND, ST. JAMES'. An interesting sword of fine workmanship, but fitted with a replaced chain knuckle guard and earlier rapier blade.

£1,000 — £1,500

202. English brass-hilted small-sword

Length 38ins. (96.5cm) About 1780

A plain sword of reasonable quality in good condition.

£150 — £200

201

202

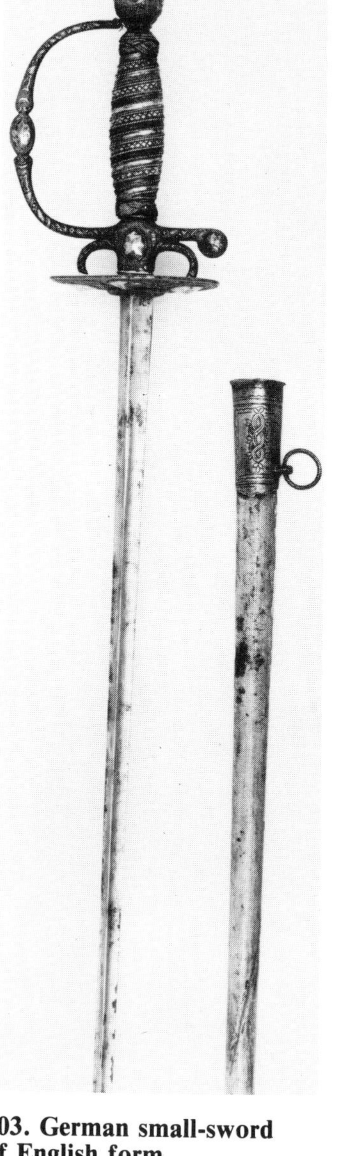

200. English silver-hilted small-sword

Length 38¼ins. (97.2cm)

London, about 1780-1785

The silver hilt made by John Perry is similar in form to 196. Good condition.

£400 — £500

203. German small-sword of English form

Length 38ins. (96.5cm) About 1780

The hilt chiselled and gilt, cut with designs simulating precious stones. Shark-skin covered scabbard with engraved steel mounts. Very good quality, a little worn overall.

£300 — £400

Photographs: 200, 202 and 203 Sotheby's; 201 Christie's

204

204. French silver-gilt hilted small-sword
Paris, about 1785-1790
The hilt cast and chased with designs in sharp relief. The oval cartouches enclose scenes of French heavy cavalrymen (see detail). The remainder of the hilt is decorated with trophies of war and peace, cherubs and foliage. Fine quality and condition. The blade a little worn.
£1,000

205

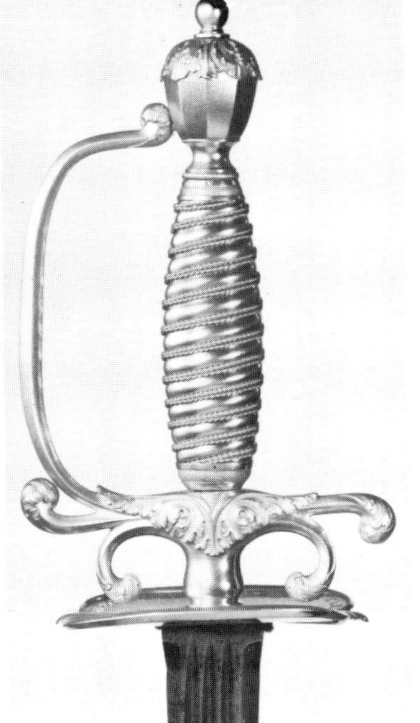

205. Russian sword of honour
Blade 34½ins. (87.6cm)
St. Petersburg, 1788
Gold hilt inscribed (in Russian) on the shell guards 'FOR FORTITUDE SHOWN IN BATTLE, JUNE 7, 1788, IN THE GULF OF OCHAKOV, SWORD PRESENTED TO SIR SAMUEL BENTHAM'. The pierced rapier blade is etched with the cypher of Catharine II. The sword was presented by the Czarist government to Samuel Bentham, brother of the philosopher Jeremy Bentham, who went to Russia in 1780. It is accompanied by a document signed by Prince Potemkin, Commander-in-Chief of the Russian armies, telling of the bravery shown by Bentham in actions against the Turks. Rare and of fine quality.
£12,000+

206

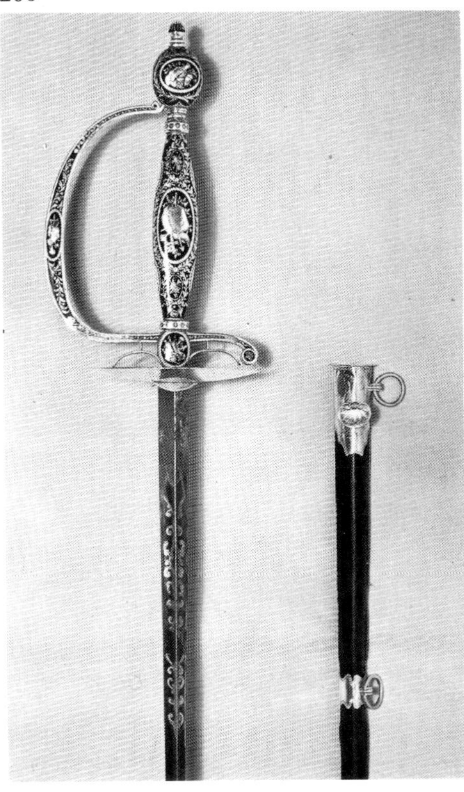

206. Gold and enamel hilted presentation small-sword
Length 39½ins. (100cm)
London, 1793-1794
The oval shell guard inscribed 'IN REMEMBRANCE OF THE EMINENT SERVICES RENDERED BY MAJOR GENERAL CUYLER TO HIS COUNTRY BY THE CONQUEST OF TOBAGO IN 1793, THIS SWORD WAS PRESENTED TO HIM BY THE INHABITANTS OF THAT ISLAND, A.D. 1794.' Made by Cornelius Bland, mounted by Nathl. Jeffreys, Dover Street. Fine quality and condition. A little worn on the blued and gilt blade. Also shown in Colour Plate 3.
£6,000 — £8,000

Photographs: 204 Peter Dale Ltd.; 205 Christie's; 206 Sotheby's

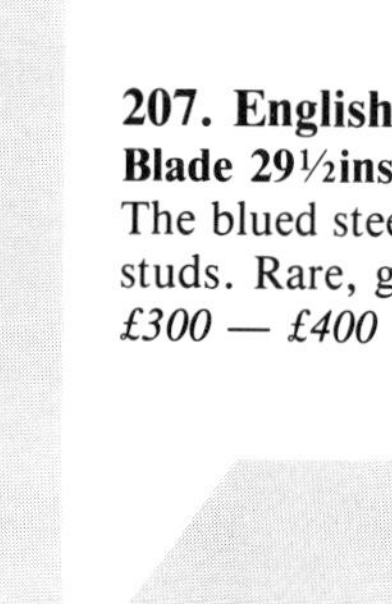

207

207. English small-sword
Blade 29½ins. (75cm) Last quarter 18th century
The blued steel hilt encrusted with silver flowers and faceted studs. Rare, good condition.
£300 — £400

208

208. English small-sword
Last quarter 18th century
Steel hilt faceted and brightly polished in the style of swords made by Matthew Boulton in Birmingham. Good quality and condition.
£200

209

210

210. English cut-steel small-sword for court use
Blade 33¼ins. (84.3cm)
About 1800
A very fine example of this style of sword, modelled on those designed and made by Matthew Boulton. Complete with steel-mounted fish-skin covered scabbard inscribed on the locket 'R. JOHNSON, LATE BLAND & FOSTER, Sword Cutler & Belt Maker to HIS MAJESTY, 68, ST. JAMES'S ST., LONDON.'
£500 — £700

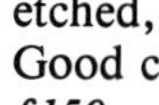

209. English court small-sword
Blade 33½ins. (85cm) Last quarter 18th century
Cut steel hilt decorated with numerous faceted beads. The etched, blued and gilt blade is of incurved triangular section. Good condition.
£150 — £200

Photographs: 207, 209, 210 Christie's; 208 Peter Dale Ltd.

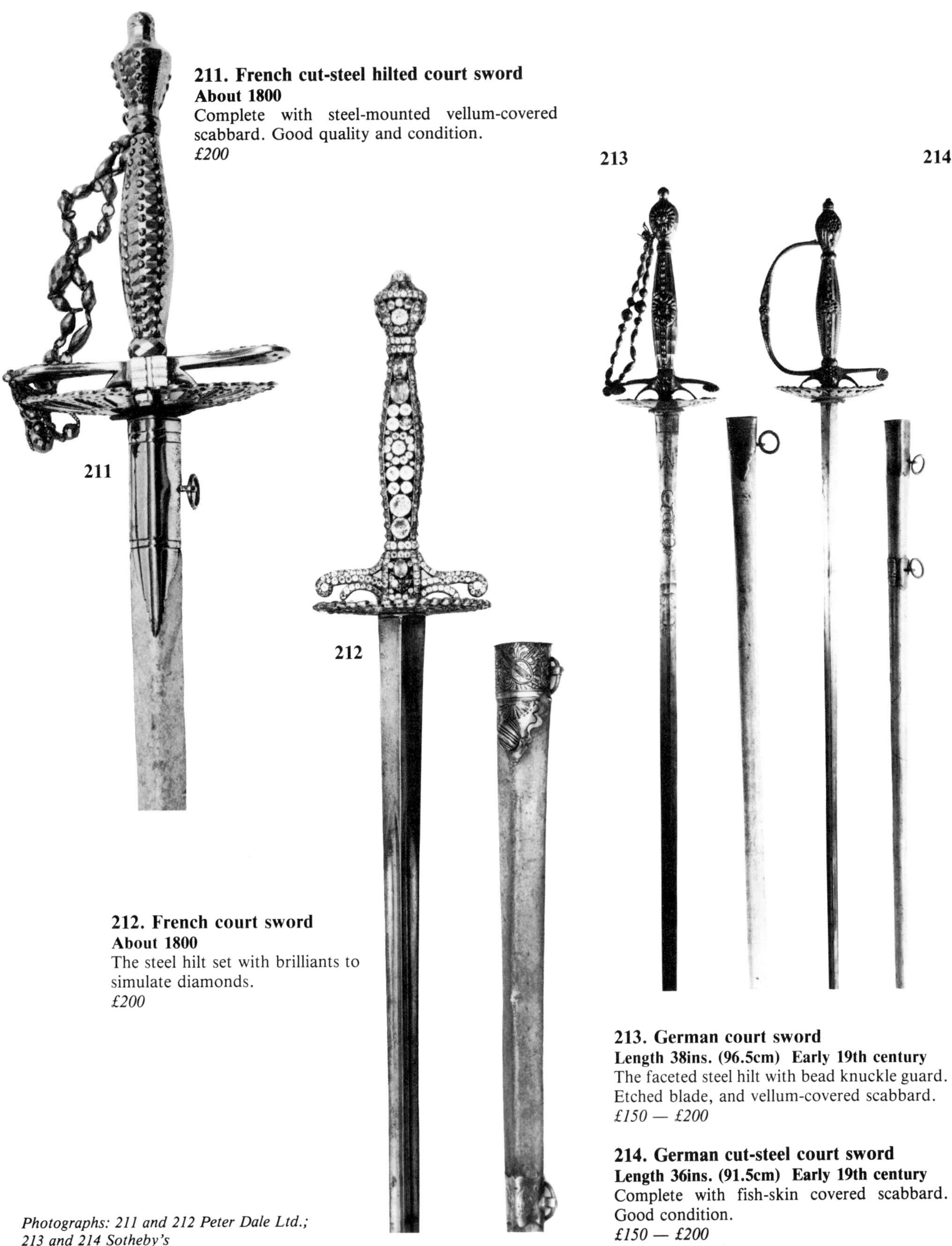

211. French cut-steel hilted court sword
About 1800
Complete with steel-mounted vellum-covered scabbard. Good quality and condition.
£200

212. French court sword
About 1800
The steel hilt set with brilliants to simulate diamonds.
£200

213. German court sword
Length 38ins. (96.5cm) Early 19th century
The faceted steel hilt with bead knuckle guard. Etched blade, and vellum-covered scabbard.
£150 — £200

214. German cut-steel court sword
Length 36ins. (91.5cm) Early 19th century
Complete with fish-skin covered scabbard. Good condition.
£150 — £200

Photographs: 211 and 212 Peter Dale Ltd.; 213 and 214 Sotheby's

215

215. Admiral Sir William Cornwallis's small-sword
Blade 34¾ins. (88.3cm) London, 1797-1798
The hilt and scabbard mounts of silver gilt were made by Francis Thurkle. The vellum-covered scabbard is engraved with the owner's arms on the locket, and inscribed 'DAVIES, SWORD CUTLER TO HIS MAJESTY, ST JAMES', who mounted the sword. Fine quality, the blued and gilt blade a little worn.
£3,500 — £4,000

Photographs: 215 Christie's; 216 Sotheby's

216

216. Sword of honour
Length 41½ins. (104.1cm) London, 1799-1800
The gold hilt is beautifully enamelled with plaques decorated with naval accoutrements, the recipient's arms and, on the upper side of the oval guard, the naval engagement for which the sword was awarded. The underside is inscribed: 'PRESENTED TO CAPTN LUCIUS FERDINAND HARDYMAN BY THE INSURANCE OFFICE OF MADRAS FOR HIS GALLANT CONDUCT IN THE CAPTURE OF THE FRENCH FRIGATE LA FORTE, ON THE NIGHT OF THE 28th FEBRUARY 1799.' Complete with gold-mounted scabbard. Made by John Ray and James Montague, and mounted by Jeffreys & Gilbert, London. A sword of the finest quality. Hardyman was presented with a second sword for the same action, see 282.
£15,000+

217 **218**

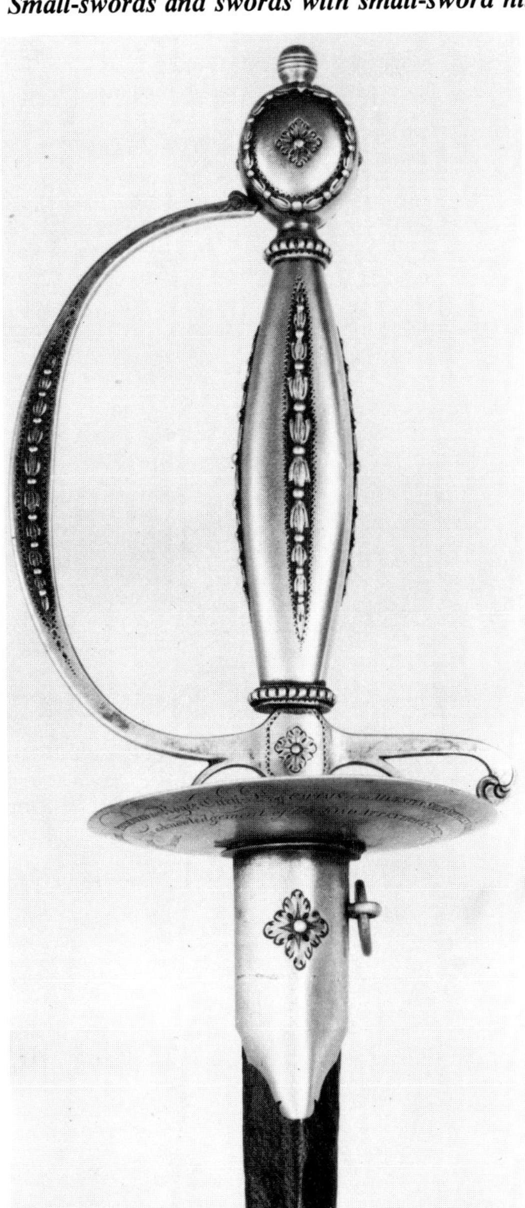

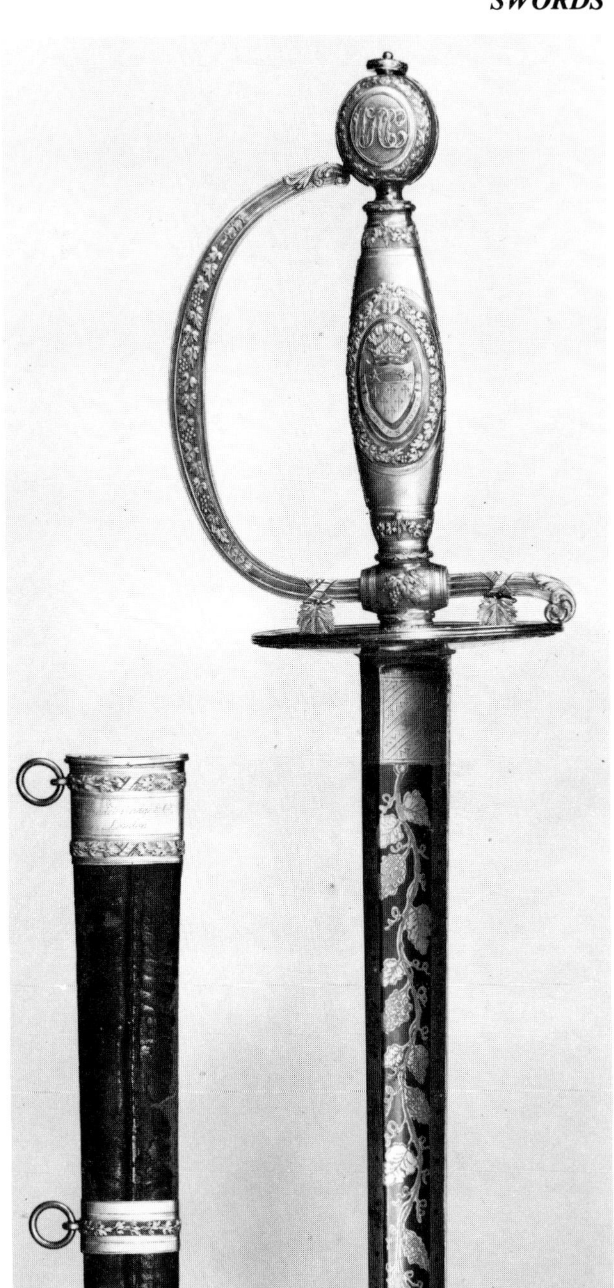

217. Presentation small-sword
Blade 32½ins. (82.7cm) London, 1801-1802
The hilt and scabbard mounts of silver-gilt are struck with an unidentified maker's mark 'CB'. The oval guard inscribed 'PRESENTED TO ROGER CURTIS, ESQ., CAPTAIN OF HIS MAJESTY'S SHIP SUFFOLK, BY JANE ROBERTSON, WIDOW OF THE LATE ARCHIBALD HAMILTON ROBERTSON, CAPTAIN OF THE ROYAL ARTILLERY, IN ACKNOWLEDGEMENT OF HIS KIND ATTENTION AND CIVILITY TO THEM ON A PASSAGE FROM THE CAPE OF GOOD HOPE TO ENGLAND, MAY, 1802.' Sword mounted by Philip Gilbert, Goldsmith to the King, Cockspur St. A fine and attractive sword. The scabbard has been repaired and the tang button replaced.
£600 — £1,000

218. Presentation sword
London, 1802-1803
The hilt and scabbard mounts of two-colour gold were made by John Ray and James Montague and the sword assembled by Rundell & Bridge, London, the royal goldsmiths. The etched, blued and gilt spadroon blade is inscribed 'TO BRIGADIER GENERAL W.H. CLINTON FROM THE BRITISH CONSUL AND FACTORY IN MADEIRA.' Like 216, this example is of the finest quality. Now in the National Army Museum, London (6007-49).
£10,000

Photographs: 217 Christie's; 218 Peter Dale Ltd.

219

219. City of London sword of honour
Length 42⅜ins. (107.6cm) London, 1807-1808
Like 216 and 218, this fine gold-hilted sword was made by John Ray and James Montague. It was mounted and retailed by Goodbehere, Wiggan & Bolt, 86 Cheapside, London, whose name appears on the gold locket. The hilt is cast and chased with trophies of arms and oak leaves. On the grip, two diamond-studded enamelled cartouches bear the arms of the City and those of the recipient, Rear Admiral Stirling (showing in the illustration). The oval shell guard is inscribed beneath: 'LEIGHTON MAYOR RESOLVED UNANIMOUSLY AT A COMMON COUNCIL HELD IN GUILDHALL, LONDON, SEPTEMBER 15th, 1807, THAT THE FREEDOM OF THIS CITY AND A SWORD VALUE TWO HUNDRED GUINEAS TO BE PRESENTED TO REAR ADMIRAL STIRLING AS A TESTIMONY OF THE ESTEEM THIS COURT ENTERTAINS OF HIS GALLANT AND MERITORIOUS CONDUCT AT THE CAPTURE OF THE FREEDOM OF MONTEVIDEO ON THIRD FEB. LAST.'
£15,000+

Photographs: 219 Christie's; 220 Sotheby's

220

220. French gold and enamel hilted small-sword
Length 37¾ins. (96cm) Early 19th century
The gold hilt, with shells of pelta form, is without arms (see detail). It is set with panels of lapis lazuli on the pommel and decorated with mythological figures. The gold-mounted fish-skin covered scabbard, with carrier, is inscribed on the locket 'MANUFR. A VERSAILLES, ENTERPRISE BOUTET, PARIS' (Made at Versailles, by Boutet & Co., Paris) and struck with an unidentified hilt maker's mark, 'JM' between two stars in a lozenge. A superb sword, reputedly made for the Duc de Cambacérès (1757-1824). Also shown in Colour Plate 4.
£12,000+

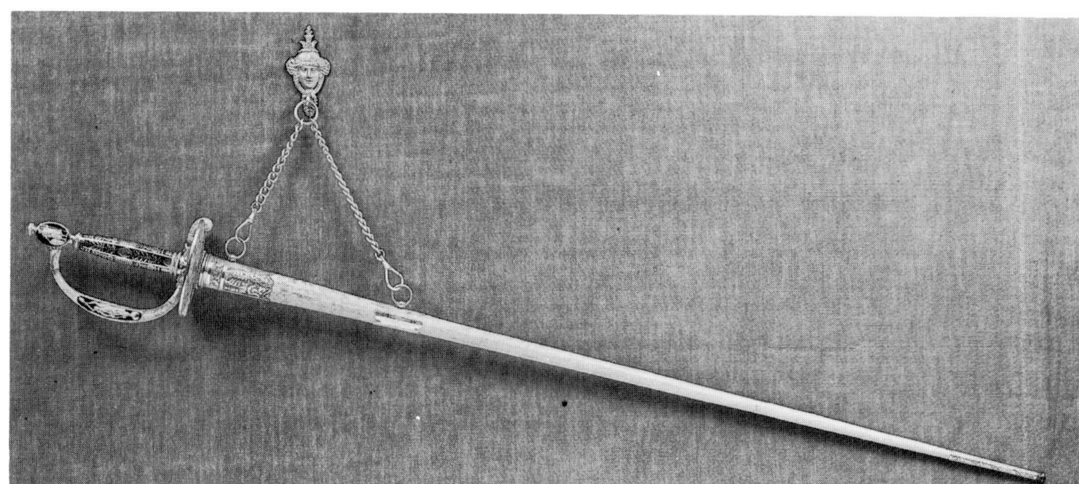

221. French presentation sword
1815
The hilt of gold is decorated with mythological figures on the pelta-shaped half shell guard and has mother-of-pearl plaque grips. The etched blued and gilt blade is inscribed 'A MONSIEUR LE COLONEL FRUEHARD, COMMANDANT SUPERIEUR EN 1815, LA VILLE DE TOUL RECONNAISSANTE' (To Colonel Freuhard, Commander-in-Chief in 1815, from the City in gratitude for everything). Very fine quality and condition.
£3,000+

221

222. Gold-mounted presentation dress small-sword
Length 38½ins. (96.5cm) London, 1821-1822
The cast and chased gold hilt with single shell, double quillons and knuckle guard. The slender blade inscribed 'PRESENTED BY THE PLANTERS RESIDENT IN GREAT BRITAIN TO SIR S. WHITTINGHAM, G.C.H. IN TESTIMONY OF HIS SERVICES DURING HIS RESIDENCE AND GOVERNMENT AS HIS MAJESTY'S REPRESENTATIVE IN DOMINICA, JANUARY 31st 1822.' The gold locket inscribed 'PROSSER, CHARING CROSS, LONDON.' A fine quality sword in very good condition, with later restoration. Now in the Tower of London Armouries (IX-1785).
£1,500 — £2,000

Photographs: Sotheby's

222

223. English sword
Early 17th century
Iron hilt decorated with silver encrustation. The two-edged blade of about 1635, stamped 'FECIT HOUNSLO'. Rare, fine quality, good condition. Now in the Tower of London Armouries (IX-1354).
£800 — £1,500

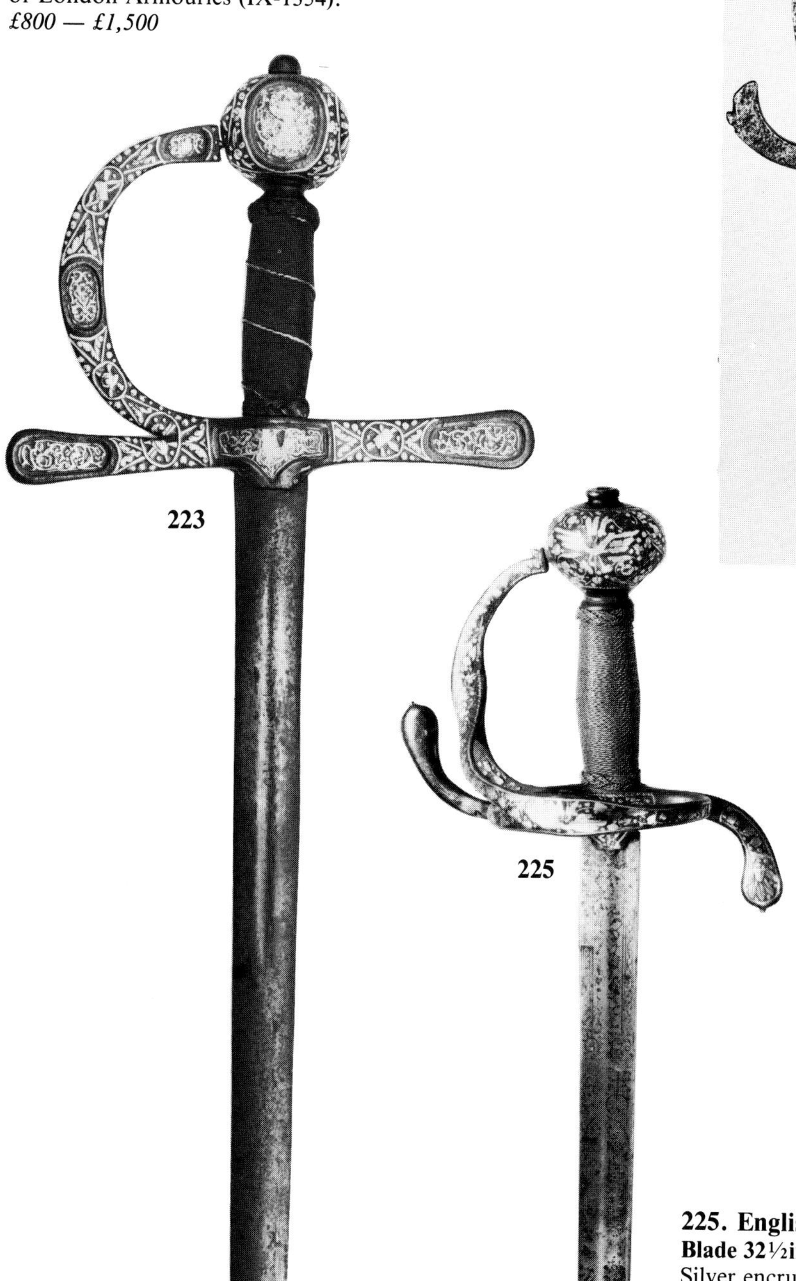

224

224. English broadsword
About 1600
The iron hilt has a pommel of flattened disc form and retains some of its original grip binding. A rare sword but heavily pitted on the hilt and blade. Now in the Tower of London Armouries (IX-840).
£500

225. English sword
Blade 32½ins. (82.5cm) Early 17th century
Silver encrusted iron hilt. The side ring has a curved bar linking it to the knuckle guard. The etched blade with orb and cross mark stamped 'PETER VON MEIGEN BRAS'. The forward quillon and thumb ring have been replaced and the grip rebound. Rare and fine quality. Condition good.
£600 — £1,000

Photographs: 223 and 224 Peter Dale Ltd.; 225 Christie's

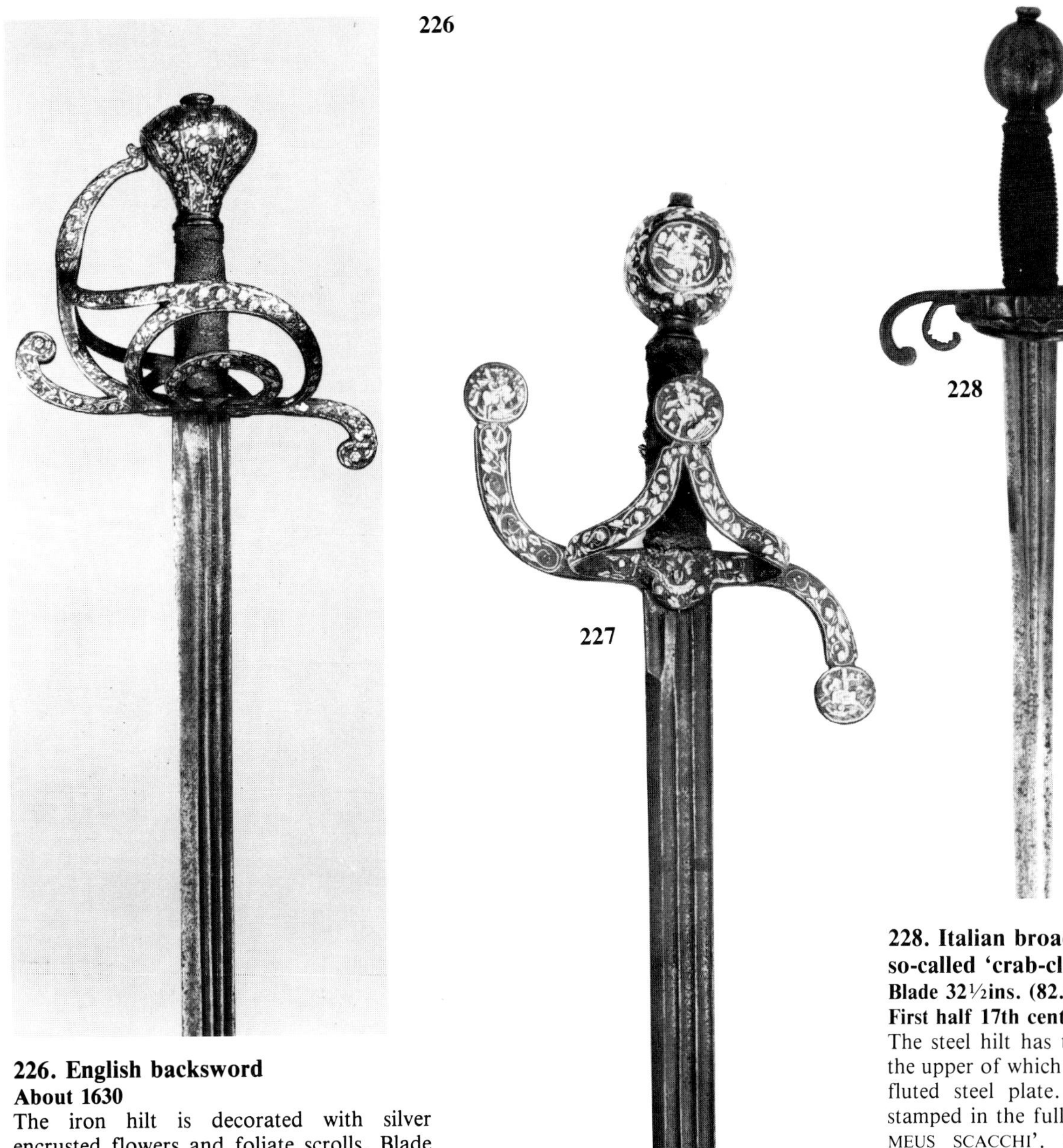

226. English backsword
About 1630
The iron hilt is decorated with silver encrusted flowers and foliate scrolls. Blade stamped 'JACOB BRACH'. Fine quality, good condition, grip re-bound.
£1,000

228. Italian broadsword with so-called 'crab-claw hilt'
Blade 32½ins. (82.5cm)
First half 17th century
The steel hilt has two side rings, the upper of which is fitted with a fluted steel plate. The blade is stamped in the fuller 'BARTHOLOMEUS SCACCHI'. Quite a rare sword in good condition, the grip replaced.
£500 — £800

Photographs: 226 and 227 Peter Dale Ltd.; 228 Christie's

227. English backsword
Early 17th century
The silver encrusted iron hilt is decorated on the pommel and on the rondels with St. George slaying the Dragon. The fullered blade is stamped 'ME FECIT SOLINGEN'. Very rare and of fine quality. Good condition. Now in the Tower of London Armouries (IX-1355).
£1,000 — £1,500

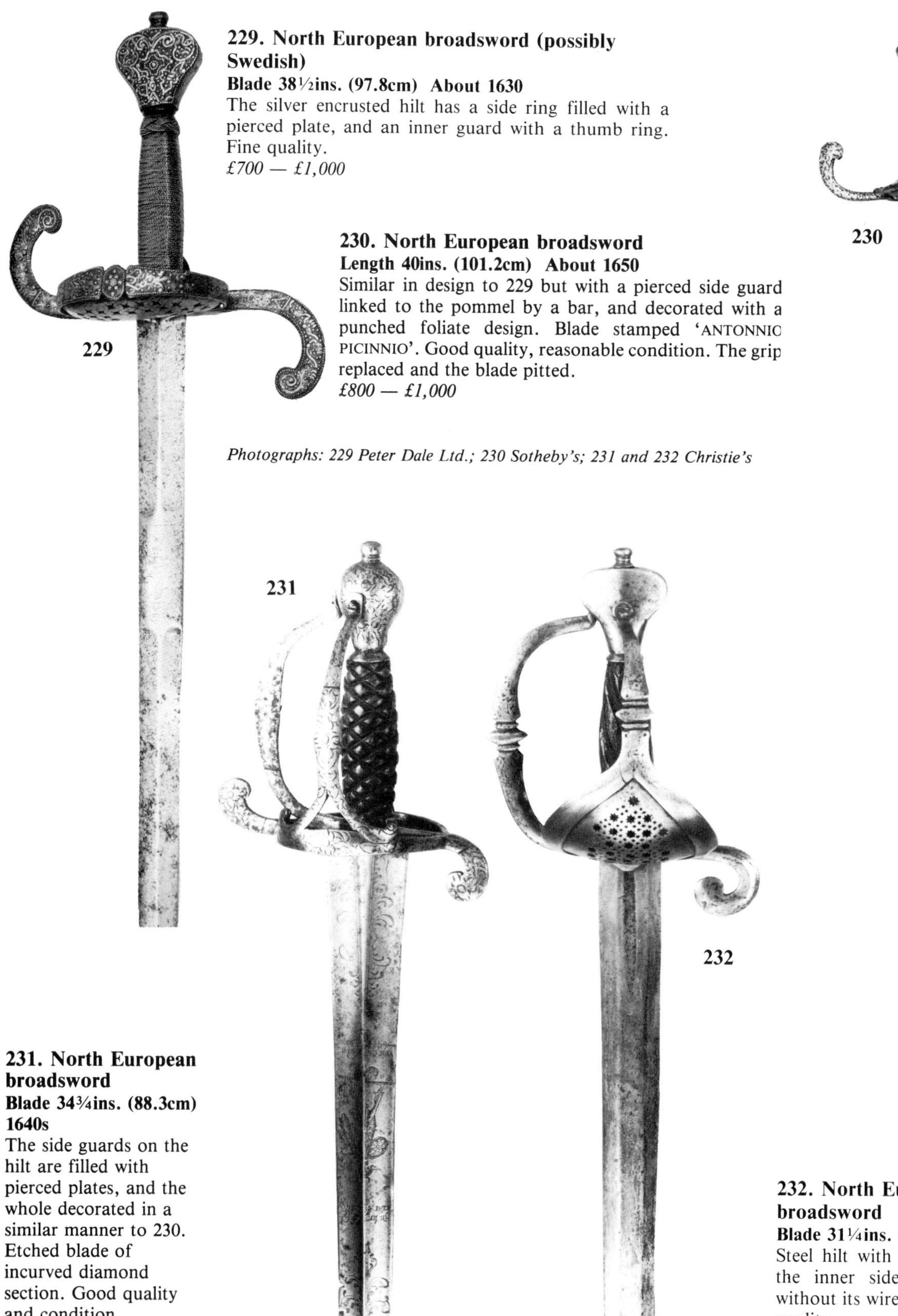

229. North European broadsword (possibly Swedish)
Blade 38½ins. (97.8cm) About 1630
The silver encrusted hilt has a side ring filled with a pierced plate, and an inner guard with a thumb ring. Fine quality.
£700 — £1,000

230. North European broadsword
Length 40ins. (101.2cm) About 1650
Similar in design to 229 but with a pierced side guard linked to the pommel by a bar, and decorated with a punched foliate design. Blade stamped 'ANTONNIC PICINNIO'. Good quality, reasonable condition. The grip replaced and the blade pitted.
£800 — £1,000

Photographs: 229 Peter Dale Ltd.; 230 Sotheby's; 231 and 232 Christie's

231. North European broadsword
Blade 34¾ins. (88.3cm) 1640s
The side guards on the hilt are filled with pierced plates, and the whole decorated in a similar manner to 230. Etched blade of incurved diamond section. Good quality and condition.
£500 — £800

232. North European broadsword
Blade 31¼ins. (79.2cm) 1640s
Steel hilt with thumb ring on the inner side. The grip is without its wire binding. Good quality.
£500 — £800

233. Dutch or English loop-guard hilted sword
Blade 33½ins. (85cm) About 1640
The hilt of steel chiselled with grotesque masks and profile heads in high relief. Etched blade. A sword of fine quality but worn. It lacks its original thumb ring on the inner side, and the small plate guard inside the loop is probably a replacement and should also turn down towards the blade (compare 234).
£300 — £350

234. North European sword
Blade 34½ins. (87.5cm) Dated 1658
Steel hilt with incised decoration similar to 230 and 231. The etched two-edged blade dated 1658. Good quality and condition.
£400 — £500

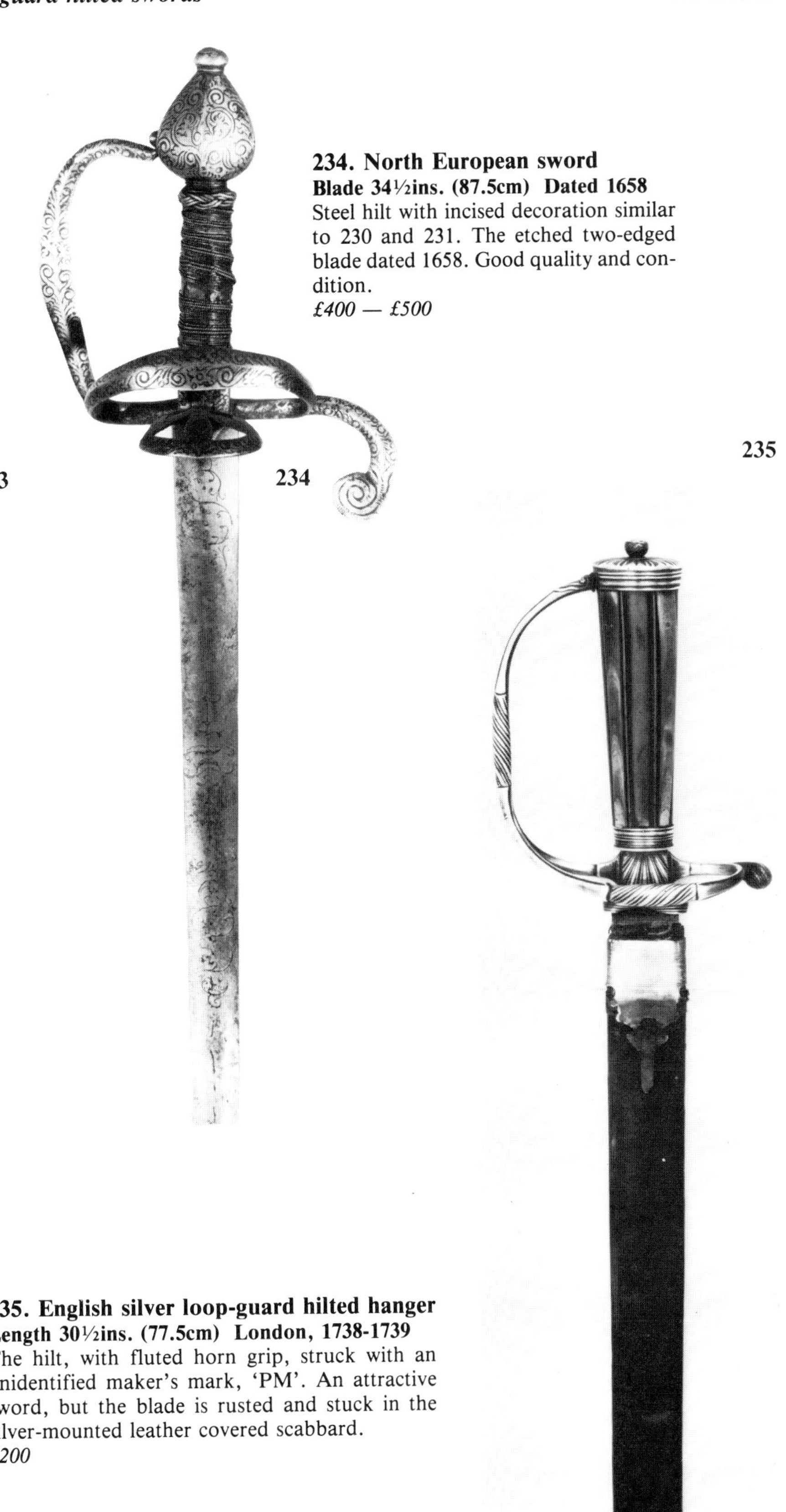
233 234 235

235. English silver loop-guard hilted hanger
Length 30½ins. (77.5cm) London, 1738-1739
The hilt, with fluted horn grip, struck with an unidentified maker's mark, 'PM'. An attractive sword, but the blade is rusted and stuck in the silver-mounted leather covered scabbard.
£200

Photographs: Christie's

236

236. English backsword
Blade 29½ins. (75cm)
About 1650
Gilded iron hilt with pierced guards, the inner guard with thumb ring. Silver wire-bound grip. The etched and gilt blade inscribed (in German) 'THE HUNTED BEAR NEVER LOSES HEART, WHEN HOUNDS COME CLOSE, HE TURNS THEM AWAY WITHOUT CEREMONY.' Fine quality. The gilding a little worn. Now in the Tower of London Armouries (IX-1327).
£2,000 — £3,000

237

237. English broadsword
Dated 1648
Gilded steel hilt chiselled with acanthus leaves and with pierced guards. The blade with running wolf mark inscribed 'FECIT SOLINGEN ANNO 1648' (Made in Solingen, 1648). Fine quality, very good condition.
£1,200 — £2,000

238

238. Dutch military broadsword with Walloon hilt
About 1660
Blackened steel hilt with side guards filled with pierced plates (one missing). A thumb ring is on the inner side. Two-edge blade with running wolf mark inscribed 'SAHAGOM'. A familiar sword in particularly good condition. Tower of London Armouries (IX-173).
£600 — £700

Photographs: 236 and 237 Christie's; 238 Crown Copyright

240

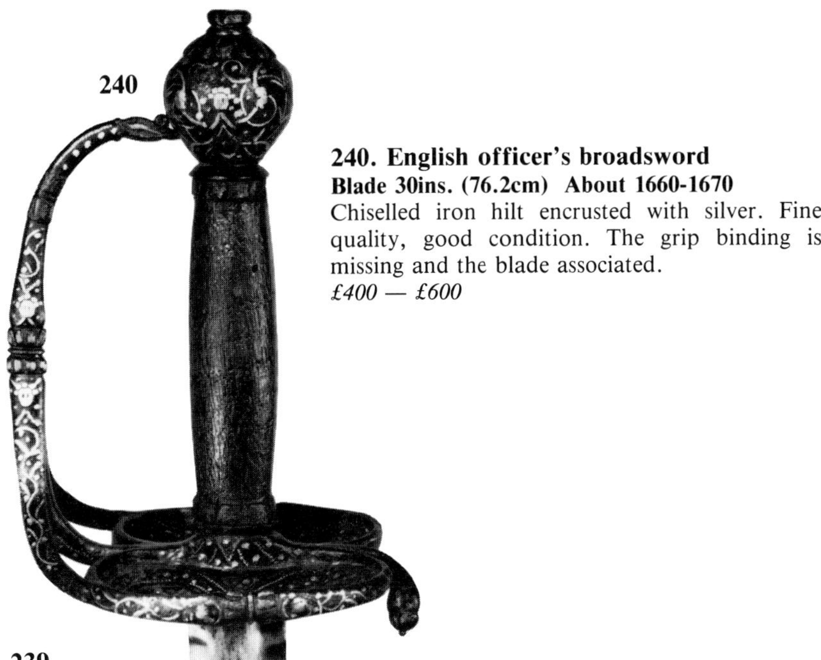

240. English officer's broadsword
Blade 30ins. (76.2cm) About 1660-1670
Chiselled iron hilt encrusted with silver. Fine quality, good condition. The grip binding is missing and the blade associated.
£400 — £600

239. North European cavalry broadsword
Blade 35ins. (89cm)
Second half 17th century
Hilt of steel with side ring filled with a pierced plate, and with a thumb ring on the inner side. The blade struck with the king's head mark of the Wundes family. Reasonable condition.
£300 — £400

239

241

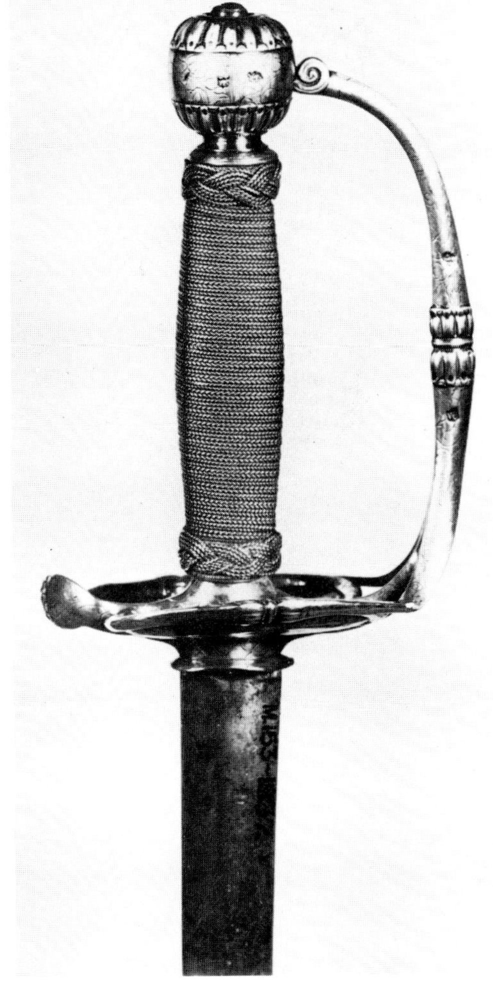

241. English silver-hilted light sword of military form
Length 36⅝ins. (93cm)
London, 1676-1677
The silver hilt with unidentified maker's mark, 'WB' in a shield. Rare and of fine quality. Victoria and Albert Museum (M.153-1937).
£600 — £800

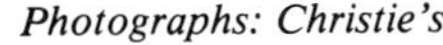

Photographs: Christie's

242

242. English brass-hilted officer's sword
About 1680
The hilt cast in relief with masks, figures and foliage. The pommel with the royal crown supported by the lion and unicorn. Two-edged blade of incurved triangular section etched at the forte. Fine quality, good condition. The blade worn.
£500 — £800

243

244

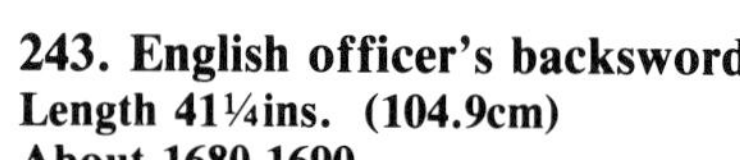

243. English officer's backsword
Length 41¼ins. (104.9cm)
About 1680-1690
Black japanned and gilded hilt with side rings filled with steel plates. The heavy blade fluted along the back-edge. Fine quality and condition. The fish-skin covered grip without its wire binding. Tower of London Armouries (IX-944).
£1,000 — £1,800

244. British infantry private's hanger
Blade 25ins. (63.5cm) Mid-18th century
A robust, brass-hilted regulation sword of the type issued before 1768. Good condition. National Army Museum (6312-251-122).
£80 — £120

Photographs: 242 Peter Dale Ltd.; 243 Crown Copyright

245

246

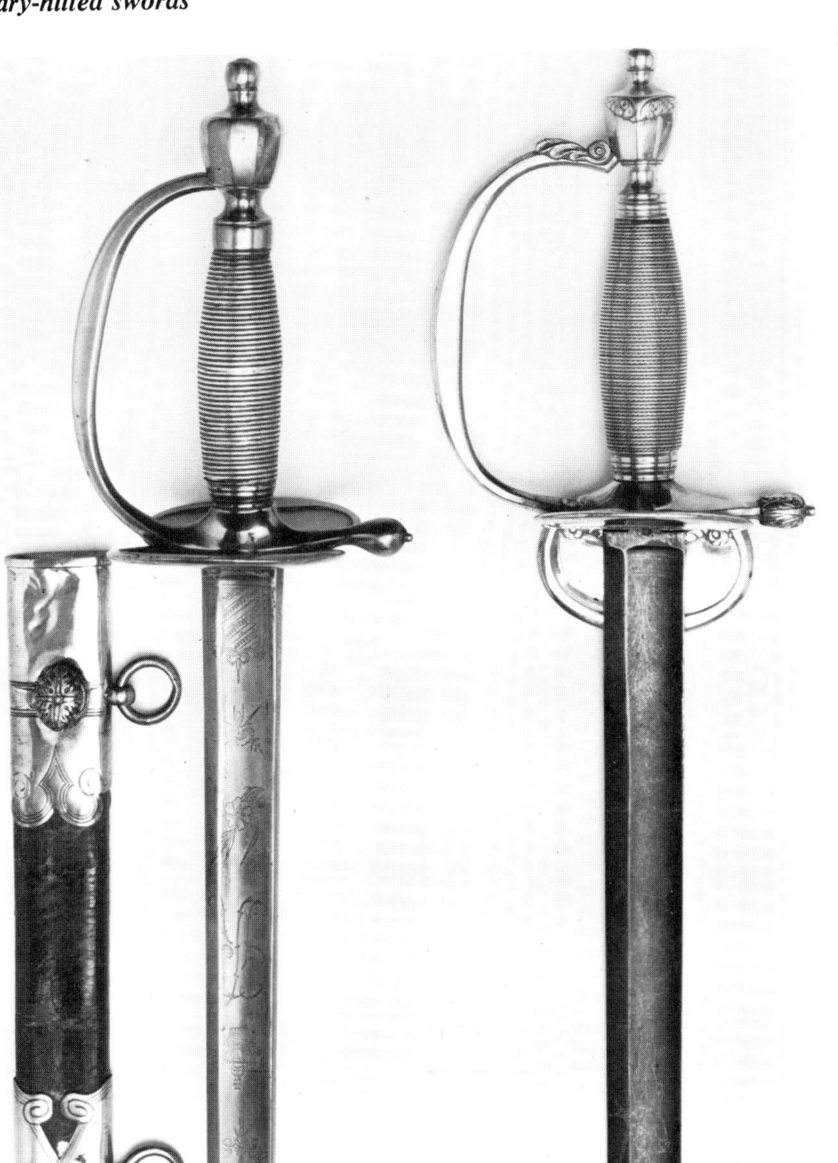

247

245. British infantry officer's sword, 1796 pattern
Blade 32ins. (81.2cm)
The hilt and scabbard mounts of gjlt-brass. Single-edged spadroon blade etched with the Georgian cypher. One of the most commonly found of all the early patterned swords. Good condition.
£80 — £100

246. British infantry officer's sword, 1796 pattern
Blade 32ins. (81.3cm)
Hilt of gilt-brass; etched spadroon blade. The inner shell is hinged to fold downwards, when not in use, to prevent rubbing. Good condition.
£70 — £90

247. Silver-hilted infantry officer's sword, 1796 pattern
Blade 32½ins. (82.5cm) London, 1797-1798
Made by Francis Thurkle. An elegant sword but the inner guard is bent, the blade is pitted, and the chape is missing.
£200 — £300

Photographs: Christie's

248. Sword of an officer of the Scottish 1st (or Royal) Regiment of Foot, 1796 pattern

Blade 32ins. (81.3cm) 1797-1812

Gilt-brass hilt with the regimental badge on the upper side of the shell guards, and the same device etched on the tapered two-edged blade. This fine example is complete with gilt-brass mounted leather scabbard inscribed on the locket 'PROSSER, CHARING CROSS, LONDON'.

£500

249. Presentation-type sword, based on the British infantry officer's 1796 pattern

Blade 31½ins. (80cm) Early 19th century

Gilt-brass hilt and scabbard mounts, the latter decorated with the labours of Hercules. Blued and gilt single-edged spadroon blade. Fine quality.

£500 — £600

249

248

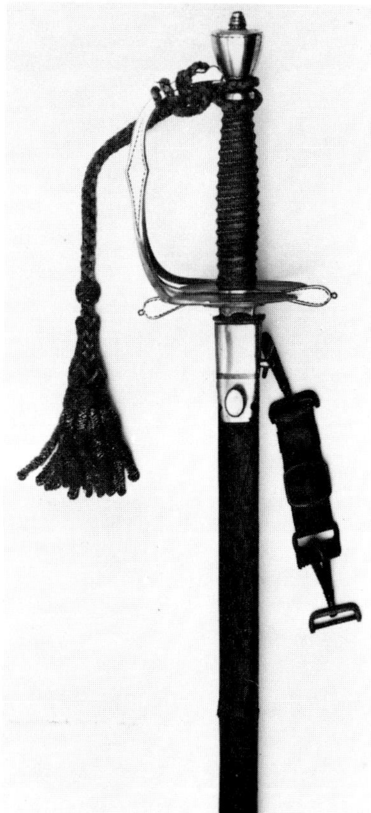

250. British officer's dress sword

Blade 31¼ins. (74.4cm) About 1800

Gilt-brass hilt and straight single-edged blade. The gilt-brass mounted scabbard signed on the locket 'PROSSER, LATE CULLUM, SWORDCUTLER, CHARING CROSS, LONDON'. A good example of a commonly found sword.

£150 — £250

250

Photographs: 248 and 250 Christie's; 249 Peter Dale Ltd.

251

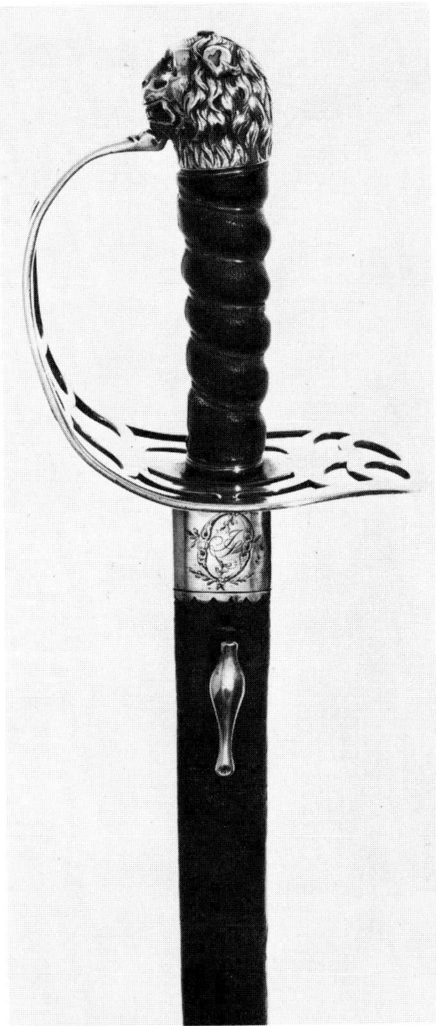

251. English silver-hilted sword
Blade 33½ins. (85cm) About 1770
The hilt, with lion's head pommel and leather-covered grip bound with silver strip, is struck with maker's mark 'GF', probably for George Fayle. Slightly curved single-edged blade. Mounted by Jeffery's, Cutler to His Majesty, Strand. Fine quality.
£1,000 — £1,500

252

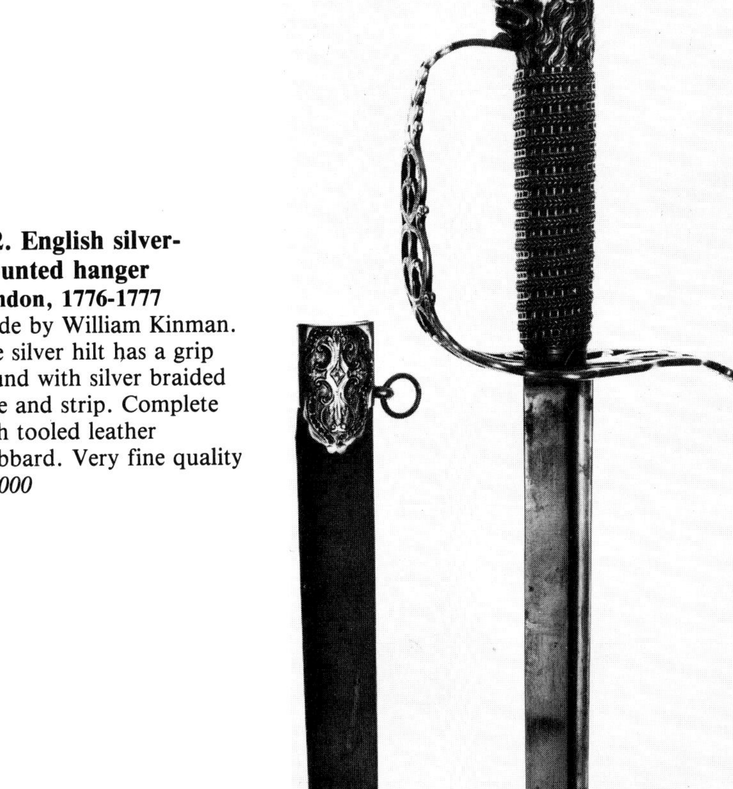

252. English silver-mounted hanger
London, 1776-1777
Made by William Kinman. The silver hilt has a grip bound with silver braided wire and strip. Complete with tooled leather scabbard. Very fine quality
£1,000

253

253. British naval officer's gilt-brass hilted hanger
About 1780
A clear view of the slotted hilt incorporating the naval fouled anchor in its design. Lion's head pommel and spirally fluted hard-wood grip bound with copper strip. Curved single-edged blade. Good condition.
£150 — £200

Photographs: 251 Christie's; 252 and 253 Peter Dale Ltd.

254. French officer's sabre
Blade 32¾ins. (83.2cm) 1780s
Gilt-brass hilt with copper wire bound grip and moving guard. The curved blade etched, gilt and blued at the forte. Good quality, reasonable condition.
£300 — £400

254

256

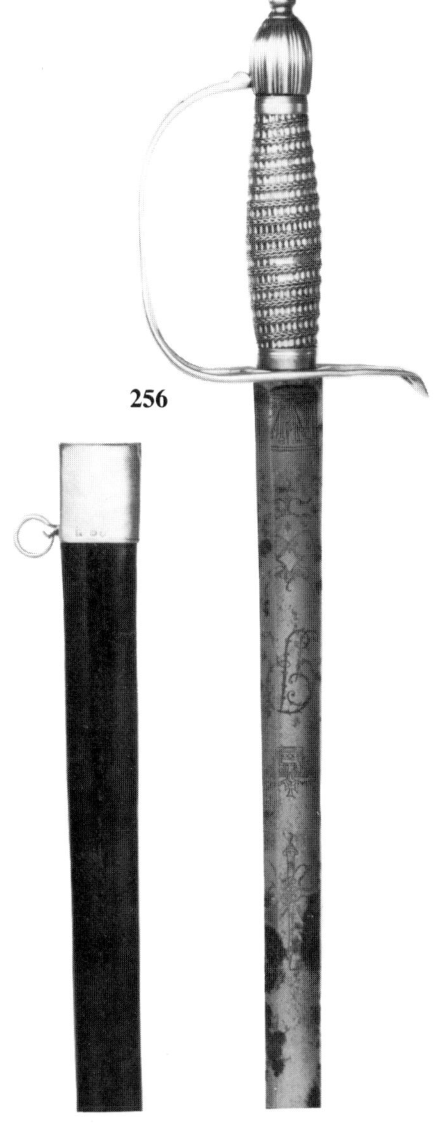

255

256. English silver-hilted officer's spadroon
Blade 32½ins. (82.5cm) London, 1793-1794
Made by Francis Thurkle. Similar to 255 but with a straight single-edged blade and in better condition.
£200 — £300

255. English silver-hilted officer's hanger
Blade 27¾ins. (70.7cm) London, about 1780
Made by William Kinman. A later inscription on the blade records that the sword was given by the gun room officers of H.M.S. *Piedmontaise* and *Barracouta* to Captain Christopher Cole of the *Caroline,* following his capture of the Island of Banda on 9th August, 1810. The sword is badly pitted on the blade and the inscription is, in parts, illegible.
£200 — £250

Photographs: Christie's

257. British naval officer's sword
Blade 28ins. (71.1cm)
Early 19th century
Gilt-brass hilt and scabbard mounts, ivory grip. The curved single-edged blade is etched with Britannia and inscribed 'OSBORN'. Good condition.
£300 — £400

257

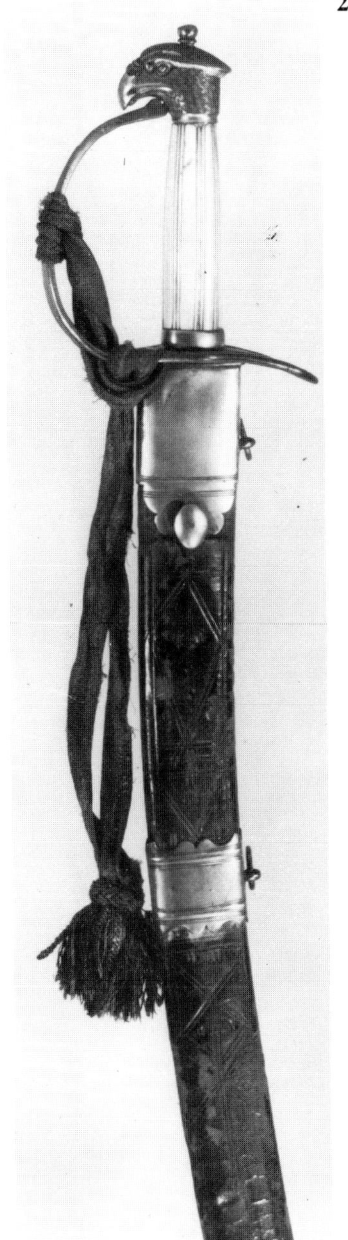

258. Officer's spadroon made for the American market
Blade 31½ins. (80cm) Birmingham, 1806-1807
Silver hilt, ivory grip, struck with an unidentified maker's mark 'TB'. The straight single-edged blade with American symbols and mottoes. A rare sword of fine quality, but now worn, especially on the blade which has lost much of its gilt and blued finish.
£200 — £300

Photographs: 257 Christie's; 258 Sotheby's; 259 Sotheby, Parke-Bernet, LA

258

259

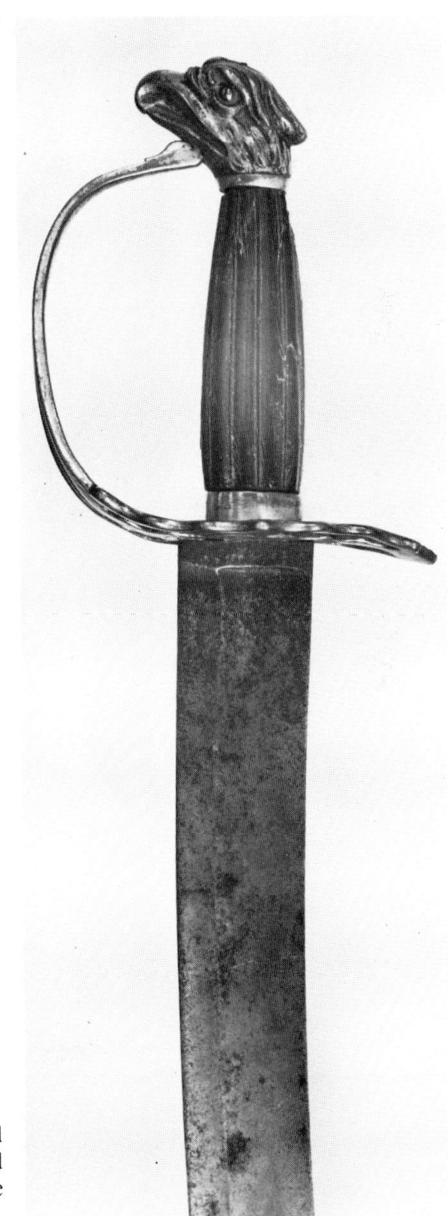

259. American officer's sabre
Length 33¼ins. (84.5cm)
Early 19th century
Gilt-brass 'slotted' hilt with eagle-head pommel and fluted horn grip. Plain curved single-edged blade. Quite rare, reasonable condition.
£150 — £200

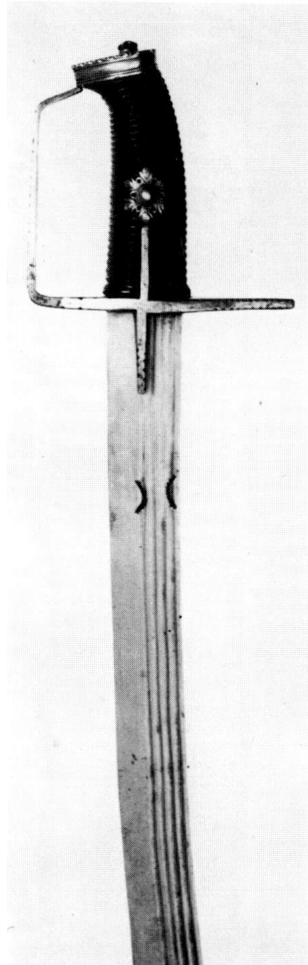

260

260. Polish stirrup-hilted sabre
Blade 29¾ins. (75.5cm) Late 17th century
Hilt of steel with leather-covered grip and brass pommel cap. The curved fullered blade with eyelash marks. Quite rare, good condition.
£500 — £700

261. French hussar officer's sabre
Length 40¾ins. (103.5cm) About 1780
The hilt and scabbard mounts of gilt-copper, the curved single-edged blade etched, blued, and gilt at the forte. Good condition.
£600 — £700

261

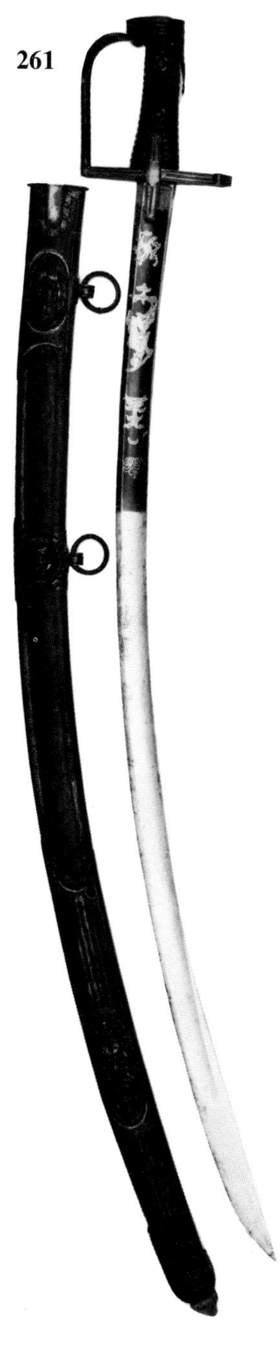

263

262

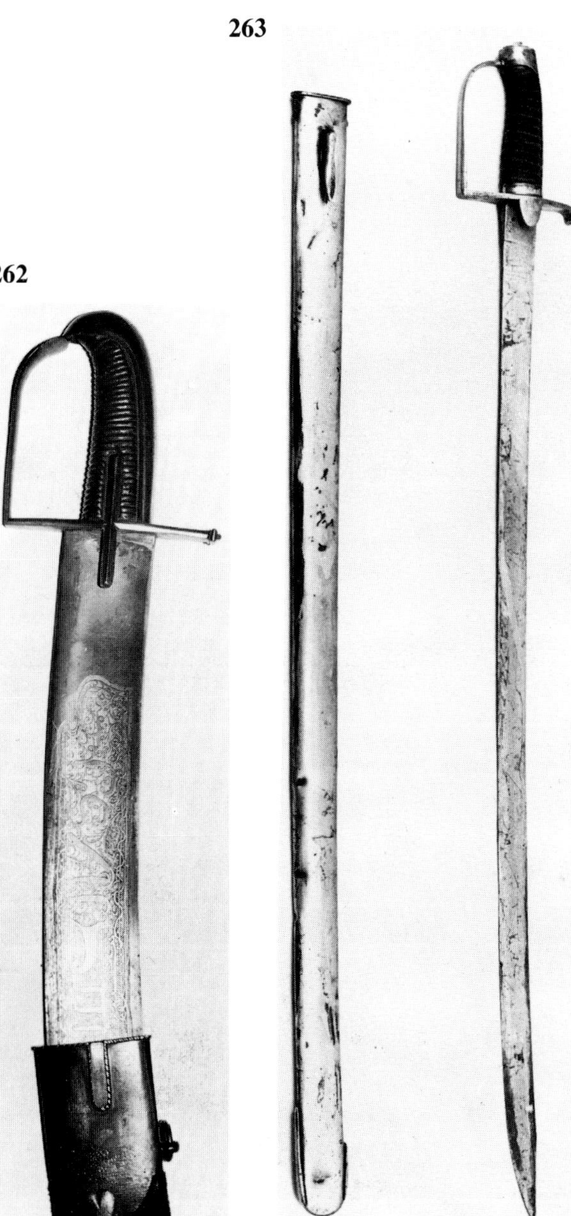

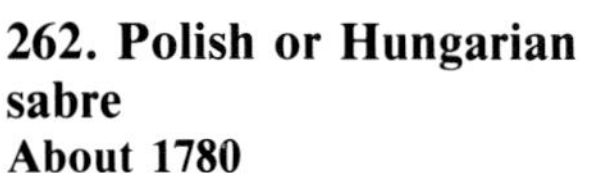

262. Polish or Hungarian sabre
About 1780
The unusually broad curved blade is deeply etched with script in the Islamic style. Good condition.
£500

263. British light cavalry trooper's sword
Length 40¾ins. (103.7cm)
About 1780-1788
The hilt and scabbard of brass. Regulation issue, good condition. National Army Museum (7205-7-43).
£150 — £200

Photographs: 260 Christie's;
261 Sotheby's;
262 Michael C. German Ltd.

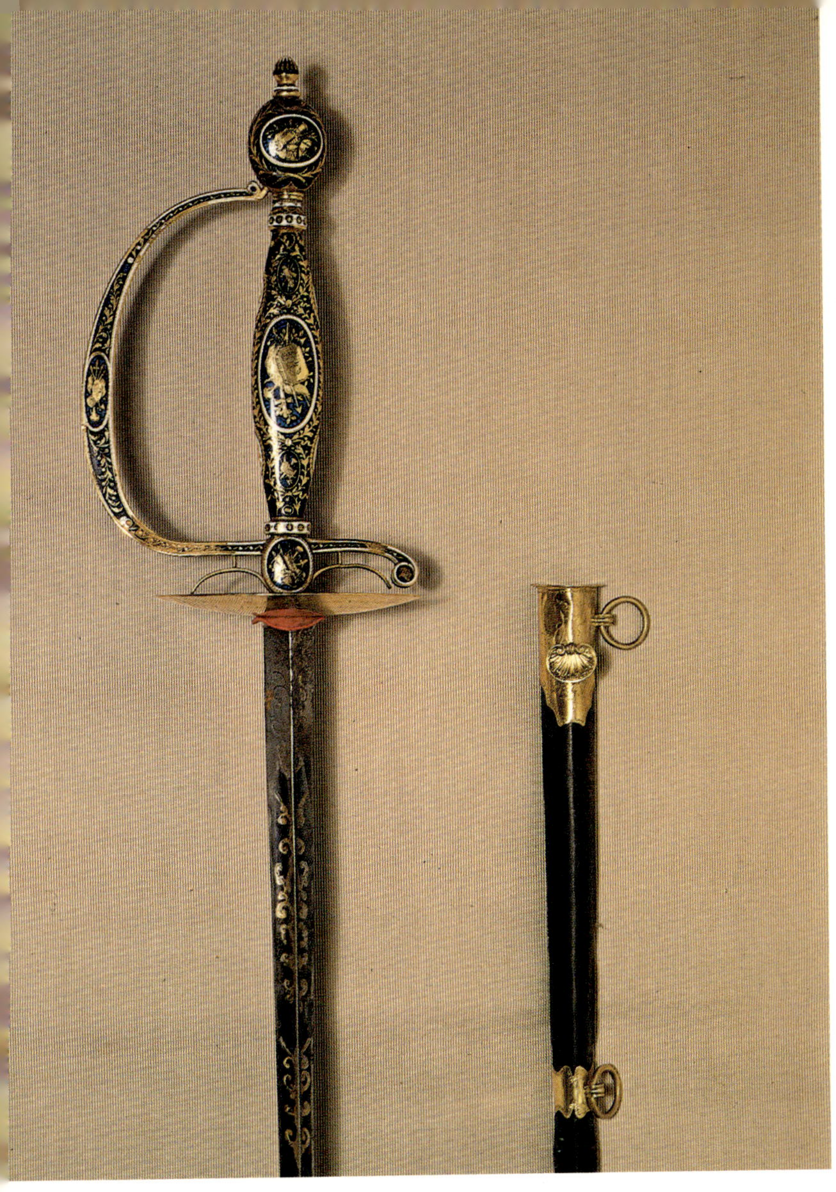

Colour Plate 3. *Gold and enamel hilted presentation small-sword, London, 1793-1794. For details see no. 206.*
Sotheby's

Colour Plate 4. *French gold and enamel hilted small-sword, early 19th century. For details see no. 220.*
Sotheby's

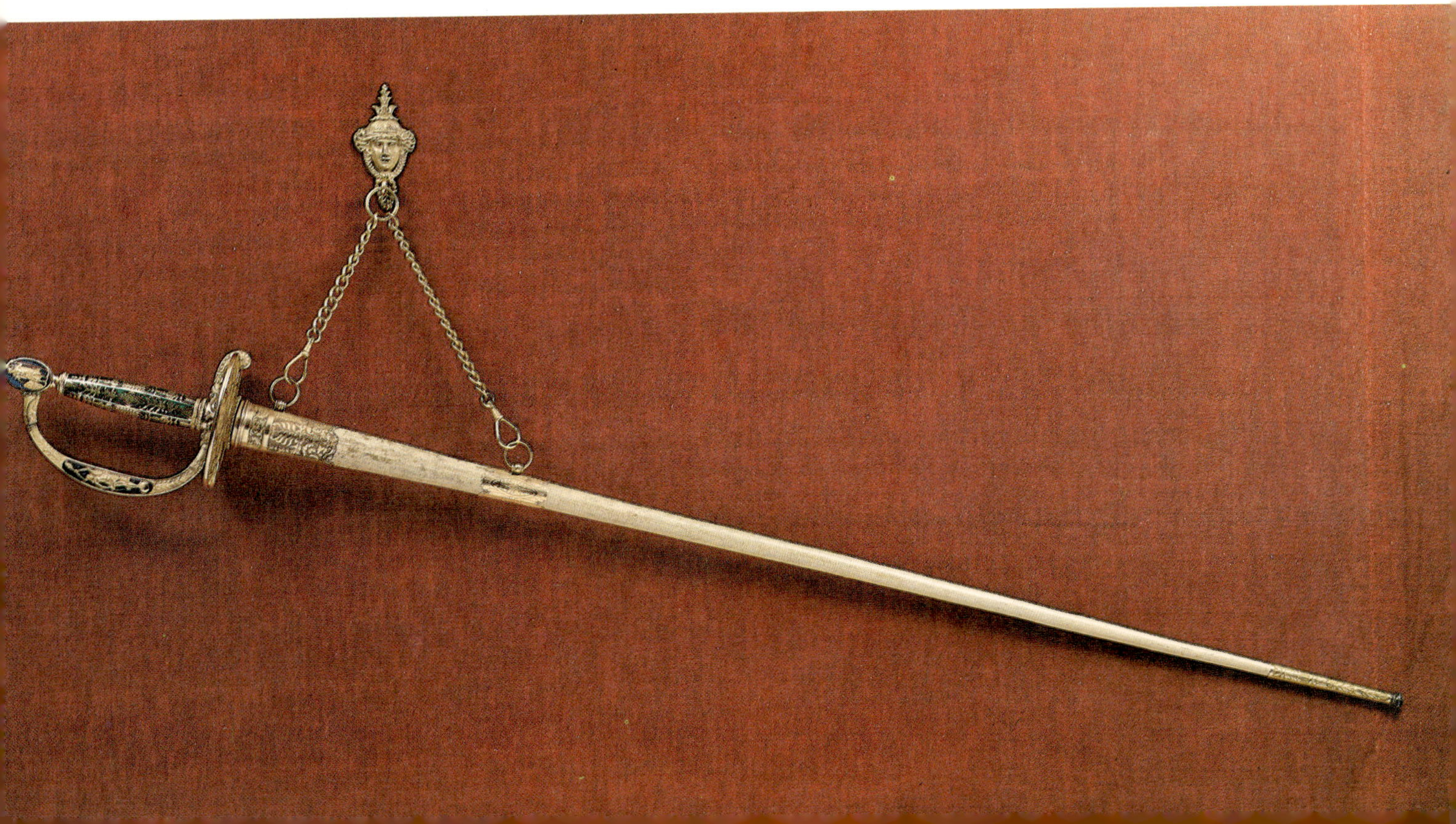

264

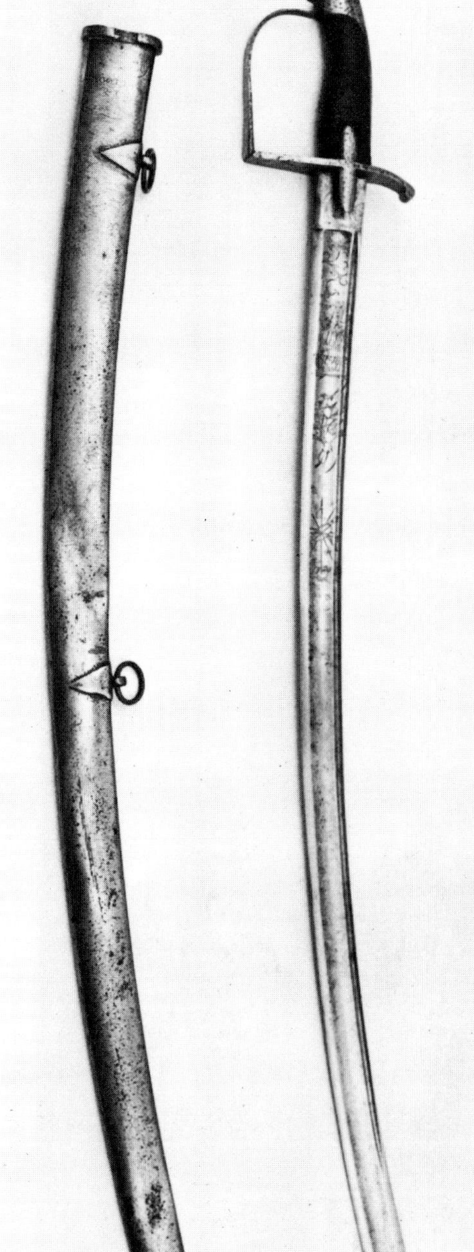

264. Sabre of an officer of the 16th or Queens Own Light Dragoons, light cavalry pattern 1788
Blade 36ins. (91.5cm)
Steel hilt with leather-covered grip. The etched curved blade inscribed with regimental title. Good condition. National Army Museum (6005-22).
£150 — £200

265

265. Indian sabre made for export to Europe
Blade 32½ins. (82.5cm) Late 18th century
Gold damascened hilt with horn grip bound with silver wire. Blade of watered steel. The scabbard mounts are decorated *en suite* with the hilt. Rare and of fine quality. Now in the Tower of London Armouries (XXVI.173S).
£400 — £600

Photograph 265 Christie's

266

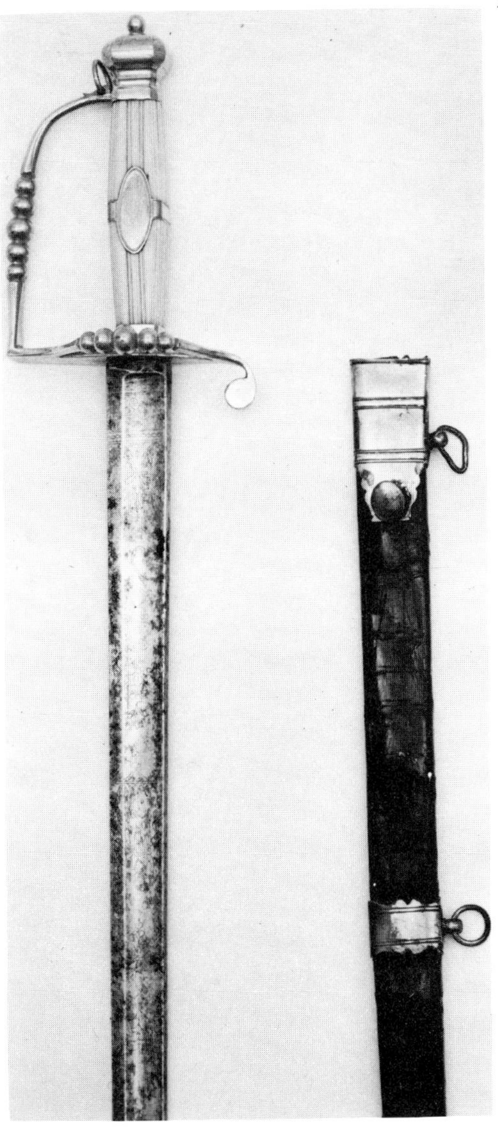

266. British infantry officer's spadroon
Blade 32ins. (81.3cm) About 1790
The gilt-brass bead-pattern hilt has five graduated beads on the knuckle guard and side ring (this type of hilt is also known as a five-ball hilt). The etched single-edged spadroon blade is of the type adopted for use on infantry officers' swords in 1786. A good example of a popular and commonly found sword.
£120 — £200

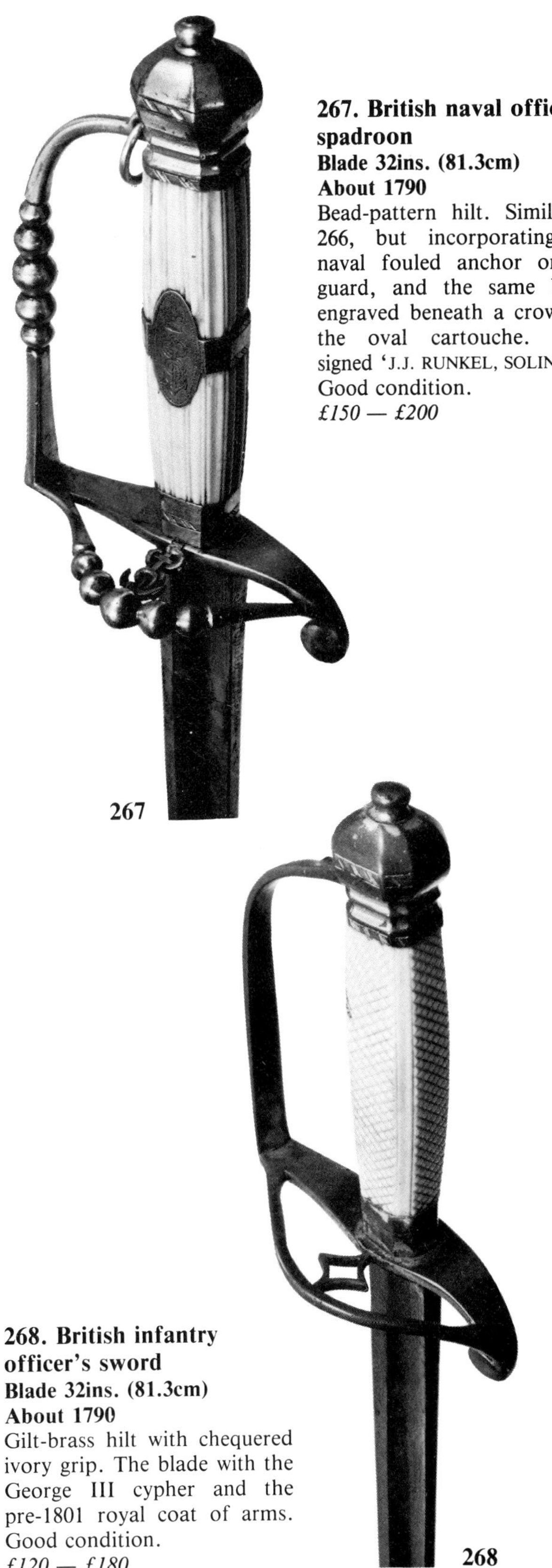

267. British naval officer's spadroon
Blade 32ins. (81.3cm)
About 1790
Bead-pattern hilt. Similar to 266, but incorporating the naval fouled anchor on the guard, and the same badge engraved beneath a crown on the oval cartouche. Blade signed 'J.J. RUNKEL, SOLINGEN'. Good condition.
£150 — £200

267

268. British infantry officer's sword
Blade 32ins. (81.3cm)
About 1790
Gilt-brass hilt with chequered ivory grip. The blade with the George III cypher and the pre-1801 royal coat of arms. Good condition.
£120 — £180

268

Photographs: Peter Dale Ltd.

Photographs:
269 Peter Dale Ltd.;
270 and 271 Christie's

269

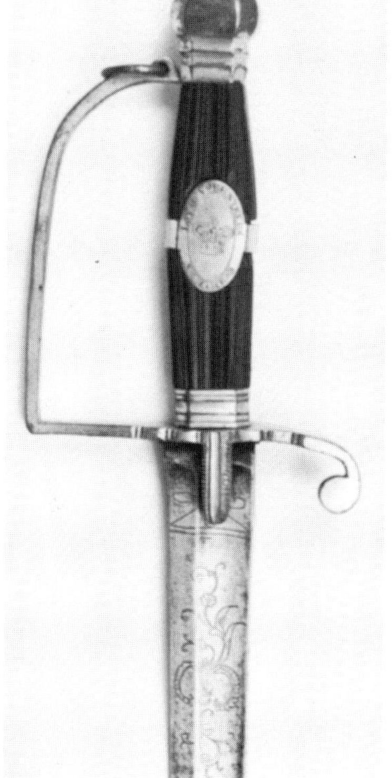

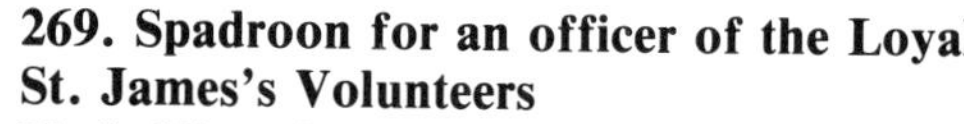

269. Spadroon for an officer of the Loyal St. James's Volunteers
Blade 32ins. (81.2cm) About 1800
Gilt metal hilt with fluted ebony grip, the cartouche engraved with a crown and the regimental title. Good quality but with some wear.
£200 — £250

270

270. British officer's sword
Blade 27¾ins. (70.5cm) About 1790
The brass hilt with shaped reeded ivory grip, and with an etched blued and gilt curved blade. Scabbard locket engraved 'BLAND & FOSTER, ST. JAMES'S'. Very good condition.
£300 — £400

271

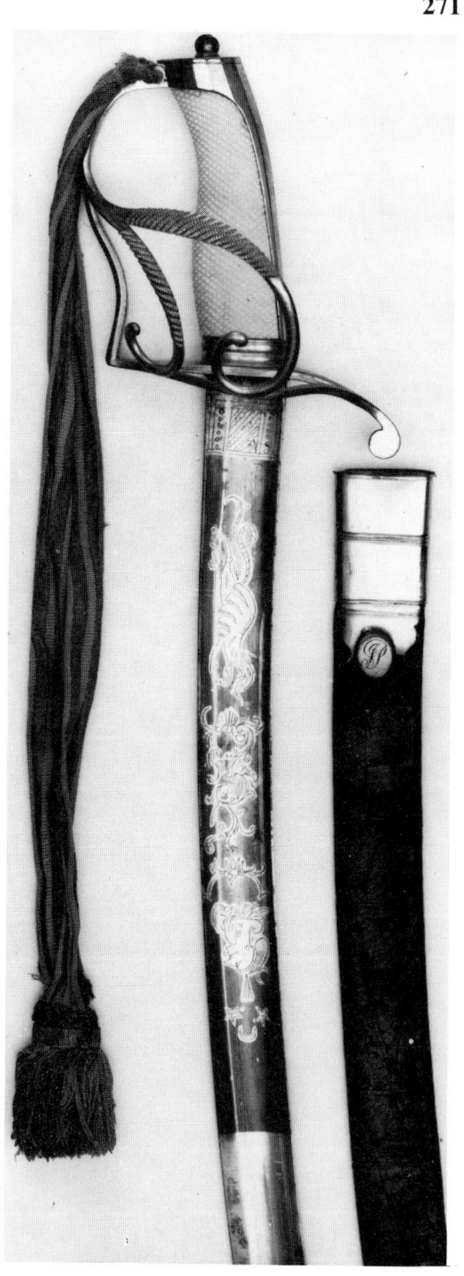

271. British officer's sword
Blade 28¾ins. (73cm)
About 1792-1806
The gilt-brass stirrup hilt with two scrolled side guards and chequered ivory grip. The locket engraved 'JOHNSON, SWORD CUTLER, Nº 8 NEWCASTLE STREET, STRAND'. An attractive sword in very good condition.
£400 — £450

274

273. British cavalry officer's sabre
Blade 31¼ins. (80.6cm) 1790s
A more ornate version of 272 with engraved gilt-brass hilt and scabbard mounts. Very good condition.
£400 — £500

274. British light cavalry trooper's sabre, 1796 pattern
Blade 33½ins. (85cm)
The steel stirrup-hilt has a reeded wooden grip. Normally this would be overlaid with leather and bound with wire. Plain curved single-edged blade. Probably the most familiar of all British regulation pattern swords. Reasonable condition.
£80 — £180

272

273

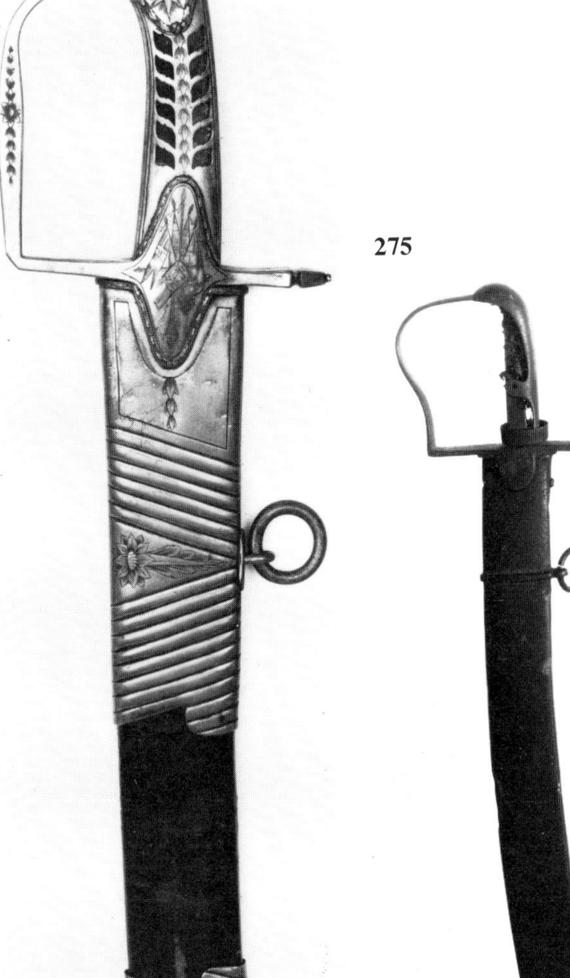

275

272. Sabre of an officer of the 7th Light Dragoons
Blade 36½ins. (93cm) 1790s
The hilt of steel with reeded ebony grip. The pitted and worn blade etched with the George III cypher. Reasonable condition.
£200 — £250

275. British light cavalry trooper's sabre, 1796 pattern
Blade 32ins. (81.3cm)
An example in very poor condition. The hilt, blade and scabbard are rusted, the grip is missing and the tang of the blade is tenuously attached to the back-plate.
£15 — £30

Photographs: Christie's

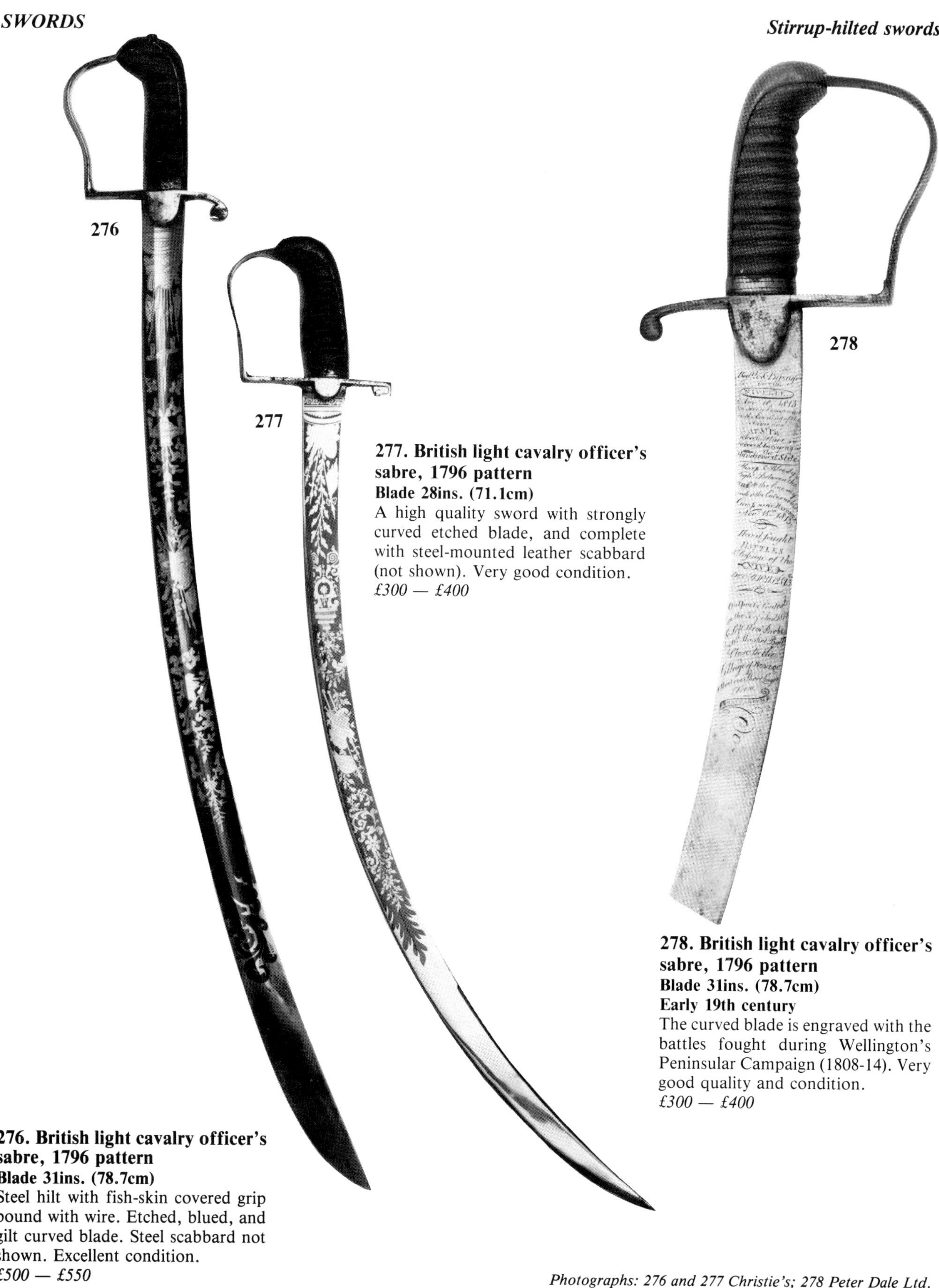

276. British light cavalry officer's sabre, 1796 pattern
Blade 31ins. (78.7cm)
Steel hilt with fish-skin covered grip bound with wire. Etched, blued, and gilt curved blade. Steel scabbard not shown. Excellent condition.
£500 — £550

277. British light cavalry officer's sabre, 1796 pattern
Blade 28ins. (71.1cm)
A high quality sword with strongly curved etched blade, and complete with steel-mounted leather scabbard (not shown). Very good condition.
£300 — £400

278. British light cavalry officer's sabre, 1796 pattern
Blade 31ins. (78.7cm)
Early 19th century
The curved blade is engraved with the battles fought during Wellington's Peninsular Campaign (1808-14). Very good quality and condition.
£300 — £400

Photographs: 276 and 277 Christie's; 278 Peter Dale Ltd.

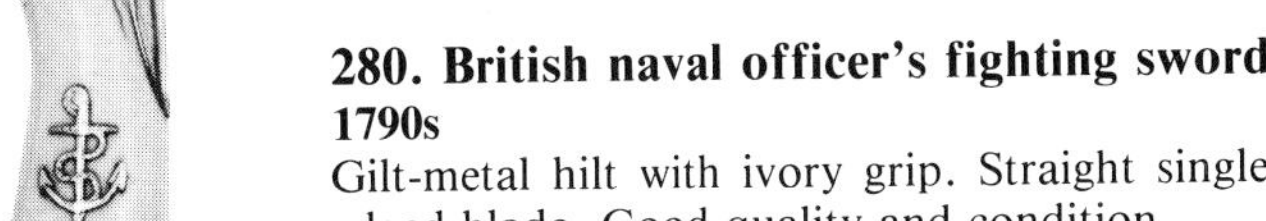

280

280. British naval officer's fighting sword
1790s
Gilt-metal hilt with ivory grip. Straight single-edged blade. Good quality and condition.
£200 — £300

279. British heavy cavalry trooper's sword, 1796 pattern
Blade 35ins. (89cm)
Steel hilt with pierced oval guard and wooden grip originally overlaid with leather. The straight single-edged blade has a hatchet point (see 300 for a clearer view of this type of blade). Similar examples have blades with spear points. Regulation issue, reasonable condition.
£150 — £180

279

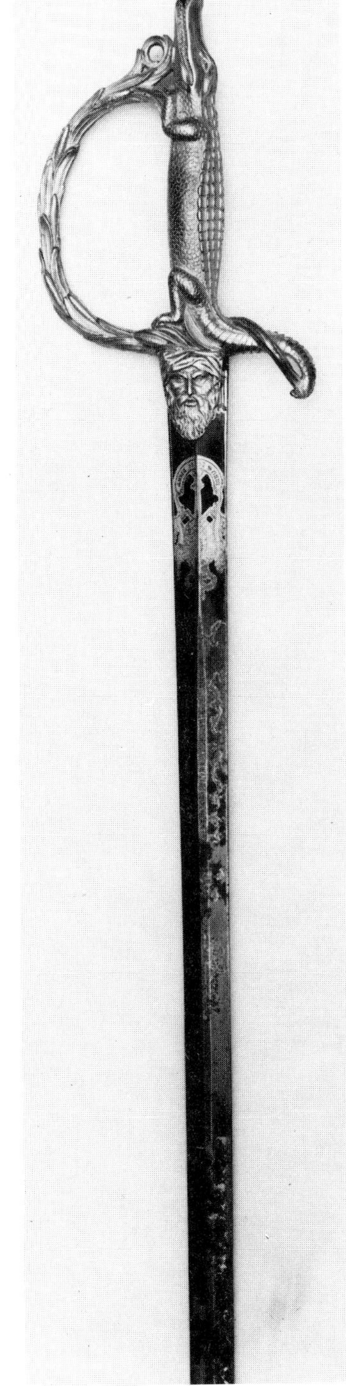

281

281. Battle of the Nile (1798) commemorative sword
Length 38½ins. (97.8cm) About 1798-1800
The gilt-metal hilt is cast with a crocodile and river gods and the knuckle guard is in the form of a laurel wreath. The straight blued and gilt two-edged blade is inscribed 'FOR MY COUNTRY AND KING'.

The sword is modelled on a gold-hilted sword given to Admiral Nelson by members of the Egyptian Club, formed by the captains of the British fleet who had fought under his command at the Nile. Several officers subsequently ordered gilt-metal copies to be made to commemorate the occasion. This rare example was ordered from Prosser, Charing Cross, London, by Robert Cuthbert, 1st Lieutenant on H.M.S. *Majestic,* who took over command of the ship when its captain, George Westcott, was killed.
£500+

Photographs: 279 Christie's; 280 Peter Dale Ltd.; 281 Sotheby's

282

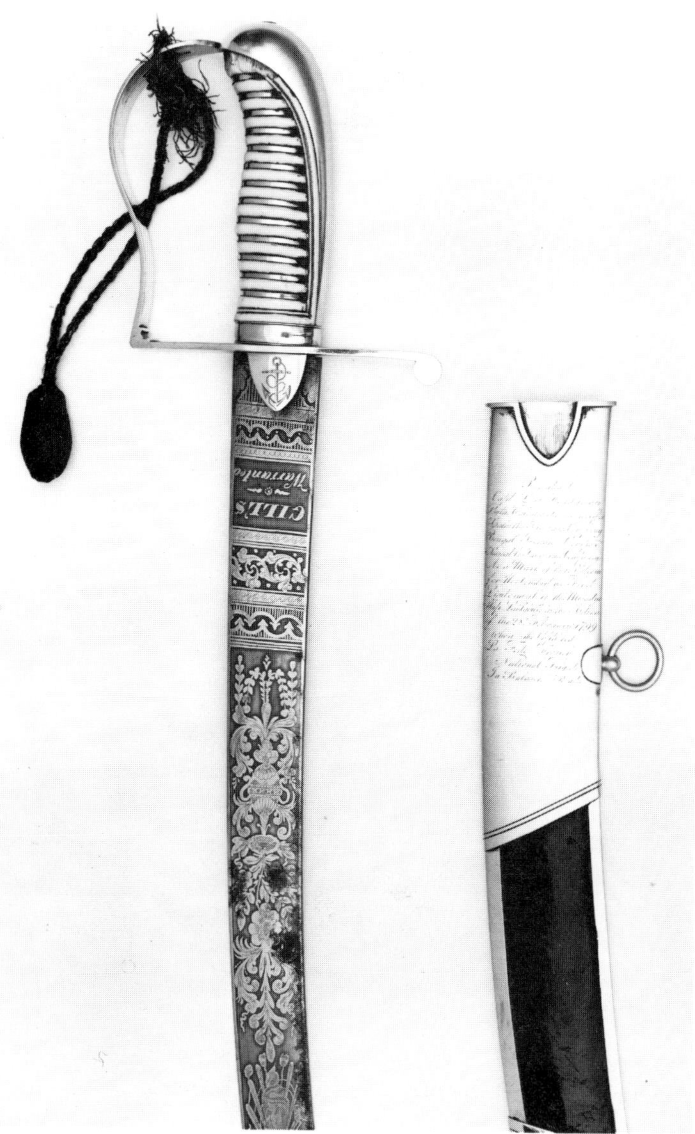

283. Gold-mounted presentation sabre
Blade 31ins. (78.8cm) 1802
Gold hilt. The blade is etched with the arms of the recipient, the Georgian cypher, and the bladesmith's signature 'MOYES EDINR.' The gold-mounted tooled-leather scabbard inscribed 'A. CUNNINGHAM, JEWELLER, SOUTH BRIDGE, EDINBURGH'. The presentation inscription reads: 'THE BERWICKSHIRE YEOMANRY CAVALRY OFFER THIS TO GEORGE BUCHANAN, ESQR. OF KELLO, THEIR MAJOR COMMANDANT, AS A TOKEN OF THEIR GRATITUDE AND ESTEEM, 1802'. Fine quality.
£5,000

283

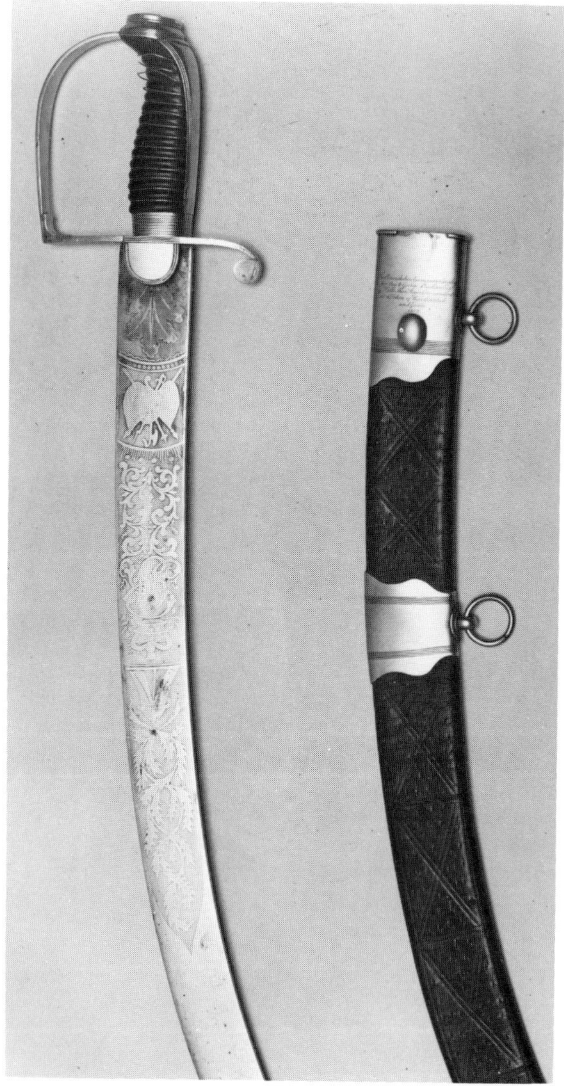

282. Gold-mounted naval presentation fighting sabre
Length 36½ins. (92.7cm)
Unmarked, probably London, 1799-1800
The gold hilt, with ivory grip, is modelled on the 1796 light cavalry pattern, which had been adopted for naval use by the late 1790s. The etched, single-edged blade is inscribed 'GILL'S WARRANTED'. The gold-mounted leather-covered scabbard is inscribed on the locket: 'PRESENTED TO CPTN. L.F. [Lucius Ferdinand] HARDYMAN BY THE CALCUTTA INSURANCE COMPANY, BENGAL INSURANCE COMPANY AND AMICABLE INSURANCE COMPANY, AS A MARK OF THEIR ESTEEM FOR HIS CONDUCT AS FIRST LIEUTENANT OF HIS MAJESTY'S SHIP LA SYBILLE IN THE ACTION OF THE 28 FEBRUARY, 1799, WHEN SHE CAPTURED LA FORTE, FRENCH NATIONAL FRIGATE, IN BELASORE ROADS'. Fine quality and condition. See 216 for the other sword presented to Hardyman for the same action.
£5,000

Photographs: 282 Sotheby's; 283 Christie's

285

285. French gilt-brass mounted boy's sabre
Blade 17½ins. (44.5cm)
Early 19th century
The sword is complete with shoulder strap and sabretache decorated with silver braid and an applied gilt-brass imperial eagle. Good condition, blade later.
£600 — £800

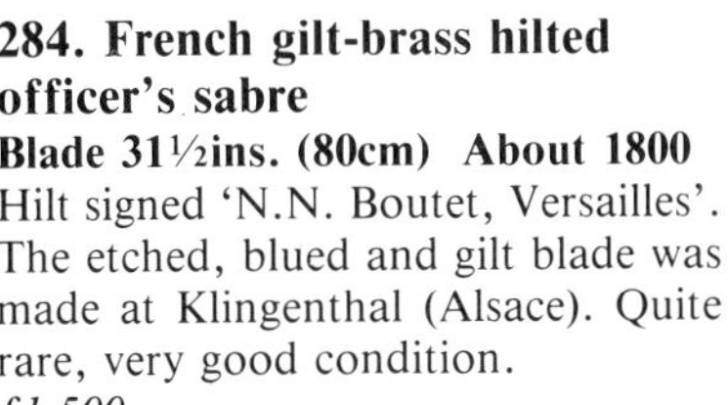

284. French gilt-brass hilted officer's sabre
Blade 31½ins. (80cm) About 1800
Hilt signed 'N.N. Boutet, Versailles'. The etched, blued and gilt blade was made at Klingenthal (Alsace). Quite rare, very good condition.
£1,500

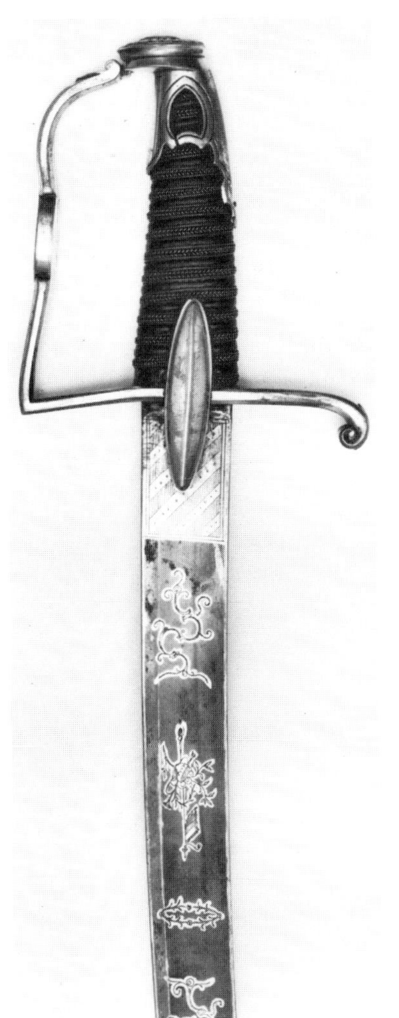

284

286

286. British Flank Company officer's sabre, 1803 pattern
Blade 30¼ins. (77cm)
Gilt-brass hilt with Georgian cypher on the knuckle guard. Reeded ivory grip. The blade etched, blued, and gilt, and inscribed 'WOOLLEY & SARGANT, WARRANTED'. A familiar sword in good condition.
£300 — £450

Photographs: Christie's

289

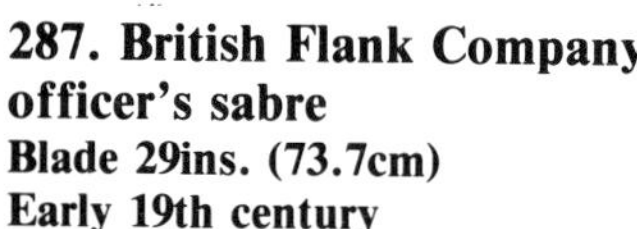

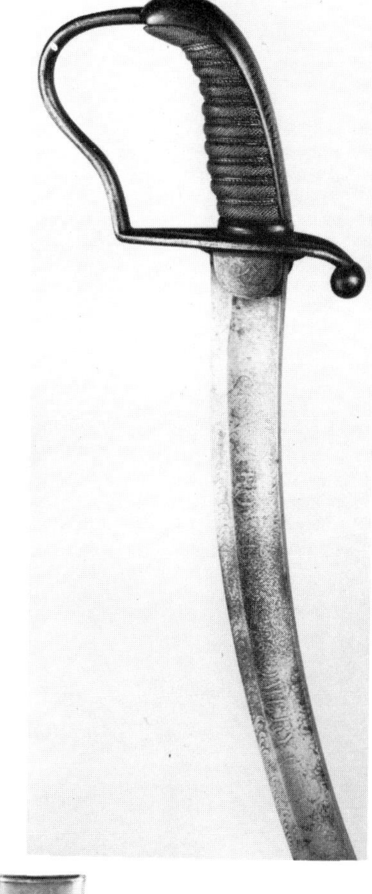

287

287. British Flank Company officer's sabre
Blade 29ins. (73.7cm)
Early 19th century
Gilt-brass stirrup hilt with chequered ivory grip. The curved single-edged blade is etched with the Georgian cypher and an officer. Good condition, blade worn.
£200 — £250

289. Sabre of an officer of the Royal Montgomery Light Infantry
Blade 29ins. (74cm)
Early 19th century
Steel hilt. Fish-skin covered grip. The curved, worn, blade etched on both sides with the regimental title.
£150

290

288

290. Silver-mounted Flank Company officer's sabre
Blade 30ins. (76.3cm)
London, 1806-1807
The hilt stamped with unidentified silver maker's mark 'GT'. Fine quality. The blued and gilt decoration on the blade is very worn.
£400 — £500

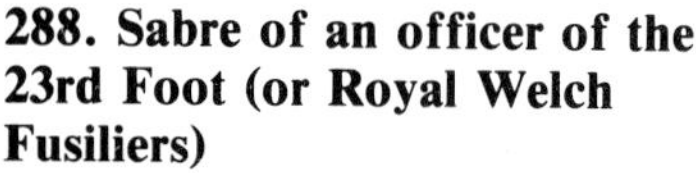

288. Sabre of an officer of the 23rd Foot (or Royal Welch Fusiliers)
Blade 29¾ins. (75.5cm) About 1803
Gilt-brass hilt and scabbard mounts with the regimental badge and title on the langets. The locket engraved 'HUME, PERCY ST., LONDON'. Very good condition.
£300 — £400

Photographs: Christie's

291 **292**

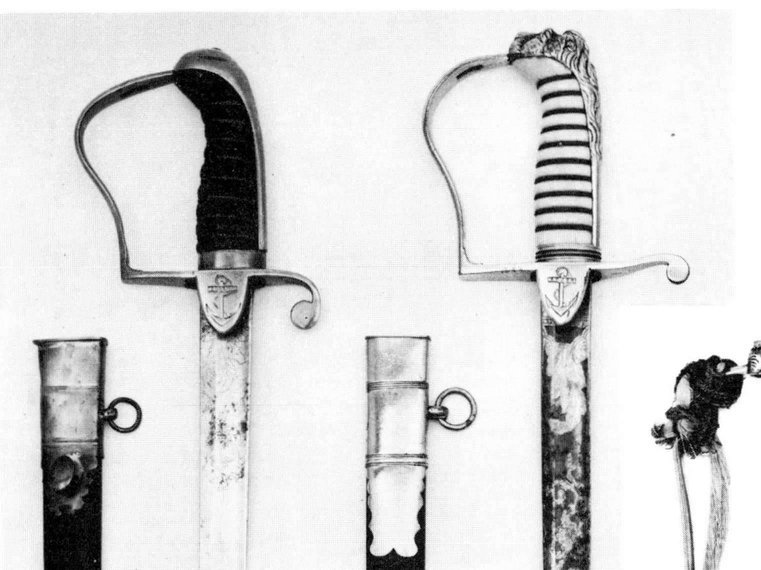

293. British customs officer's sword, 1805 pattern
Length 37⅛ins. (94.3cm)
The gilt-brass hilt engraved with the Customs House badge on the langet. Etched, blued and gilt straight blade. Locket inscribed 'HOUGH, HIGH ST., PORTSMOUTH'. Very good condition. The upper part of the ivory grip is missing.
£150 — £200

293

294

291. British naval sword for lieutenants and midshipmen, 1805 pattern
Blade 32¼ins. (82cm)
The gilt metal hilt with fish-skin covered grip is engraved with fouled anchor badge on the langet. Straight single-edged etched blade. Good condition.
£100 — £120

292. British naval sword for commanders and higher ranks, 1805 pattern
Blade 32¼ins. (82cm)
Gilt metal hilt with reeded ivory grip and lion's head pommel. The blued and gilt blade worn. Good condition.
£100 — £150

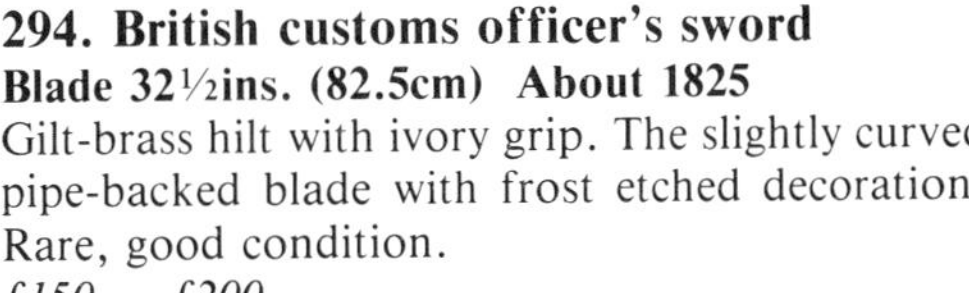

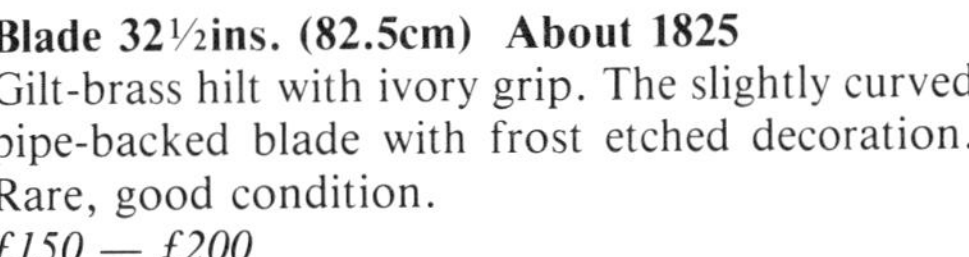

294. British customs officer's sword
Blade 32½ins. (82.5cm) About 1825
Gilt-brass hilt with ivory grip. The slightly curved pipe-backed blade with frost etched decoration. Rare, good condition.
£150 — £200

Photographs: 291, 292 and 294 Peter Dale Ltd.; 293 Sotheby's

295

295. Lloyds Patriotic Fund presentation sword of one hundred pound type
Length 34½ins. (87.6cm) 1804
Sword with gilt-metal hilt and scabbard made by R. Teed, Sword-Cutler, Lancaster Court, Strand. The near perfect blued and gilt blade inscribed: 'FROM THE PATRIOTIC FUND AT LLOYDS TO CONWAY SHIPLEY, ESQ^R COMMANDER OF H.M.S. HIPPOMENES OF 18 GUNS ON THE 27TH MARCH, 1804, WHEN SHE CHACED AND CAPTURED L'EGYPTIENNE, F.F.P. OF 36 GUNS, AS RECORDED IN THE LONDON GAZETTE OF 19TH MAY.' A very fine example of the highest grade of sword awarded by the Fund (compare condition with 296).
£10,000

296

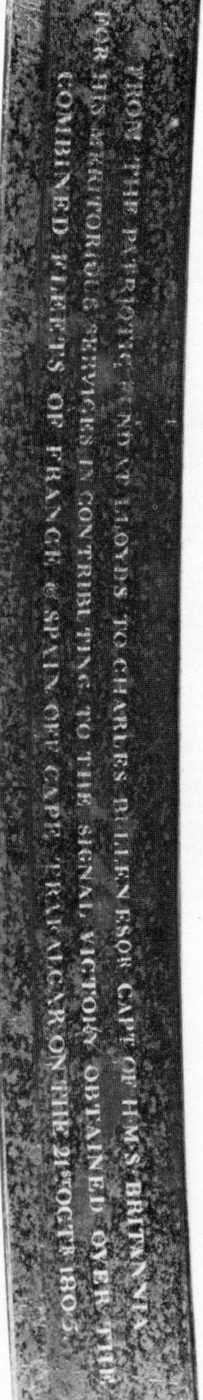

296. Lloyds Patriotic Fund presentation Trafalgar sword
Length 36⅛ins. (91.7cm) 1805
Another example of the one hundred pound type but not in such good condition. The blade, for example, has lost most of its blued finish (see detail). Inscribed 'FROM THE PATRIOTIC FUND AT LLOYDS TO CHARLES BULLEN, ESQ^R, CAPT. OF H.M.S. BRITANNIA, FOR HIS MERITORIOUS SERVICES IN CONTRIBUTING TO THE SIGNAL VICTORY OBTAINED OVER THE COMBINED FLEETS OF FRANCE AND SPAIN OFF CAPE TRAFALGAR ON 21ST OCT^R 1805.'
£8,000

Photographs: Sotheby's

297

297. Lloyds Patriotic Fund presentation sword of fifty pound type

Blade 31ins. (78.7cm) 1806

The most noticeable difference in the grades of swords given by the Patriotic Fund, lies in the scabbard. Compare with 295, 296 and 298. The blued, gilt and etched blade is inscribed: 'FROM THE PATRIOTIC FUND AT LLOYDS TO LIEUT. SIR WILM. GEO. PARKER, BART. OF H.M.S. RENOMMEE, FOR HIS GALLANT CONDUCT IN BOARDING AND CARRYING IN THE BOATS BELONGING TO THAT SHIP FROM UNDER THE GUNS OF THE TOWN AND TOWER OF VIEGA, HIS CATHOLIC MAJESTY'S SCHOONER GIGANTA OF 9 GUNS & 38 MEN, ON THE 4TH MAY, 1806, AS RECORDED IN THE LONDON GAZETTE OF 8TH JULY.' Excellent condition.

£8,000

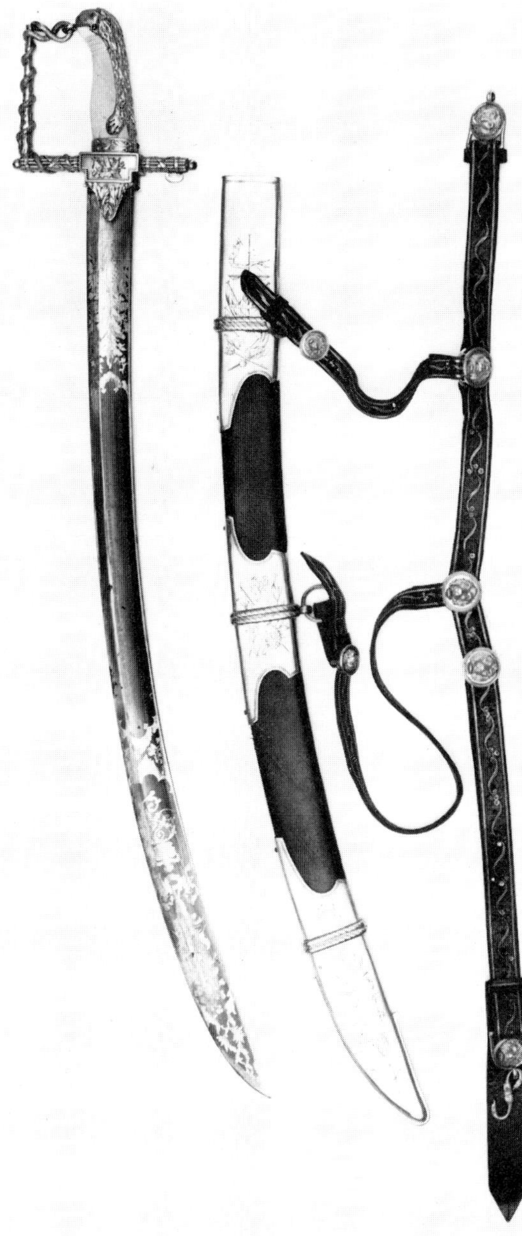

298

298. Lloyds Patriotic Fund presentation sword of thirty pound type

Length 35¼ins. (89.5cm) 1807

The lowest grade of Lloyds sword is less common than the fifty pound and one hundred pound types. The blade on this example is worn and the leather on the scabbard has been replaced. Inscribed 'FROM THE PATRIOTIC FUND AT LLOYDS TO MR JOHN GREEN, MASTER'S MATE OF H.M.S. GALATEA, FOR HIS GALLANTRY AND PERSEVERANCE WHEN COMMANDING A BOAT BELONGING TO THAT SHIP, IN BOARDING AND CARRYING THE FRENCH NATIONAL CORVETTE LYNX OF 16 GUNS & 161 MEN, AS RECORDED IN THE LONDON GAZETTE OF THE 14TH APRIL, 1807.'

£5,000 — £6,000

Photographs: 297 Christie's; 298 Sotheby's

299

300

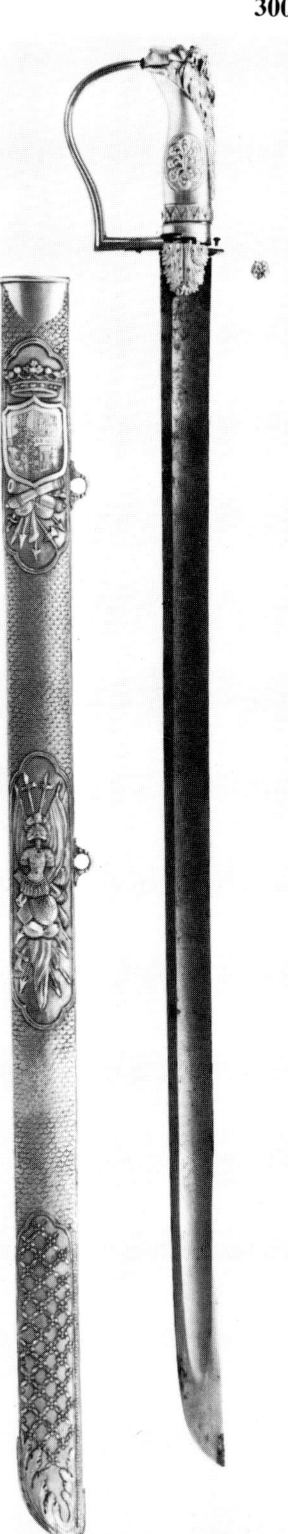

299. City of London One Hundred Guinea sword of honour
Blade 32ins. (81.2cm)
London, 1806-1807
Hilt and scabbard mounts of silver gilt stamped with maker's mark 'RT', probably for Richard Teed, the Lloyds Patriotic Fund sword maker. Ordered and mounted by Prosser of London, and presented to Thomas Masterman Hardy, Captain of Nelson's flagship, H.M.S. *Victory*. The straight two-edged blade inscribed: 'TRUMPHANS TRAFALGAR: T.M. HARDY NAVIS BRITANNICE VICTORIAE PREFECTO IN PRELIO TRAFALGAR XXI OCT.R. MDCCCV. INSIGNITER MERITO CIVITAS LONDINENSIS HOC TESTIMONIUM SUMMAE EXISTINATIONIS D.D.MDCCCVI' (Triumphant at Trafalgar: To T.M. Hardy, Commander of the British Ship *Victory* at the Battle of Trafalgar, 21st Oct. 1805, where he performed markedly well, the City of London gave this testimony of their highest esteem, 1806). Also shown in Colour Plate 5.
£20,000

Photographs: Christie's

300. Silver-gilt mounted presentation cavalry sword
Blade 32ins. (81.3cm) London, 1805-1806
Made by John Ray and James Montague, mounted by Rundell, Bridge & Rundell, London. The stirrup hilt incorporates in the knuckle guard two other bars which can be released to form side guards. The finely decorated scabbard bears the unidentified coat of arms of the recipient, and the sword also bears a French provincial warranty mark introduced in May 1838 (see Blair, 1972, pp. 49-51, no. 32). The 1796 Heavy Cavalry pattern blade is inscribed 'WARRANTED' and signed 'J.J. RUNKEL, SOLINGEN'. Very fine quality. Blade worn.
£3,000 — £5,000

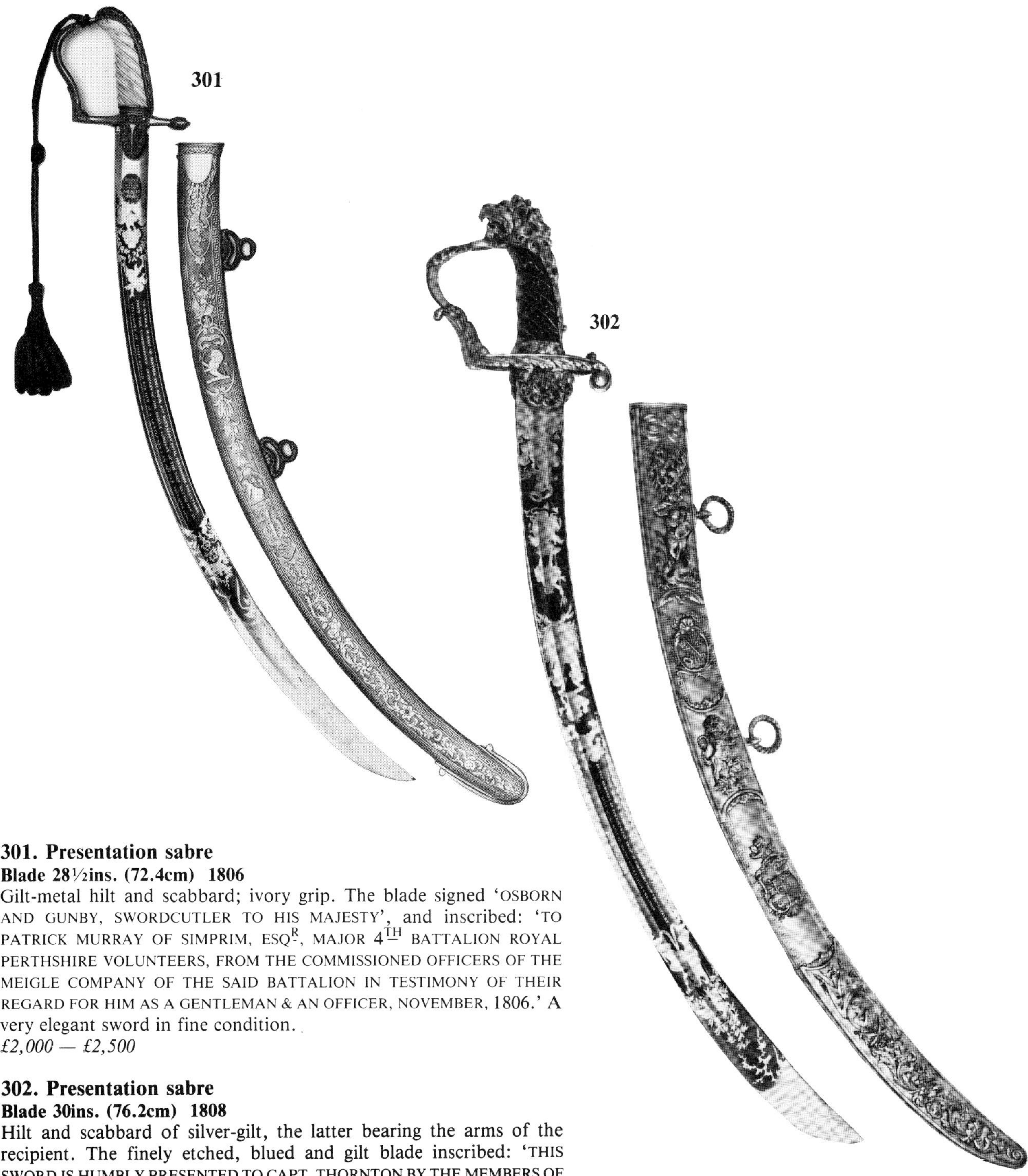

301. Presentation sabre
Blade 28½ins. (72.4cm) 1806
Gilt-metal hilt and scabbard; ivory grip. The blade signed 'OSBORN AND GUNBY, SWORDCUTLER TO HIS MAJESTY', and inscribed: 'TO PATRICK MURRAY OF SIMPRIM, ESQ^{R}, MAJOR 4TH BATTALION ROYAL PERTHSHIRE VOLUNTEERS, FROM THE COMMISSIONED OFFICERS OF THE MEIGLE COMPANY OF THE SAID BATTALION IN TESTIMONY OF THEIR REGARD FOR HIM AS A GENTLEMAN & AN OFFICER, NOVEMBER, 1806.' A very elegant sword in fine condition.
£2,000 — £2,500

302. Presentation sabre
Blade 30ins. (76.2cm) 1808
Hilt and scabbard of silver-gilt, the latter bearing the arms of the recipient. The finely etched, blued and gilt blade inscribed: 'THIS SWORD IS HUMBLY PRESENTED TO CAPT. THORNTON BY THE MEMBERS OF THE DAVENTRY TROOP OF NORTHAMPTON^{SR} YEO. CAVALRY, AS A MARK OF THE MOST PROFOUND VENERATION & RESPECT, JUNE 4TH, 1808.' Fine quality, excellent condition.
£2,000 — £3,000

Photographs: 301 Christie's; 302 Peter Dale Ltd.

303

303. Presentation sabre

Blade 34ins. (86.3cm) About 1807

Gilt-brass hilt and scabbard mounts. Horn grip. The etched and gilt blade (worn) inscribed: 'PRESENTED TO MAJOR CAMPBELL BY THE OFFICERS OF THE 2nd BATTALION LXIInd REGIMENT [Wiltshire Regiment], AS A MARK OF RESPECT FOR HIS MANY VIRTUES THAT ADORN HIS CHARACTER AS AN OFFICER AND A GENTLEMAN.' Locket signed 'PROSSER, CHARING CROSS, LONDON'. Very good quality. The leather on the scabbard is replaced.

£500 — £800

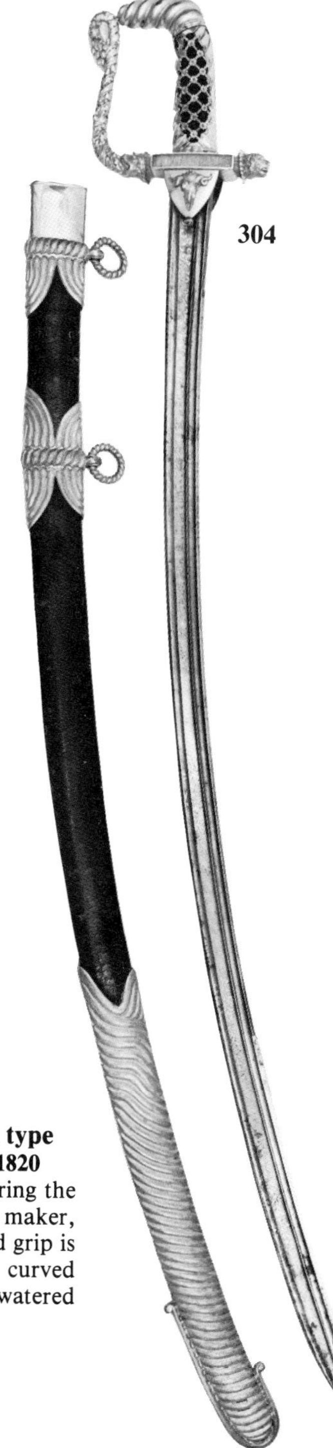

304

304. English sabre of presentation type

Blade 32½ins. (82.6cm) About 1805-1820

A more ornate version of 303 and bearing the signature of the same London sword maker, Prosser. The gilt-brass hilt with pierced grip is underlaid with purple velvet. The curved fullered blade is etched to simulate watered steel. Very good condition.

£700 — £900

Photographs: 303 Christie's; 304 Peter Dale Ltd.

305. French boy's sword for a member of the Imperial Guard of the King of Rome
Blade 20ins. (51cm) About 1814
Brass hilt with leather-covered grip. The curved blued blade inscribed 'GARDE IMPERIALE DU ROI DE ROME'. The sword was intended to be used by a member of a guard, formed of pupils from the four Paris lycées, which Napoleon planned to create for his son in 1814. The project appears to have remained unrealised (see Dufty & Borg, 85c). Quite rare, good condition.
£600 — £800

305

Photographs: 305 Christie's; 306 Sotheby's; 307 Peter Dale Ltd.

307

306

306. Presentation sabre
Length 41ins. (104cm) 1814
The hilt and scabbard of gilt brass, with chequered horn grip. The etched, blued and gilt blade with Georgian cypher inscribed: 'THIS SWORD IS PRESENTED BY THE NON-COMMISSION'D OFFICERS, AND PRIVATES OF C TROOP, IN THE 1ST REGT. OF LIFE GUARDS, TO LIEUTENANT SULIVAN OF THE SAME REGT. AS A TOKEN OF THEIR HIGH ESTEEM OF HIM AS AN OFFICER AND A GENTLEMAN. ST. JEAN DE LUZ, FRANCE, MARCH 24TH 1814.' Worn overall.
£1,500

307. Presentation sabre
Blade 32ins. (81.3cm) About 1814
Signed 'HAMLET, PRINCES ST., LEICESTER SQ., LONDON'. Gilt-metal hilt and scabbard mounts, the guard in the form of a scrolling serpent. The etched, blued and gilt blade inscribed: 'THIS SWORD WAS PRESENTED TO JAS. COOKE, ESQR, LIEUT. COL. COMMANDANT OF THE TRAFFORD HOUSE & HULME LOCAL MILITIA, BY THE OFFICERS UNDER HIS COMMAND, AS A TESTIMONY OF THEIR HIGH OPINION OF HIS MILITARY TALENTS AND UNWEARY'D EXERTIONS FOR THE DISCIPLINE & WELFARE OF THE REGIMENT.' Fine quality. The blade and leather covering on the scabbard a little worn.
£2,000

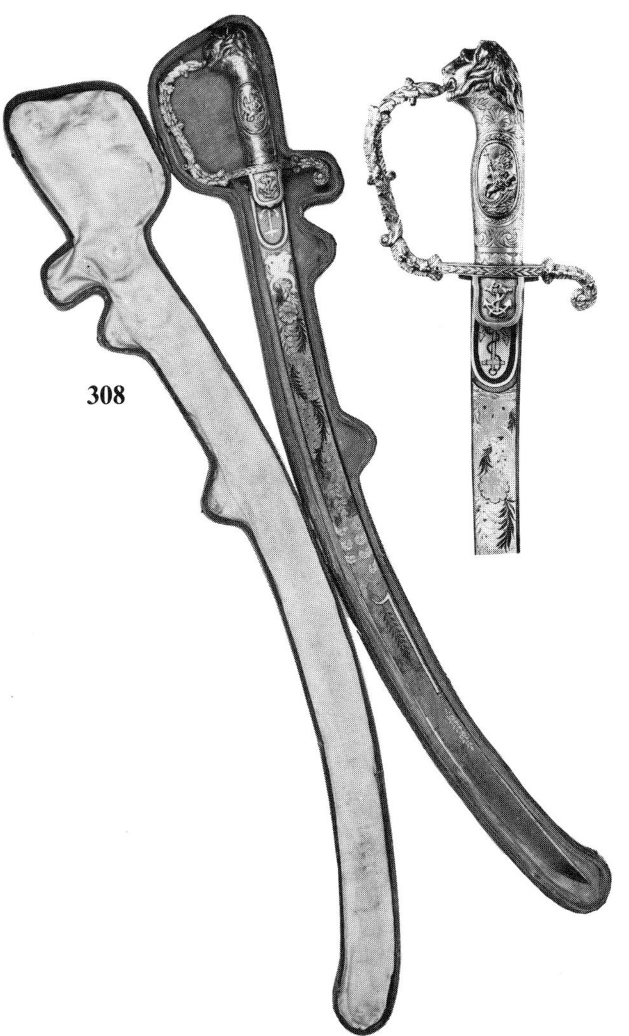

308. Presentation sword

Blade 29ins. (73.7cm) 1814

Silver-gilt hilt with unidentified maker's mark 'TP'. The gilt, blued and frosted blade inscribed: 'PRESENTED TO JOHN BULL, ESQ^{R}., COMMANDER OF H.M. PACKET MARLBOROUGH BY THE PASSENGERS ON BOARD AS A TOKEN OF HIS GALLANT CONDUCT IN SUCCESSFULLY DEFENDING HIS VESSEL AGAINST A SHIP OF MUCH SUPERIOR FORCE, 12TH MARCH, MDCCCXIV, 1814, IN A VOYAGE FROM FALMOUTH TO LISBON.' A fine quality sword but without its scabbard. Complete with velvet-lined case.
£1,500 — £2,000

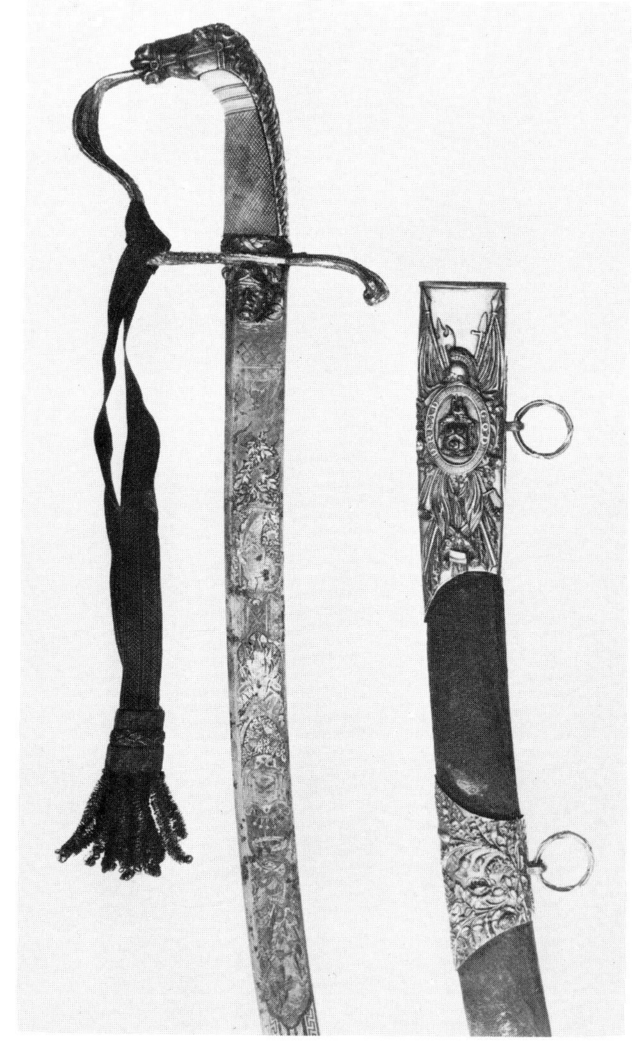

309. Presentation sabre

Blade 31¼ins. (79.5cm) 1817

Gilt-brass hilt and scabbard mounts; chequered ivory grip. The etched, blued and gilt blade signed 'GILL, N° 6, PRINCES ST., LONDON', and inscribed: 'TO THE HONBLE. ROBERT GORDON IN TOKEN OF THE ESTEEM & APPROBATION OF HIS SERVICES DURING A LONG & ACTIVE LIFE, PARTICULARLY, AS COLONEL OF THE NORTH REGIMENT OF MILITIA OF ST. VINCENT, DURING THE INSURRECTION OF THE FRENCH & CHARAIDS IN THE COLONY, A.D. 1795. SENATUS SANCTI VINCENTII DEDIT, A.D. 1817 (The Council of St. Vincent gave this, A.D. 1817). Very good condition.
£2,000 — £2,500

Photographs: 308 Peter Dale Ltd.; 309 Christie's

310

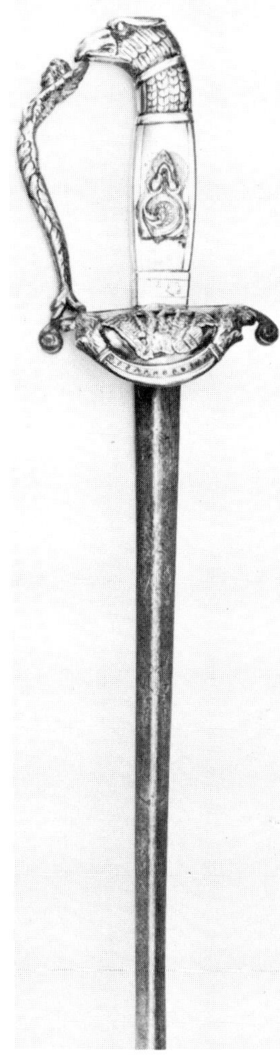

311

310. American naval officer's sword
Blade 32¼ins. (82cm) 1815-1830

Cast gilt-brass hilt with ivory grip and silver-plated single shell guard. Blued and gilt, straight single-edged blade. Good condition. Complete with silver-plated scabbard (not shown).
£120 — £180

311. Austrian silver-hilted dress sword
Length 37½ins. (95.2cm)
Italian hallmarks, about 1848-1860

Silver hilt with the cypher of Emperor Franz Joseph (1848-1916) on the single shell guard. Straight blade of diamond section by P.D. Moll of Solingen. Fair condition.
£200 — £250

312 313

312. British pioneer sword
Length 22ins. (56cm) About 1820-1830

Brass hilt and curved saw-backed blade. Regulation issue. Tower of London Armouries (IX-411).
£40 — £50

313. British pioneer sword of regulation pattern
Blade 22½ins. (57cm) 1856-pre 1904

All-brass hilt and saw-backed blade. The first and only pattern of British pioneer sword, introduced in 1856. Tower of London Armouries (IX-413).
£40 — £50

Photographs: 310 Sotheby, Parke-Bernet, LA; 311 Sotheby's 312 and 313 Crown Copyright

Colour Plate 5. *City of London One Hundred Guinea sword of honour, presented to Thomas Masterman Hardy, Captain of Nelson's flagship,* H.M.S. Victory *at the Battle of Trafalgar, 1805. For details see no. 299.*

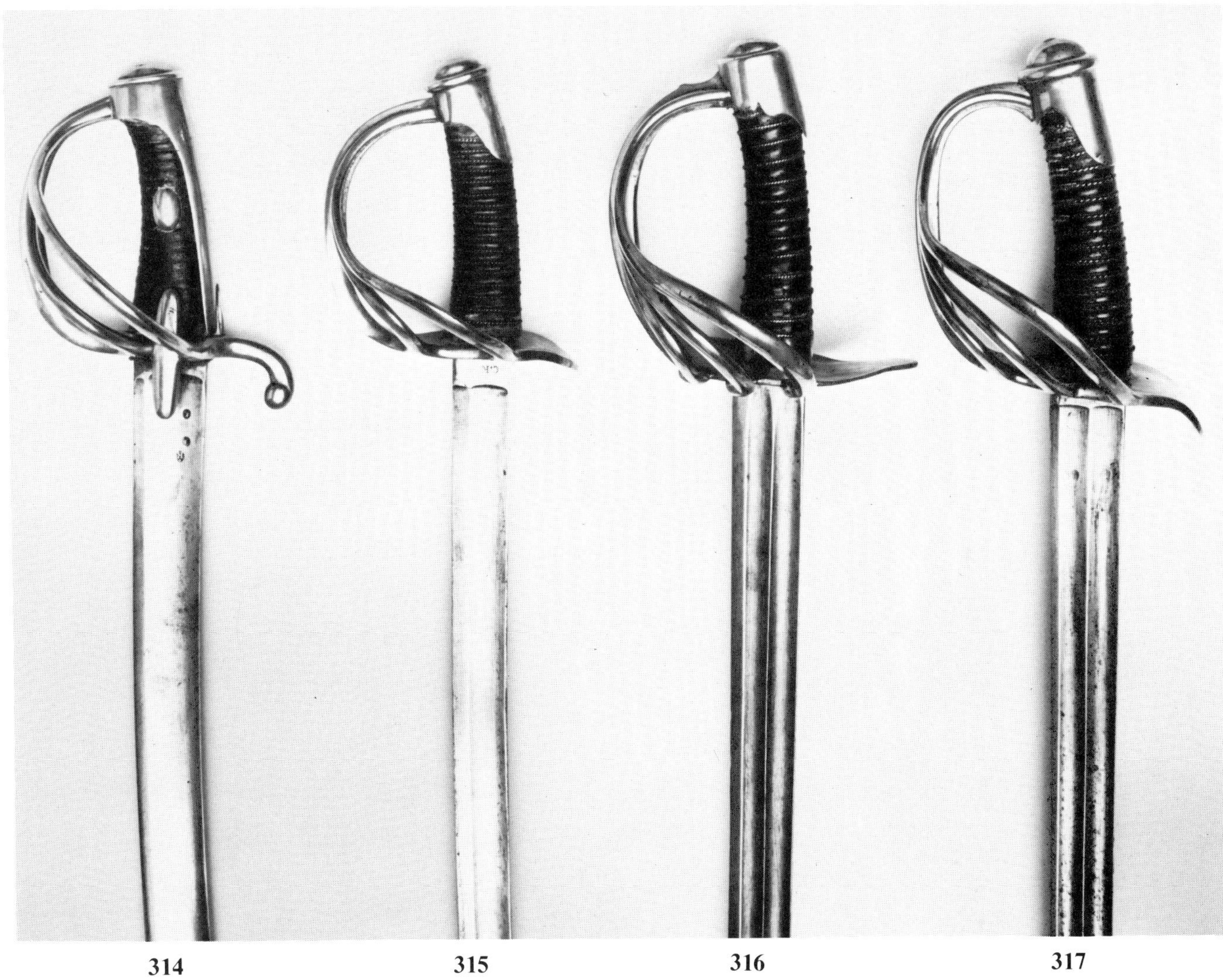

314 315 316 317

314. French light cavalry sabre, An. XI (1802-3) pattern
Blade 34⅝ins. (88cm)
Brass hilt with three-bar guard, leather-covered wooden grip and curved single-edged blade. Regulation issue. Reasonable condition. Steel scabbard not shown.
£80 — £100

315. French light cavalry sabre, 1822 pattern
Blade 35¼ins. (89.5cm)
Brass hilt with three-bar guard and leather-covered grip. Regulation issue. Good condition.
£60 — £80

316. French heavy cavalry sword, An. XI (1802-3) pattern
Blade 38⅜ins. (97.5cm)
Brass hilt with four-bar guard and leather-covered grip. Distinctive single-edged straight blade with double fullers on each side. Regulation issue, good condition. Steel scabbard not shown.
£60 — £100

317. French heavy cavalry sword, 1816 pattern
Blade 36½ins. (92.7cm)
Brass hilt with four-bar guard and leather-covered grip. Blade similar to 316. Steel scabbard not shown. Regulation issue, good condition.
£150

Photographs: Christie's

318. American Mounted Artillery officer's sabre
Blade 33½ins. (82.5cm) 1815-1830
Gilt-brass hilt of French design, with fish-skin covered grip. Curved single-edged Solingen blade etched, blued and gilded with American devices and mottoes. These swords were made in France for export to the United States (see Peterson, 1965, 98, p. 107/8). Rust patches on the blade and on the brass scabbard.
£400 — £500

319. British light cavalry trooper's sword, 1821 pattern
Blade 35ins. (89cm)
Hilt of steel with reeded wooden grip originally overlaid with leather. Single-edged slightly curved blade. Steel scabbard not shown. Regulation issue. Reasonable condition.
£40 — £60

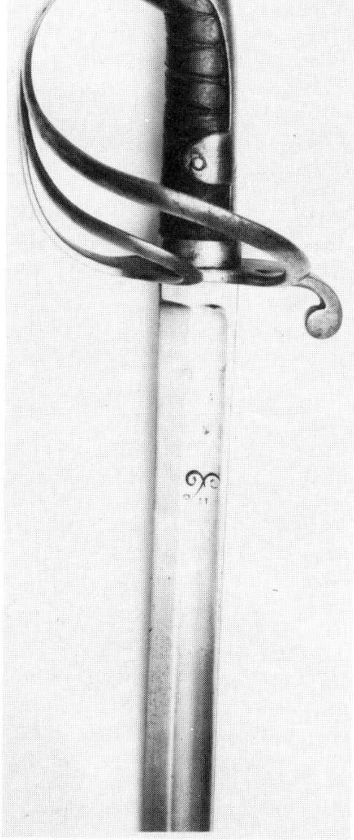

319

Photographs: Christie's

320. British Royal Artillery officer's sword
Blade 33½ins. (85cm) About 1850
Steel hilt with three-bar guard modelled on the previous sword. Fish-skin covered grip. Slightly curved etched blade. Steel scabbard. A very common sword in reasonable condition.
£60 — £80

321. Presentation sword
Blade 32¾ins. (83.2cm) 1876
Silver plated hilt and scabbard; ivory grip. The etched single-edged blade inscribed: 'PRESENTED TO CAPTN. GEO. G. ADAMS (LATE COMDG) BY THE NON-COMMISSIONED OFFICERS AND GUNNERS OF THE 1ST LONDON ARTILLERY VOLR. CORPS AS A TOKEN OF RECOGNITION FOR THE ENERGY DISPLAYED IN THE RESUSCITATION OF THE REGIMENT, 1ST MAY, 1876.' Very good quality and condition.
£500 — £600

318

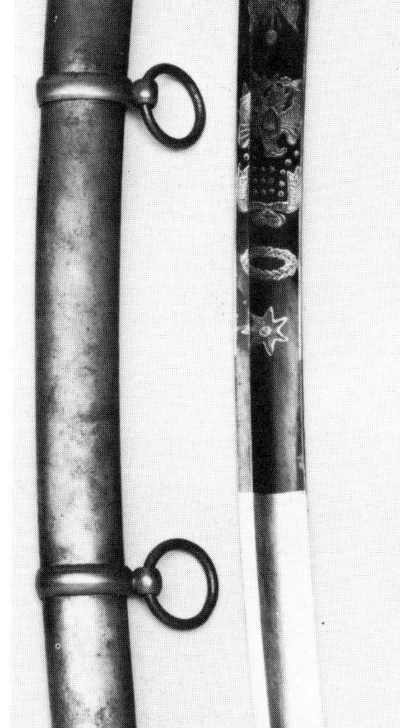

320

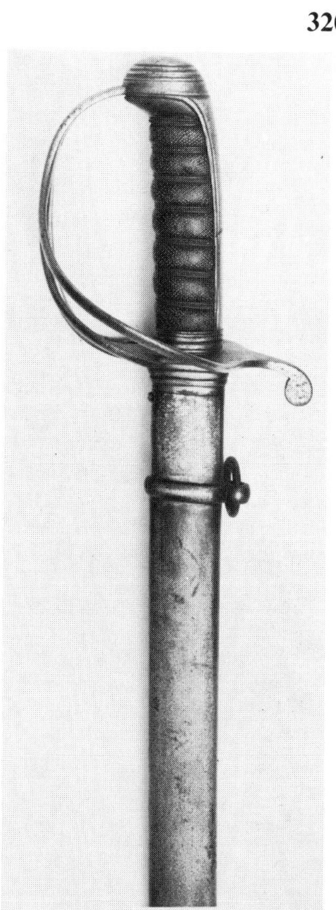

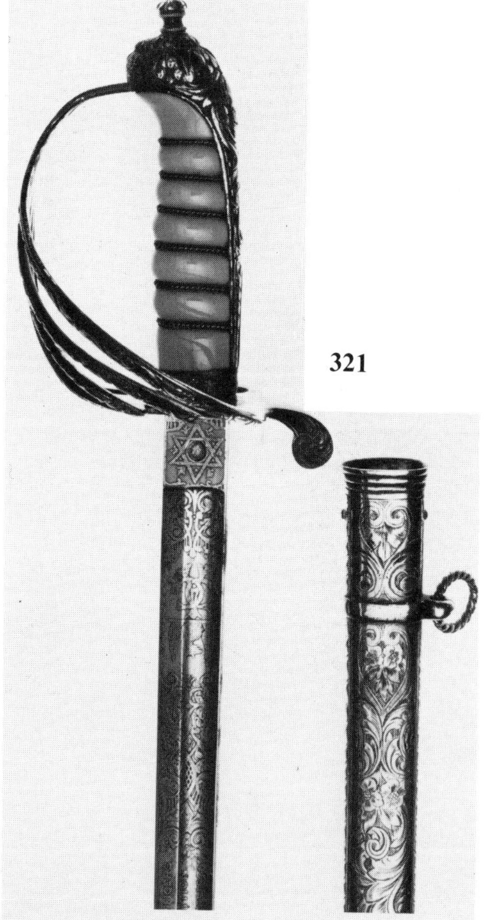

321

322. British 1822 pattern infantry officer's combined sword and percussion pistol
Blade 32ins. (81.3cm) About 1830
Gilt-brass Gothic hilt with folding inner guard and with George IV cypher. The box-lock mechanism of the pistol forming the base of the grip. Breech signed 'JOHNSTON, NEWCASTLE STREET'. Barrel on the right side of the pipe-backed blade. Rare and in good condition.
£700 — £800

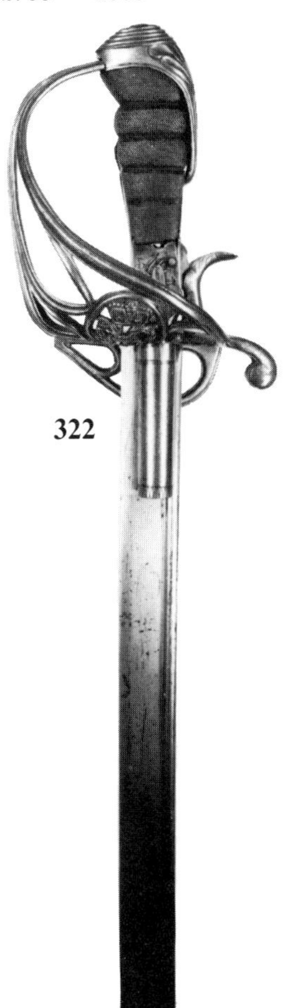

322

323

323. British infantry officer's levée sword, 1822 pattern hilt
Blade 32½ins. (82.5cm) Second half 19th century
A very light sword with the Victorian cypher on the gilt-brass hilt. The etched single-edged Wilkinson blade is of the type adopted in 1845. Very good condition.
£60 — £80

324. British infantry officer's sword, 1822 pattern hilt
Blade 32½ins. (82.5cm) Second half 19th century
Brass hilt with Victorian cypher. As with 323, this example is fitted with a Wilkinson blade (adopted in 1845). A very common sword in reasonable condition.
£50 — £80

324

325

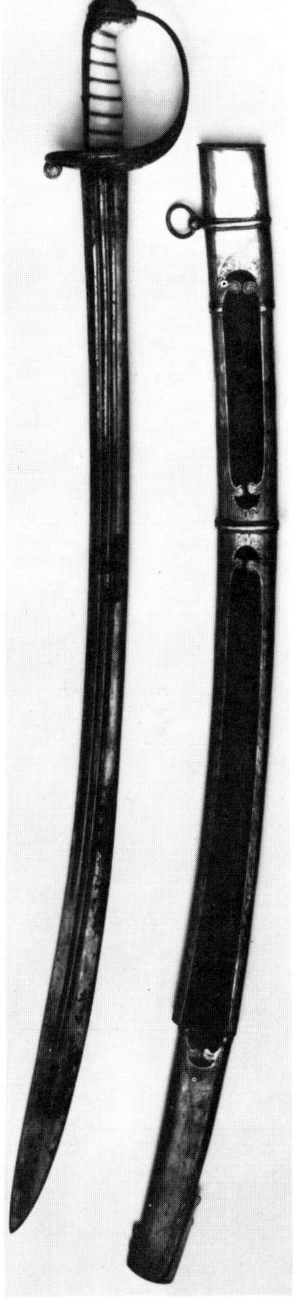

325. Left-handed officer's sword, variation on 1822 infantry pattern
Blade 33ins. (83.8cm)
Mid-19th century
The steel hilt incorporates the coat of arms of the owner, Sir Hugh Seymour Blane (see detail), who succeeded to the baronetcy of Blane (Blanefield, Co. Ayr) in 1834. Ivory grip bound with silver wire. The sword is fitted with a 17th century blade stamped 'ANDRIA FERARA' and is complete with silver-mounted scabbard. Unusual and of fine quality. Blade worn. The hilt with surface dirt.
£300 — £500

Photographs: Christie's

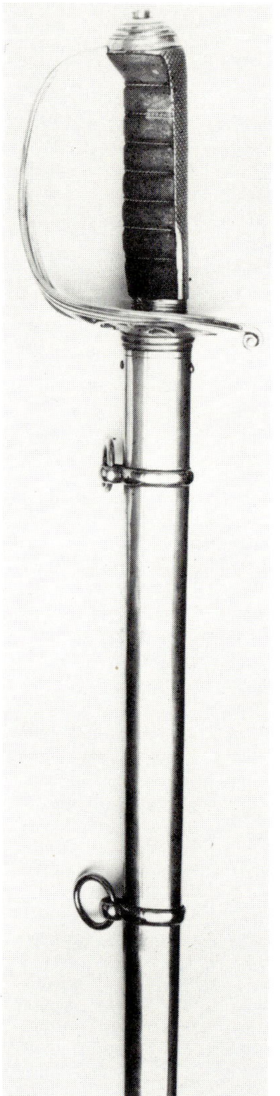

326

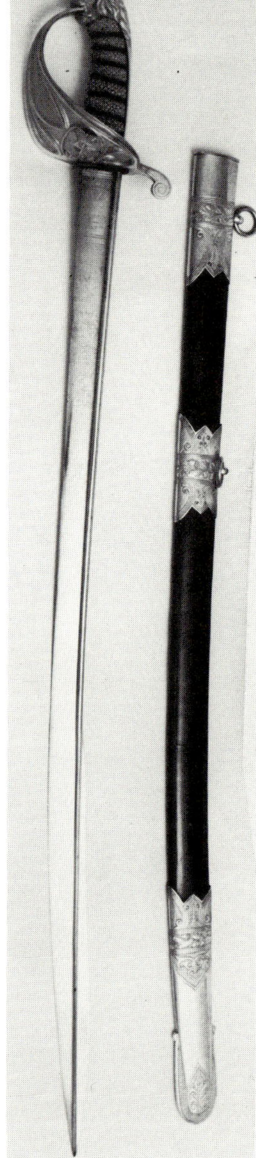

327

Photographs: 326 and 328 Christie's; 327 Peter Dale Ltd.; 329 Sotheby's

326. British rifle regiment officer's presentation sword, 1892 pattern
Blade 32½ins. (82.5cm) 1896
Plated steel hilt of Gothic form with fish-skin covered grip. The etched straight blade signed 'HOBSON & SON, 135 LEXINGTON ST., LONDON W' and inscribed 'PRESENTED TO LIEUT. WM. SCOTT WYLIE BY THE SERGTS. OF F. COMPANY, MAY 1896'. Good condition.
£70 — £100

327. Admiral Sir James Saumarez's sword, naval pattern 1827
Blade 30ins. (76.2cm)
Gilt-metal hilt of solid Gothic form incorporating the naval anchor badge on the guard. Ivory grip and etched pipe-backed blade. The scabbard is a flag officer's pattern of 1832. A familiar sword in good condition. Its association with one of the most prominent of British naval captains of the late 18th/early 19th century increases the value.
£300 — £400

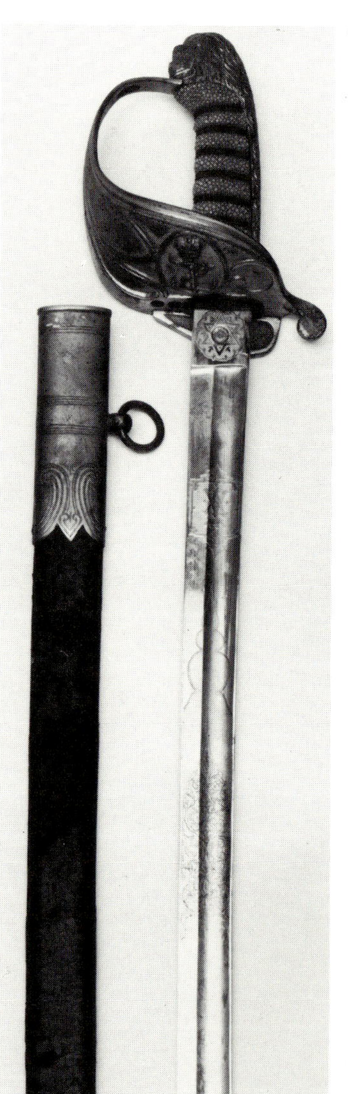

328

329

328. British naval officer's sword
Blade 32ins. (81.3cm) Second half 19th century
The major differences between this sword and 327 are the Wilkinson flat-backed sword blade, No. 23017 (introduced in 1846), the folding inner guard, and the extended lion's mane on the back-strap. The last is a feature found on many post-1846 examples.
£120 — £150

329. Danish naval officer's sword (Søofficerssabel) 1840 pattern
Length 36ins. (91.5cm)
Gilt-copper hilt of solid Gothic type with mother-of-pearl grip. Pipe-backed blade. Reasonable condition, blade worn.
£40 — £80

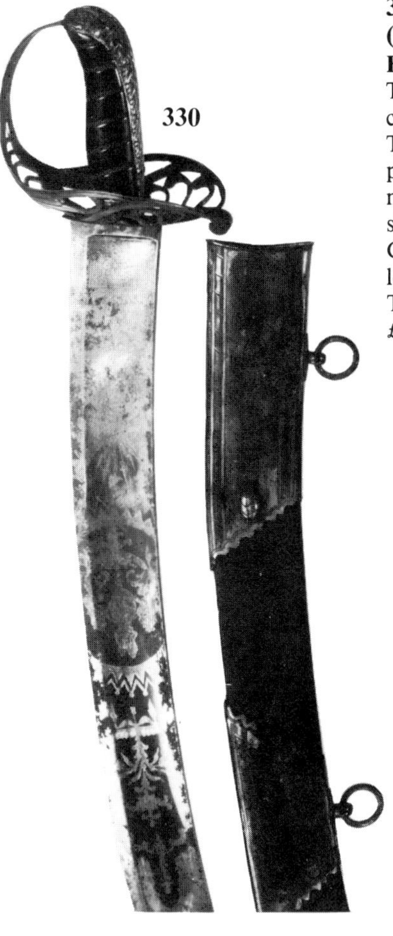

330

330. British heavy cavalry officer's sword (variation on 1796 pattern)
Blade 35¼ins. (89.5cm) Early 19th century
The gilt-brass pierced hilt is the same as the heavy cavalry officer's undress sword hilt design of 1796. The wide, curved, blued, and gilt blade (with post-1801 royal arms) is unusual. The type of blade normally fitted to this pattern of hilt is straight, single-edged with a spear or hatchet point (see 331). Gilt-brass mounted scabbard is inscribed on the locket 'BROWN, Nº 104, STRAND'. Fair condition. The blade very worn.
£200 — £250

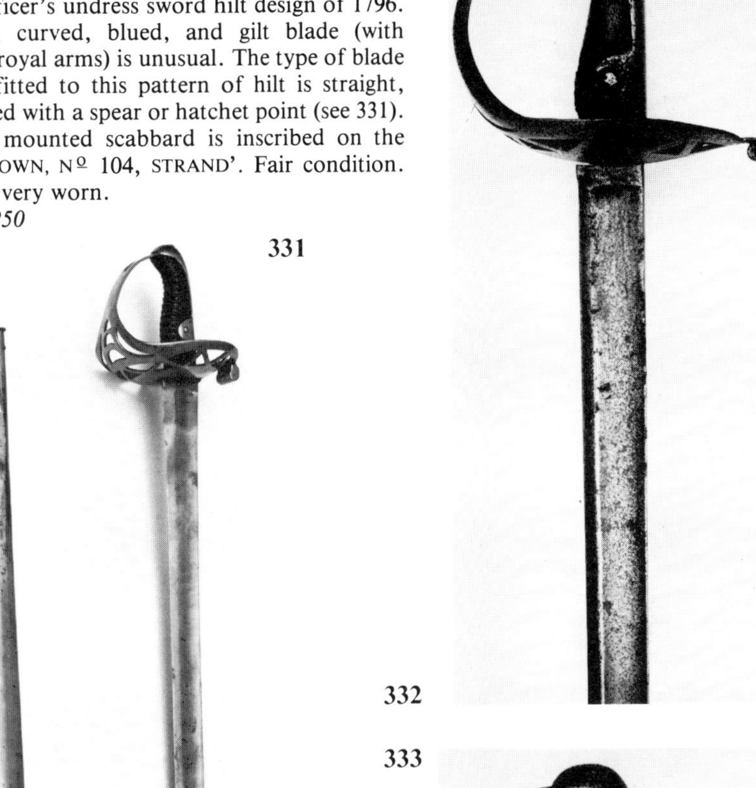

331

332

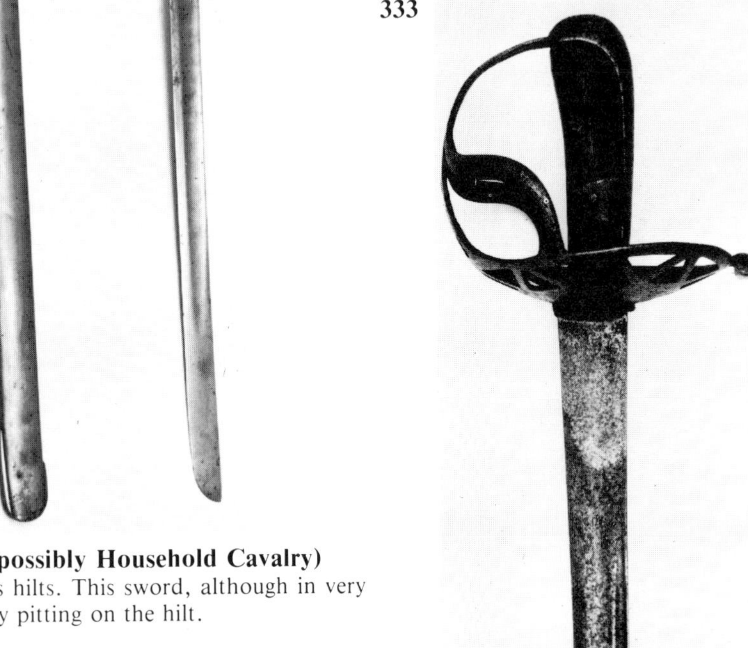

333

331. British heavy cavalry trooper's sword (possibly Household Cavalry)
Blade 35ins. (89cm)
About 1808-1818
Brass hilt with reeded leather-covered shaped grip. Blade of 1796 heavy cavalry pattern, signed 'I. GILL'. Brass scabbard. Regulation issue. Very good condition. National Army Museum (7205-7-5).
£200 — £250

332. British heavy cavalry trooper's sword (possibly Household Cavalry)
A rare version of 331. Most examples have brass hilts. This sword, although in very poor condition, has a hilt of steel. Note the heavy pitting on the hilt.
£200 — £250

333. British heavy cavalry trooper's sword (possibly Royal Horse Guards)
Blade 34½ins. (87.5cm) About 1820
Steel hilt and single-edged fullered blade. A very rare sword but in poor condition. Wooden grip replaced.
£200 — £250

Photographs: 330 Christie's; 332 and 333 Sotheby's

334. Sword of a private of the 6th Dragoon Guards, heavy cavalry pattern 1821
Blade 36½ins. (92.7cm)
Steel guard engraved '6-D' and 'BALACLAVA OCTR. 25th, 1854'. Slightly curved single-edged blade. Regulation issue. Fair condition.
£120 — £200

335

334

336. British naval cutlass, 1858 pattern
Blade 26ins. (66cm)
All-steel hilt. Single-edged blade with later presentation inscription. Regulation issue. Fair condition.
£60 — £80

336

337

335. Brigadier General John Jacob's sword
Blade 36½ins. (92.7cm) 1850s
Steel hilt with pierced scroll, or honeysuckle, designs. The Wilkinson single-edged blade is etched with Indian battle honours and inscribed 'JOHN JACOB, BOMBAY ARTILLERY, COMMANDANT OF THE SINDE IRREGULAR HORSE'. The sword type is not unusual, being the same as the Royal Engineer's Officer pattern of 1857; but its association with the inventor of the Jacob rifle increases the value.
£800

337. Dress sword of an officer of the 2nd Life Guards
Blade 38ins. (96.5cm) About 1865-1922
Pierced steel guard with regimental crest and brass rivets. The straight single-edged blade signed 'HAMBURG, ROGERS & CO., 50 KING ST., COVT. GD. LONDON'. A common sword in poor condition, being heavily pitted on the hilt and steel scabbard.
£100 — £150

Photographs: Christie's

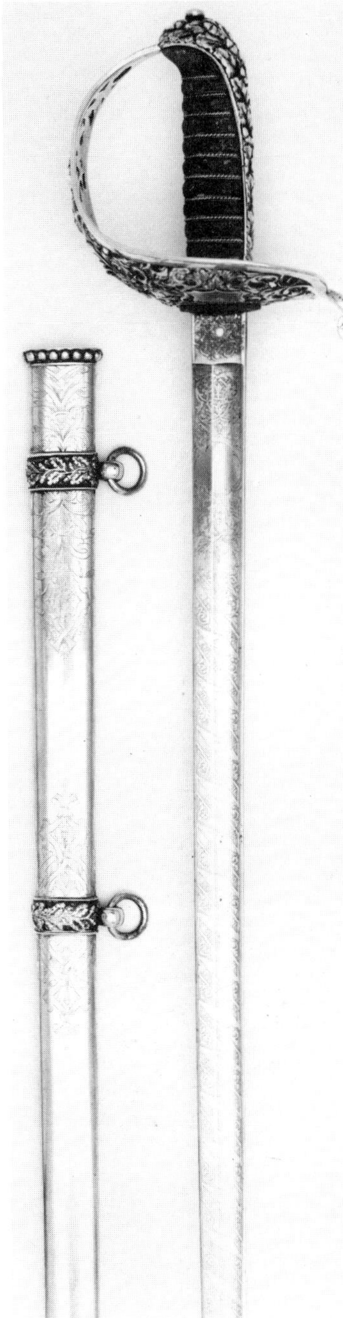

338

338. Presentation sword
Length 38¾ins. (98.5cm) London, 1876-1877
Silver hilt and scabbard decorated with oak leaves and acorn motifs. The guard with the crest of the recipient and the crowned bugle. Etched single-edged blade inscribed: 'PRESENTED TO CAPTN. E.H. BUSK, ON HIS PROMOTION TO THE RANK OF MAJOR, BY THE PRESENT AND PAST MEMBERS OF D. COMPANY, OF THE ARTISTS RIFLE CORPS [Middlesex 38th (The Artists) Rifle Volunteers] IN RECOGNITION OF THE ZEAL AND COURTESY HE DISPLAYED WHILST IN COMMAND OF THE COMPANY, MAY 26TH 1877.' Fine quality and condition.
£500

339. British cavalry trooper's sword, 1882 pattern (short)
Blade 33ins. (83.8cm)
Steel bowl guard pierced with a Maltese cross. Single-edged curved blade. From 1853 swords for privates of both regiments of British cavalry (heavy and light) were of the same design. Regulation issue. Poor condition, the guard heavily pitted.
£40 — £80

339

340

341

340. British heavy cavalry officer's sword, 1887 pattern
Blade 35¼ins. (89.5cm)
Plated steel hilt and scabbard. The etched single-edged blade with owner's initials (the Earl of Shaftesbury). Reasonable condition. Rust patches on guard and scabbard.
£60 — £100

341. British naval cutlass, 1889 pattern
Blade 28ins. (71cm)
All-steel hilt. Leather scabbard with steel mounts. Regulation issue. Poor condition.
£50 — £80

Photographs: 338 Sotheby's; 339-341 Christie's

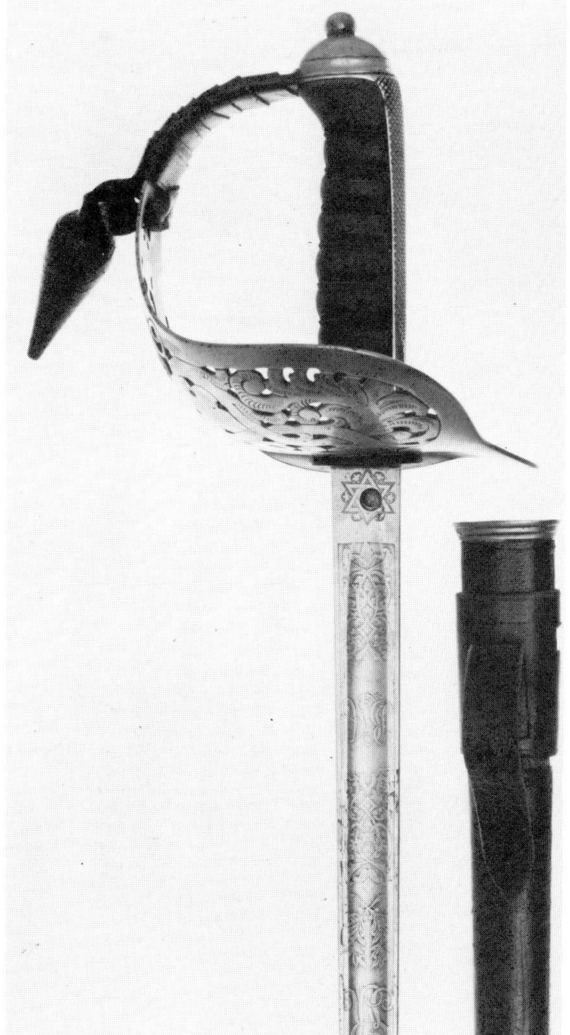

342

342. Montgomery's sword, British infantry officer pattern 1897

Blade 32¼ins. (83.2cm) 1911-1914

Plated steel hilt. Etched blade with owner's initials, 'B.L.M.' and George V cypher. Leather-covered steel scabbard. This very familiar type of sword has greater interest and value because it was owned and carried by Bernard Law Montgomery, later Field-Marshal Montgomery of Alamein, at the battles of Le Coteau and Meteren in 1914.

£500

343 344

343. British cavalry trooper's sword, 1908 pattern

Blade 35¼ins. (89.5cm)

Hilt of steel with chequered plastic grip. Straight blade. Regulation issue. Good condition.

£100 — £120

344. British cavalry officer's sword, 1908 pattern

Blade 35½ins. (90.2cm)

Engraved plated steel hilt, with fish-skin covered grip. The straight etched blade signed 'HENRY WILKINSON, PALL MALL, LONDON'. Complete with leather-covered scabbard, frog and belt. A familiar sword in fine condition.

£100 — £150

Photographs: Christie's

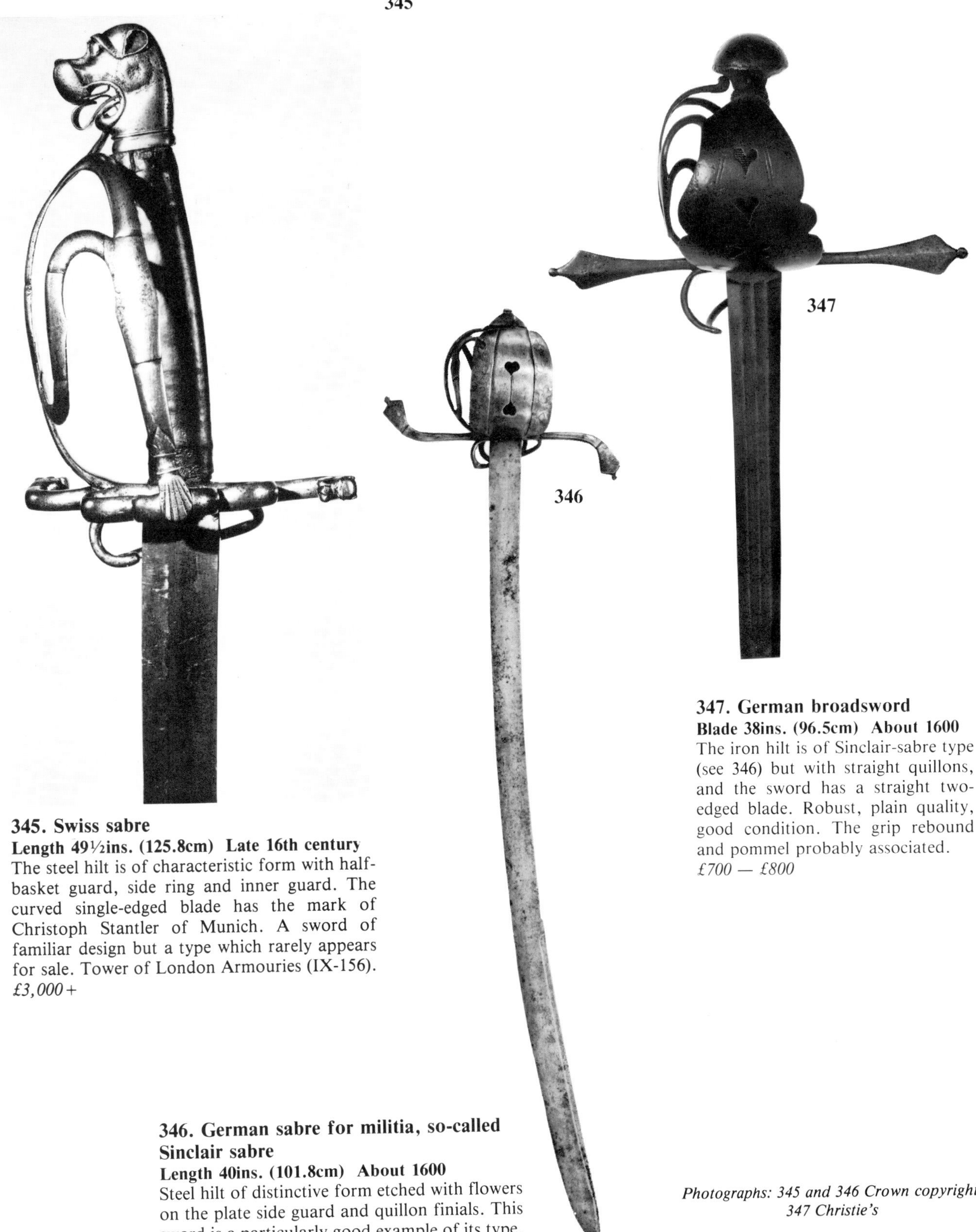

345. Swiss sabre
Length 49½ins. (125.8cm) Late 16th century
The steel hilt is of characteristic form with half-basket guard, side ring and inner guard. The curved single-edged blade has the mark of Christoph Stantler of Munich. A sword of familiar design but a type which rarely appears for sale. Tower of London Armouries (IX-156).
£3,000+

346. German sabre for militia, so-called Sinclair sabre
Length 40ins. (101.8cm) About 1600
Steel hilt of distinctive form etched with flowers on the plate side guard and quillon finials. This sword is a particularly good example of its type. Tower of London Armouries (IX-1013).
£1,000+

347. German broadsword
Blade 38ins. (96.5cm) About 1600
The iron hilt is of Sinclair-sabre type (see 346) but with straight quillons, and the sword has a straight two-edged blade. Robust, plain quality, good condition. The grip rebound and pommel probably associated.
£700 — £800

Photographs: 345 and 346 Crown copyright; 347 Christie's

348. English cavalry officer's backsword
About 1630
Steel hilt with ivory grip. The single-edged, fullered blade stamped 'HOUNSLOE'. Very good quality and condition. Tower of London Armouries (IX-1388).
£600

Photographs: 348 and 349 Crown copyright; 350 Christie's

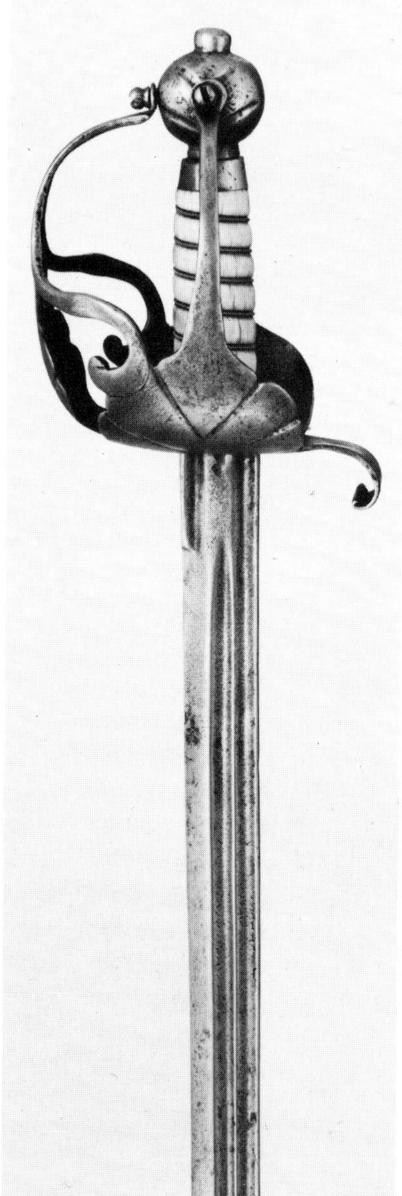

348

349

349. English cavalry officer's mortuary-hilted backsword
Length 37$\frac{3}{8}$ins. (97.4cm)
Mid-17th century
A fine example of the distinctive English Civil War period sword. The iron hilt is chiselled with portraits of Charles I and Britannia, and with winged cherubs' heads on the bars. The single-edged German blade is inscribed 'IHN SOLINGEN'. Tower of London Armouries (IX-1086).
£2,000

350

350. English cavalry officer's mortuary-hilted broadsword
Blade 33$\frac{1}{2}$ins. (85cm) About 1640
The hilt was originally black japanned and retains traces of its original gilding. The blade with three short fullers is struck with three crescent moons and stamped 'HOUNSLO'. Fine quality, worn overall.
£700 — £800

351. English cavalry backsword with mortuary hilt
Blade 35ins. (89cm) Mid-17th century
Iron hilt crudely chiselled with roses and foliage. The blade stamped 'IINKEK' in the fullers. Good quality and reasonable condition.
£600 — £800

351

353. English broadsword
Blade 32ins. (81.4cm)
Mid-17th century
The hilt has bars on one side only. On the inner side is a thumb ring. Very poor condition. It is worn and pitted overall and is without its grip.
£200 — £250

352

353

352. English cavalry mortuary-hilted backsword
Blade 34½ins. (88cm) Mid-17th century
Chiselled iron hilt decorated with foliage and crude bearded heads on the side guards. The blade with sickle marks and stamped 'ANDREA FERARA'. Good quality but worn overall.
£600

Photographs: Christie's

354. English cavalry officer's mortuary-hilted backsword

Blade 36¾ins. (93.5cm) About 1650

The iron hilt is chiselled and pierced with a variety of martial motifs, and is complete with leather hilt liner. A fine quality sword. It was possibly originally gilded although no trace remains. Very good condition. The langets (a distinctive feature of the mortuary hilt) have been reduced.

£1,500 — £2,000

354

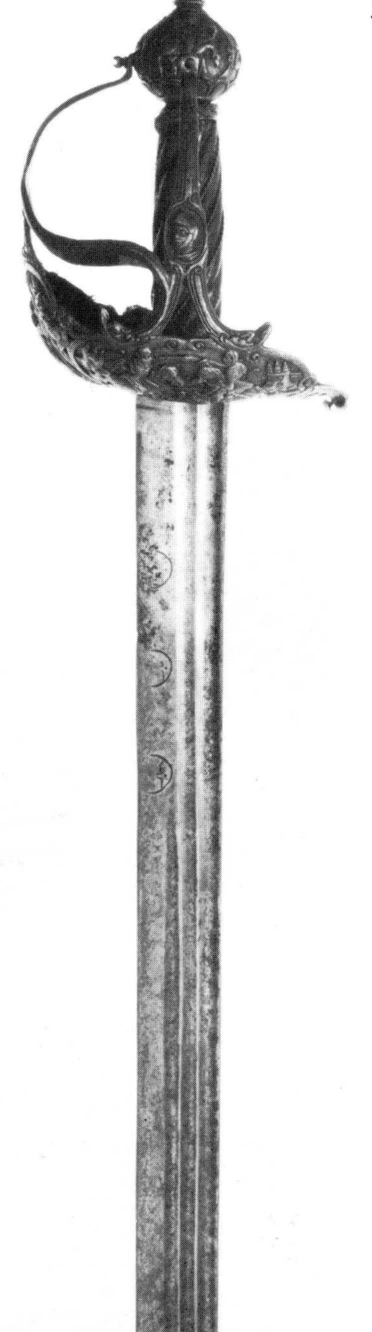

Photographs: Christie's

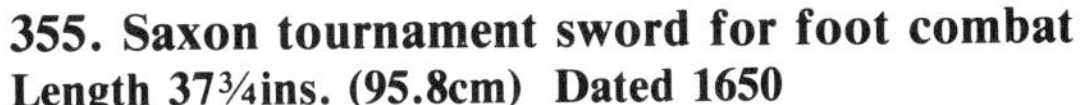

355. Saxon tournament sword for foot combat
Length 37¾ins. (95.8cm) Dated 1650
Blackened iron hilt of half-basket form with double shell guards. The blade with rebated edges and rounded point is dated 'ANNO 1650' and struck with a bladesmith's mark, 'M', above a hunting horn in a shield. Fine condition.
£4,000 — £5,000

355

356. English officer's backsword
Blade 35½ins. (90.5cm) About 1720
Brass hilt. The grip binding is missing and the rear quillon broken. Etched blade with Georgian cypher and the motto 'GOD BLESS KING GEORGE AND HIS RAGEL FAMILIE'. Reasonable condition.
£200

356

357

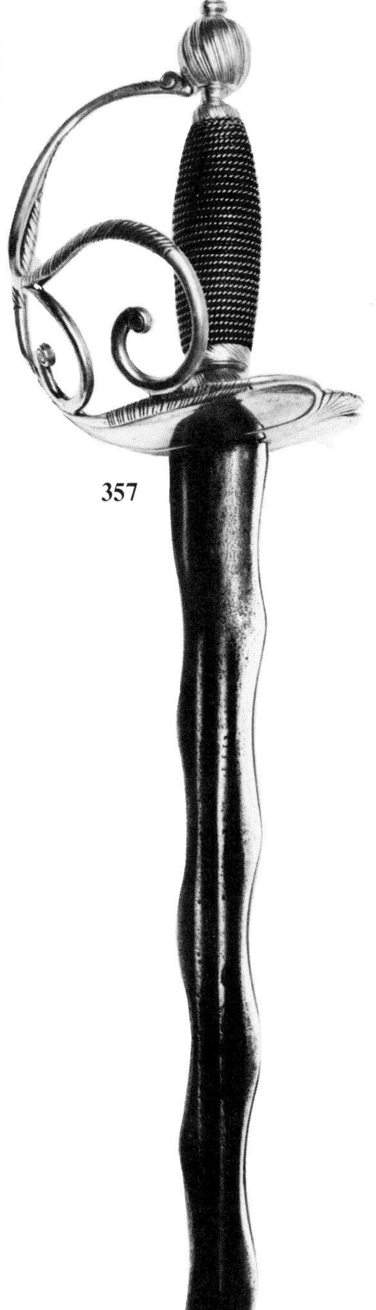

357. English silver-hilted officer's sword
London, 1744-1745
Silver hilt with heart-shaped guard and two scrolled side guards. Silver wire-bound grip. The earlier flamboyant blade (worn) stamped 'ANDRIA FERARA'. Fine quality.
£400 — £500

Photographs: 355 Sotheby's; 356 Christie's; 357 Peter Dale Ltd.

358

358. Indian hanger made for the European market
Third quarter 18th century
Gold damascened, blued steel hilt. The scabbard mounts on the leather-covered wooden scabbard decorated *en suite* with the hilt. Rare and of fine quality.
£400

359

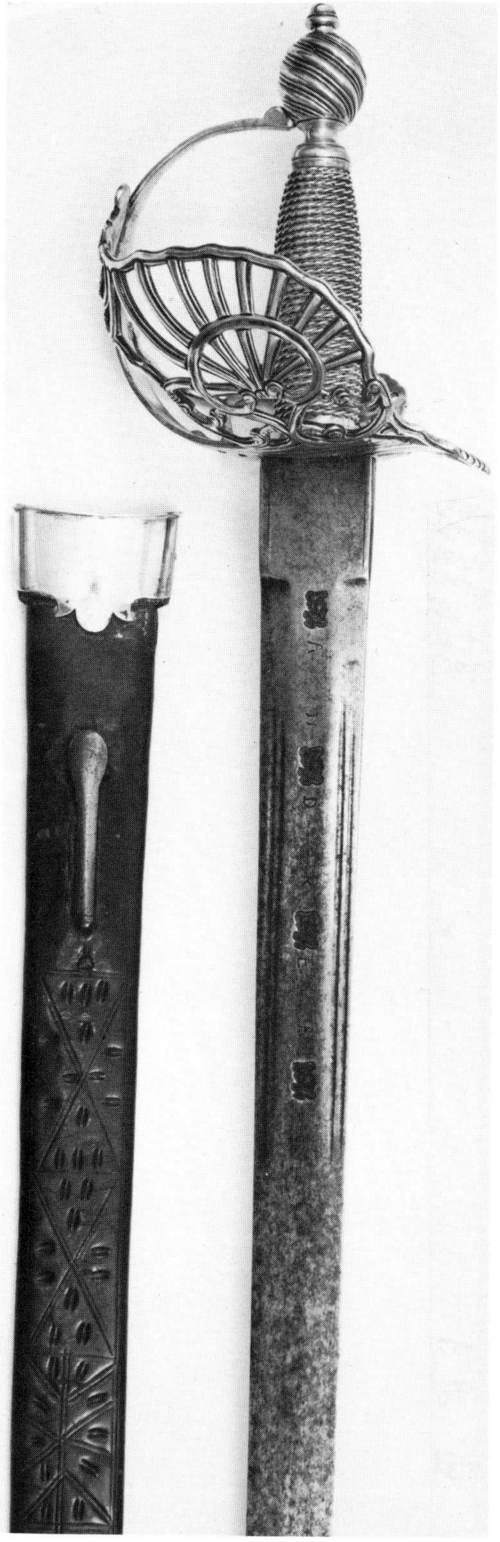

359. English silver-hilted officer's broadsword
London, about 1750-1760
Silver hilt with pierced shell-like side guard and silver wire-bound grip. The earlier two-edged blade stamped with four Turk's head marks and inscribed 'ANDRIA FERARA'. Silver-mounted tooled leather scabbard. Fine quality, very good condition. Blade worn.
£400 — £500

Photographs: Peter Dale Ltd.

360

360. Backsword of an officer of the 1st Troop of Horse Guards
Blade 34ins. (86.4cm)
About 1750-1780
Hilt of steel with fish-skin covered grip. Plain fullered blade. Good condition.
£400 — £500

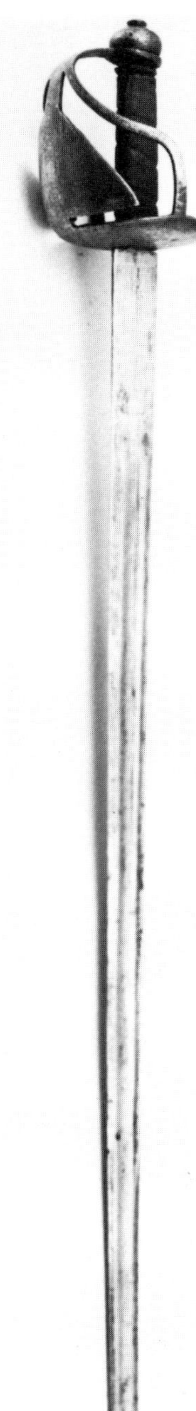

361

361. English cavalry trooper's backsword
Length 41⅝ins. (105.7cm) About 1760
Robust hilt of steel forged in one piece. Quite rare, good condition. National Army Museum (7205-7-32).
£180 — £250

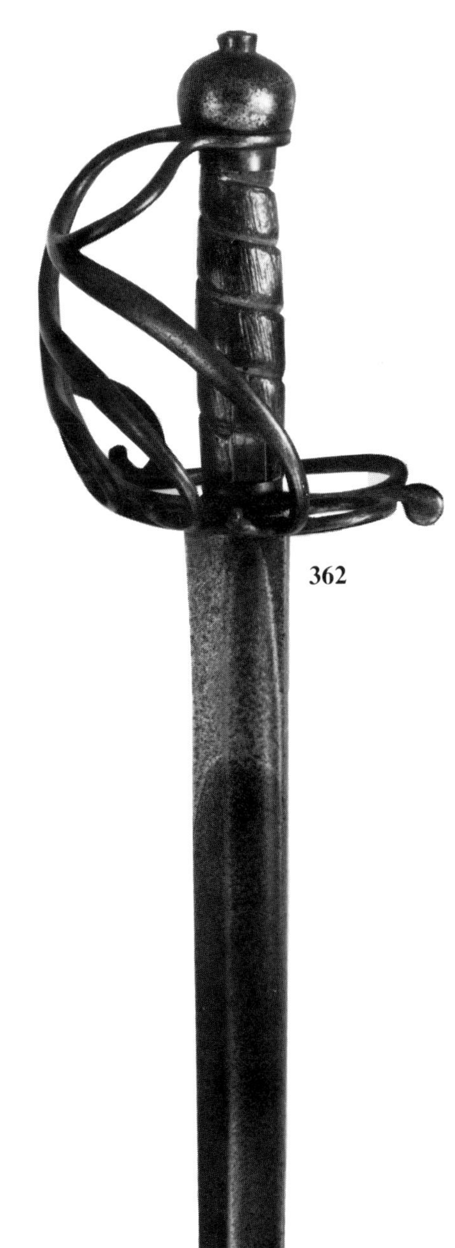

362

362. Backsword of a private of the 2nd Troop Horse Grenadier Guards
Blade 38ins. (96.5cm) About 1770-1780
Steel hilt engraved '61 2nd T P G G D S'. The grip is without its covering and wire binding. Reasonable condition.
£400

Photographs: 360 and 362 Christie's

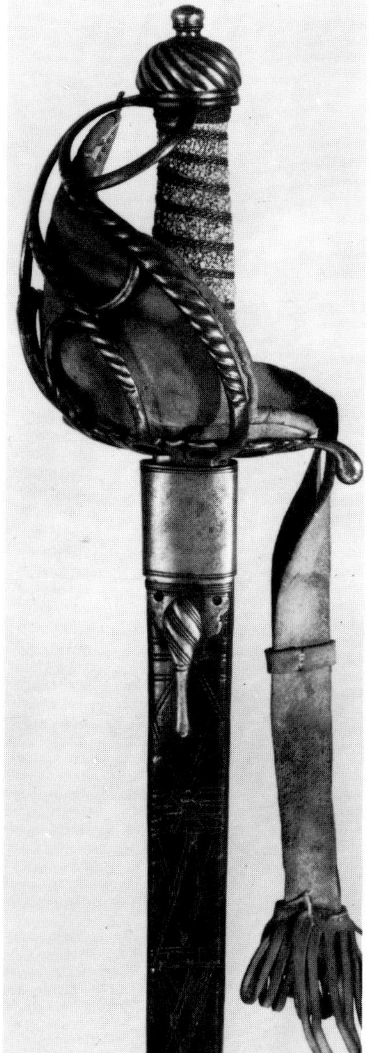

363

363. English cavalry officer's backsword
Blade 36ins. (91cm)
About 1766-1788
Hilt of bright steel decorated with writhen fluting. Fish-skin covered grip. Complete with hilt liner, sword knot, and steel-mounted tooled leather scabbard. The locket inscribed 'BIBB, NEWPORT ST.' Very good quality and condition.
£700

364

364. English cavalry officer's broadsword
Blade 33ins. (83.8cm)
Third quarter 18th century
Bright steel hilt with the side bars in the form of scrolled serpents. Grip bound with copper wire and strip. Complete with steel-mounted, leather-covered wooden scabbard. Fine quality.
£650

365

365. Sword of an officer of the 3rd King's Own Dragoons, heavy cavalry pattern 1788
Blade 37¼ins. (94.6cm) 1792-1796
Steel hilt with fish-skin covered grip. The etched, straight, single-edged blade inscribed 'LIEUTENANT. COL. CALLOW, 3rd KOD'. Rare, reasonable condition. One of the bars of the guard is missing. National Army Museum (6005-7).
£300 — £400

Photographs: 363 and 364 Christie's

366

367

368. 2nd Life Guards trial pattern sword of French type
Length 42½ins. (108cm)
Late 18th century
Etched gilt-brass hilt. The partly blued and gilt blade inscribed 'GILL'S WARRANTED'. Unusual. Very good condition.
£500 — £700

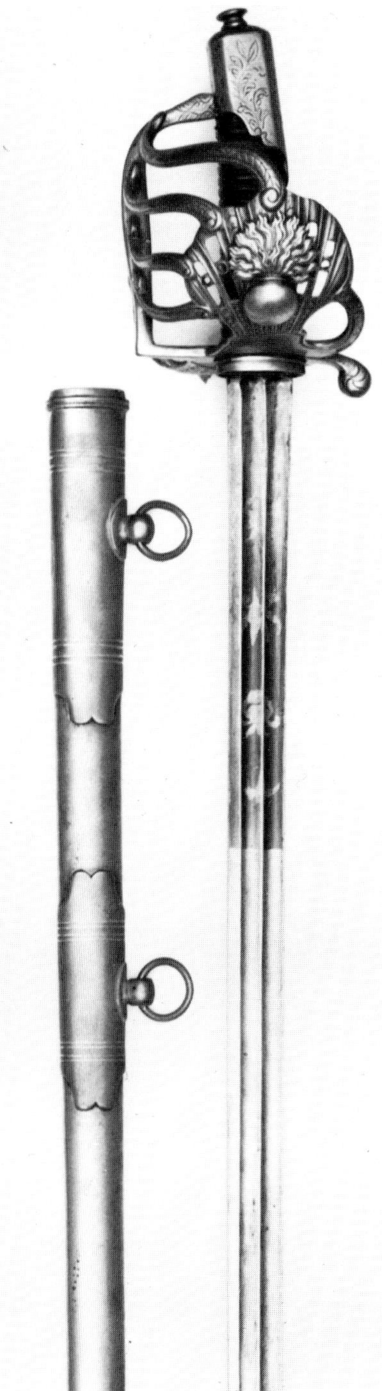

368

366. Danish cavalry officer's sword (Officerspallask)
Blade 34ins. (86.3cm) Mid-18th century
Hilt of brass (formerly gilt) with embossed side guard and pommel. Fish-skin covered grip. Etched straight two-edged blade. Good quality and condition.
£750

367. French cavalry officer's sword, 1779 pattern
Blade 38⅜ins. (97.5cm)
Steel hilt with leather-covered grip bound with wire. Straight single-edged fullered blade. Good condition. Blade worn. Tower of London Armouries (IX-614).
£600 — £800

Photographs: 366 Christie's; 367 Crown Copyright; 368 Sotheby's

371

372

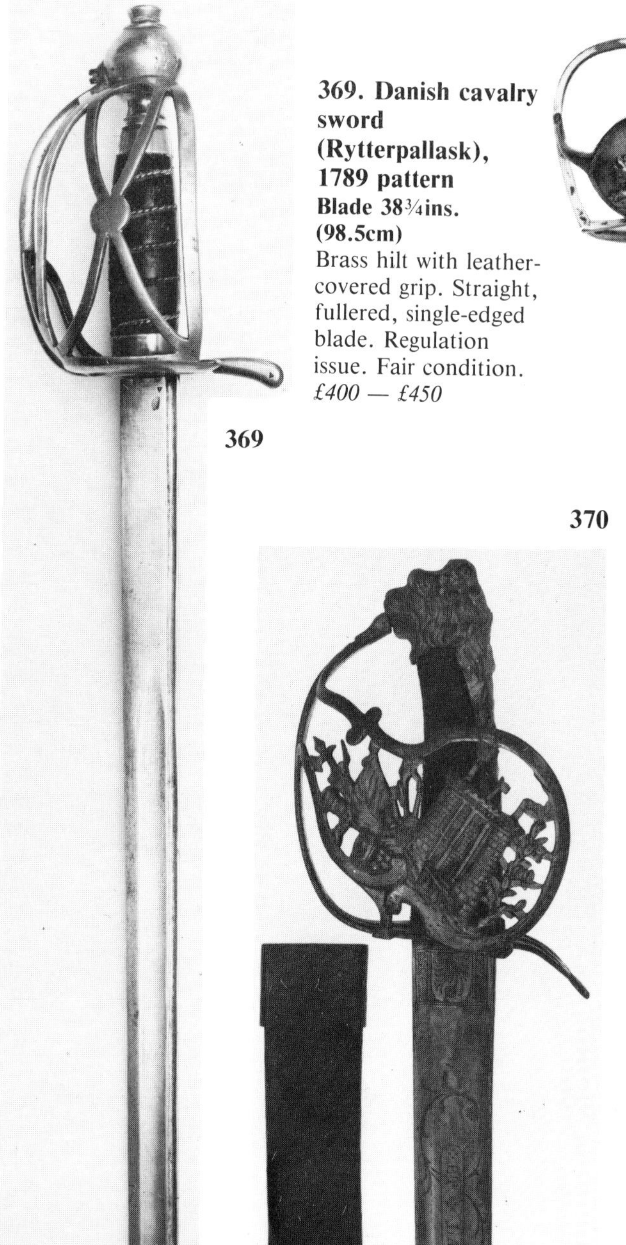

369

370

369. Danish cavalry sword (Rytterpallask), 1789 pattern
Blade 38¾ins. (98.5cm)
Brass hilt with leather-covered grip. Straight, fullered, single-edged blade. Regulation issue. Fair condition.
£400 — £450

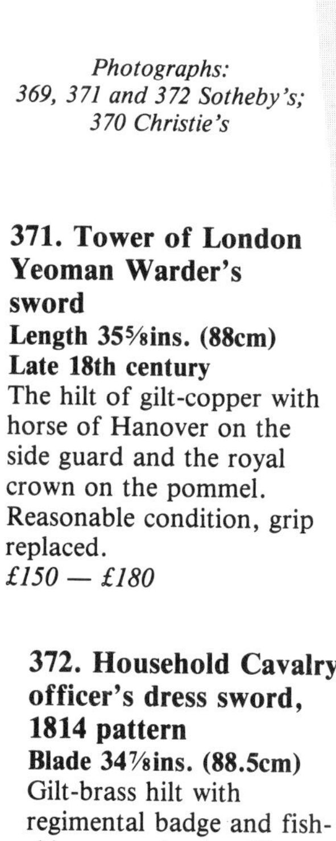

Photographs:
369, 371 and 372 Sotheby's;
370 Christie's

370. French gilt-brass hilted sword
Blade 30½ins. (77.5cm) Late 18th century
Hilt with pierced side guard decorated with trophies of arms and the Bastille. The etched blade inscribed 'LA VIGILANCE ET LA FORCE' (Watchfulness and Strength). Good quality and condition.
£800 — £1,000

371. Tower of London Yeoman Warder's sword
Length 35⅝ins. (88cm)
Late 18th century
The hilt of gilt-copper with horse of Hanover on the side guard and the royal crown on the pommel. Reasonable condition, grip replaced.
£150 — £180

372. Household Cavalry officer's dress sword, 1814 pattern
Blade 34⅞ins. (88.5cm)
Gilt-brass hilt with regimental badge and fish-skin covered grip. Gilt-brass mounted scabbard with fish-skin backing. A familiar sword in very good condition.
£250 — £300

374

374. German backsword
Blade 37ins. (94cm)
Last quarter 16th century
Steel basket hilt fitted to two plate side guards at the front and rear. Leather-covered grip. The fullered blade with two-edged point. Robust quality and good condition.
£800

373

373. German basket-hilted broadsword
Blade 37¾ins. (95.8cm) Late 16th century
Robust hilt of steel comprising a trelliswork of bars linked to side rings, arms and quillons. The pommel is probably associated. Quite rare, good condition.
£800

375

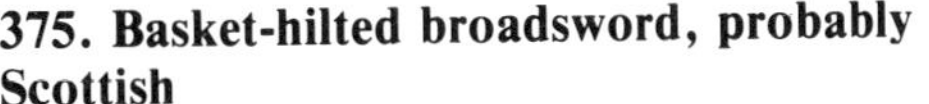

375. Basket-hilted broadsword, probably Scottish
Blade 32½ins. (82.7cm) About 1600
Steel hilt of ribbon form, with recurved quillons. The blade struck with a bladesmith's mark (a cross with split stave in a shield). Grip missing. A rare, early, example, but now very worn.
£800 — £1,000

Photographs: 373 and 374 Peter Dale Ltd.; 375 Christie's

378. English broadsword with silver-encrusted hilt
Blade 33½ins. (85cm) About 1610
Fine quality. The broad two-edged blade with half-moon marks. The hilt liner and the grip binding are later. Good condition.
£1,000

376

377

378

379

376. English basket-hilted broadsword
About 1600-1625
Ribbon basket hilt with long quillons. Blade with half-moon mark. Like 375 this is a rare example, originally of fine quality, but now pitted and worn.
£1,000 — £1,200

377. English basket-hilted broadsword
Length 39ins. (99.1cm) About 1610
Iron hilt retaining traces of original damascened decoration. The fullered two-edged blade stamped 'ANDREA FERARA'. A fine quality sword in reasonable condition, but without its grip binding. Now in the Tower of London Armouries (IX-1114).
£800 — £1,200

379. West Highland basket-hilted broadsword
Blade 37½ins. (95.2cm) About 1660
The sword is in a rather worn and rough state. The blade, stamped 'ANDREA FERARA', is associated, and the pommel and grip are later.
£500 — £600

Photographs: Christie's

380

380. Scottish silver basket-hilted presentation broadsword
Blade 33ins. (83.8cm) Elgin, 1701

The basket hilt has the crowned cypher of Charles II, and an inscribed panel describing the event for which the sword was awarded (see 381). The pommel is also inscribed 'TAKEN AT DUMBLAIN BY ONE OF EVAN'S DRAGOONS'. The silver maker's mark, 'VS' in monogram, is probably for William Scott of Elgin (see Christie's Arms and Armour Catalogue, 21 December, 1977, Lot 261). This sword is of high value as it is one of only a small number known to exist and because of the exceptional weight and quality of the silver. Also shown in Colour Plate 7.
£20,000

381

381. Scottish silver-hilted broadsword
Detail of the inscribed panel on the hilt of 380. It reads: 'ATT HUNTLY CASTLE THE SECOND FRYDAY OF SEPT.R 1701. WONNE AT KING CHARLES THE $2^{ND.S}$ FARE ALL HORSES NOT EXCEIDING ONE 100 MARKS PRYCE WERE ADMITTED, THE RYDERS STAIKING CROWNS, WHICH WAS GIVEN TO THE POORE WHO WERE OBLIDGED TO PRAY THAT THE MONARCHRIE AND ROYALL FAMELIE MAY BE LASTING AND GLORIOUS IN THES KINGDOMS'. Above and at the side of the marks is also written 'WONE BE JA: DRUMMOND IN DRMMA QUHANCE'.

382

382. Scottish basket-hilted horseman's broadsword
About 1700

Front view of a steel hilt made by John Simpson (the Elder) of Glasgow. It is inlaid with a silver shield bearing the arms of the Earls of Balcarres, probably of Colin, the third Earl, a staunch supporter of the House of Stuart. Scottish swords with the marks of known makers are not uncommon, but they do not appear for sale often. This is a particularly fine example.
£2,000 — £2,500

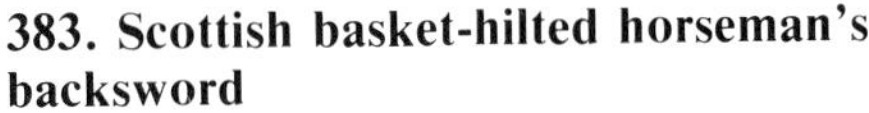

383. Scottish basket-hilted horseman's backsword
Length 39¾ins. (101cm) About 1715

Profile view of a hilt similar to 382 and possibly by the same maker. The maker's mark on this example is indistinct. Blade associated, reasonable to good condition.
£1,500 — £2,000

383

Photographs: 380, 381 and 383 Christie's; 382 Peter Dale Ltd.

386

384

384. Scottish basket-hilted horseman's backsword
Blade 34ins. (86.3cm)
About 1715-1720
A fine sword with hilt of bright steel made by John Simpson (the Younger) of Glasgow. Etched blade. Complete with original liner and wrist thong.
£2,500 — £3,000

385

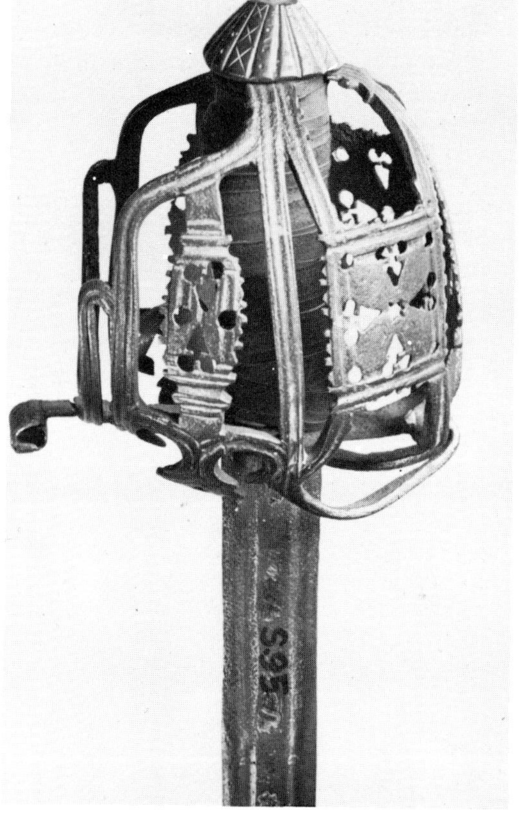

385. Scottish basket-hilted broadsword
Blade 33ins. (83.8cm)
About 1720-1730
Another sword by John Simpson (the Younger) of Glasgow, but in a poorer condition than 384, with a later grip and pommel (without button). Of high value because of the known maker.
£1,500

386. Scottish basket-hilted broadsword
Blade 34½ins. (87.6cm)
About 1720-1730
Made by Thomas Gemmill of Glasgow. The two-edged blade stamped 'ANDRIA FARARA'. Fine quality, good condition.
£2,000 — £2,200

Photographs: Christie's

387

387. Basket guard from a Scottish sword hilt
Height 6ins. (15.2cm)
Signed and dated 1731
A rare and fine brass inlaid steel guard signed 'JOHN ALLAN, STIRLING, FECIT 1731', and struck with the maker's mark 'JAS'. The mark and signature are probably those of John Allan, Senior, of Stirling (see Christie's Arms Catalogue, 6 March, 1974, Lot 110).
£3,000 — £4,000

389

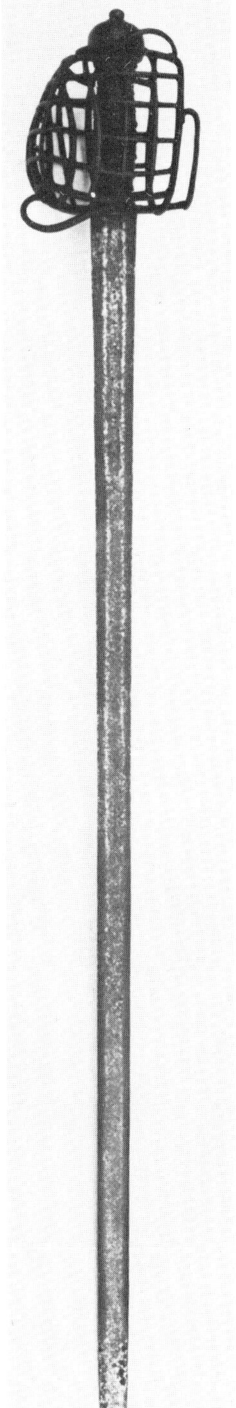

388

388. Scottish broadsword with Anti-Union (Jacobite) blade
Hilt about 1740
Basket hilt of steel. The two-edged German (Solingen) blade of earlier date (about 1710) is etched with portraits of James Stuart, the Old Pretender (1688-1766) and St. Andrew, and inscribed 'PROSPERITY TO SCHOTLAND, NO UNION', and 'GOD SAVE KING JAMES YE VIII'. Quite rare, good condition.
£600 — £800

389. English cavalry broadsword
About 1740
Robust blackened steel basket hilt with a wooden grip bound with wire. The fullered two-edged blade worn and pitted. National Army Museum (6408-77-8).

£350 — £400

Photographs: 387 and 388 Christie's

390

391

391. English cavalry officer's backsword
About 1740-1745
Basket hilt of steel with lion's head pommel. The panels of the hilt are chiselled and pierced with trophies of arms and linked to each other by diagonal bars in the form of serpents. A fine sword.
£1,200+

390. English cavalry backsword with brass basket hilt
Blade 34½ins. (87.6cm) About 1740
Fish-skin covered grip bound with wire. The single-edged blade with ?anchor mark. Good condition.
£400 — £450

Photographs: 390 Christie's; 391 Peter Dale Ltd.

392

392. Scottish basket-hilted backsword
Length 38½ins. (97.8cm)
About 1735-1760
Made by Walter Allan of Stirling. The single-edged blade stamped 'ANDRIA FARARA'. Fine quality and of higher value because of the well-known maker's mark on the hilt.
£2,000

395

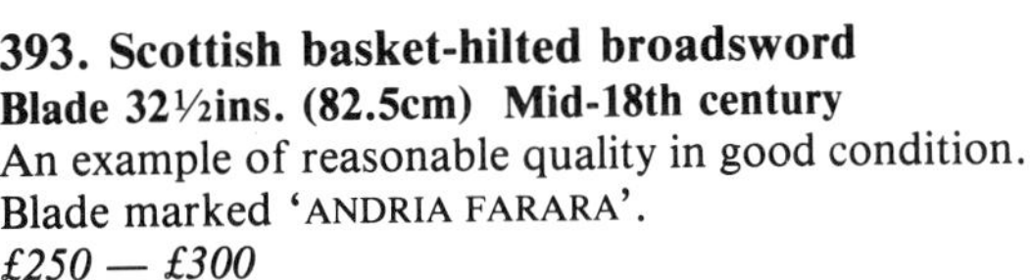

393. Scottish basket-hilted broadsword
Blade 32½ins. (82.5cm) Mid-18th century
An example of reasonable quality in good condition. Blade marked 'ANDRIA FARARA'.
£250 — £300

394. Scottish military backsword, possibly for a Royal Highland Regiment
Blade 31ins. (78.7cm) Mid-18th century
A rather ordinary example. The blade stamped 'ANDRIA FARARA'.
£250 — £300

395. Scottish brass basket-hilted broadsword
Blade 35½ins. (90.2cm)
About 1750-1760
A better quality example with a two-edged blade marked 'ANDREA FERARA'. The hilt liner is later.
£600 — £800

393 394

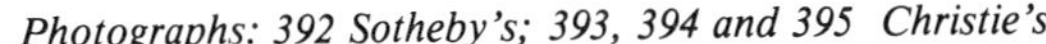

Photographs: 392 Sotheby's; 393, 394 and 395 Christie's

396. English officer's basket-hilted backsword
Blade 33½ins. (85.1cm)
Third quarter 18th century
A good quality sword with a steel hilt fitted with a fish-skin covered grip. The single-edged, fullered blade inscribed 'ME FECIT SOLINGEN.'
£400 — £500

398. Scottish basket-hilted backsword
Blade 33ins. (84cm) Third quarter 18th century
Steel hilt. Single-edged blade with the mark 'SH' in a running wolf, probably of S. Harvey of Birmingham.
£400 — £500

399. Scottish basket-hilted broadsword
Length 32¾ins. (83.2cm)
About 1750-1760
An example of fine quality with a hilt in the manner of those made by Walter Allan of Stirling. Blade stamped 'ANDREA FERARA'.
£800 — £1,000

396

398

397

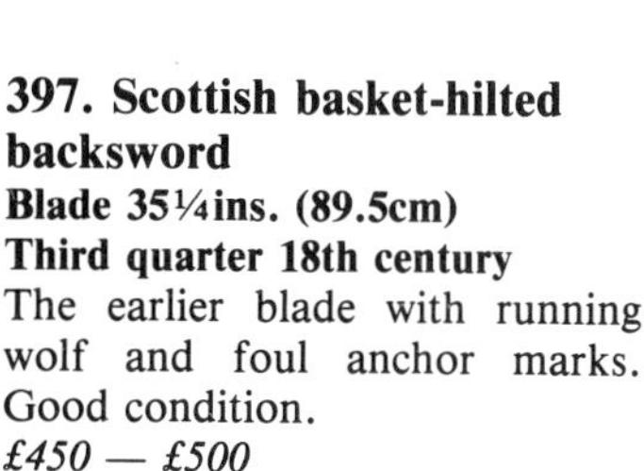

397. Scottish basket-hilted backsword
Blade 35¼ins. (89.5cm)
Third quarter 18th century
The earlier blade with running wolf and foul anchor marks. Good condition.
£450 — £500

Photographs: Christie's

Photographs: 400 Sotheby's; 401 and 402 Christie's

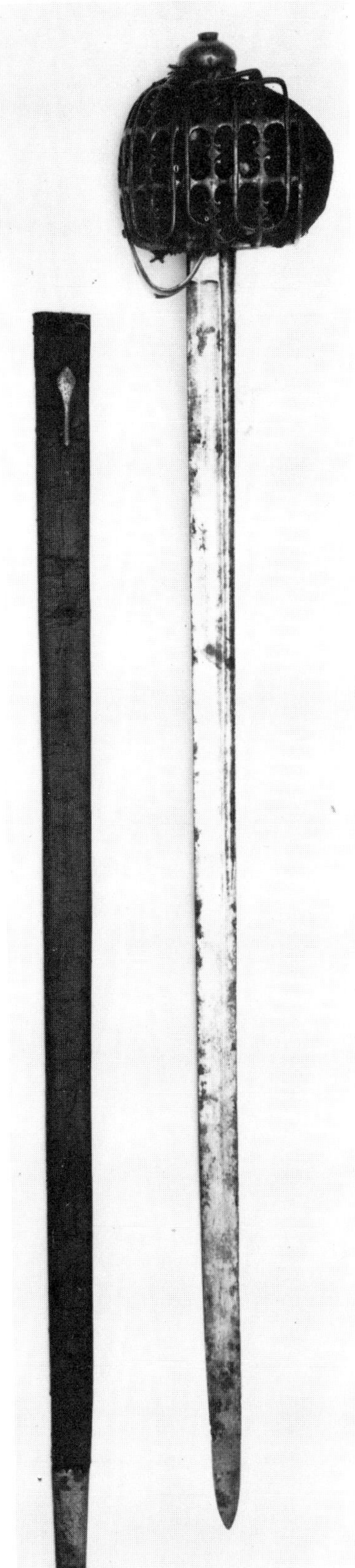

400. Scottish basket-hilted officer's backsword
Length 40⅞ins. (103.8cm) About 1770
Finely formed steel hilt of military type with fish-skin covered grip and liner. The single-edged blade has traces of engraved decoration. A very good quality sword, but worn on the blade.
£800 — £1,000

401

401. Scottish basket-hilted officer's backsword
Blade 32½ins. (82.5cm) About 1770
Detail of a military basket hilt similar to 400 but with a down-turned rear guard or quillon. A particularly good example. The single-edged blade with patches of wear.
£800 — £1,000

402

402. Danish cavalry sword (Rytterpallask), 1773 pattern
Blade 39ins. (99cm)
Robust hilt of brass with leather-covered grip. Straight, fullered, single-edged blade. Regulation issue. Good condition.
£450 — £480

400

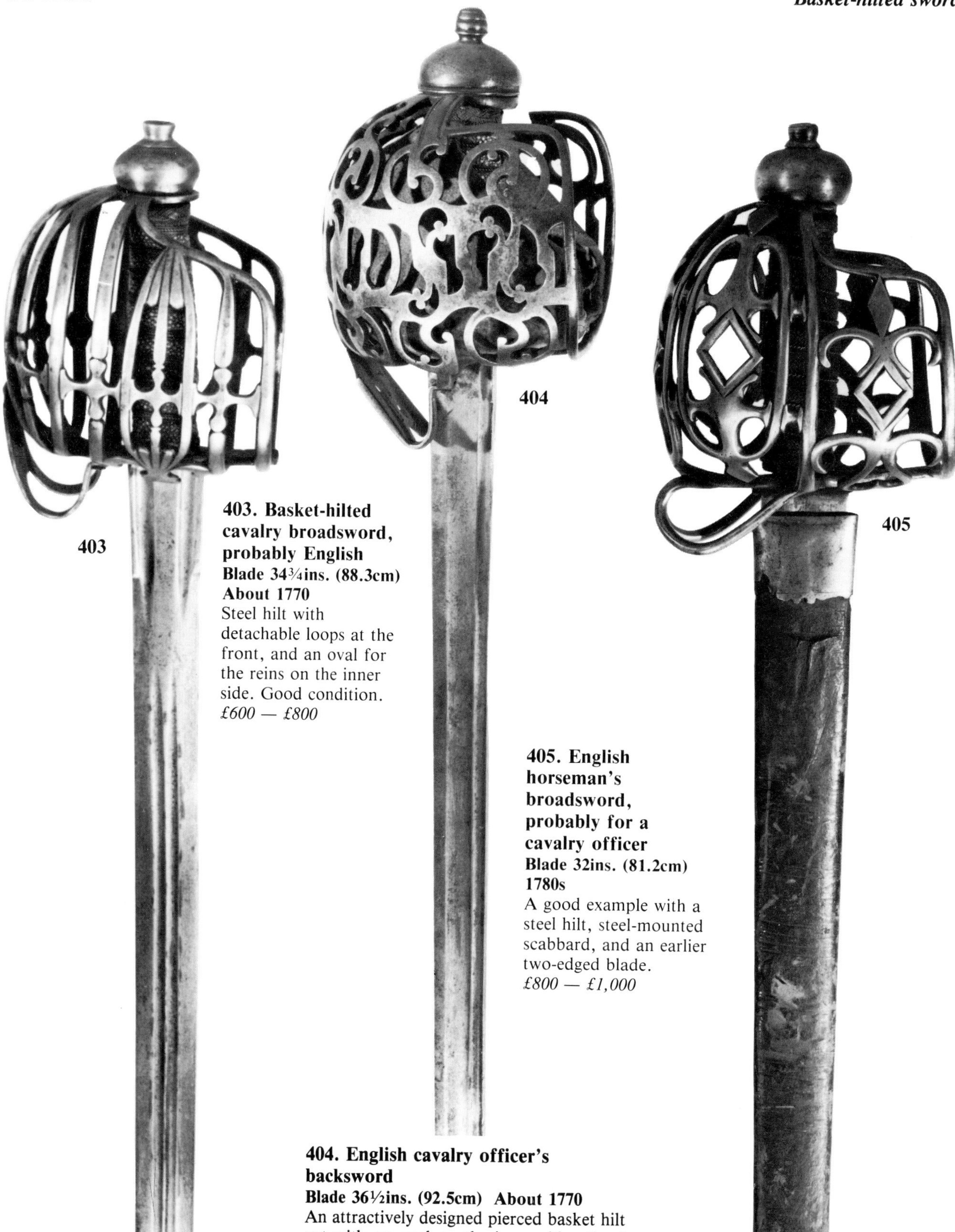

403. Basket-hilted cavalry broadsword, probably English
Blade 34¾ins. (88.3cm)
About 1770
Steel hilt with detachable loops at the front, and an oval for the reins on the inner side. Good condition.
£600 — £800

405. English horseman's broadsword, probably for a cavalry officer
Blade 32ins. (81.2cm)
1780s
A good example with a steel hilt, steel-mounted scabbard, and an earlier two-edged blade.
£800 — £1,000

404. English cavalry officer's backsword
Blade 36½ins. (92.5cm) About 1770
An attractively designed pierced basket hilt cut with an oval on the inner side. Good condition.
£800 — £1,000

Photographs: Christie's

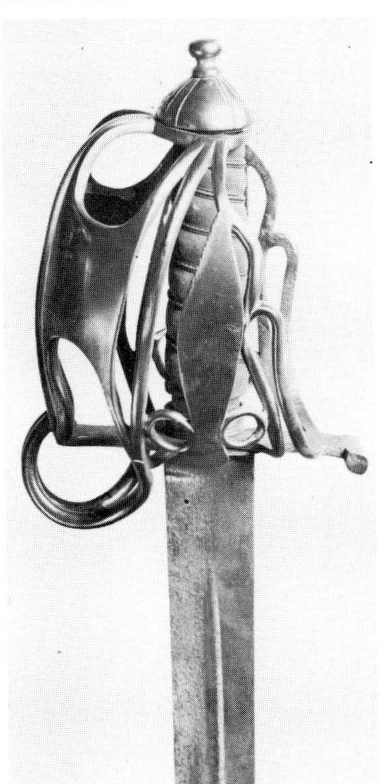

406

406. Scottish brass basket-hilted officer's broadsword
Blade 35ins. (88.9cm)
Early 19th century
Plain hilt and blade. Fish-skin covered grip.
£200

407

407. Sword of an officer of a Scottish volunteer regiment
Blade 33ins. (83.8cm) About 1800
Basket hilt of polished steel incorporating a regimental badge (thistle in a garter with crown above) and the motto 'PRO ARIS ET FOCIS' (For [our] altars and [our] hearths). The single-edged blade stamped 'ANDRIA FERARA'. Good condition.
£400

408

408. Scottish backsword
Blade 32ins. (81.3cm)
Early 19th century
Steel basket-hilt with Cairngorm pommel set in silver. Single-edged blade stamped 'ANDRIA FARARA'.
£500

409

409. Silver basket-hilted sword of Sir Joseph Radcliffe
Blade 33ins. (83.8cm)
Edinburgh, 1826-1827
Hilt and scabbard mounts of silver with unidentified maker's mark, 'TR'. Cairngorm pommel. The design of the hilt incorporates a cartouche, with the figure of St. Andrew holding his cross, set with gems (see detail). The etched two-edged blade bears the owner's coat of arms. A sword of high quality in excellent condition.
£4,000 — £5,000

Photographs: Christie's

410

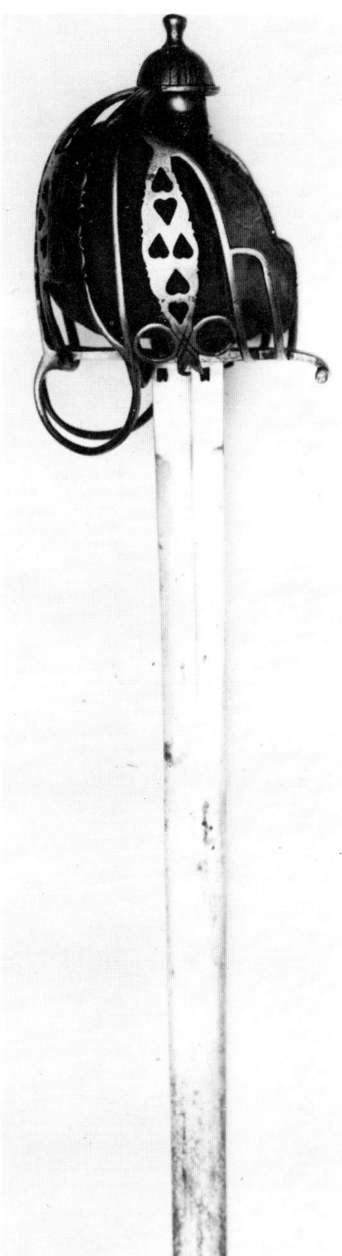

410. Highland regimental broadsword
Length 39½ins. (100.3cm)
Second quarter 19th century
A regulation pattern of familiar type in reasonable condition.
£200

411

411. Scottish silver-mounted broadsword
Blade 30ins. (76.2cm) Edinburgh, 1847-1848
Basket hilt and scabbard of silver, struck with an unidentified maker's mark, 'JK', and inscribed 'MORTIMER, EDINBURGH'. The 17th century blade (worn) stamped 'THEILL KEULLER ME FECIT SOLINGEN'. Fine quality.
£1,000

Photographs: 410 Sotheby's; 411 and 412 Christie's

412

412. Officer's sword of the Queen's Own Cameron Highlanders, 1865 pattern
Blade 32¼ins. (82cm)
A regulation sword fitted with a two-edged Wilkinson blade etched with the Victorian cypher. Good condition.
£200

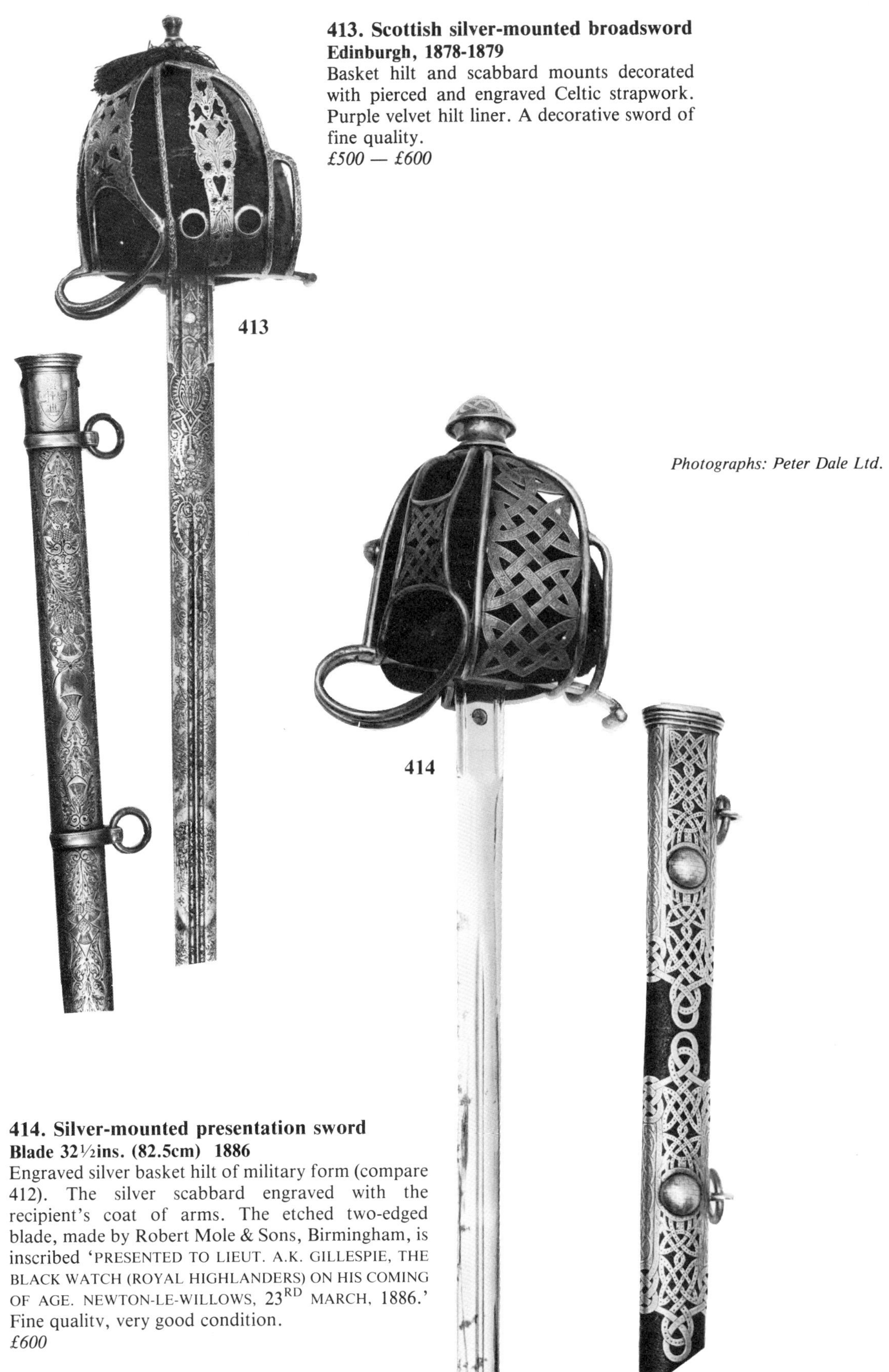

413. Scottish silver-mounted broadsword
Edinburgh, 1878-1879
Basket hilt and scabbard mounts decorated with pierced and engraved Celtic strapwork. Purple velvet hilt liner. A decorative sword of fine quality.
£500 — £600

413

Photographs: Peter Dale Ltd.

414

414. Silver-mounted presentation sword
Blade 32½ins. (82.5cm) 1886
Engraved silver basket hilt of military form (compare 412). The silver scabbard engraved with the recipient's coat of arms. The etched two-edged blade, made by Robert Mole & Sons, Birmingham, is inscribed 'PRESENTED TO LIEUT. A.K. GILLESPIE, THE BLACK WATCH (ROYAL HIGHLANDERS) ON HIS COMING OF AGE. NEWTON-LE-WILLOWS, 23RD MARCH, 1886.' Fine qualitv, very good condition.
£600

415. Venetian schiavona
Blade 35½ins. (90.2cm) 17th century
Steel hilt with a thumb ring on the inner side. Reasonable condition with a heavily pitted blade. These early schiavonas are less frequently found than 18th century examples.
£800 — £850

416. Venetian schiavona
Blade 33ins. (83.8cm) About 1700
A more characteristic example but in poor condition. The steel hilt is badly corroded and the later pommel is of the wrong type.
£250

415

416

418

417

417. Venetian schiavona
Blade 35¼ins. (89.5cm)
First half 18th century
Hilt of steel with so-called brass cat's-head pommel. A better quality example, but with wear on the blade.
£500

418. Venetian schiavona
Blade 37ins. (94cm)
Second half 18th century
Fully developed basket hilt of steel with a brass shield-shaped pommel and fish-skin covered grip. Blade inscribed 'IN SOLINGEN'. A good solid example.
£500 — £600

Photographs: Christie's

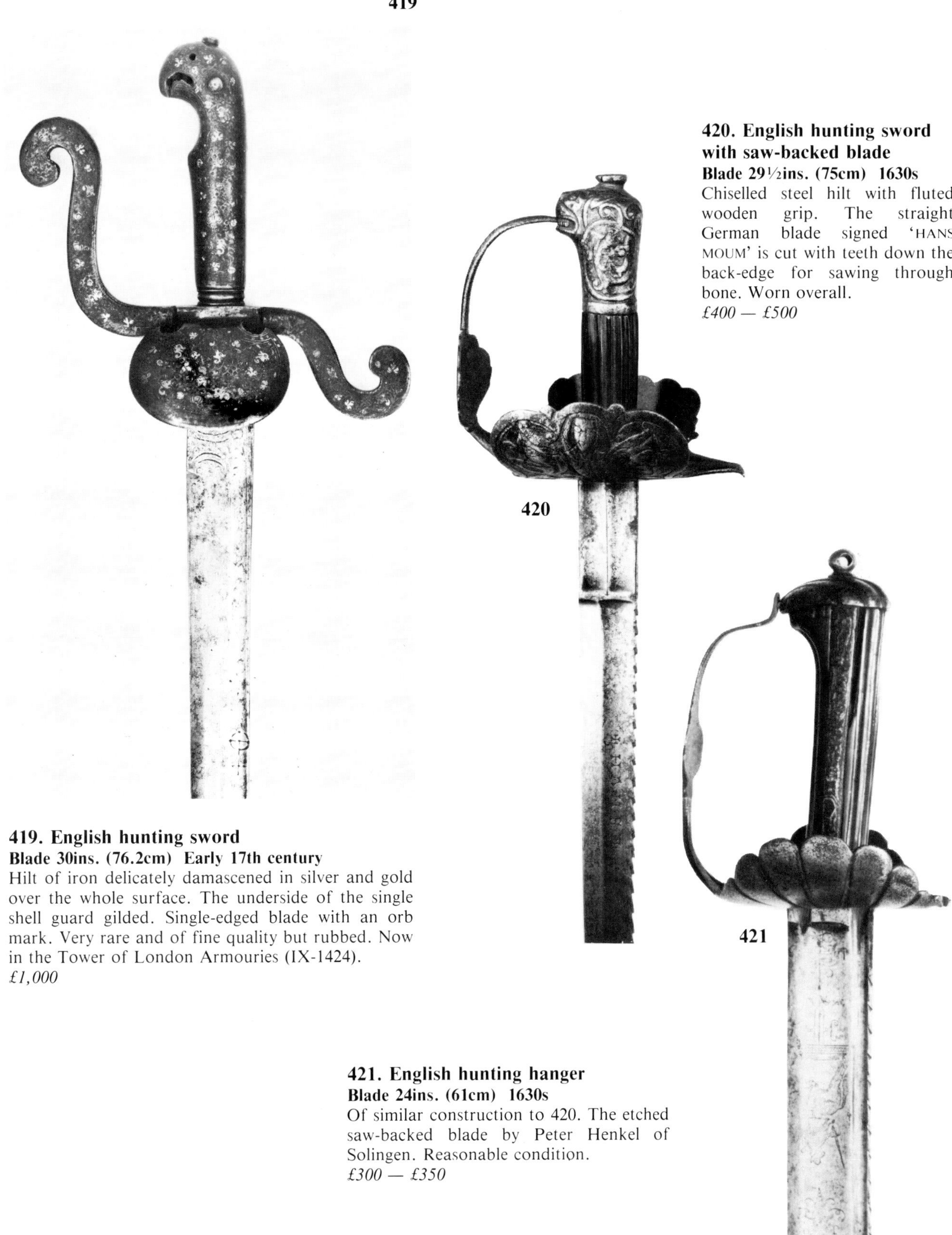

420. English hunting sword with saw-backed blade
Blade 29½ins. (75cm) 1630s
Chiselled steel hilt with fluted wooden grip. The straight German blade signed 'HANS MOUM' is cut with teeth down the back-edge for sawing through bone. Worn overall.
£400 — £500

419. English hunting sword
Blade 30ins. (76.2cm) Early 17th century
Hilt of iron delicately damascened in silver and gold over the whole surface. The underside of the single shell guard gilded. Single-edged blade with an orb mark. Very rare and of fine quality but rubbed. Now in the Tower of London Armouries (IX-1424).
£1,000

421. English hunting hanger
Blade 24ins. (61cm) 1630s
Of similar construction to 420. The etched saw-backed blade by Peter Henkel of Solingen. Reasonable condition.
£300 — £350

Photographs: Christie's

422. English hunting hanger
Blade 27¾ins. (70.5cm)
About 1630
Steel hilt, with wooden grip, pierced and chiselled with bold scrollwork on the guards. The curved fullered blade bears the running wolf mark. Rare. Good condition.
£400 — £500

424. English hunting hanger
Blade 25¼ins. (64.2cm)
Mid-17th century
Similar to 423 but with a different design of silver encrustation, and a replacement wooden grip (compare 423 and 426). Blade pitted.
£400 — £450

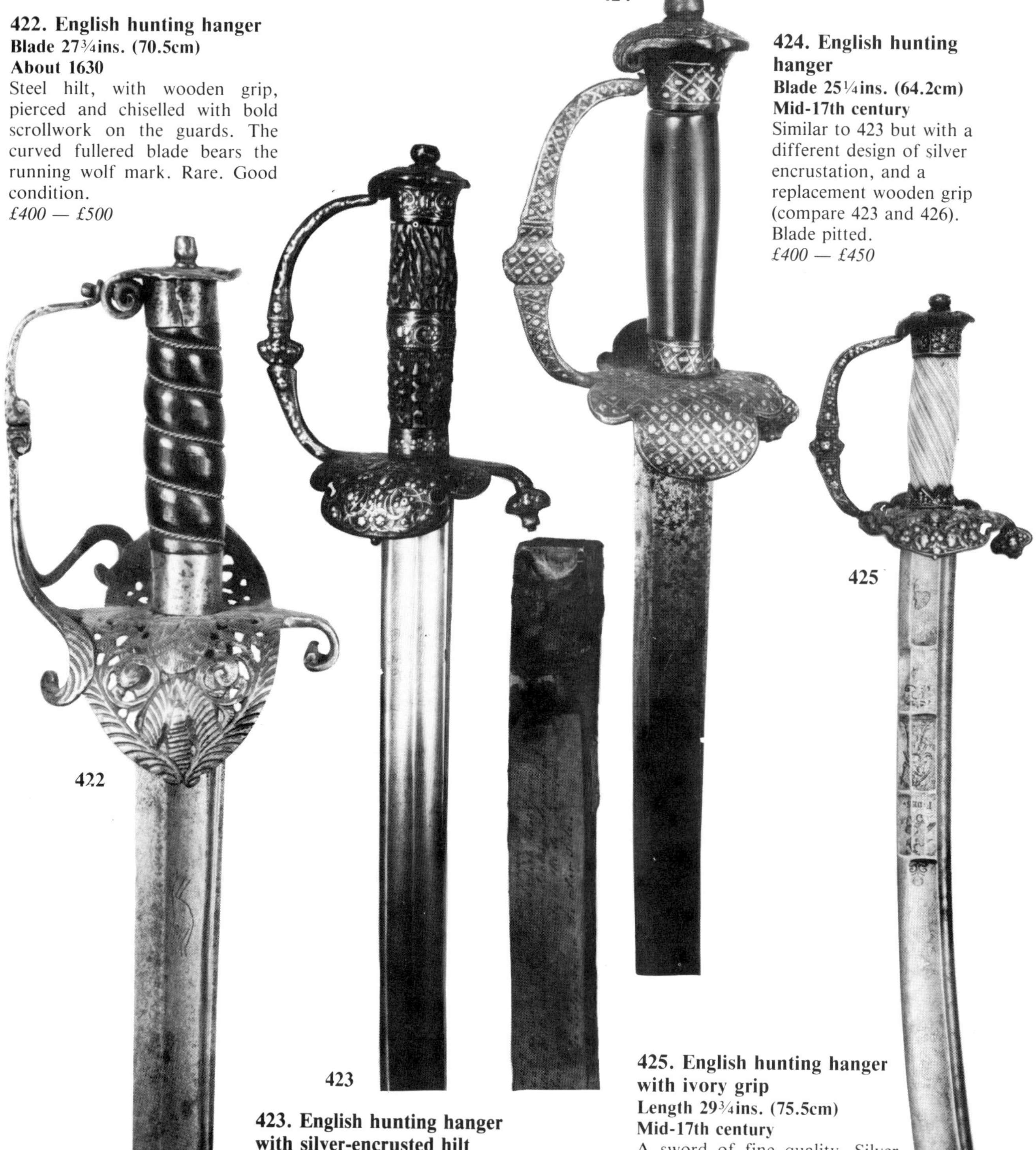

423. English hunting hanger with silver-encrusted hilt
Blade 25¼ins. (64.2cm)
Mid-17th century
A fine example of a very characteristic English weapon with stag-horn grip and curved fullered blade. Reputedly once owned by Captain John Jackson, Royal Navy, retired 1710.
£800 — £1,000

425. English hunting hanger with ivory grip
Length 29¾ins. (75.5cm)
Mid-17th century
A sword of fine quality. Silver-encrusted hilt chiselled with flowers and foliage. The curved, panelled blade (probably German) etched with the figures of FIDES (Faith) and PRUDENTIA (Prudence).
£1,000 — £1,500

Photographs: 422-424 Christie's; 425 Sotheby's

428

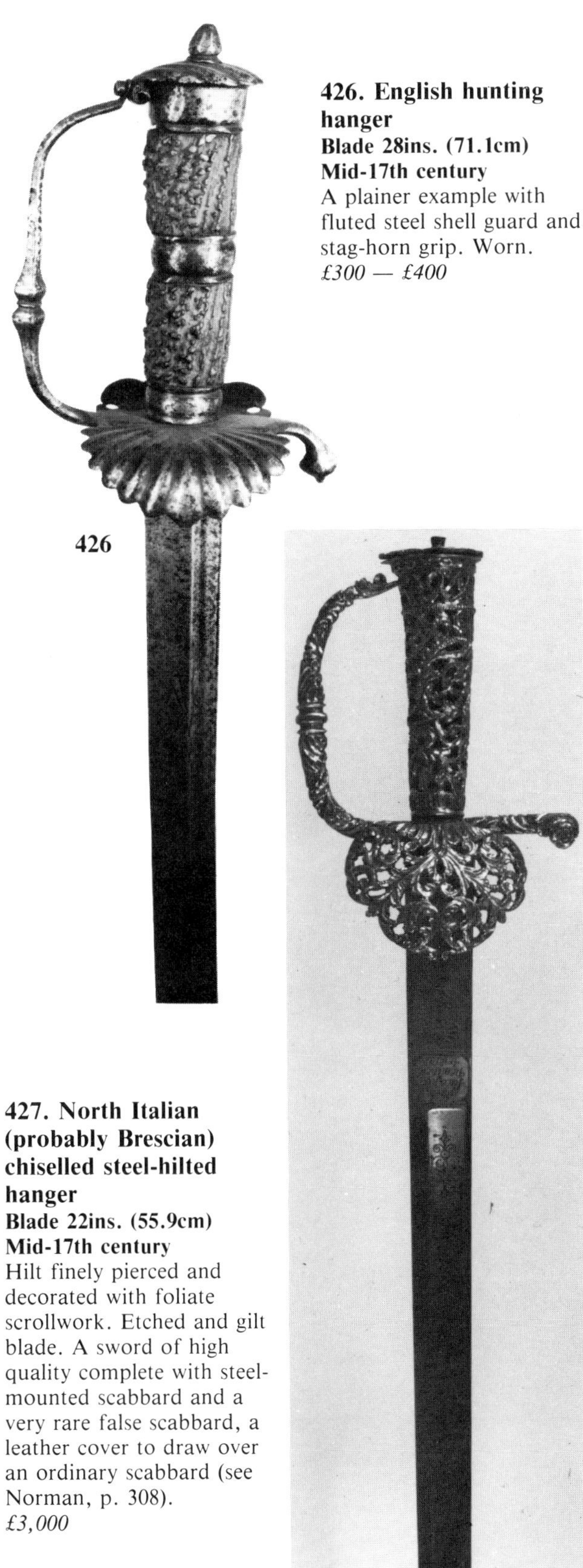

426

427

426. English hunting hanger
Blade 28ins. (71.1cm)
Mid-17th century
A plainer example with fluted steel shell guard and stag-horn grip. Worn.
£300 — £400

427. North Italian (probably Brescian) chiselled steel-hilted hanger
Blade 22ins. (55.9cm)
Mid-17th century
Hilt finely pierced and decorated with foliate scrollwork. Etched and gilt blade. A sword of high quality complete with steel-mounted scabbard and a very rare false scabbard, a leather cover to draw over an ordinary scabbard (see Norman, p. 308).
£3,000

428. Cingalese carved ivory-hilted hanger
Length 29ins. (73.6cm) Mid-17th century
Hilt boldly carved to represent a rampant lion fighting with hounds. Probably made for the Dutch East India Company and for eventual sale in Europe.
£500 — £600

Photographs: 426 and 427 Christie's; 428 Peter Dale Ltd.

429

432. English silver-hilted hanger
Blade 18½ins. (47cm)
About 1690
A fine example with stag-horn grip and silver-mounted, leather-covered scabbard. Unidentified silver maker's mark, 'RF' in a shield.
£200 — £250

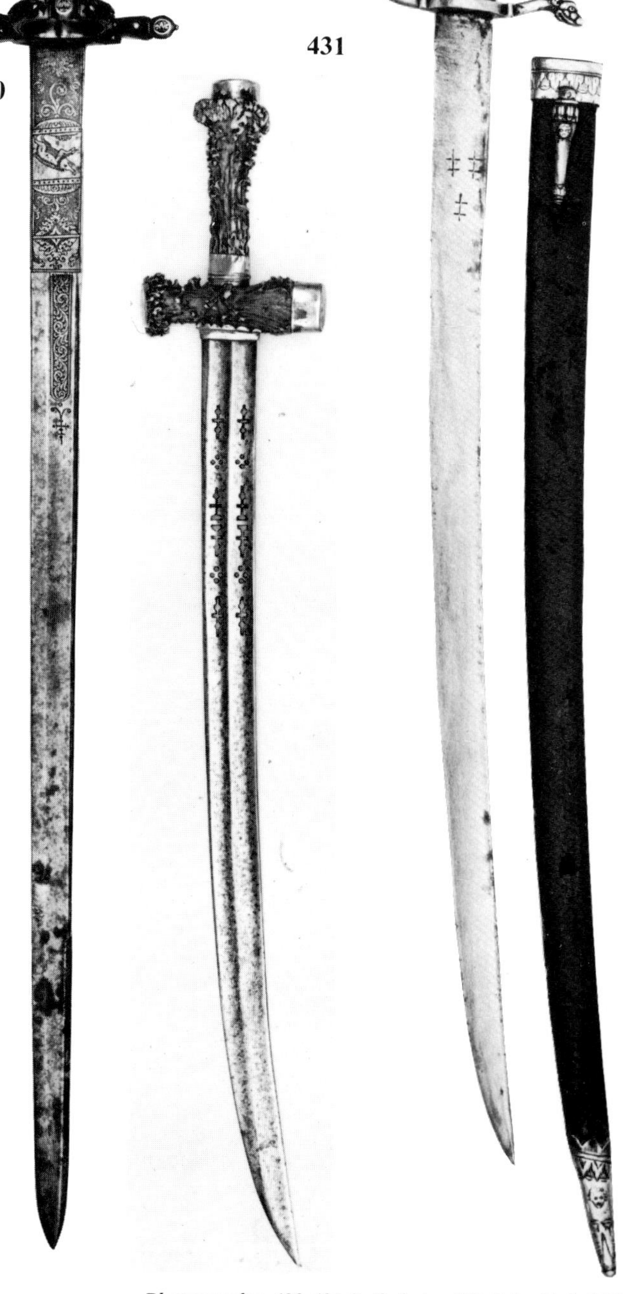

430 431 432

429. Saxon hunting sword
Length 39ins. (99cm) Dated 1662
The steel hilt has a side ring filled with a plate, and an additional guard beneath the rear quillon. Grip faced with horn plaques. The steel-mounted scabbard (worn) is dated on the locket and fitted with a compartment for the knives and file. A fine example. The sword forms a garniture with the woodknife shown in 665.
£5,000

430. Italian hunting sword with brass hilt
Length 30ins. (76.2cm) About 1660
Constructed in a similar way to 429 but without the plate in the side ring. The hilt faced with stag horn. The down-curved guard is missing. Good condition, without scabbard.
£500 — £600

431. English buck-horn hilted hunting hanger
Length 24¾ins. (62.8cm) About 1675
The hilt with silver mounts. A familiar sword of good quality with pierced blade.
£200 — £250

Photographs: 429-431 Sotheby's; 432 Peter Dale Ltd.

433. English brass-hilted hunting hanger
Blade 17¾ins. (45.1cm) About 1700
Hilt with stag-horn grip and pierced shell decorated with hunting scenes. Single-edged blade with the king's head mark. Very good quality.
£200 — £250

434. Dutch or English hunting hanger
About 1700
This high quality sword, with carved ivory grip, may have been made in Holland for the English market, or it may be an English sword fitted with a Dutch grip. The single-edged curved blade is struck with the king's head mark.
£800 — £1,000

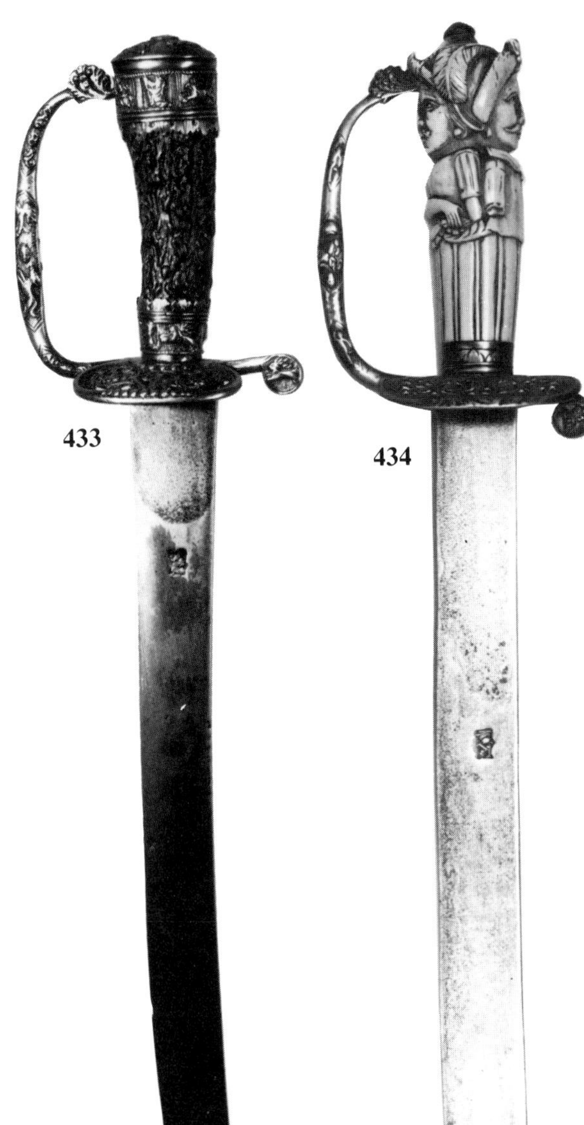

433 434

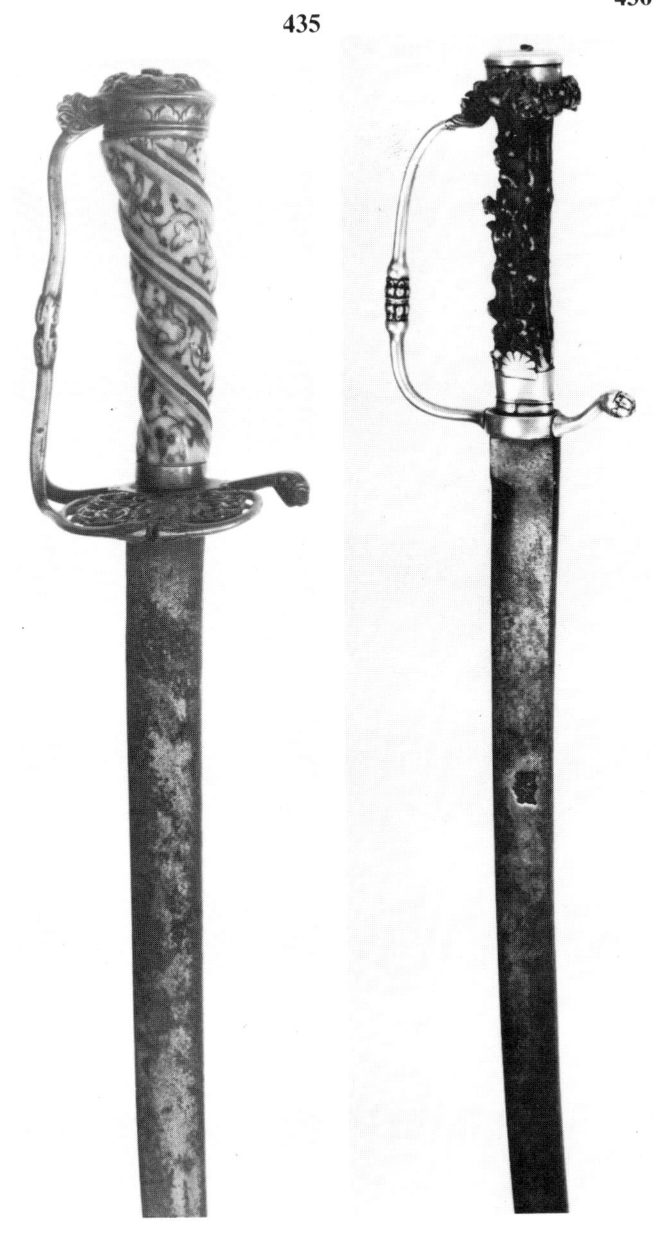

435 436

435. English brass and ivory hilted hunting hanger
Blade 21½ins. (54.6cm) About 1700
The ivory grip is probably Dutch. Very good quality. Blade worn. Reputedly once owned by Admiral Cockcraft.
£300 — £400

436. English silver-hilted hanger
Blade 20½ins. (52cm) About 1700
Hilt with buck-horn grip. The maker's mark appears to be 'IH'. Curved single-edged blade (worn) with the king's head mark. Fine quality. The quillon is bent and the worn scabbard (not shown) has lost its chape.
£200

Photographs: Christie's

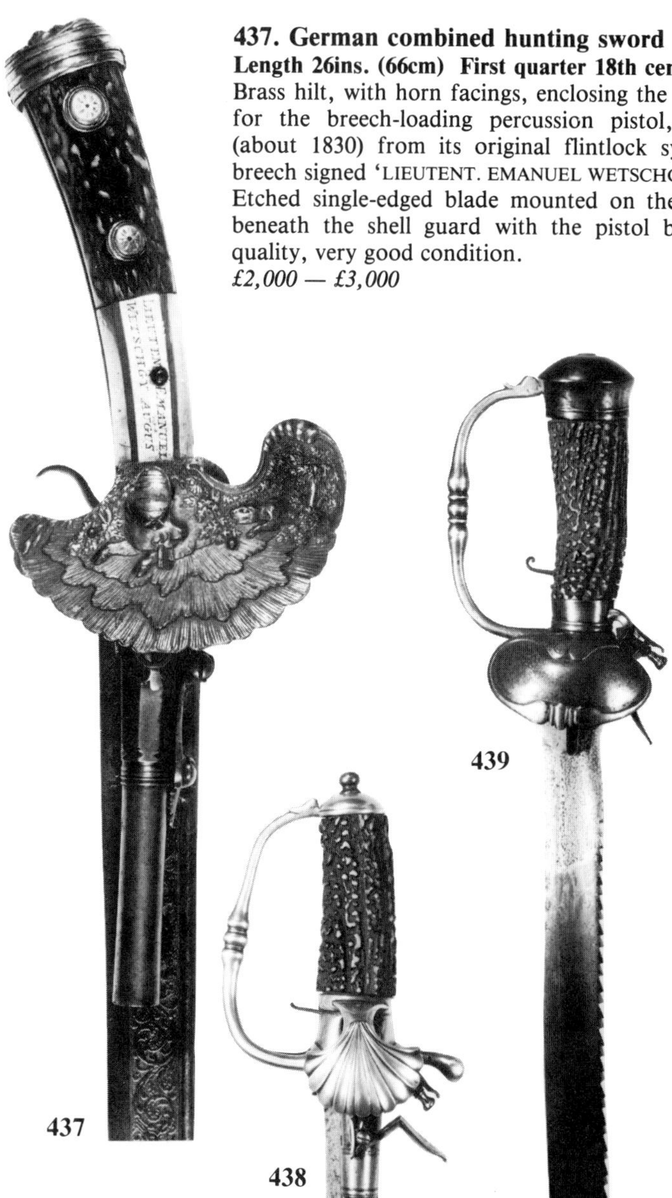

437. German combined hunting sword and pistol
Length 26ins. (66cm) First quarter 18th century
Brass hilt, with horn facings, enclosing the mechanism for the breech-loading percussion pistol, converted (about 1830) from its original flintlock system. The breech signed 'LIEUTENT. EMANUEL WETSCHGY, AUGUS'. Etched single-edged blade mounted on the right side beneath the shell guard with the pistol barrel. Fine quality, very good condition.
£2,000 — £3,000

440. English combined hunting sword and flintlock pistol
Length 30¼ins. (76.8cm)
Second quarter 18th century
Brass hilt with stag-horn grip. The pistol barrel mounted on the right of the single-edged blade and struck with a barrel-smith's mark, 'TR'. Good quality but worn on the blade and with some gun parts restored.
£800 — £850

438. English combined hunting sword and pistol
Length 27½ins. (69.8cm)
London, first quarter 18th century
Silver hilt with single shell covering the flintlock pistol mechanism. Stag-horn grip. The turn-off barrel is fitted to the right side of the blade and signed on the breech 'VANDEBAISE, LONDON'. Fine quality. The blade worn.
£2,000 — £2,500

439. English combined hunting sword and flintlock pistol
Length 30½ins. (77.5cm)
First quarter 18th century
A very good quality example with steel hilt and curved saw-backed blade.
£800 — £1,000

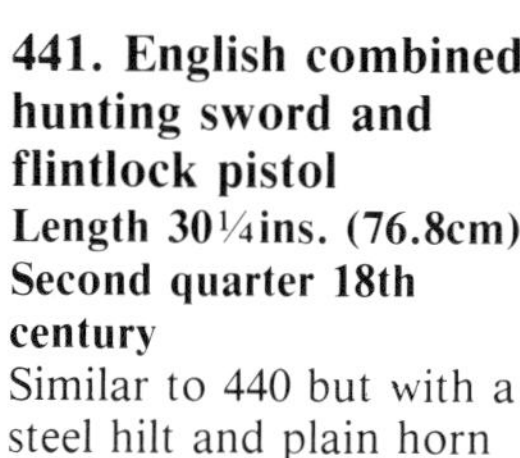

441. English combined hunting sword and flintlock pistol
Length 30¼ins. (76.8cm)
Second quarter 18th century
Similar to 440 but with a steel hilt and plain horn grip.
£800

Photographs: 437 Sotheby's; 438-441 Christie's

442. English silver-hilted hanger with stag-horn grip
Blade 20½ins. (52cm)
London, 1731-1732
A fine piece but with a shortened and worn saw-backed blade. Maker's mark indistinct.
£150 — £180

444. English silver-hilted hanger with agate grip
Blade 22½ins. (57.2cm)
About 1740
The knuckle guard with unidentified maker's mark, 'WS' with a pellet below. The worn blade with running wolf mark. Fine quality. Complete with scabbard (not shown).
£400 — £500

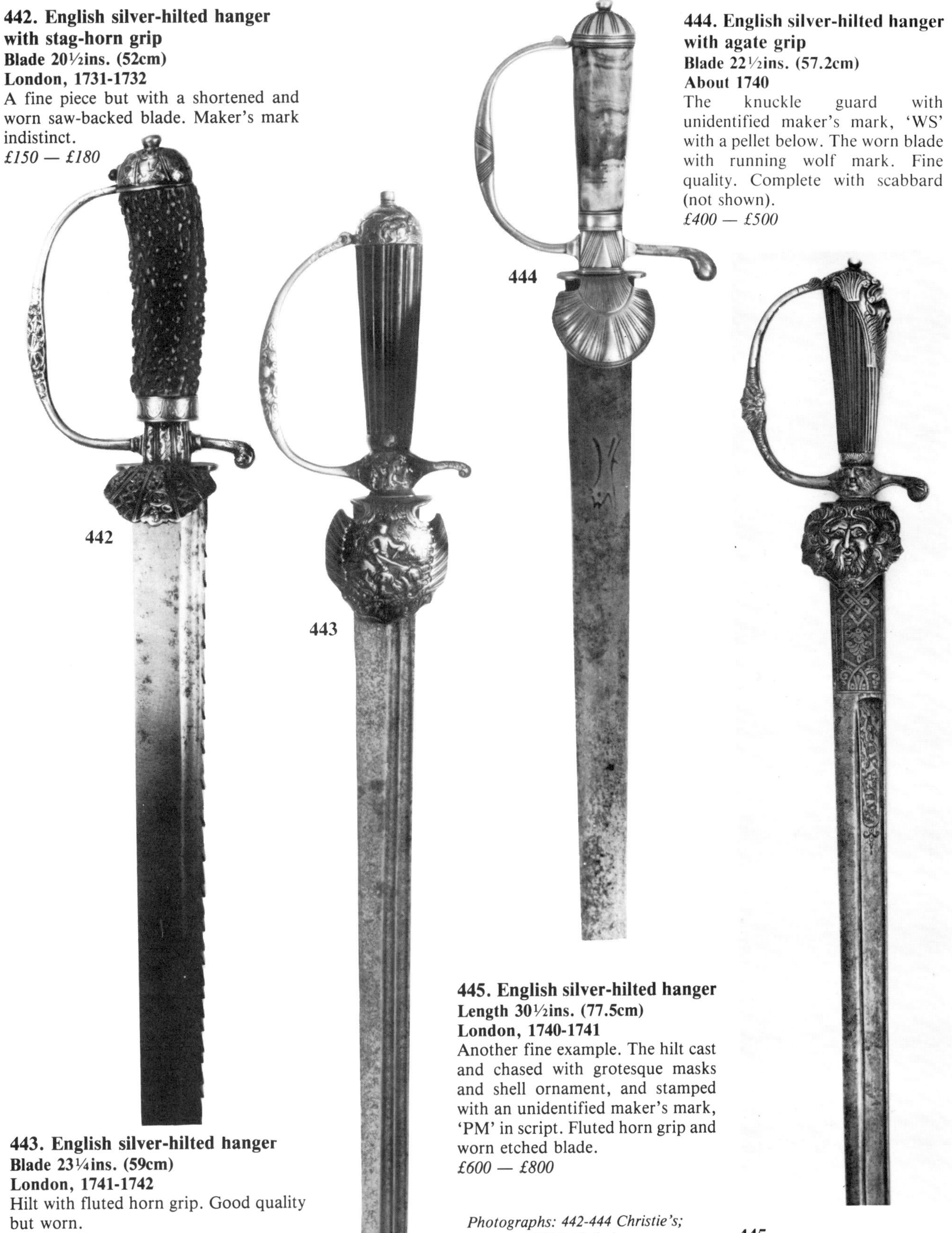

445. English silver-hilted hanger
Length 30½ins. (77.5cm)
London, 1740-1741
Another fine example. The hilt cast and chased with grotesque masks and shell ornament, and stamped with an unidentified maker's mark, 'PM' in script. Fluted horn grip and worn etched blade.
£600 — £800

443. English silver-hilted hanger
Blade 23¼ins. (59cm)
London, 1741-1742
Hilt with fluted horn grip. Good quality but worn.
£250 — £300

Photographs: 442-444 Christie's; 445 Sotheby's

446

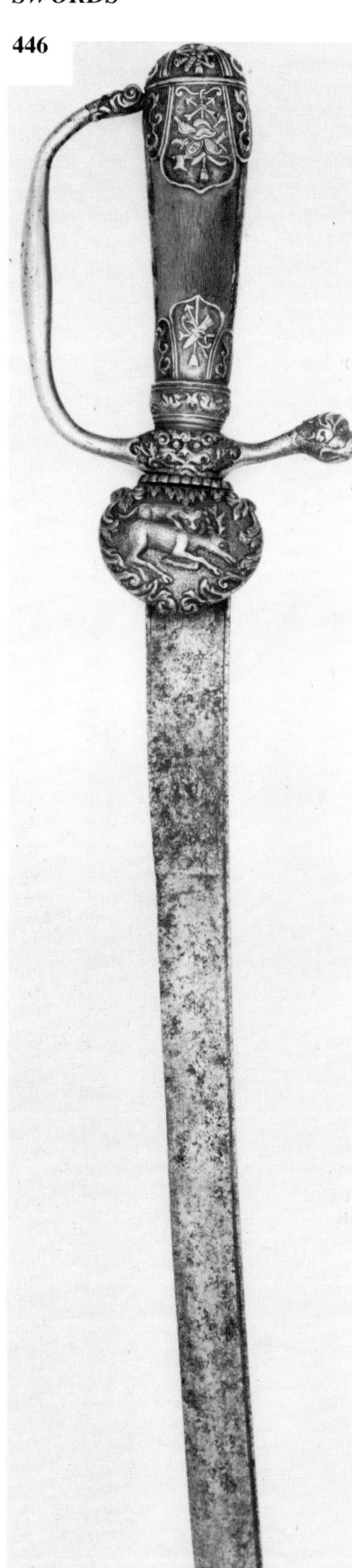

446. German brass-mounted hunting hanger
Length 27½ins. (69.8cm) Mid-18th century
A good example. The blade is worn and the wooden grip without its original covering.
£120 — £160

447. German silver-hilted hunting hanger
Length 26½ins. (67.3cm) Mid-18th century
Ivory grip finely carved to represent hounds attacking a bear. Single shell guard. The blade is etched with the monogram 'EA' and inset with two portrait miniatures, possibly of the Elector Ernst August of Hanover and his wife. Unidentified silver maker's mark, 'CS' in a heart. Fine quality.
£3,000

447

448

448. Continental hunting hanger, possibly Polish
Blade 20ins. (50.8cm)
Mid-18th century
Silver mounted. Hilt of karabela form mounted with horn scales. Watered steel blade inlaid with gold Turkish inscriptions. Good condition.
£250 — £300

Photographs: 446 and 447 Sotheby's; 448 Christie's

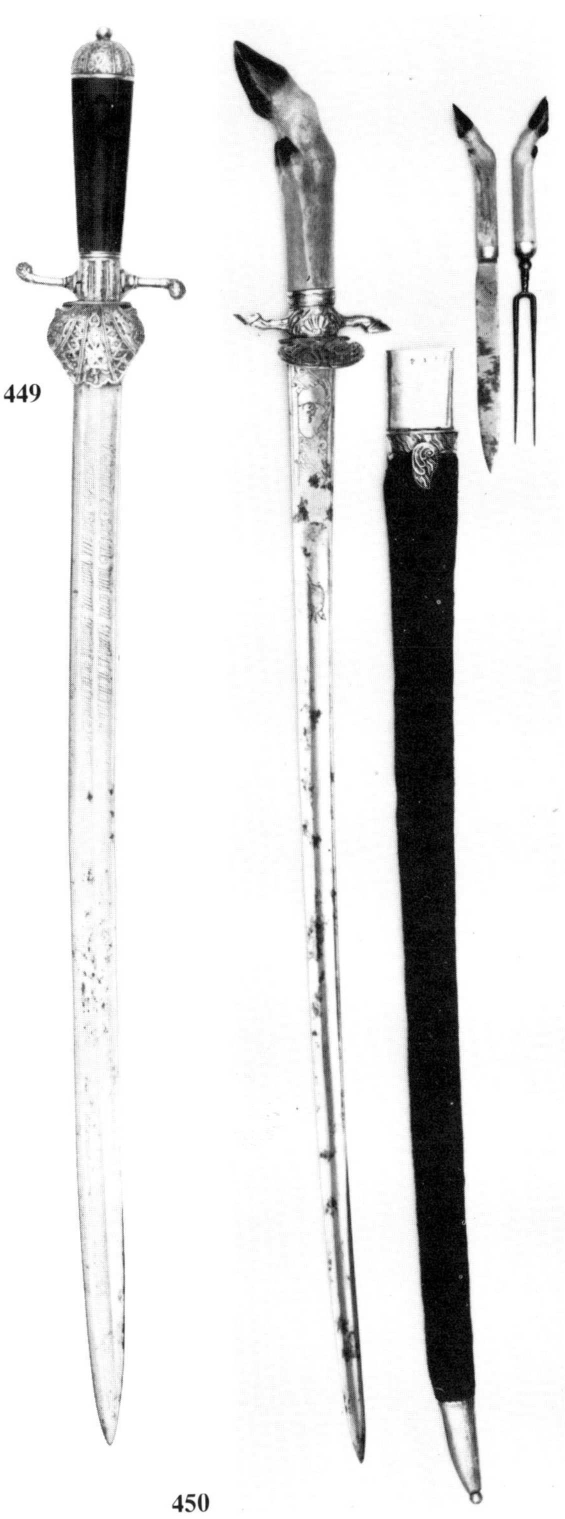

449

450

450. Saxon porcelain-hilted hunting hanger

Length 28½ins. (72.4cm) Dresden, mid-18th century

The hilts of the sword, knife and fork are made of silver and Meissen porcelain in the form of deer hooves. The locket has the Dresden mark as well as an unidentified maker's mark, 'FRS'. A delicate and decorative item in good condition. The velvet covering the scabbard and the chape are later.

£1,000

451. English silver-hilted hanger

Length 27¾ins. (70.5cm) Mid-18th century

Agate grip. The quillon block is decorated on one side with Neptune and on the other with Romulus, Remus and the She-Wolf. Locket inscribed 'B. GODDE' or 'R. GODDEN' of Hemmings Row. Scabbard and blade worn.

£400 — £500

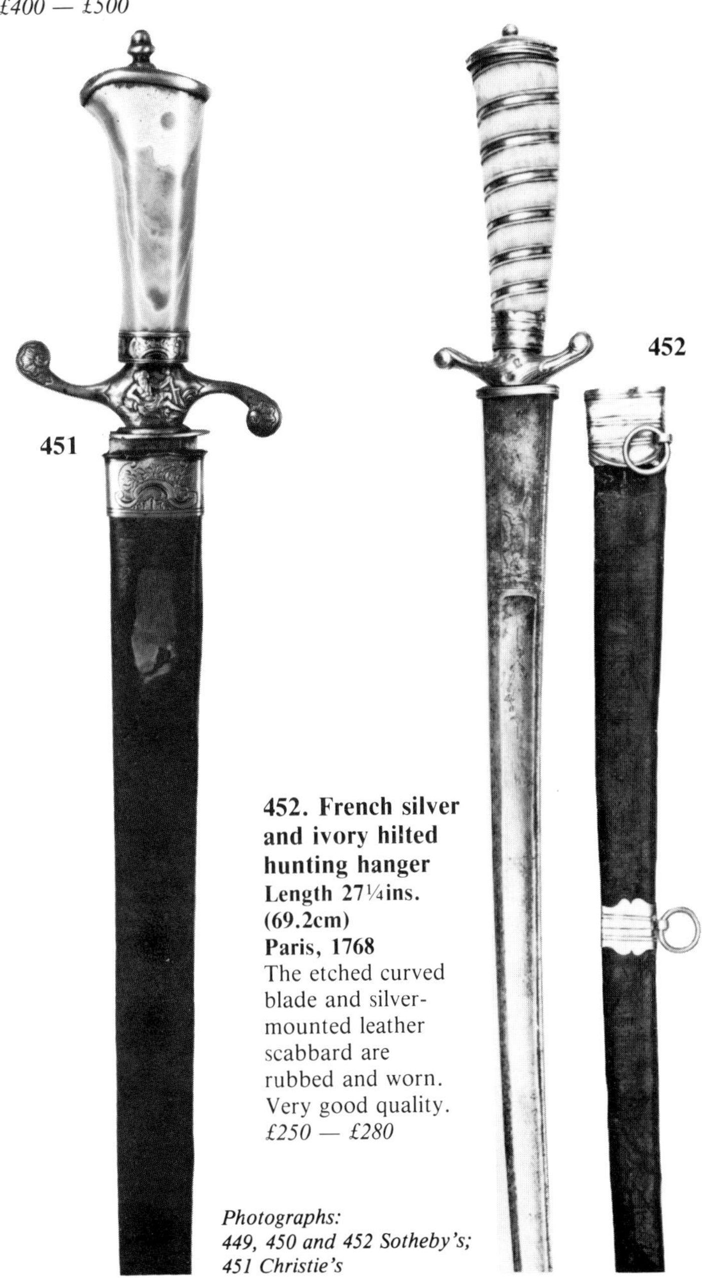

451

452

452. French silver and ivory hilted hunting hanger

Length 27¼ins. (69.2cm)

Paris, 1768

The etched curved blade and silver-mounted leather scabbard are rubbed and worn. Very good quality.

£250 — £280

Photographs:
449, 450 and 452 Sotheby's;
451 Christie's

449. German silver-mounted hunting hanger

Length 25½ins. (64.7cm) Mid-18th century

Ebony grip. A good example but with pitting on the etched blade and restored leather covering on the scabbard (not shown).

£200 — £300

Photographs: 453 Peter Dale Ltd.; 454 and 455 Christie's

453

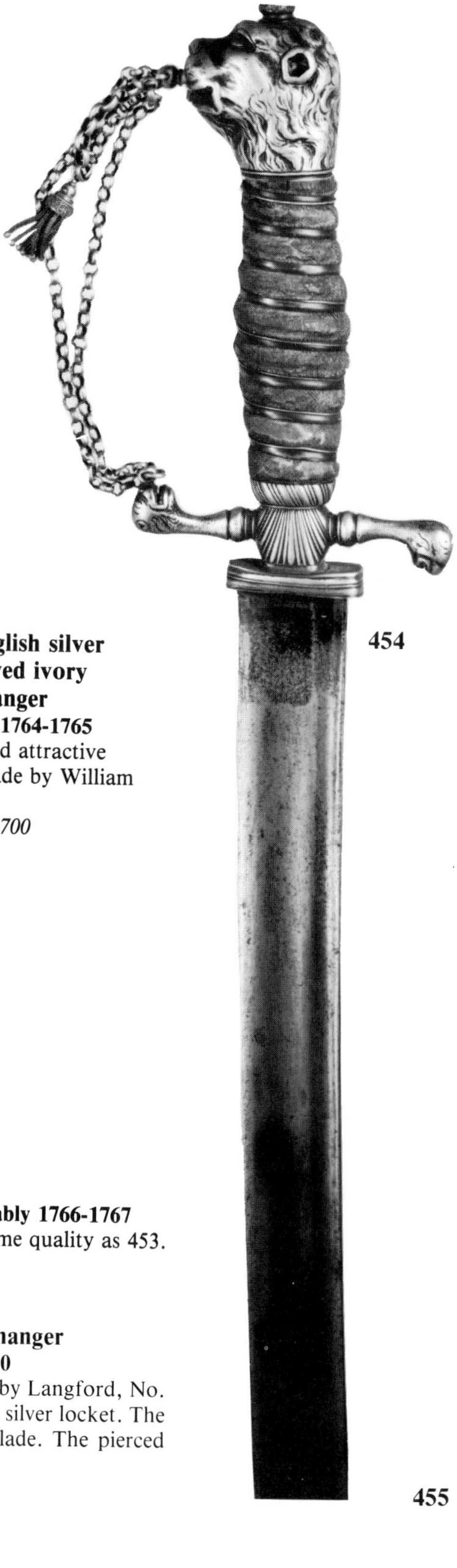

453. English silver and carved ivory hilted hanger
London, 1764-1765
A fine and attractive sword made by William Kinman.
£500 — £700

454

455

454. English silver-hilted hanger
Blade 23¾ins. (60.4cm) London, probably 1766-1767
Made by William Kinman and of the same quality as 453. The grip is covered with fish skin.
£400 — £600

455. English silver and ivory hilted hanger
Blade 26ins. (66cm) London, about 1770
Made by William Kinman and mounted by Langford, No. 50, Fleet St., whose name appears on the silver locket. The grip is of stained green ivory. Etched blade. The pierced guard is slightly damaged.
£400 — £500

456

456. French combined hunting sword and pistol
Blade 23½ins. (56.7cm) About 1770
Steel hilt with wooden grips. Straight two-edged blade inscribed 'VIVE LA CHASSE' (Long live the hunt) and mounted on the right side with a flintlock pistol. Very good quality. A little worn. The single shell guard replaced.
£600 — £800

457

457. French silver-mounted hunting sword and pistol
Blade 23ins. (58.4cm) Paris, 1771
Ivory hilt with silver guard and shell in the form of a dolphin. The flintlock pistol mounted on the right side of the etched, gilt and blued blade. The silver mounts stamped with the discharge mark of Julien Alaterre. An example of very fine quality, reputedly made for the Dauphin of France.
£6,000 — £8,000

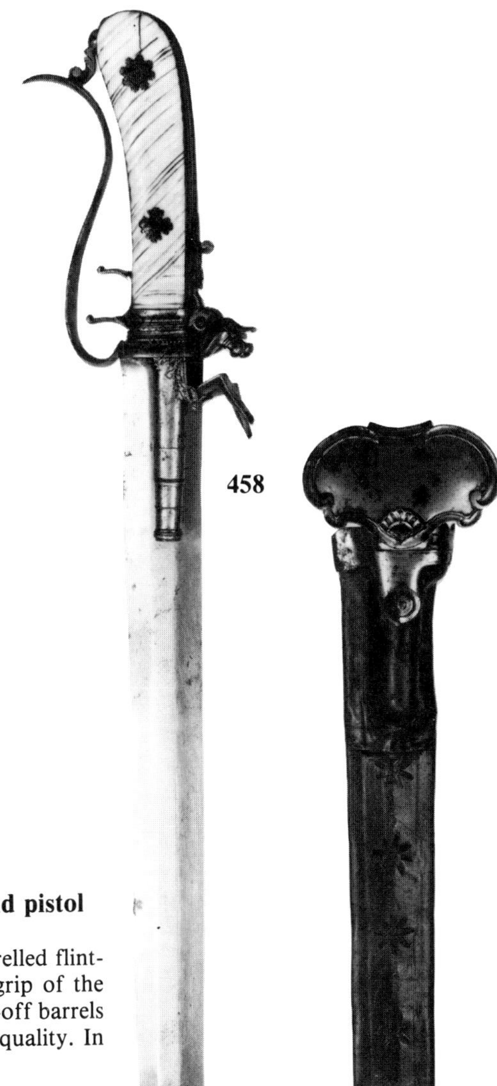
458

458. Italian combined hunting sword and pistol
Length 28ins. (71cm) About 1760
Made by Guiseppe Averani. The double-barrelled flint-lock pistol actions are enclosed within the grip of the steel hilt and covered by ivory plaques. Turn-off barrels on either side of the two-edged blade. Fine quality. In steel-mounted, tooled-leather scabbard.
£2,000

Photographs: Christie's

Photographs: 459-460, 462 Sotheby's; 461 Christie's

459

460

461. German combined hunting sword and pistol
Blade 24½ins. (62.2cm)
Third quarter 18th century
Brass hilt with stag-horn grip facings. The flint-lock pistol barrel mounted on the right side of the curved blade. Brass-mounted scabbard not shown. Good quality. Blade worn.
£700 — £900

462

459. English silver-mounted hunting sword pistol
Length 34ins. (86.3cm)
London, about 1770
The hilt is a flintlock box-lock pistol fitted beneath the breech with a single-edged blade. The lock signed 'GRIFFIN & TOW, LONDON'. The silver mounts with maker's mark 'IK' (?John King). Fine quality and very good condition.
£1,200 — £1,500

461

462. Austrian combined hunting sword and pistol
Blade 20¼ins. (51.5cm)
About 1780
Similar to 461 but with a percussion pistol, converted from the original flintlock about 1830. Very good quality. The curved blade worn.
£800

460. English hunting sword pistol
Length 34½ins. (87.6cm) About 1770
Similar to 459 but mounted in brass and in poorer condition. The lock is signed 'WALSINGHAM'.
£600 — £800

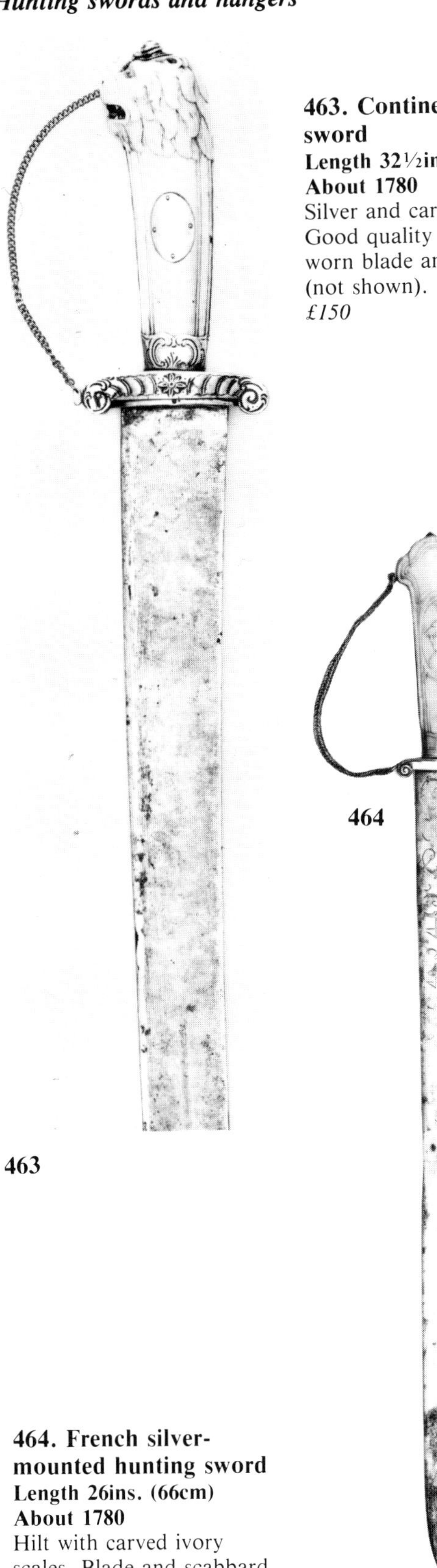

463

463. Continental hunting sword
Length 32½ins. (82.5cm)
About 1780
Silver and carved ivory hilt. Good quality but with a worn blade and scabbard (not shown).
£150

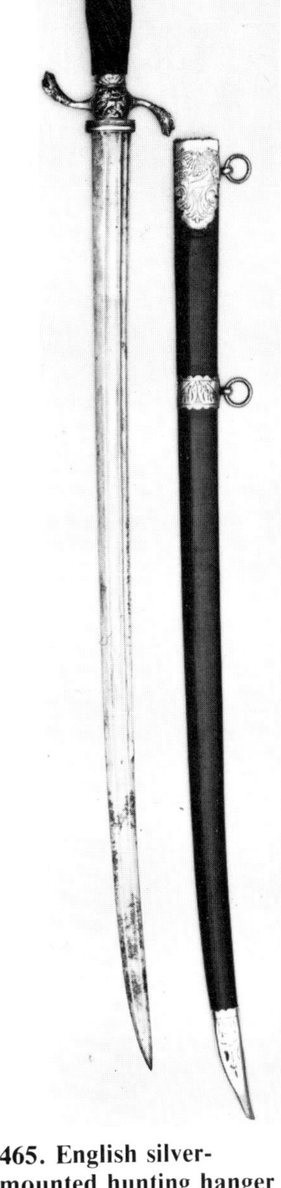

465

465. English silver-mounted hunting hanger
Length 28½ins. (72.4cm)
About 1780
Hilt with eagle's head pommel and stained ivory grip. The locket inscribed 'FLEUREAU, HAYMARKET'. Good quality.
£300 — £400

464

464. French silver-mounted hunting sword
Length 26ins. (66cm)
About 1780
Hilt with carved ivory scales. Blade and scabbard worn.
£120 — £140

466

466. Silver-mounted hunting hanger, possibly French
Length 28½ins. (72.4cm)
Late 18th century
Another good example with a guard of slotted form, and a parchment-covered scabbard.
£250 — £300

Photographs: Sotheby's

467

467. French (Dieppe) ivory-mounted hunting sword
Early 19th century
A sword of high quality carved on the grip and scabbard with scenes of the chase in high relief. Hilt and scabbard mounts of steel.
£1,500

468

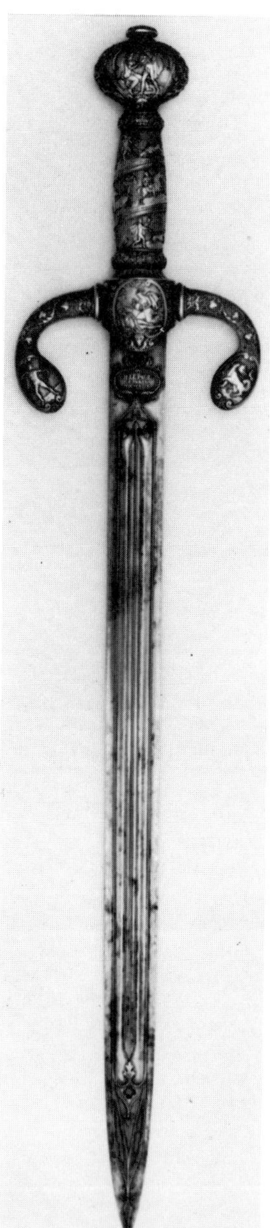

469

Photographs: 467 Michael C. German Ltd.; 468-469 Sotheby's

468. French (Dieppe) ivory-mounted hunting sword
Length 29ins. (73.7cm) First half 19th century
Like the previous item, it is the high quality ivory carving which gives the sword its value. The carving depicts grotesque masks and symbols of the hunt and of the sea. The etched blade and velvet covering on the scabbard are worn.
£700 — £900

469. French hunting sword in the form of a late 16th century dagger
Length 28½ins. (72.4cm) Dated 1829
Hilt of gilt copper decorated with hunting and classical scenes. The fullered blade signed 'H. LE PAGE A PARIS, MDCCCXXIX'. Fine quality.
£1,500 — £2,000

470

470. French silver-mounted hunting sword
Length 27ins. (68.5cm) 1852-1870
Hilt of silver finely cast and chased with intertwined branches of oak and vine. The guard with an unidentified coat of arms, and the pommel formed as a coronet. Etched flamboyant blade signed 'GASTINNE RENETTE, ARQ^{ER} DE S.M. L'EMPEREUR A PARIS' (Gastinne Renette, Gunmaker of His Majesty the Emperor [Napoleon III], Paris).
£2,000 — £3,000

471. French silver-mounted hunting sword
Blade 17¾ins. (45cm) 1865
Silver-gilt hilt modelled to show a huntsman calling to his hounds beneath an oak tree (see detail). The blade signed 'MARREL AINE & FILS. FR. BTE DE S.M. L'EMPEREUR & DE S.M. L'IMPERATRICE, PARIS' and the locket inscribed 'COURSES DU CAMP DE CHALONS, PRIX DONNE PAR L'EMPEREUR, 1865' (Emperor's prize given for the Châlons Military Camp races, 1865).
£1,500 — £1,800

471

Photographs: 470 Sotheby's; 471 Christie's

472

473

474

472. Polish sabre
About 1620-1650
A rare, 'classic' horseman's sabre with long curved single-edged blade. Steel hilt with chainlet and leather-covered wooden grip. Worn. Tower of London Armouries (IX-656).
£1,000+

473. Polish sabre of Hungarian type
Blade 27½ins. (69.8cm) Dated 1655
Chiselled steel hilt and scabbard mounts retaining some original gilding. Etched blade dated 1655. Quite rare, reasonable condition.
£700 — £1,000

474. Polish sabre of Hungarian type
About 1600
A full-length view of a sword similar to 473. The single-edged blade on this example however has a 'false edge' (sharpened section on the blunted edge) one third from the point. National Museum, Cracow.
£800 — £1,000

Photographs: 472 Crown Copyright; 473 Christie's

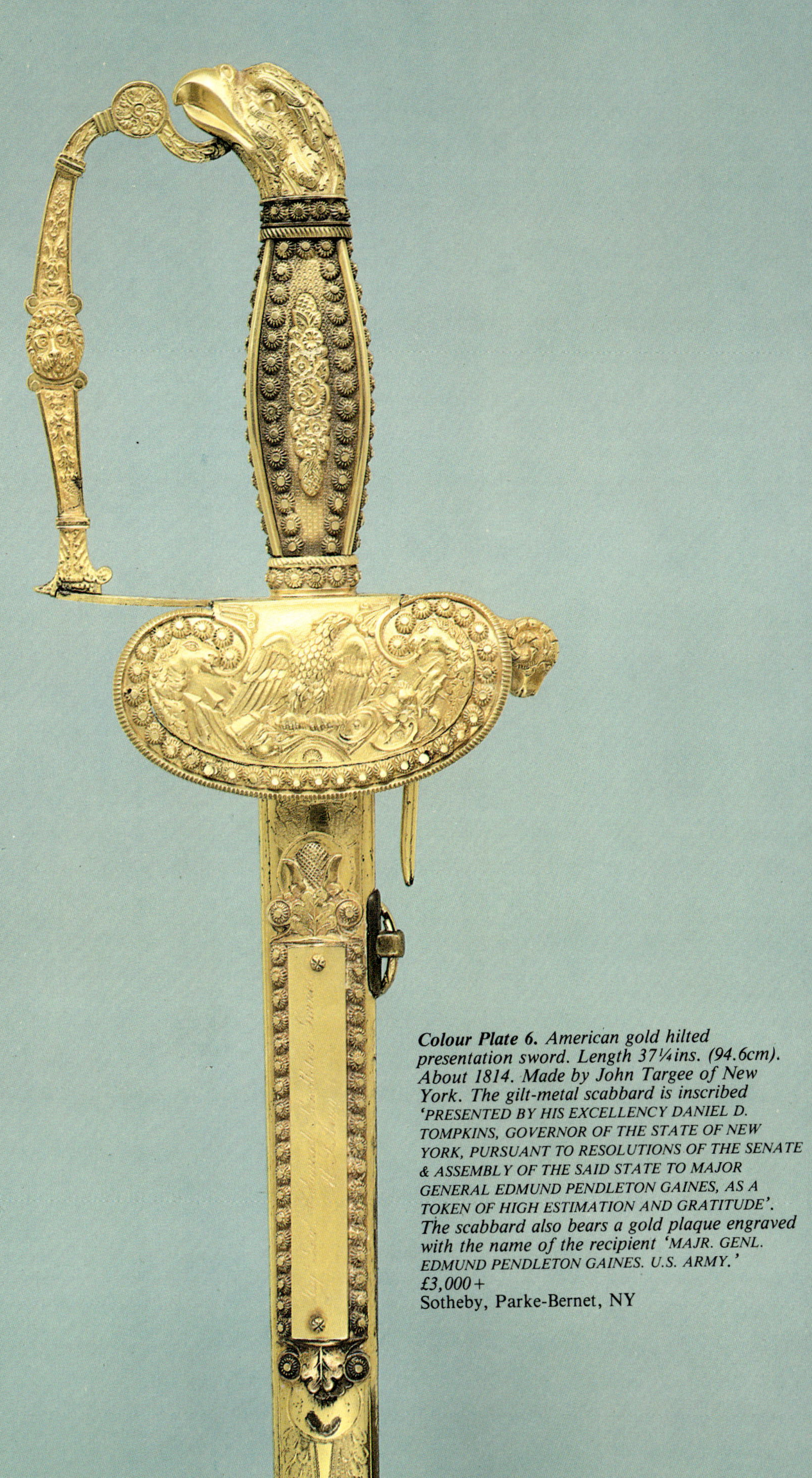

Colour Plate 6. *American gold hilted presentation sword. Length 37¼ins. (94.6cm). About 1814. Made by John Targee of New York. The gilt-metal scabbard is inscribed '*PRESENTED BY HIS EXCELLENCY DANIEL D. TOMPKINS, GOVERNOR OF THE STATE OF NEW YORK, PURSUANT TO RESOLUTIONS OF THE SENATE & ASSEMBLY OF THE SAID STATE TO MAJOR GENERAL EDMUND PENDLETON GAINES, AS A TOKEN OF HIGH ESTIMATION AND GRATITUDE*'. The scabbard also bears a gold plaque engraved with the name of the recipient '*MAJR. GENL. EDMUND PENDLETON GAINES. U.S. ARMY.*'
£3,000+*
Sotheby, Parke-Bernet, NY

475

476

475. Polish pallash
Blade 33ins. (83.8cm) Late 17th/early 18th century
Hilt with guard of silver and fitted with wooden grip scales. Straight single-edged blade. Reasonable condition.
£400 — £500

476. Polish pallash
Blade 31½ins. (80cm) Late 17th/early 18th century
Similar to 475 but with horn grips and steel guard. The straight blade commemoratively inscribed with the words of King Sobieski after the Battle of Vienna: 'VENIMUS, VIDIMUS DEUS VICIT, 1683' (We came, we saw and God conquered). Reasonable condition.
£800

477. Polish karabela with silver-encrusted mounts
Blade 31¼ins. (79.4cm)
Late 17th/early 18th century
Hilt of stylised birds's-head form fitted with horn grip scales. The curved blade inlaid with silver and gold. Good quality.
£300 — £500

477

478

478. Polish silver-mounted karabela
Blade 29½ins. (74.9cm)
Early 18th century
The silver quillons and scabbard mounts embellished with niello. Very good quality and condition.
£300 — £400

Photographs: Christie's

479. Polish sabre of karabela type
Blade 31¼ins. (79.4cm)
18th century
All-steel hilt and scabbard mounts inlaid with gold. Blade of watered steel. This high quality, but worn, sword differs from other karabelas in not having scales of horn, ivory or some other material riveted to the tang to form the grip.
£300 — £350

480. Polish silver-mounted karabela
Blade 31ins. (78.7cm) Late 18th century
Grip fitted with walrus ivory scales. The earlier Persian blade of watered steel inlaid with gold Koranic inscriptions. Fine quality and condition.
£1,000 — £1,500

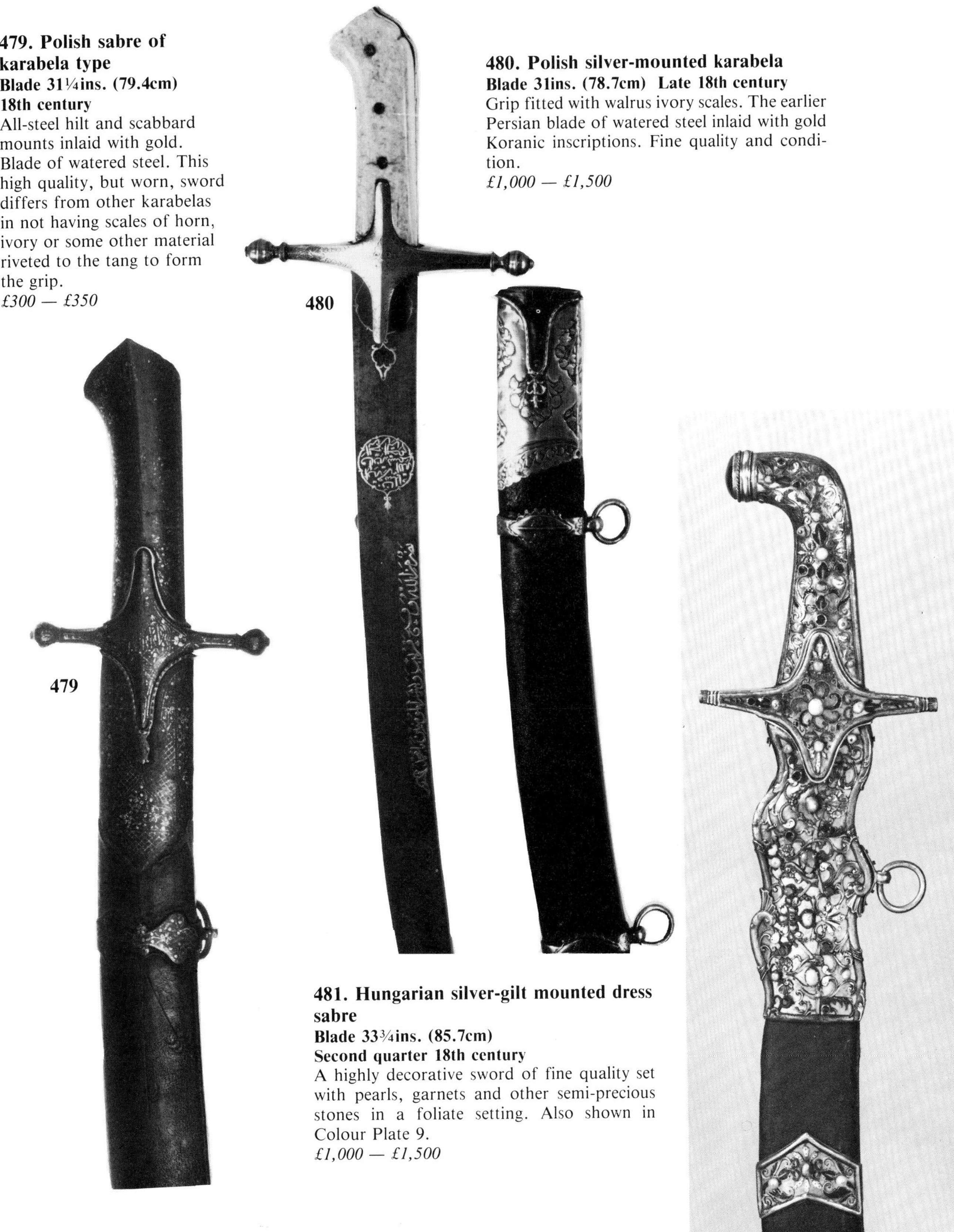
480
479

481. Hungarian silver-gilt mounted dress sabre
Blade 33¾ins. (85.7cm)
Second quarter 18th century
A highly decorative sword of fine quality set with pearls, garnets and other semi-precious stones in a foliate setting. Also shown in Colour Plate 9.
£1,000 — £1,500

481

Photographs: 479, 480 Christie's; 481 Howard Ricketts Ltd.

482

482. Polish silver-mounted sabre
Blade 29½ins. (75cm)
18th century
A good quality sword. The repaired hilt has horn grips. The chainlet is missing.
£300 — £400

483. Polish gilt-bronze mounted officer's sabre
Blade 32ins. (81.3cm)
Early 19th century
Quite a rare sword in very good condition with wooden scales on the grip and a blade of kilij form.
£300 — £500

483

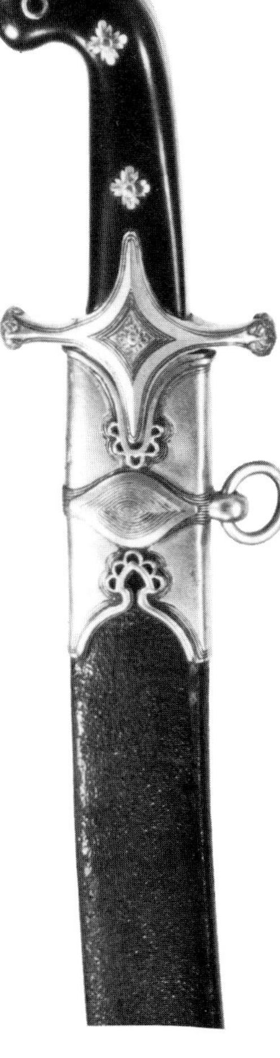

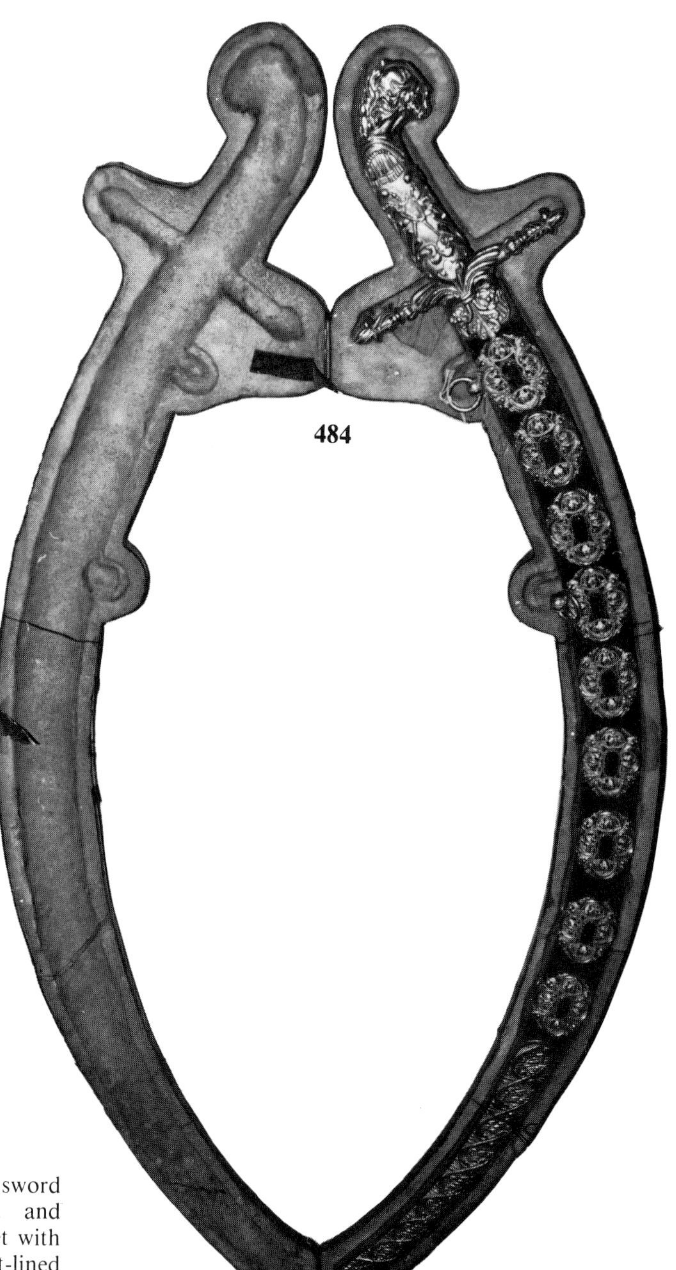

484

484. Hungarian gilt-bronze mounted dress sabre
About 1850
An elaborate and high quality sword with cast and chased hilt and scabbard mounts, the latter set with semi-precious stones. In velvet-lined outer case.
£900 — £1,200

Photographs: 482-483 Christie's; 484 Michael C. German Ltd.

485

485. Russian silver-mounted presentation sabre
Length 40¾ins. (103.5cm)
19th century
The silver hilt and scabbard mounts embellished with niello. Quillons inscribed (in Russian) 'FOR BRAVERY'. A sword of good quality with a chiselled Turkish blade.
£300

486

487

487. Russian shashqua
19th century
Silver and niello decorated, it is of the same high quality as 486.
£500

488

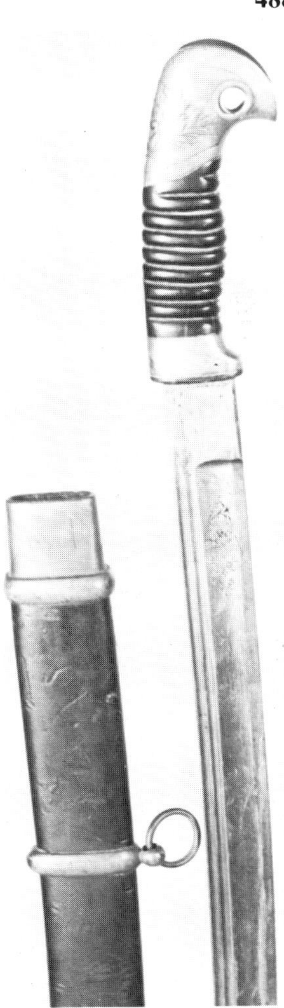

486. Russian silver-mounted presentation shashqua
Blade 29¾ins. (75.5cm) 19th century
Silver and nielloed hilt of characteristic form with the cypher of Alexander III on the pommel surmounted by the inscription (in Russian) 'FOR BRAVERY'. Presented to Commander O.S. Locker-Lampson by the Russian Government in 1917. The scabbard mounts are inscribed 'G.M. TROTSKY, VLADIKAVKAZ, 1917' and 'TO COL. LOCKER-LAMPSON'. Etched blade bearing the cypher of Nicholas II and the makers name GUZUNOV. Fine quality. A little worn on the blade.
£500 — £800

488. Russian cossack officer's shashqua, 1881 pattern
Blade 31ins. (78.7cm)
Brass hilt and scabbard mounts, reeded horn grip. Reasonable condition. Weller and Dufty Ltd.
£80

Photographs: 485 Sotheby's; 486-487 Christie's

489. Turkish silver-gilt mounted yataghan with ivory hilt
Length 35½ins. (90.2cm) Early 19th century
Of characteristic form and of fine quality. The hilt and scabbard are overlaid with silver and finely decorated with flowers and foliage. Gold inlaid blade.
£2,000

490

489

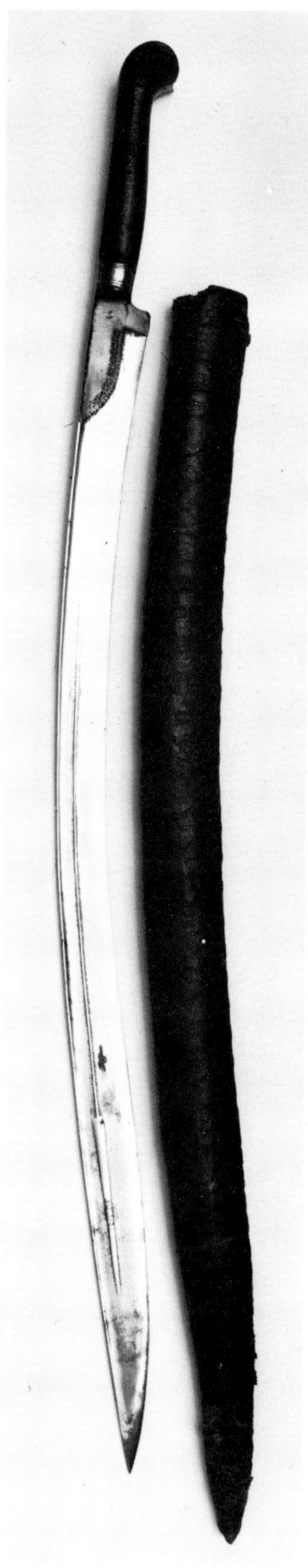

490. Turkish silver-mounted yataghan
19th century
Hilt and scabbard encased in embossed silver sheet. Decorated in a more familiar manner than 489 but still of very good quality.
£200 — £300

491. Turkish horn-hilted yataghan
Length 32¼ins. (82cm)
19th century
A plain, poor quality example with leather-covered wooden scabbard.
£25 — £30

Photographs: 489 and 491 Christie's; 490 Michael C. German Ltd.

491

492

492. Bosnian dress sword
Blade 32½ins. (82.5cm) 18th century
An elaborate and ornate sword with silver-gilt hilt and scabbard mounts set with garnets and embellished with niello. Earlier two-edged blade with running wolf mark.
£1,000

493

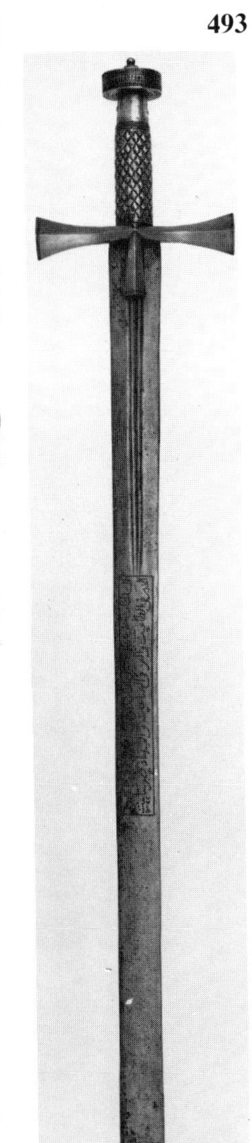

494

495

493. East Sudanese silver-hilted kaskara of Ali Dinar
Length 41½ins. (105.5cm)
Dated 1904
Cruciform silver hilt with diaper design on the grip. The two-edged blade inscribed with the genealogy of the last Sultan of Darfur, Alī Dīnār (1898-1916), and dated A.H. 1322 (A.D. 1904). Kaskaras of this quality are quite rare. Most examples are similar to 494.
£300+

494. Sudanese kaskara
Length 42ins. (106.7cm) 19th century
Hilt of steel with wooden grip bound with leather. Blade inlaid with silver. Compare 493. This is the type most frequently found. Very poor quality and condition.
£20 — £40

495. Moroccan nimcha with silver-mounted scabbard
About 1800
Iron hilt of typical form with bone grip. The slightly curved European blade has a single fuller on each side. Good quality and condition.
£100 — £120

496

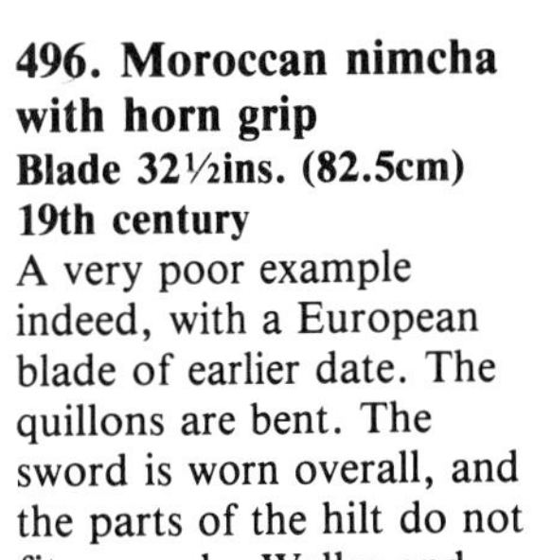

496. Moroccan nimcha with horn grip
Blade 32½ins. (82.5cm)
19th century
A very poor example indeed, with a European blade of earlier date. The quillons are bent. The sword is worn overall, and the parts of the hilt do not fit properly. Weller and Dufty Ltd.
£20 — £30

Photographs: 492 and 494 Christie's; 493 Sotheby's; 495 Michael C. German Ltd.

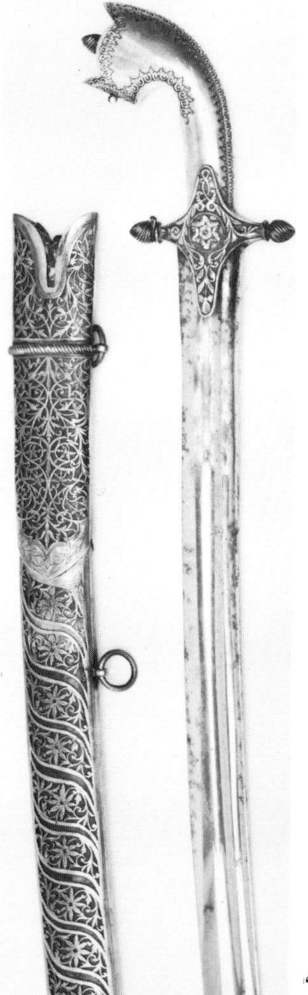

497

497. Arab silver-mounted saif

Length 35¼ins. (89.5cm) 19th century

Cast and engraved silver hilt. The wood-lined silver scabbard finely pierced with flowers and foliage.

£400

498. Turkish or Persian sabre

Blade 34¾ins. (88.3cm) 16th or 17th century

The hilt of silver gilt set with turquoise. The scabbard mounts *en suite* but further embellished with jade plaques. The curved watered-steel blade inlaid in gold at the forte with the maker's mark of Kalb Ali. A decorative sword of fine quality. Chape replaced. Also shown in Colour Plate 8.

£8,000 — £10,000

498

499. Persian royal shamshir

Blade 30¾ins. (78cm) 17th century

Hilt and scabbard mounts of steel inlaid with gold. Walrus ivory plaque grips. Quillons inscribed 'PROPERTY OF JURJYUS IBN DANYAL AB HAMILTIN' (for George, son of Daniel Hamilton). Curved blade with 'Forty Steps' (Kirk Nardaban) design signed 'WORK OF ASSADULLAH OF ISFAHAN', and with the names of former owners 'SULAYMAN, SLAVE OF THE KING OF THE UNIVERSE' (reigned 1667-94) and 'PROPERTY OF NADIR SHAH, A.H. 1155' (A.D. 1742).

A sword of high quality, very elegant and simple in design and with a blade signed by the most celebrated Persian swordsmith. George Hamilton, whose name appears on the guard, probably worked for the British East India Company. *Art of the Armourer,* 1963, cat. no. 314. Shown also in Colour Plate 10.

£1,500 — £2,000

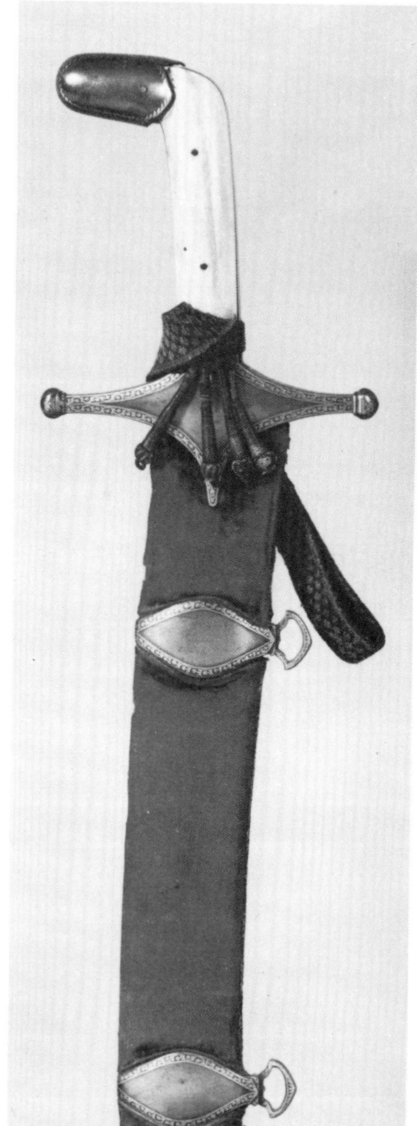

499

Photographs:
497 and 498 Sotheby's;
499 Howard Ricketts Ltd.

500

500. Persian silver and enamel mounted shamshir
Length 35½ins. (90.2cm)
17th or 18th century
Hilt, scabbard and belt mounts of enamelled silver. Walrus ivory grips damaged and bound. A high quality sword in a tooled leather scabbard. Worn.
£300 — £500

501. Indian silver and enamel hilted sword
18th century
Of fine quality. The hilt with tiger's head pommel and quillon finials. Red velvet-covered scabbard. Shown also in Colour Plate 11.
£1,000 — £1,300

501

502

502. Indian shamshir
Length 34½ins. (87.6cm)
19th century
Gilt-copper hilt set with semi-precious stones. Curved blade of watered steel, and velvet-covered scabbard, with gilt-copper mounts. Good quality and condition.
£500 — £800

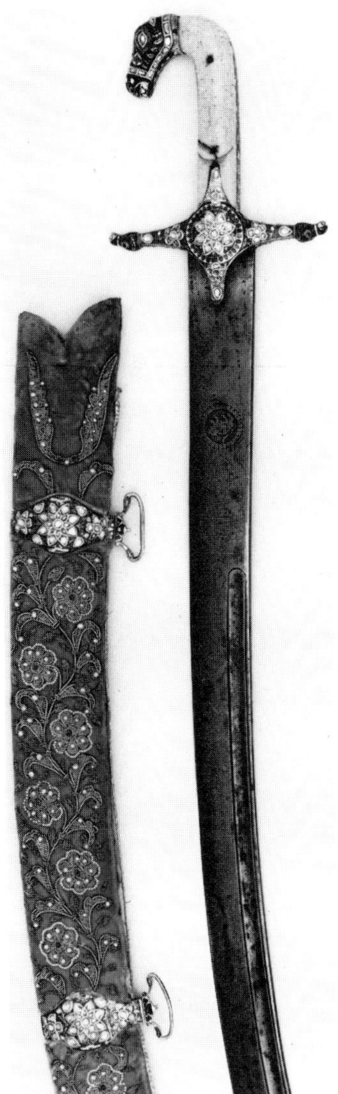

503

503. Indian gold, enamel and diamond-set shamshir
Length 43½ins. (110.5cm)
Early 19th century
Hilt of gold decorated with enamel and set with diamonds. Ivory grips. Curved 18th century single-edged Persian blade of watered steel. Velvet-covered scabbard decorated with gold floral braid and mounted *en suite* with the hilt. A fine quality sword in reasonable condition. The blade is worn and one grip is cracked. The hilt has been dismantled and the quillons replaced the wrong way round.
£5,000

Photographs: 500 and 502 Christie's; 501 Howard Ricketts Ltd.; 503 Sotheby's

504. French officer's sabre
Blade 31¾ins. (80.7cm) Early 19th century
Gilt-brass hilt with chequered horn grip. Curved blade. Embossed brass scabbard. Very good quality. Chainlet missing.
£600 — £800

504

505

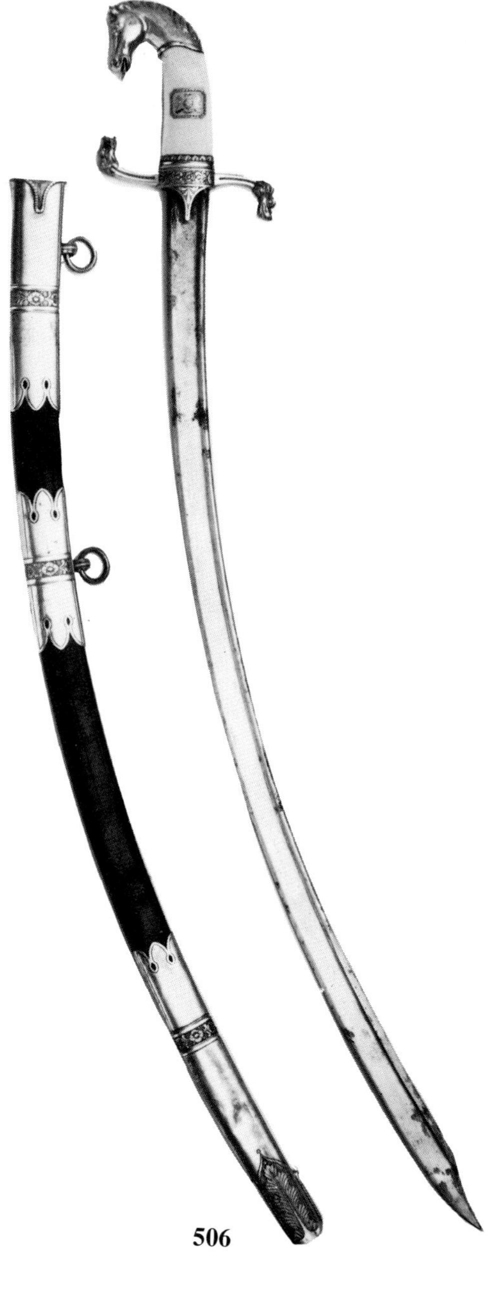

506

505. British presentation sabre
Blade 29ins. (73.6cm) 1810
Gilt-brass hilt and scabbard mounts; ivory grip. Finely etched blued and gilt curved blade with post-1801 royal coat of arms. Signed 'JOHN GILL'S Warranted' and inscribed 'PRESENTED BY THE NON COMMISSIONED OFFICERS & PRIVATES OF THE NORTON VOLUNTEER COMP.Y. TO SAMUEL SHORE ESQ.R. (CAPTAIN) AS A TOKEN OF RESPECT & ATTACHMENT TO HIS CHARACTER AS A GENTLEMAN AND A SOLDIER, 1810'. Fine quality. The chainlet is missing and the leather on the scabbard has been renewed.
£1,200 — £1,800

506. British presentation sabre
Blade 32ins. (81.2cm) Early 19th century
Hilt and scabbard mounts of gilt-brass. The ivory grip with two enamel plaques, one bearing the royal coat of arms, the other the arms of Hay of Errol. The sword is traditionally believed to have been presented to Lord James Hay, Ensign 1st Guards, who was killed at Waterloo. Fine quality. A little worn on the pipe-backed blade.
£2,000 — £2,500

Photographs: Christie's

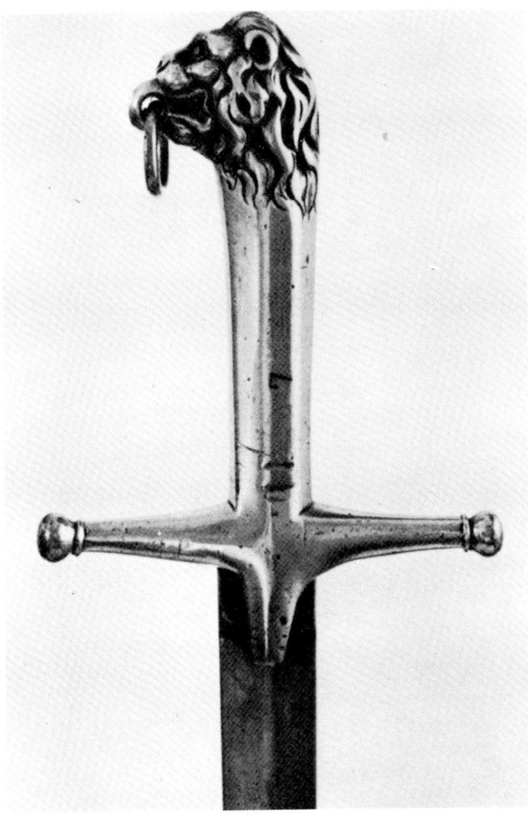

507

507. British infantry band sword
Blade 26½ins. (67.3cm) About 1820
A brass-hilted regulation sword. Tower of London Armouries (IX-431).
£50 — £80

509

509. British band sword, probably for a cavalry regiment
Blade 32⅜ins. (82.2cm) About 1820
Brass hilt stamped 'H48' on the grip. Regulation issue. Tower of London Armouries (IX-430).
£50 — £80

508

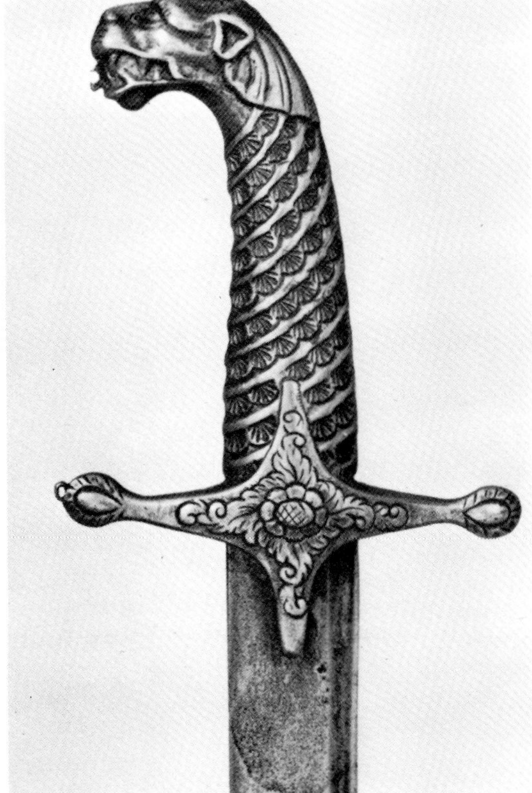

508. British infantry band sword
Blade 27⅜ins. (67.5cm) About 1820
Another brass-hilted regulation sword. Chainlet missing. Tower of London Armouries (IX-596).
£50 — £80

Photographs: Crown Copyright

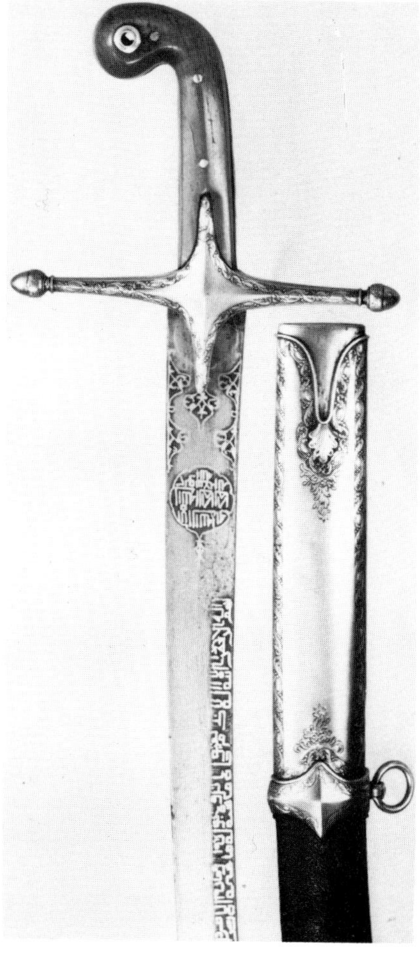

510

512

511

510. Turkish gold-mounted shamshir of Sir John Moore (1761-1809)
Blade 30ins. (76.2cm)
18th century
A fine sword, reputedly a gift from the Grand Vizier of Turkey. The curved blade is inlaid with gold calligraphy and the grips are of horn. Of value because of the quality of the sword, the gold mounts and the historical association.
£4,000 — £5,000

511. Turkish silver-mounted shamshir
Greek hallmark Early 19th century
Hilt and scabbard of silver (formerly gilt), cast and chased with arabesques. Plain curved blade. Very good quality and condition.
£600 — £700

512. Turkish silver-mounted shamshir
About 1820
An elegant weapon with engraved silver quillons and gold inlaid blade. Grips of horn. The price would increase by about a third, if it had its scabbard. Tower of London Armouries (XXIV-116S).
£400 — £500

Photographs: 510 Christie's;
511 Robert Hales Antiques Ltd.
512 Crown Copyright

Photographs: Sotheby's

513. South Russian (Turkestan) shamshir
Length 38¼ins. (97.2cm) 19th century
Hilt and scabbard decorated with turquoise, mounted in silver and embellished with niello. Watered-steel blade. A fine, decorative sword in very good condition. The blade with some wear.
£1,500

514. Indian shamshir with silver-gilt mounted scabbard
Length 36½ins. (92.1cm) Early 19th century
Gold inlaid hilt set with turquoise on the quillon finials. The earlier Persian blade of watered steel inscribed in gold 'AMAL-I ASSADULLAH ISFAHANI' (Made by Assadullah of Isfahan). See also 499.This high quality sword was presented by Tej Singh to Viscount Gough at the Treaty of Lahore, 1843.
£1,200 — £1,500

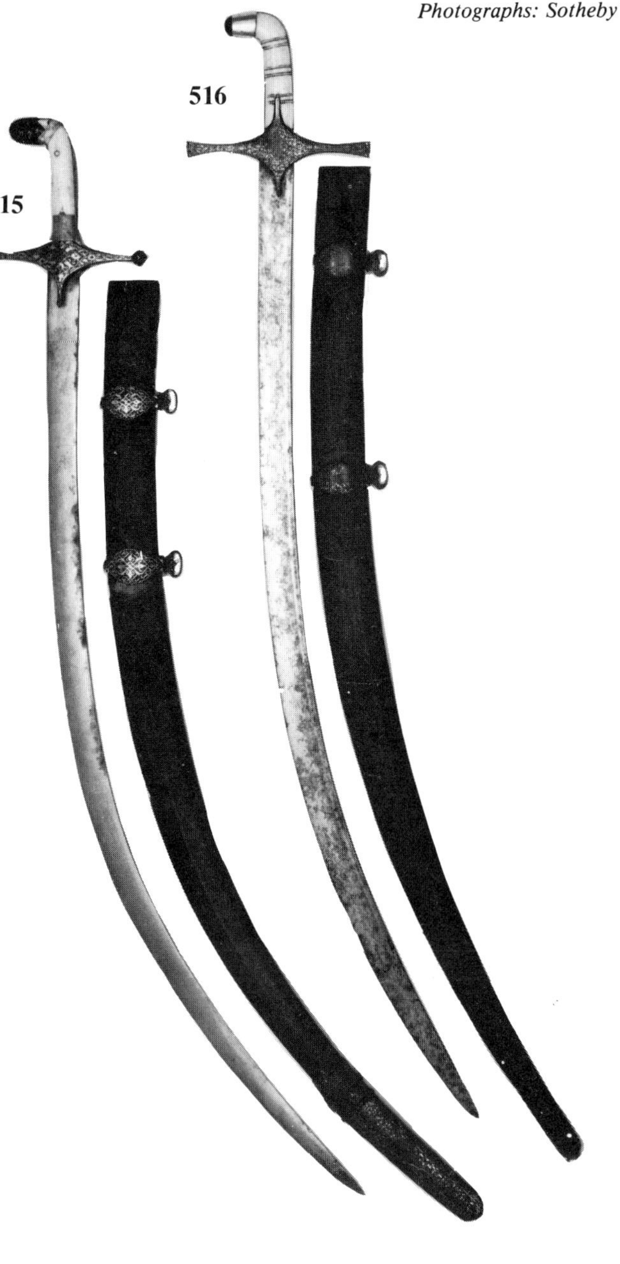

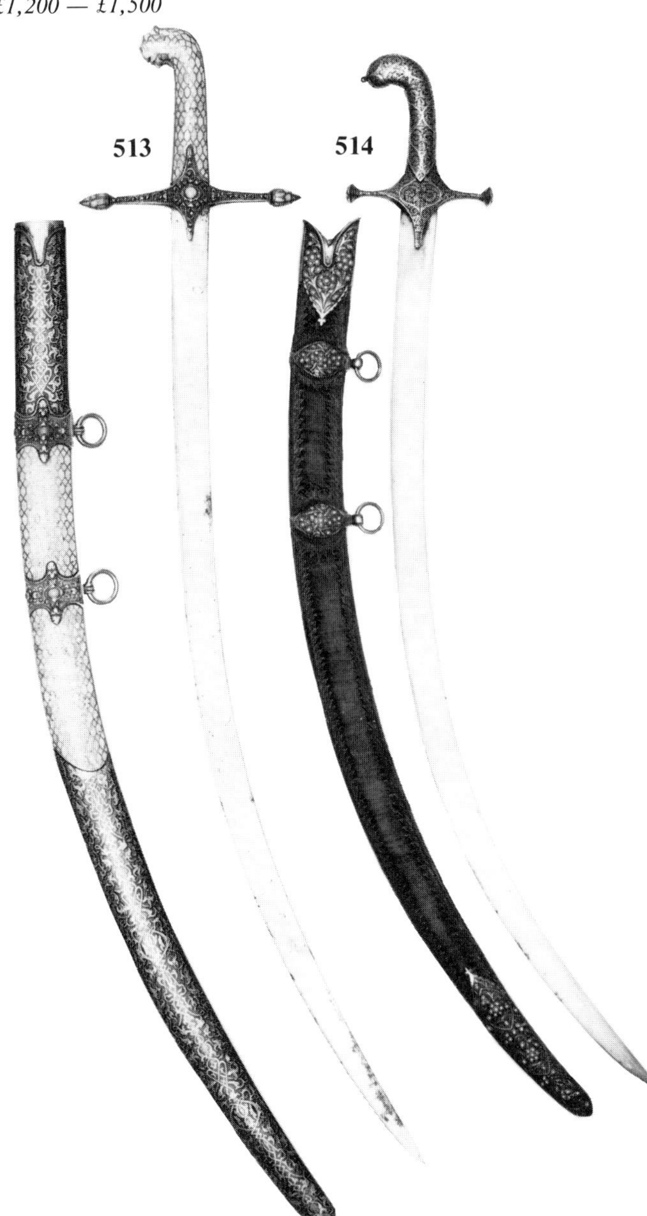

515. Persian shamshir
19th century
Another high quality sword, with gold inlaid steel mounts, but now in rather poor condition. The inlay is rubbed especially on the hilt and chape; the horn grips are fractured and bound at the guard; and the watered steel blade is worn.
£200

516. South Russian shamshir
19th century
In the same rather worn condition as 515 (clearly seen on the gold inlaid mounts and blade).
£150 — £250

517. Turkish kilij with gold-encrusted mounts
Blade 32ins. (81.3cm) Blade dated 1453
A fine sword, beautifully decorated with gold foliate arabesques on the quillons and scabbard mounts. Gold inscribed watered-steel blade dated 1453
£2,000

519. Turkish or Egyptian kilij
Length 35½ins. (90.2cm) 19th century
Quillons, scabbard mounts and blade inlaid with gold calligraphy. Horn scale grips and cloth-covered scabbard. Good quality and condition.
£600 — £800

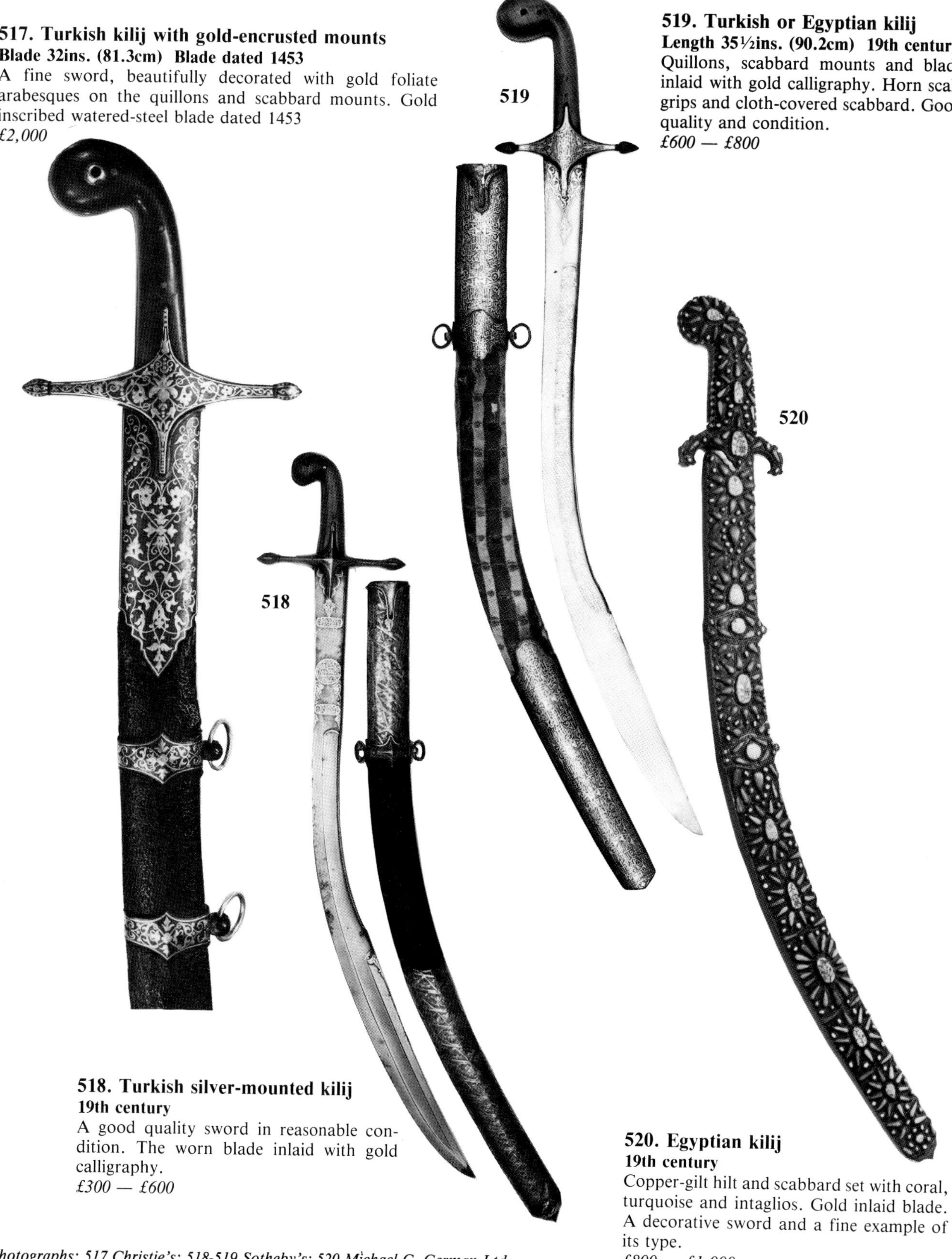

518. Turkish silver-mounted kilij
19th century
A good quality sword in reasonable condition. The worn blade inlaid with gold calligraphy.
£300 — £600

520. Egyptian kilij
19th century
Copper-gilt hilt and scabbard set with coral, turquoise and intaglios. Gold inlaid blade. A decorative sword and a fine example of its type.
£800 — £1,000

Photographs: 517 Christie's; 518-519 Sotheby's; 520 Michael C. German Ltd.

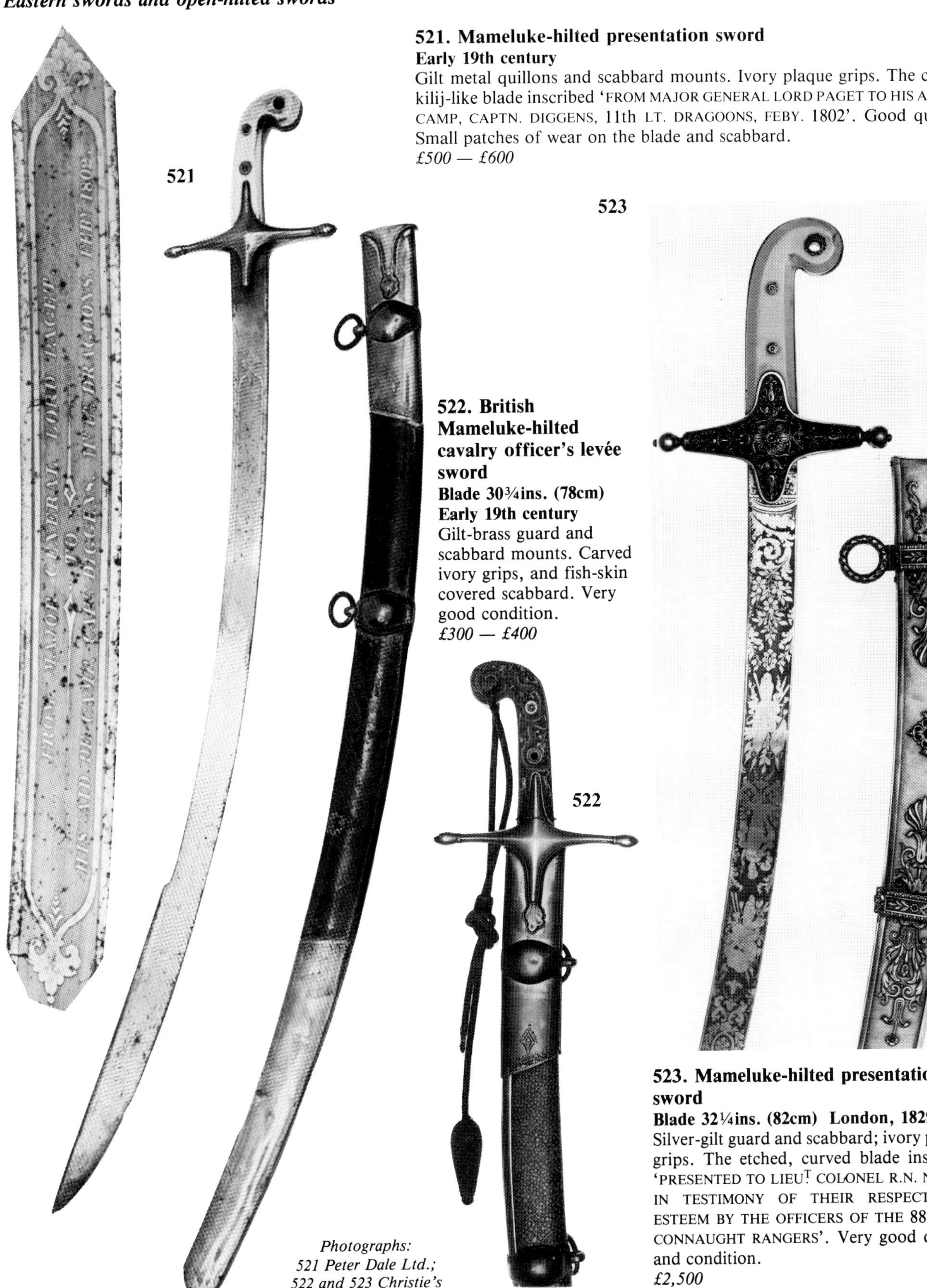

521. Mameluke-hilted presentation sword
Early 19th century
Gilt metal quillons and scabbard mounts. Ivory plaque grips. The curved kilij-like blade inscribed 'FROM MAJOR GENERAL LORD PAGET TO HIS AID-DE-CAMP, CAPTN. DIGGENS, 11th LT. DRAGOONS, FEBY. 1802'. Good quality. Small patches of wear on the blade and scabbard.
£500 — £600

522. British Mameluke-hilted cavalry officer's levée sword
Blade 30¾ins. (78cm)
Early 19th century
Gilt-brass guard and scabbard mounts. Carved ivory grips, and fish-skin covered scabbard. Very good condition.
£300 — £400

523. Mameluke-hilted presentation sword
Blade 32¼ins. (82cm) London, 1829-1830
Silver-gilt guard and scabbard; ivory plaque grips. The etched, curved blade inscribed 'PRESENTED TO LIEU^T^ COLONEL R.N. NICKLE IN TESTIMONY OF THEIR RESPECT AND ESTEEM BY THE OFFICERS OF THE 88TH, OR CONNAUGHT RANGERS'. Very good quality and condition.
£2,500

Photographs:
521 Peter Dale Ltd.;
522 and 523 Christie's

524. British general officer's sword, 1831 pattern
Blade 31ins. (78.7cm)
Mameluke hilt with gilt-brass quillons and ivory plaque grips. Etched blade. Brass scabbard. A very common sword still in use. Good condition.
£150 — £200

525. British naval sword for officers of flag rank
Blade 31ins. (78.7cm) 1842-1856
Gilt-brass quillons and scabbard mounts, the locket inscribed 'BATTEN & ADAMS' (Devonport). Ivory plaque grips. Officers of flag rank were given permission to wear Mameluke-hilted swords in 1842. The practice was abolished in 1856. Rare. Very good condition.
£400 — £500

524

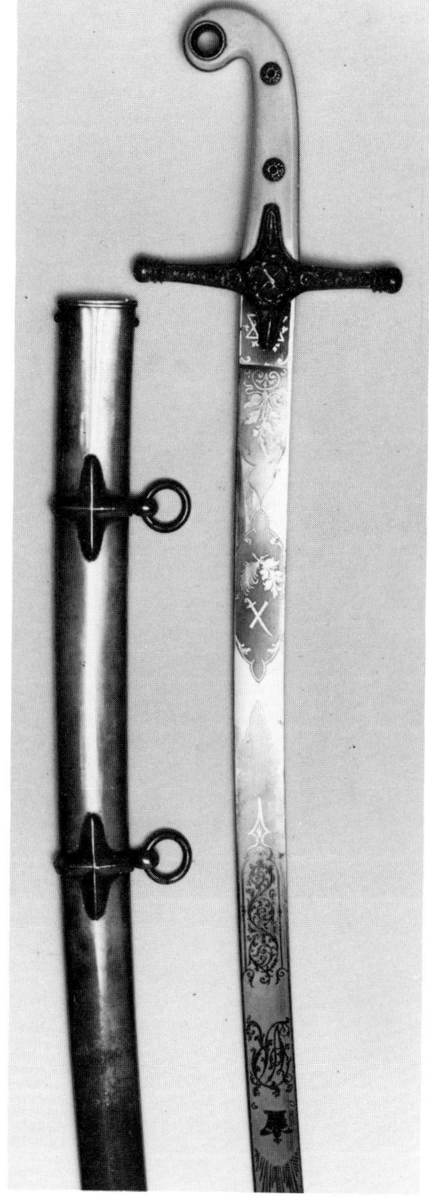

525

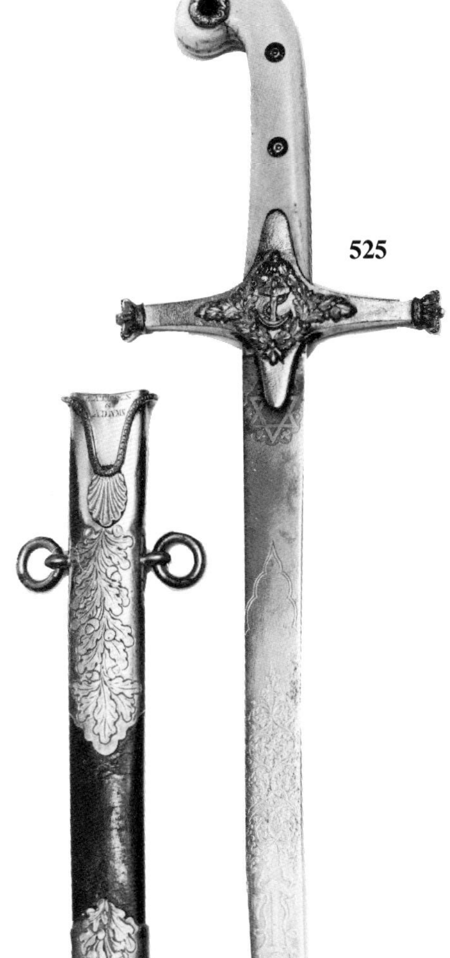

526

526. Presentation sword
Blade 31½ins. (80cm) London, 1877-1878
Silver-gilt mounted sword with maker's mark, 'RH', perhaps for Richard Hennel. Blade signed 'HENRY WILKINSON, PALL MALL, LONDON'. The portrait miniature mounted on the scabbard and the initial L on the enamel plaque on the quillon block are of the 1st Earl of Lytton, Viceroy of India 1876-80, who presented the sword at the pageant at Delhi when Queen Victoria was made Empress of India. The inscription on the blade reads 'FROM THE VICEROY, 1st JAN. 1877'. A fine quality sword complete with belt fittings, in a glazed lined case.
£800 — £900

Photographs: 524 and 526 Christie's; 525 Peter Dale Ltd.

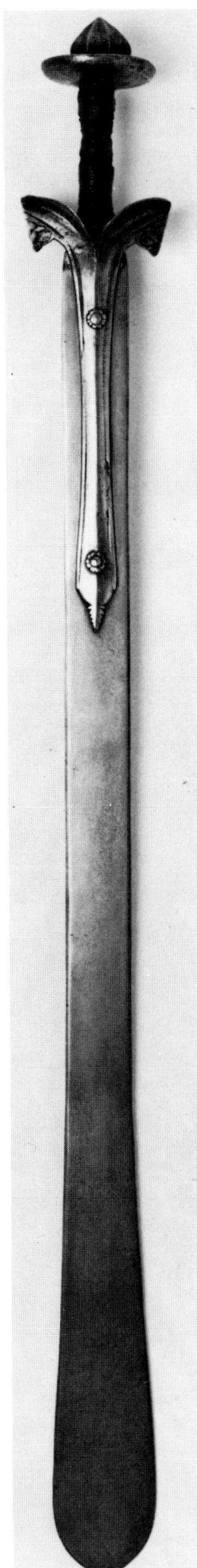

527 528

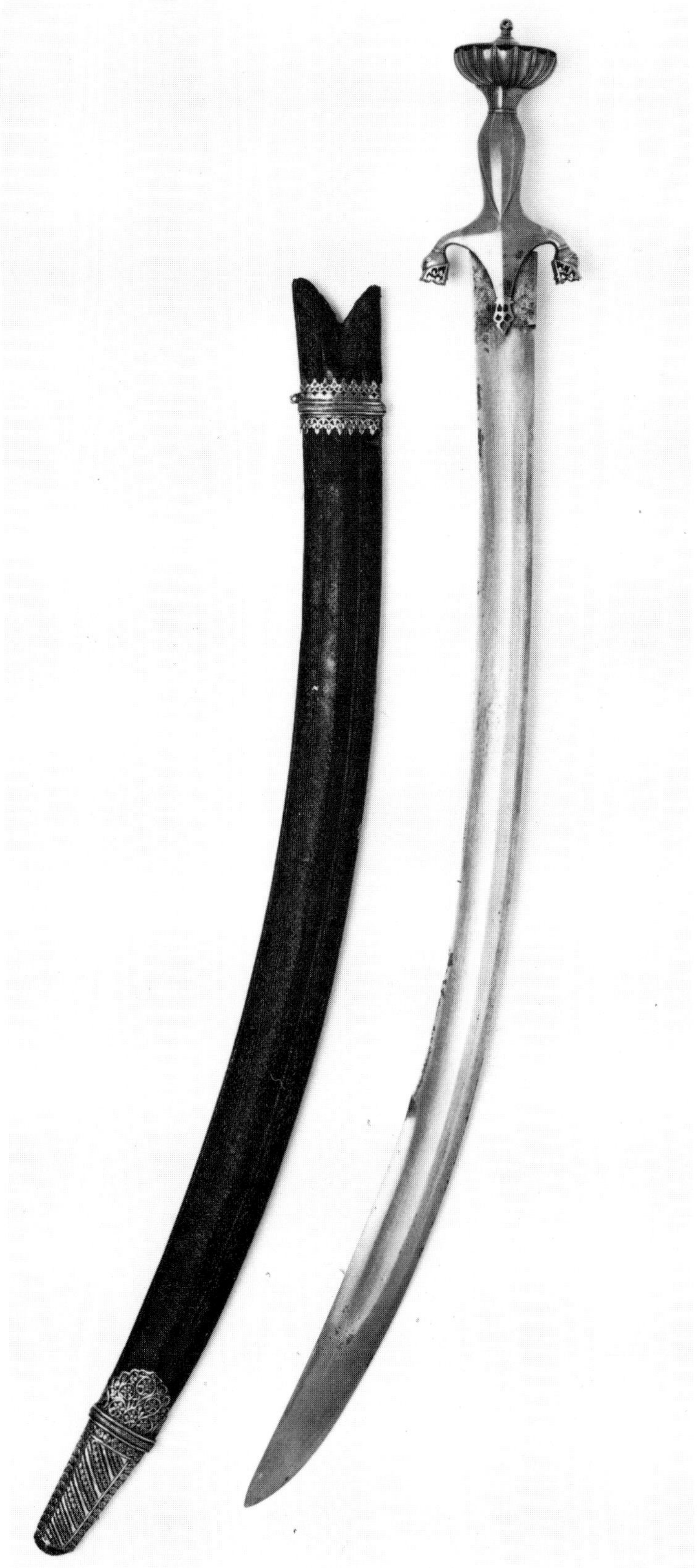

527. South Indian or Deccan sword
17th century
Steel hilt with leather-covered grip bound with cord. The two-edged blade is of spatula form.
£180 — £220

528. Afghan pulouar with silvered steel hilt
Late 17th century
Of good quality. The curved, watered steel blade with two-edged point. Tooled leather-covered scabbard stamped with scrolling foliage, and mounted with a silver locket and chape pierced with fine tracery.
£300 — £500

Photographs: Howard Ricketts Ltd.

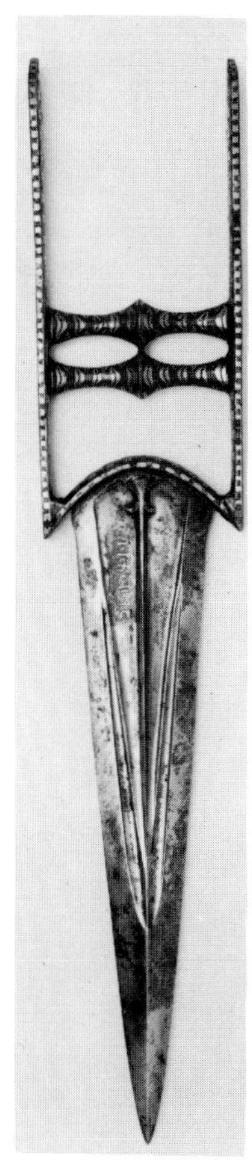

529

529. Indian tulwar and companion katar
17th or 18th century
Hilts of russet steel decorated with gold tiger-stripe inlay. Both blades inscribed in gold. Very good quality. Matching sets such as this are rare and valuable.
Sword £250 — £350
Katar £180 — £250
Together £700+

530

530. Indian silver-damascened hilted tulwar
18th century
Another very good quality example fitted with a plain, exceptionally broad blade, which is possibly original.
£300 — £350

Photographs: Howard Ricketts Ltd.

531

532. Indian tulwar with gold-mounted scabbard
Blade 34ins. (86.3cm) 18th or 19th century
Hilt of blued steel (worn) inlaid with gold flowers and leaves. The velvet-covered scabbard mounted with a finely pierced gold locket and chape. Watered steel blade. Fine quality, good condition.
£400

532

533

533. Indian tulwar
Length 35½ins. (90.2cm)
19th century
An example of good quality in a worn condition. The hilt russeted and inlaid with gold foliage and flowers.
£60 — £100

531. North Indian tulwar
Blade 29ins. (73.6cm)
18th century
Gold inlaid hilt with a knuckle guard and two side guards linked to a globular pommel. Reasonable condition.
£80 — £150

Photographs:
531-532 Christie's;
533-534 Sotheby's

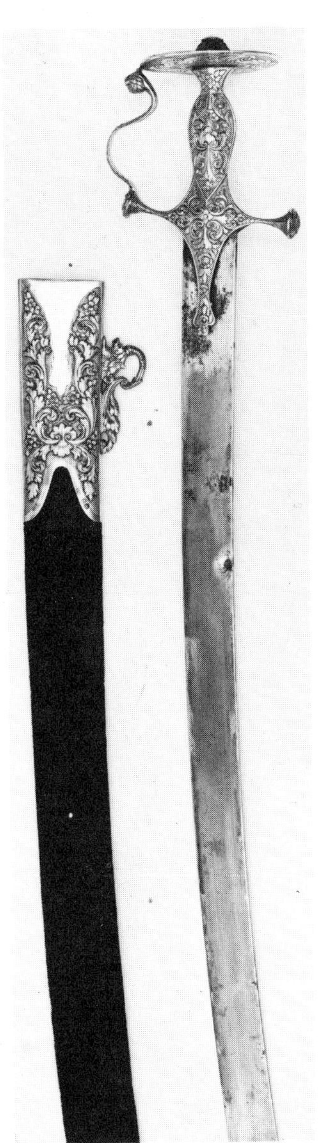

534. English silver-mounted sword modelled on an Indian tulwar
Length 38ins. (96.5cm) London, 1828-1829
Made by Samuel Whitford. Hilt and scabbard mounts of silver gilt, cast and chased with foliate and shell ornament. The worn, curved blade is associated. An unusual sword of fine quality.
£500 — £600

534

Colour Plate 7. *Scottish silver-hilted presentation broadsword, Elgin, 1701. For details see nos. 380 and 381.*
Christie's

535. Indian khanda
17th century
Hilt inlaid with gold flowers and foliage. Blade with applied pierced panels decorated *en suite*. A sword of fine quality complete with padded hilt liner, and silk-covered scabbard.
£1,000+

535

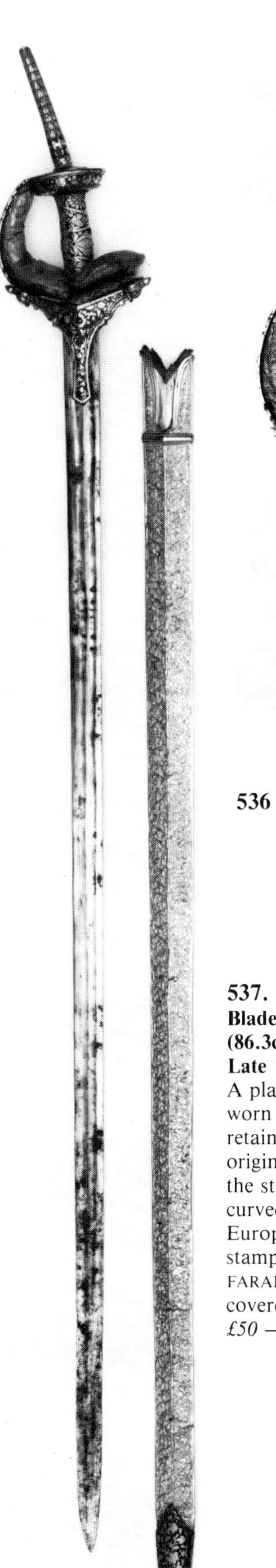

536

536. Indian firangi with gold scabbard
Length 48⅝ins. (123.5cm) 18th century
The high value of this example lies in the finely embossed gold scabbard, which is lined with wood and fitted with a gold inlaid steel chape. The gold inlay on the hilt is rubbed (see detail) and the long European single-edged blade is pitted.
£2,000 — £3,000

537. Indian firangi
Blade 34ins.
(86.3cm)
Late 18th century
A plainer, more worn example but retaining some original gilding on the steel hilt. The curved 17th century European blade stamped 'ANDRIA FARARA'. Leather covered scabbard.
£50 — £100

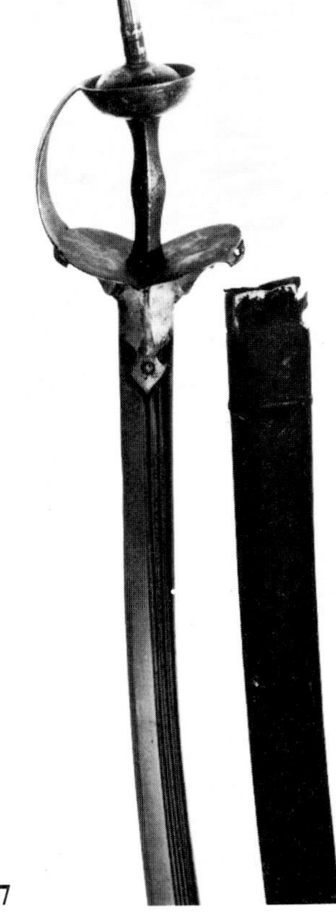

537

538. Indian case of swords
Late 18th century
Gold inlaid blued steel hilts of khanjar form. Watered-steel blades. The hilts are flattened on one side and lock together to appear as one in a single scabbard. Very rare. Fine quality.
£1,000 — £1,500

538

539. South Indian pata
Second half 18th century
Hilt of silvered steel chiselled with foliage and scrollwork. Two-edged European blade. The velvet-covered scabbard has mounts *en suite* with the hilt. Very good quality.
£600 — £1,000

539

Photographs:
538-540 Michael C. German Ltd.;
541 Christie's

540

540. South Indian pata
Second half 18th century
Brass hilt embossed in high relief with foliate panels and a grotesque mask. European blade. Good quality.
£600

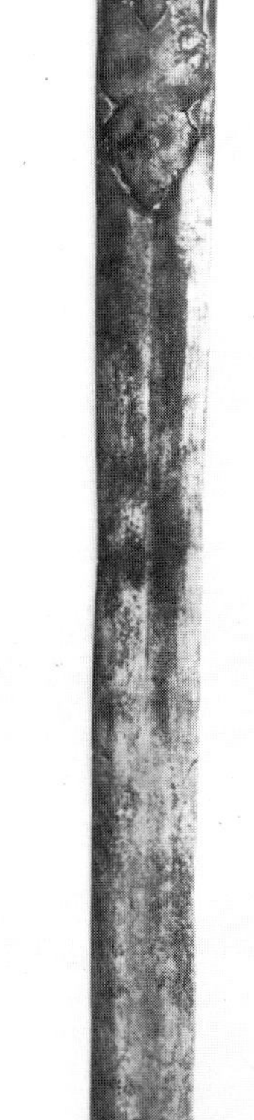

541

541. South Indian pata
Blade 38½ins. (97.8cm) 18th or 19th century
An example of reasonable quality in very poor condition. The chiselled steel hilt is rusted and corroded.
£20 — £50

543. North Indian or Nepalese ram dao (sacrificial temple sword)
19th century
Two-hand hilt of brass, with leather-covered grip. The single-edged blade finely inlaid with brass. Fine quality. Blade worn.
£280 — £300

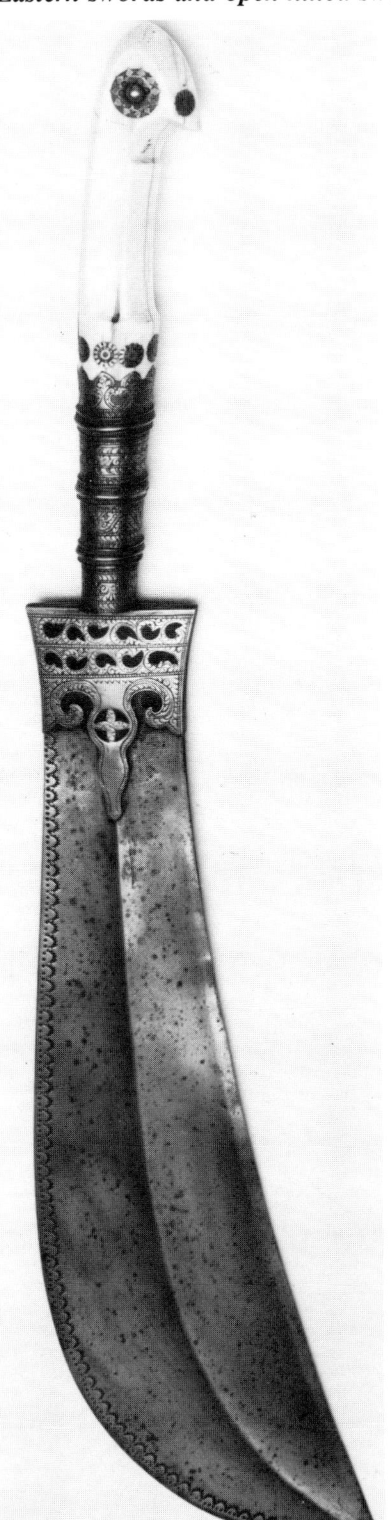

542

542. South-west Indian (Malibar coast) ivory-hilted moplah
Early 19th century
Engraved brass-mounted hilt. The shoulder of the blade encased in pierced brass and fitted with red and black enamel. Good quality. The single-edged blade with minor pitting.
£180 — £200

543

544

544. Nepalese all-steel kora
19th century
A good, fairly plain, example simply engraved on the hilt and blade.
£45 — £60

Photographs: Robert Hales Antiques Ltd.

547. Indonesian gold-mounted sword
Blade 23½ins. (59.7cm)
19th century
Hilt overlaid with embossed gold sheet. The lacquered wooden scabbard gold-mounted *en suite* with the hilt. Very good quality. The weight of gold adds value.
£300 — £400

Photographs:
545 Robert Hales Antiques Ltd.;
546-547 Christie's;
548 Michael C. German Ltd.

545. Cingalese silver-mounted kastane
Early 19th century
A fine example of a familiar and characteristic sword. The hilt and scabbard are encased in silver and decorated in relief. The eyes of the dragons' heads are set with rubies.
£450

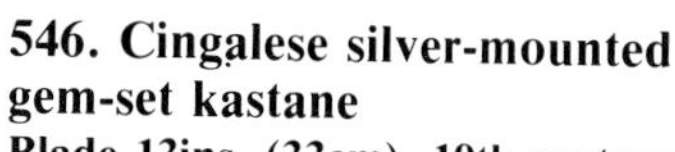

546. Cingalese silver-mounted gem-set kastane
Blade 13ins. (33cm) 19th century
A full-length view of a sword similar in form and quality to 545.
£400 — £500

548. Burmese carved-ivory ceremonial dha
Mid-19th century
Very finely pierced and carved in deep relief with monsters and animals amid foliage. Embossed silver mounts. Curved single-edged blade.
£1,000 — £1,500+

549. Burmese or Thai dha
Blade 23ins. (54.4cm) 19th century
Brass hilt with fish-skin covered grip. Cloth-covered wooden scabbard. Ordinary, and rather poor quality.
£30 — £50

550. Burmese or Thai silver-mounted dha
Length 22¼ins. (56.5cm) 19th century
The use of silver on the wooden scabbard, and on the hilt adds value. Ivory grip. Complete with carrying cord.
£40 — £80

549 550

551

552

551. Chinese brass-mounted sword
Length 29½ins. (75cm) 19th century
Hilt and scabbard mounts of brass decorated with foliage. Fish-skin covered scabbard. Good quality and condition.
£50 — £80

552. Chinese silver and jade mounted case of swords
Mid-19th century
The silver hilts are flattened on one side to enable the two swords to fit into a single scabbard. An example of fine quality, reputedly part of the Imperial wardrobe. A sword with brass fittings and with no jade plaques would be considerably less valuable.
£500+

Photographs: 549-551 Christie's; 552 Michael C. German Ltd.

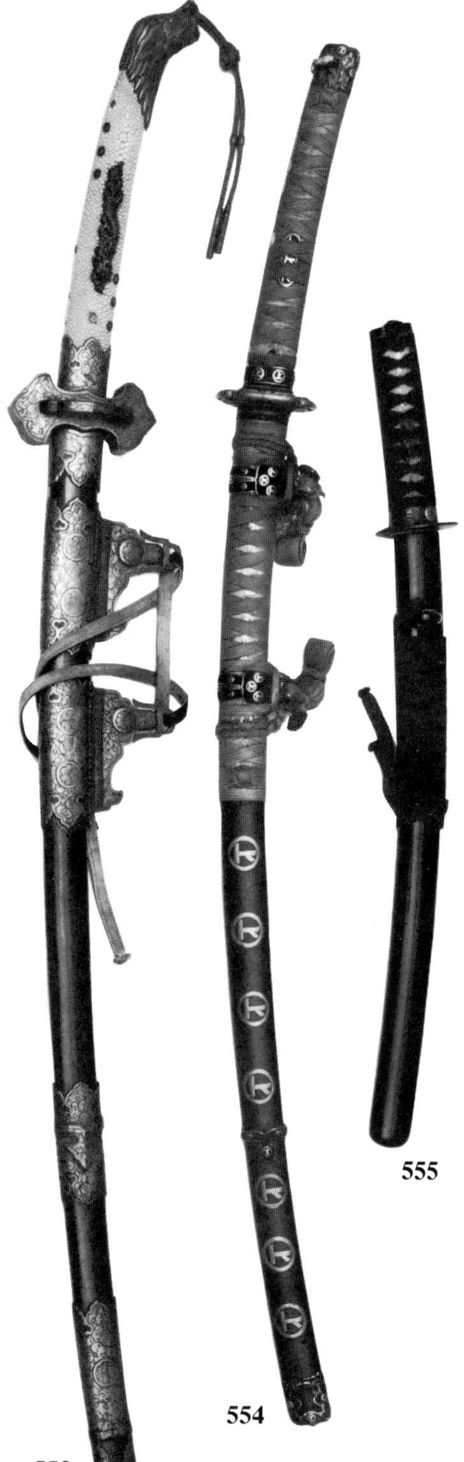

556

553. Japanese nodachi
Blade $30\frac{3}{16}$ins. (75.7cm)
Blade mid-17th century
Gilt-metal mounted hilt with fish-skin covered grip and brown lacquer scabbard mounted *en suite*. The hilt and scabbard 19th century. Blade signed 'HITACHI NO KAMI JUMYO' (of Mino).
£2,000 — £3,500

554. Japanese tachi
Blade $27\frac{9}{16}$ins. (70cm)
Blade dated 1401
Shakudo mounted hilt and scabbard 19th century. Blade signed 'BISHU OSAFUNE JU YASUMITSU' and dated 'OEI JUHACHINEN' (1401). Fine quality.
£3,000 — £4,000

555. Japanese wakizashi
Blade $15\frac{1}{2}$ins. (39.6cm)
Blade 16th century
17th century iron-mounted hilt and lacquered scabbard. The single-edged blade signed 'BISHU OSAFUNE KATSUMITSU'. Very good quality.
£400 — £600

556. Japanese katana
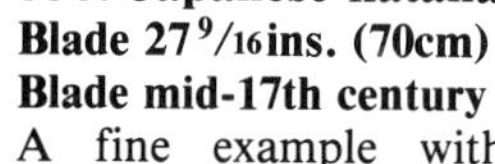
Blade $27\frac{9}{16}$ins. (70cm)
Blade mid-17th century
A fine example with 19th century shakudo-mounted hilt and scabbard of crushed shell. Blade signed 'BUNGO JU YAMASHIRO DAIJO FUJIWARA KUNIHARA.'
£2,000 — £3,000

557 558

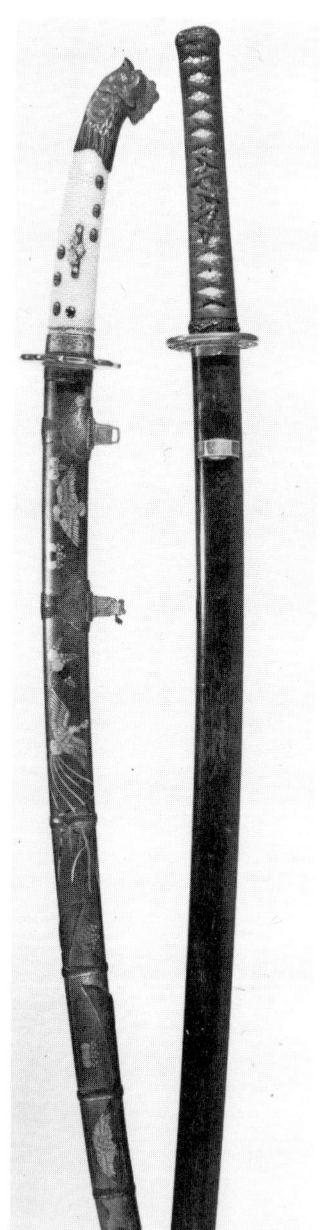

557. Japanese tachi
Blade $25\frac{1}{2}$ins. (64.8cm) Mid-17th century
A good example with metal mounts originally silvered. Blade signed 'MUSASHI NO KAMI NAGAMICHI.'
£1,000 — £3,000

558. Japanese katana
Blade $26\frac{1}{2}$ins. (67.3cm)
Blade late 17th century
Gilt-bronze tsuba (guard) and fish-skin grip bound with cord. The single-edged blade signed 'MUSASHI NO KAMI FUJIWARA KIYOSADA'. Good quality.
£1,000 — £1,500

Photographs: Christie's

2. DAGGERS, KNIVES, BAYONETS AND HUNTING ACCESSORIES — European and American

Scramasax/Baselards/Rondel daggers

559

559. Anglo-Saxon scramasax
Length 5¼ins. (13.5cm) 10th century
Iron inlaid with copper and silver and inscribed (with the name of the maker, or owner) 'OSMUND'. Rare, excavated condition. Without grip. Both sides of the scramasax are shown.
£2,000 — £2,500

562

562. French rondel dagger
Blade 15½ins. (39.4cm)
Mid-15th century
Hilt of steel with characteristic disc guard and pommel, wooden grip, and hollow ground single-edged blade. Rare. Wallace Collection, London (A726).
£1,000

560

560. Baselard
Length 14ins. (35.6cm)
14th century
Iron hilt of distinctive form overlaid with wood. Two-edged blade. Excavated condition. Quite rare.
£600 — £650

561

561. Baselard
Length 14¼ins. (36.2cm)
14th century
Similar to 560 but with a single-edged blade.
£600 — £650

563

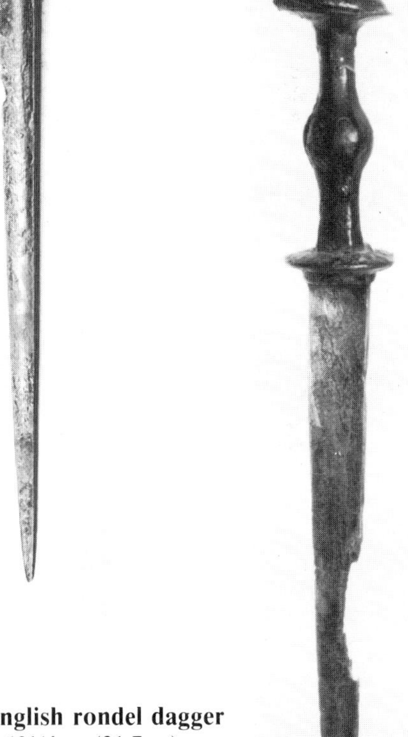

563. English rondel dagger
Length 12½ins. (31.7cm)
Mid-15th century
Steel hilt with wooden grip. Excavated condition.
£500 — £550

Photographs: 559-561 and 563 Christie's

564

564. Ballock knife, possibly English
Length 12¾ins. (32.5cm)
About 1450
Hilt of ivy root. An example in particularly good condition.
£500 — £600

565

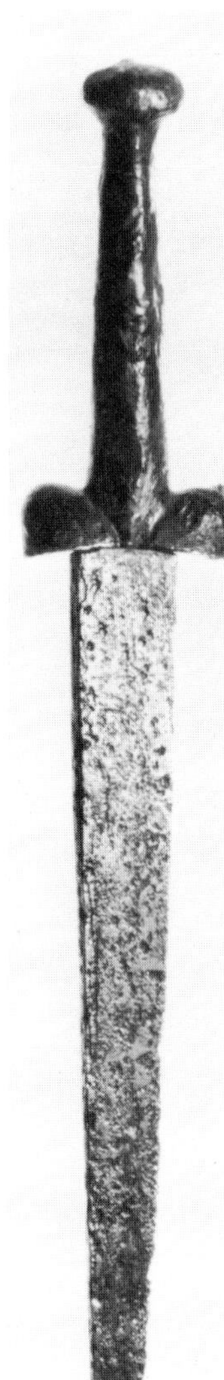

565. Ballock knife
Length 14¾ins. (37.5cm)
15th century
An example of good form with a single edged blade and a repaired wooden hilt.
£500 — £550

566 567

566. Ballock knife, possibly Flemish
Length 13ins. (33cm) 15th century
Hilt of root wood. Excavated condition.
£500 — £600

567. English ballock knife
Length 14ins. (35.5cm) 15th century
Hilt of root walnut. The heavily corroded blade has traces of gold inlay.
£300 — £400

568

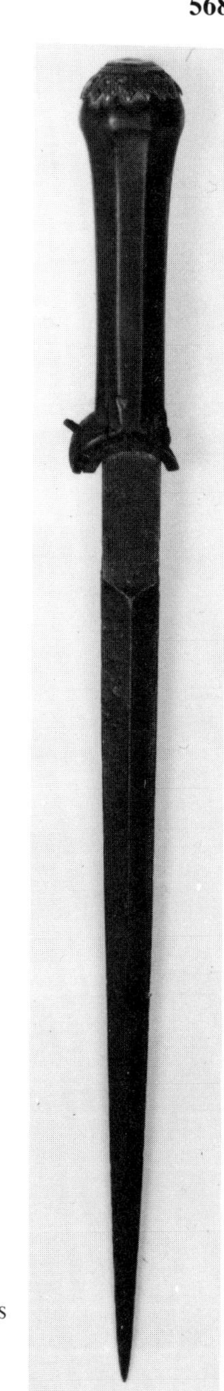

568. Scottish or English ballock knife
Length 15¼ins. (38.7cm)
About 1610-1619
Ebony hilt with some parts missing. Blade etched with the initials 'HW' conjoined, and the date 161... Rare.
£600 — £800

Photographs:
564, 566 and 567 Sotheby's;
565 and 568 Christie's

569. Venetian ear dagger
Blade 8¼ins. (21cm) About 1500
Hilt of steel mounted with horn plaques. Note the robust tang of the blade at the centre of the grip. Rare, fine quality. Wallace Collection, London (A737).
£1,000+

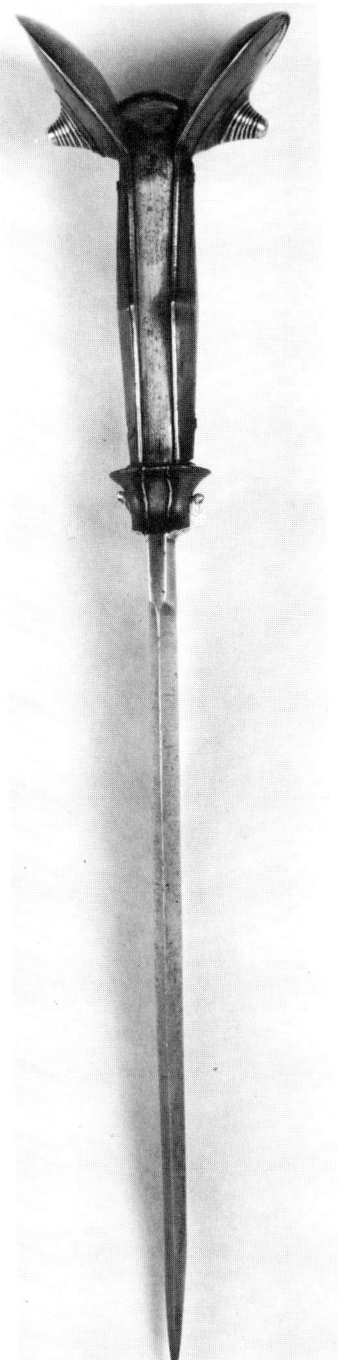

569

570. Spanish ear dagger
Length 13ins. (33cm) Late 15th century
In an excavated condition, but indicating its original fine quality by the remaining traces of gold on the grip.
£800

570

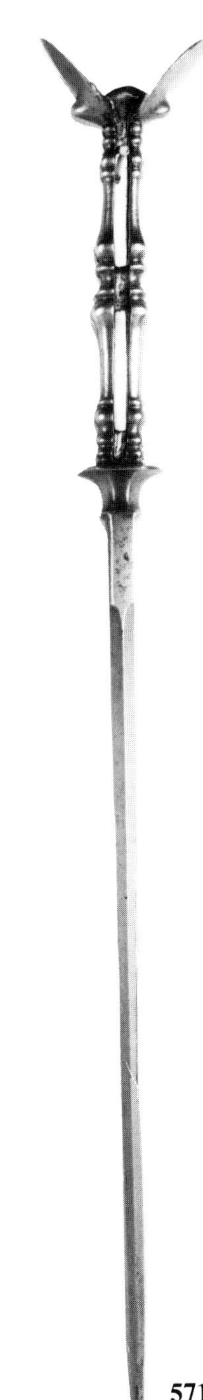

571

571. Venetian all-steel ear dagger
Blade 8¼ins. (21cm) 16th century
Steel hilt, of baluster form, wrought in one piece. Fine quality. Wallace Collection, London (A736).
£1,000+

Photograph: 570 Christie's

572

572. Brass-hilted dagger of quillon type
Length 16ins. (40.6cm) Late 15th century
A dagger of rare form with a heavily corroded blade. One quillon is incomplete.
£800 — £850

573

573. Quillon dagger, possibly Italian
Length 13¼ins. (33.6cm) About 1540
Hilt of steel with later grip.
£500

574

574. German quillon dagger
Length 14½ins. (36.8cm)
About 1525-1550
A good example but worn. The grip is probably a replacement.
£500 — £600

575

575. English quillon dagger
Length 12¼ins. (31cm) Dated 1628
Silver encrusted hilt with fluted snake-wood grip. Etched saw-edged blade with reinforced point inscribed 'OMNIA VINCIT AMOR' (Love conquers all), and 'FEARE GOD, HONOR Y KING'. A fine and rare dagger with tooled leather-covered sheath, complete with bodkin. The companion knife (or byknife) is missing. Tower of London Armouries (X-267).
£1,000+

576

576. Swiss Holbein dagger
Dated 1592
A fine and rare example with a wooden sheath overlaid in gilt metal, pierced and chased with the death of Virginia. The two small knives which fit into compartments on the sheath are missing. Victoria and Albert Museum (2188-1855).
£1,500

Photographs: 572-574 Christie's; 575 Crown Copyright

577. German Landsknecht dagger
Length 17¾ins. (45cm) Early 16th century
The grip is later. Good condition.
£800 — £1,000

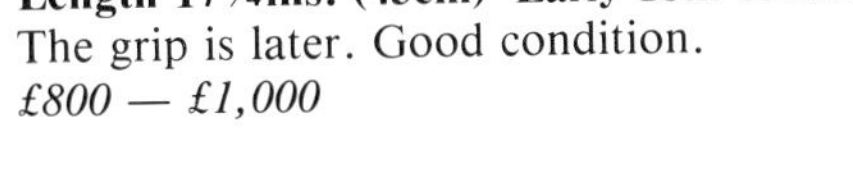

577

578

578. German Landsknecht dagger
Length 14¾ins. (37.5cm)
Early 16th century
The horn grip studded with nails. Rare and in good condition.
£700 — £800

579. German Landsknecht dagger
Length 14¼ins. (36.2cm) About 1550
An example of more familiar form with blackened steel pommel, guard and associated scabbard. The wire binding on the cone-shaped wooden grip is missing. Rare.
£900 — £1,000

579

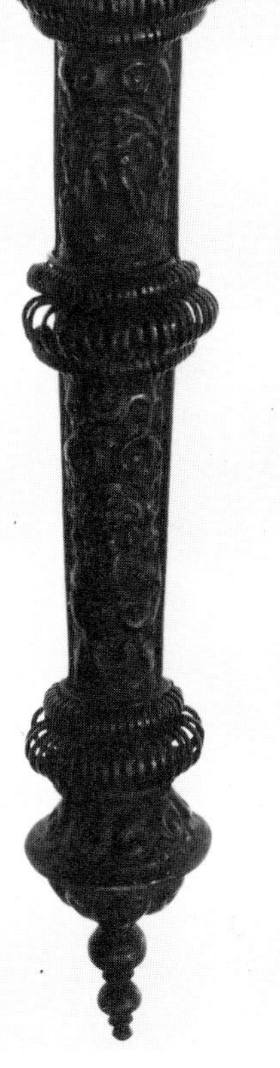

580

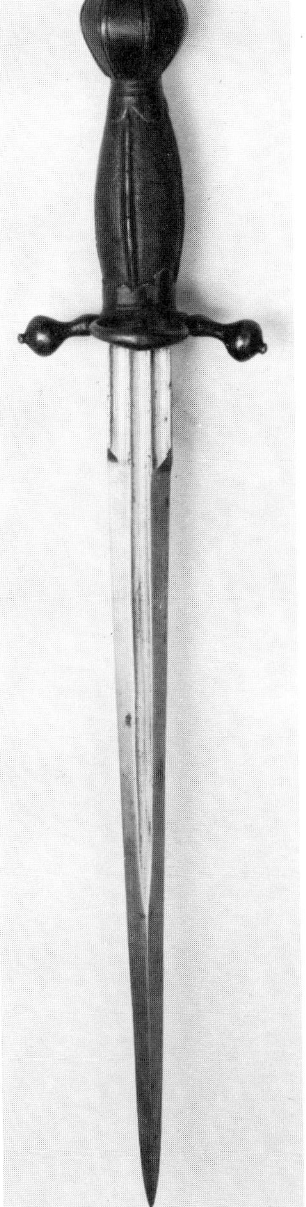

580. Saxon Landsknecht dagger
Length 15¼ins. (38.7cm) About 1570-1580
Blued steel hilt with side ring and fish-skin covered grip. The blade with reinforced armour-piercing point. A very good example.
£1,000

Photographs: Christie's

581. Left-hand dagger in the Spanish style
Length 18¼ins. (46.4cm)
Second half 16th century
Blackened hilt of steel with side ring. Robust blade with 'swordbreaker' edges. Rare, fine quality and condition. Victoria and Albert Museum (M.1-1946).
£2,000

582. Saxon left-hand dagger
Length 19½ins. (49.5cm)
About 1590-1610
Hilt of blued steel with a side ring filled with a pierced plate. Fine condition. Of the type carried by the Saxon Electoral Guard (see also 70).
£4,000 — £6,000

581

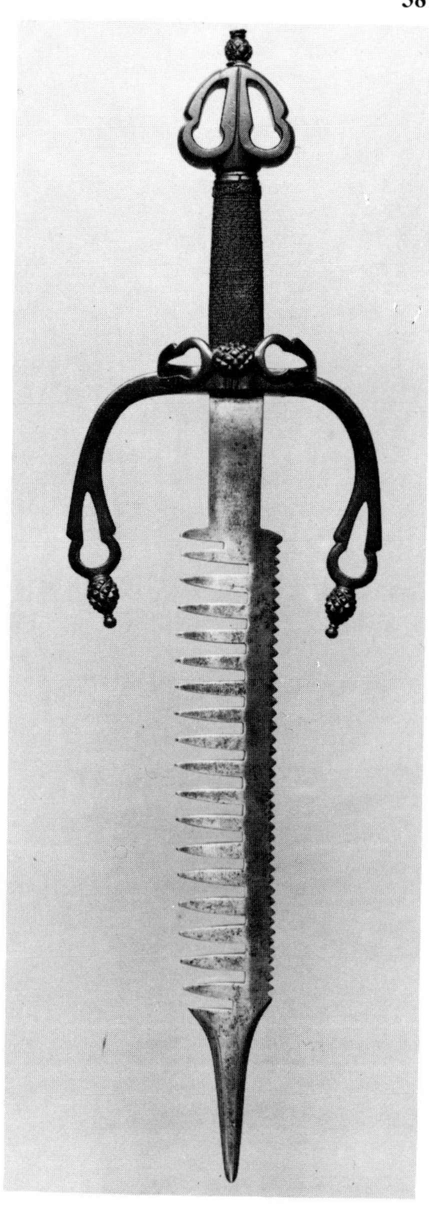

582

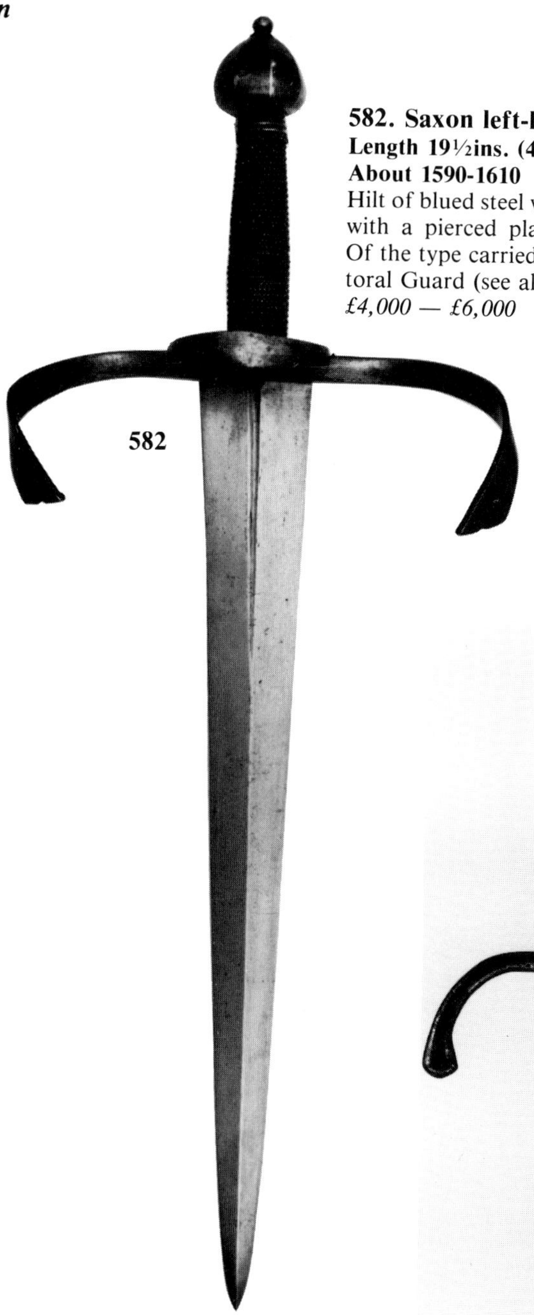

583

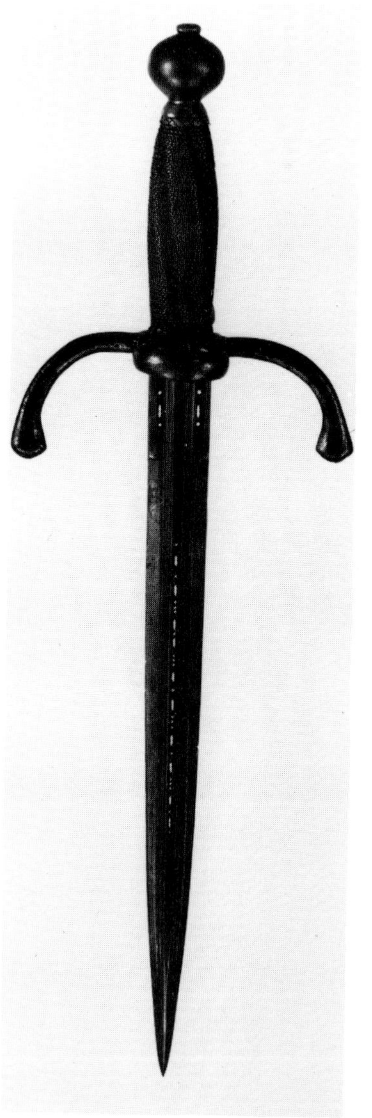

583. German left-hand dagger
Length 15¾ins. (40cm) About 1600
Steel hilt with associated pommel. Pierced and fullered blade with reinforced point. Good condition.
£600 — £800

Photographs: 582 Sotheby's; 583 Christie's

585. Saxon left-hand dagger
Length 15¼ins. (38.7cm) About 1590-1610
Silver plated steel hilt with side ring. A fine example which could form a garniture with rapier 69. Silver plating worn.
£1,000 — £1,500

586. German or English left-hand dagger
Length 15ins. (38.1cm) About 1600-1620
Silver-encrusted hilt with later copper wire binding on the grip. Associated pierced blade. Originally of fine quality.
£1,000

584. German left-hand dagger
Length 18¾ins. (47.6cm) About 1600
Hilt of steel with side ring, later grip and associated pommel. Rather poor condition.
£300 — £400

Photographs: 584 Sotheby's; 585 and 586 Christie's

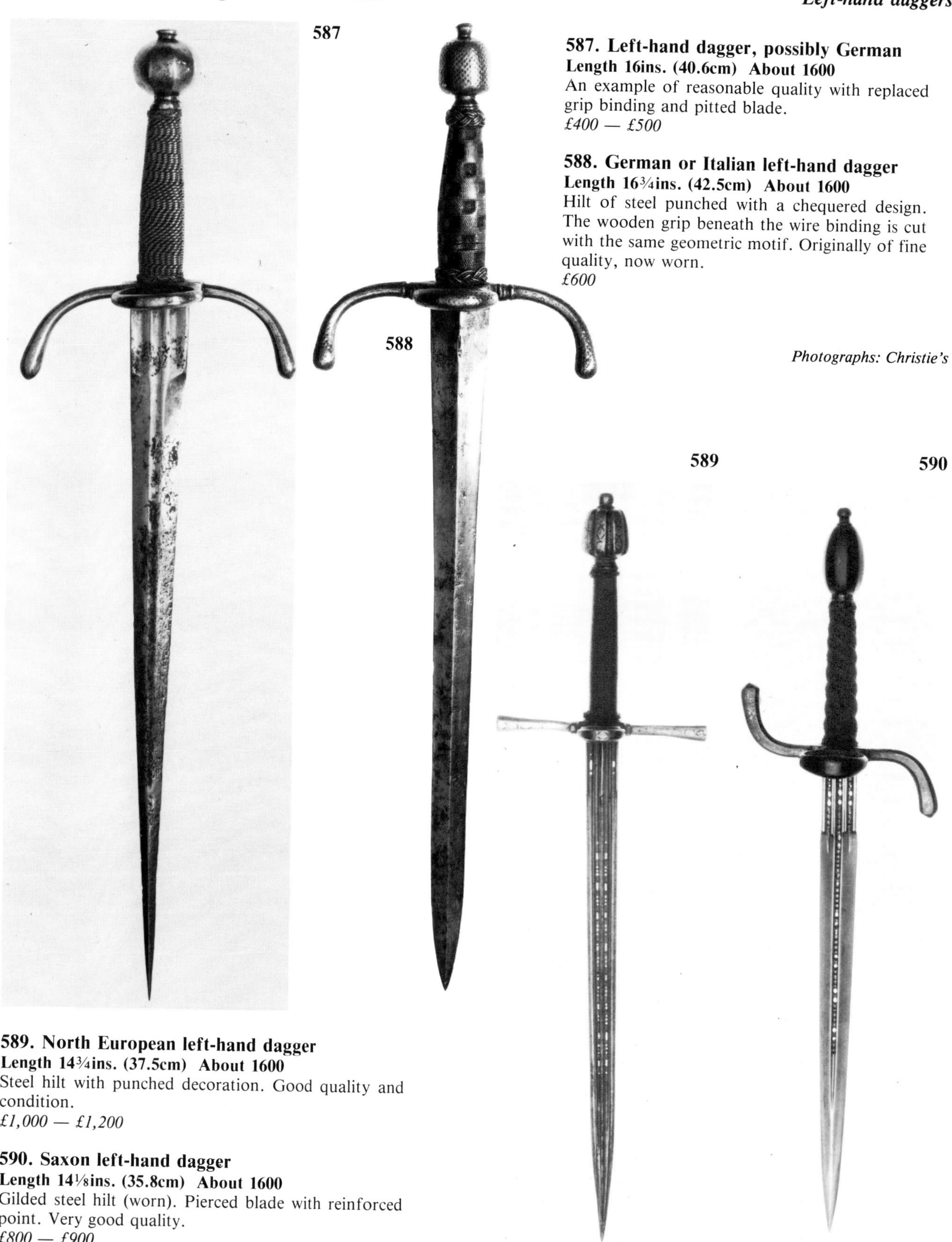

587. Left-hand dagger, possibly German
Length 16ins. (40.6cm) About 1600
An example of reasonable quality with replaced grip binding and pitted blade.
£400 — £500

588. German or Italian left-hand dagger
Length 16¾ins. (42.5cm) About 1600
Hilt of steel punched with a chequered design. The wooden grip beneath the wire binding is cut with the same geometric motif. Originally of fine quality, now worn.
£600

Photographs: Christie's

589. North European left-hand dagger
Length 14¾ins. (37.5cm) About 1600
Steel hilt with punched decoration. Good quality and condition.
£1,000 — £1,200

590. Saxon left-hand dagger
Length 14⅛ins. (35.8cm) About 1600
Gilded steel hilt (worn). Pierced blade with reinforced point. Very good quality.
£800 — £900

Photographs:
591 and 592 Christie's;
593 Peter Dale Ltd.

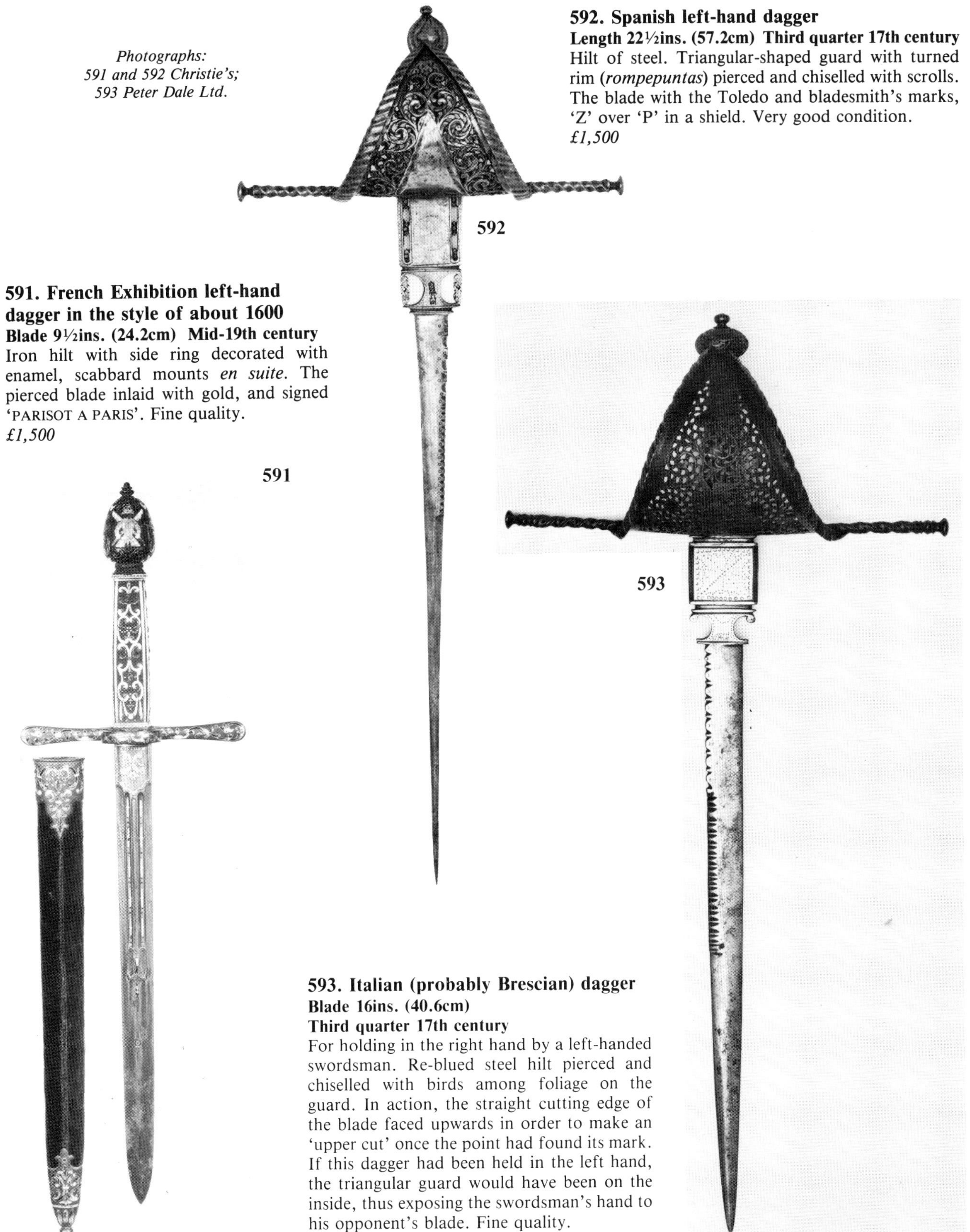

592. Spanish left-hand dagger
Length 22½ins. (57.2cm) Third quarter 17th century
Hilt of steel. Triangular-shaped guard with turned rim (*rompepuntas*) pierced and chiselled with scrolls. The blade with the Toledo and bladesmith's marks, 'Z' over 'P' in a shield. Very good condition.
£1,500

591. French Exhibition left-hand dagger in the style of about 1600
Blade 9½ins. (24.2cm) Mid-19th century
Iron hilt with side ring decorated with enamel, scabbard mounts *en suite*. The pierced blade inlaid with gold, and signed 'PARISOT A PARIS'. Fine quality.
£1,500

593. Italian (probably Brescian) dagger
Blade 16ins. (40.6cm)
Third quarter 17th century
For holding in the right hand by a left-handed swordsman. Re-blued steel hilt pierced and chiselled with birds among foliage on the guard. In action, the straight cutting edge of the blade faced upwards in order to make an 'upper cut' once the point had found its mark. If this dagger had been held in the left hand, the triangular guard would have been on the inside, thus exposing the swordsman's hand to his opponent's blade. Fine quality.
£1,500

594. Brescian left-hand dagger
Length 24¼ins. (61.5cm) Third quarter 17th century
The hilt of steel with pierced and chiselled dome-shaped guard. The forte of the blade shaped, pierced and notched for sword catching. Fine quality and condition.
£1,500

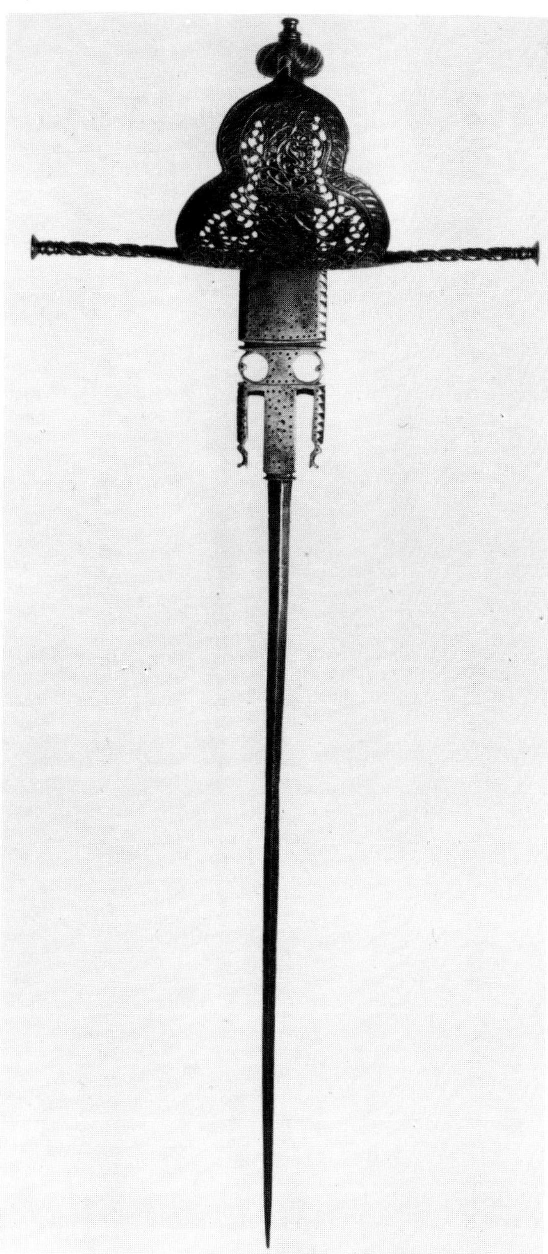

594

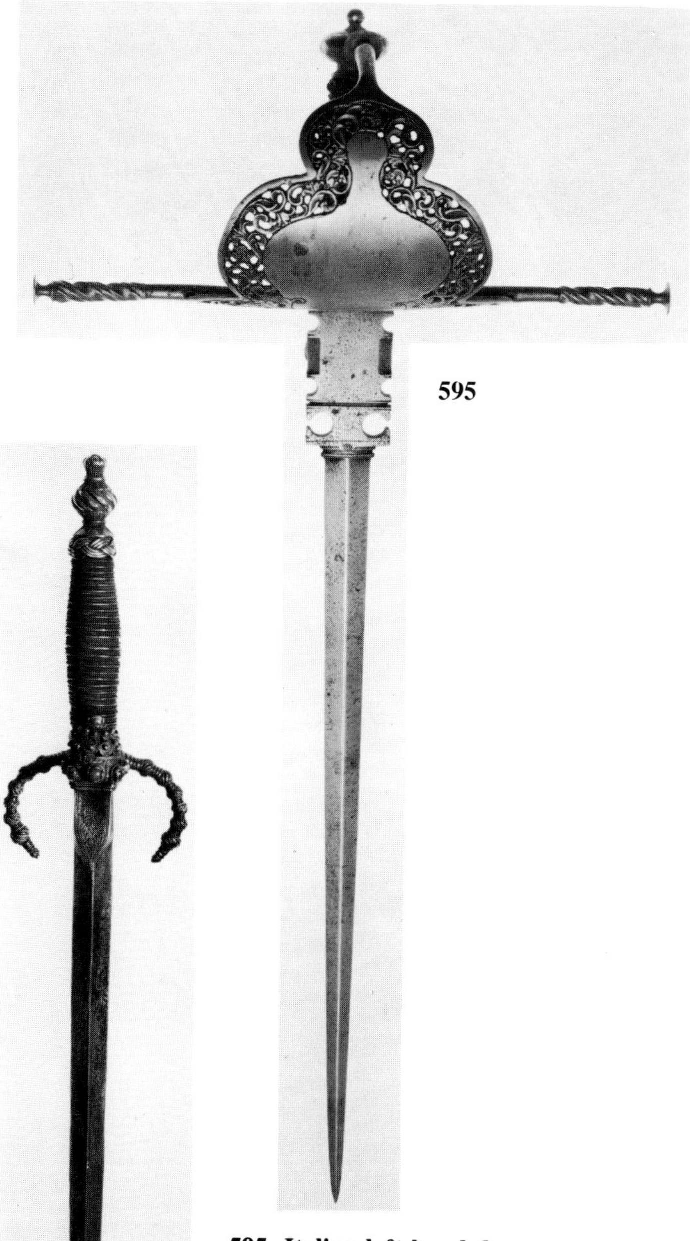

595

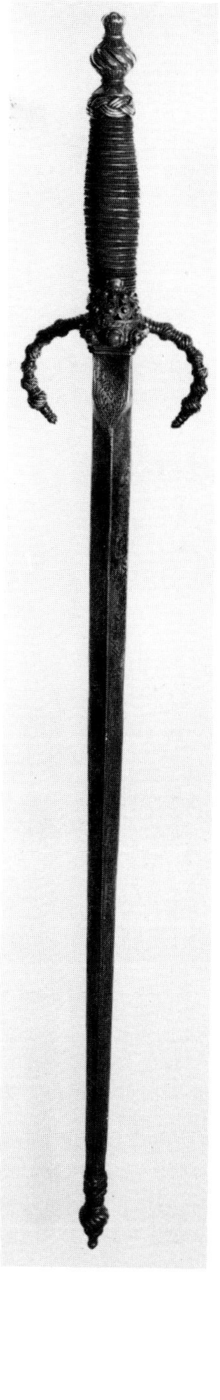

595. Italian left-hand dagger
Length 20¼ins. (51.4cm)
Third quarter 17th century
The steel hilt with guard similar to 594, chiselled and pierced on the border with foliate scrolls. Very good quality and condition.
£1,500

596. Venetian or Dalmatian schiavona dagger
Length 21¾ins. (55.2cm) Dated 1775
Silver-gilt hilt and engraved scabbard. The small dome-shaped side ring set with turquoise and decorated with filigree. The scabbard with the initials 'C.P.S' and dated 1775. Quite rare, very good condition.
£1,000 — £1,200

596

Photographs: Christie's

597. Italian all-steel stiletto
Length 10⅛ins. (26cm) 17th century
A typical example in good condition.
£300 — £400

598. Italian all-steel stiletto
17th century
Of good quality and condition.
£300 — £400

599. Italian all-steel dagger
About 1650
This good example is robust enough to have been used as a left-hand parrying dagger.
£400

600. Italian all-steel gunner's (or bombardier's) stiletto
Length 19¼ins. (48.1cm)
Second half 17th century
The narrow triangular blade is etched with a scale for converting weight of shot into calibre. Fine quality.
£600 — £700

601. Italian gunner's (or bombardier's) stiletto
Length 24ins. (61cm)
Second half 17th century
Iron hilt with writhen horn grip studded with horn pellets and brass nails. Familiar and in reasonable condition.
£350 — £400

Photographs: 597 and 598 Sotheby's; 599 Peter Dale Ltd.; 600-601 Christie's

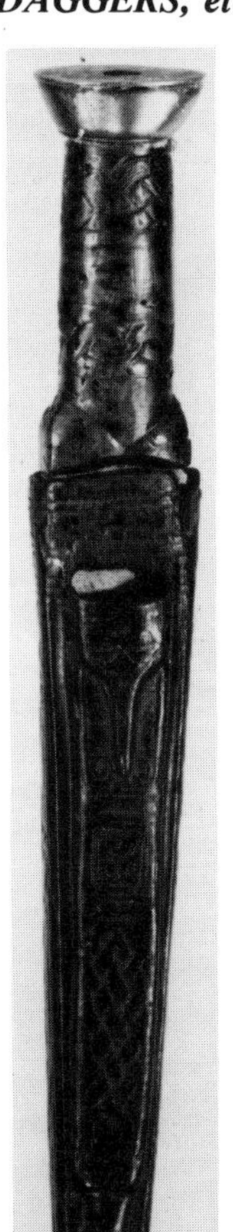

602

602. Scottish highland dirk
Blade 13ins. (33cm) Last quarter 17th century
Hilt of carved root wood. The tooled leather scabbard, with compartment for a byknife, marked with a crowned hammer between the initials 'IC'. Rare.
£400 — £450

603

603. Brass-mounted highland dirk
Length 20ins. (50.8cm)
Early 18th century
The single-edged blade with a running wolf mark has been cut down from a sword blade.
£400 — £500

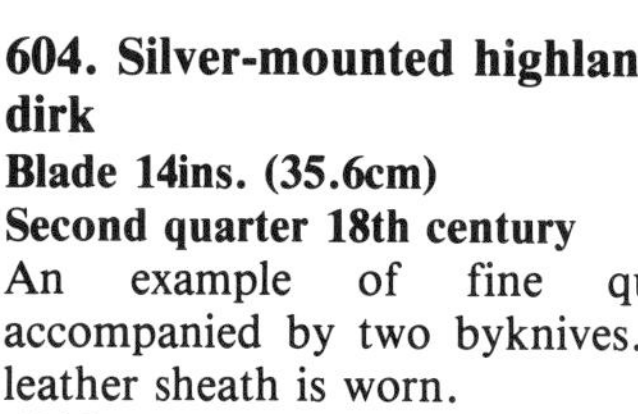

604

604. Silver-mounted highland dirk
Blade 14ins. (35.6cm)
Second quarter 18th century
An example of fine quality accompanied by two byknives. The leather sheath is worn.
£500

605. Brass-mounted highland dirk
Blade 15ins. (38.1cm)
Third quarter 18th century
Carved wooden hilt and heavily worn blade.
£300 — £400

606. Highland dirk
Blade 15½ins. (39.4cm)
Third quarter 18th century
Brass-mounted carved wooden hilt and saw-backed blade. Reasonable condition.
£300 — £400

605 606 607

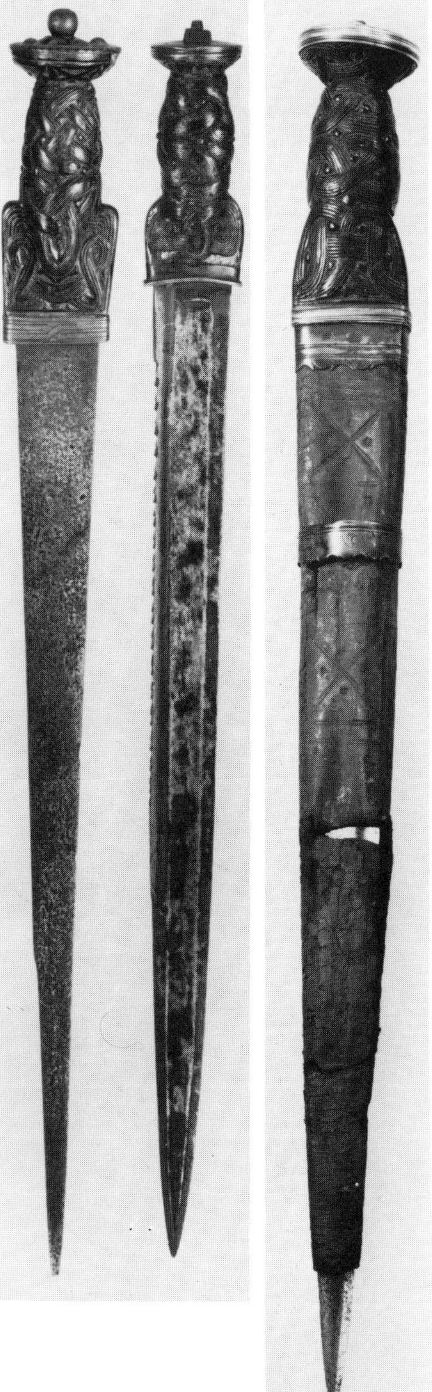

607. Silver-mounted highland dirk
Length 19ins. (48.2cm) Third quarter 18th century
Originally of fine quality but now much worn and without the byknife.
£250 — £300

Photographs: Christie's

608. Brass-mounted highland dirk
Length 18¾ins. (47.6cm) Last quarter 18th century
Carved wood hilt with brass nails and tooled leather scabbard. Very good quality.
£400 — £500

609. Silver-mounted dress dirk
Length 19ins. (48.2cm) London, 1842-1843
A fine example stamped with an unidentified maker's mark, 'WF'. The pommels of the dirk and its companion knives are set with pieces of cut glass representing cairngorms.
£500 — £600

608 **609**

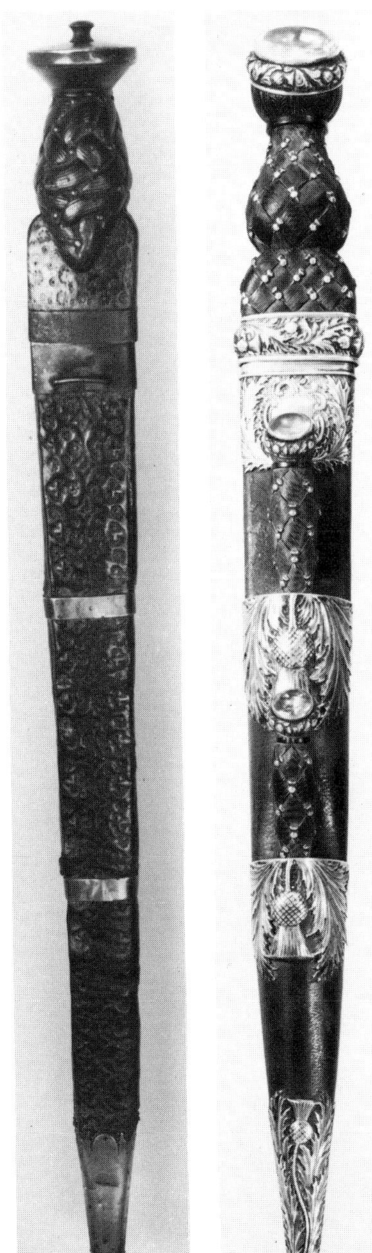

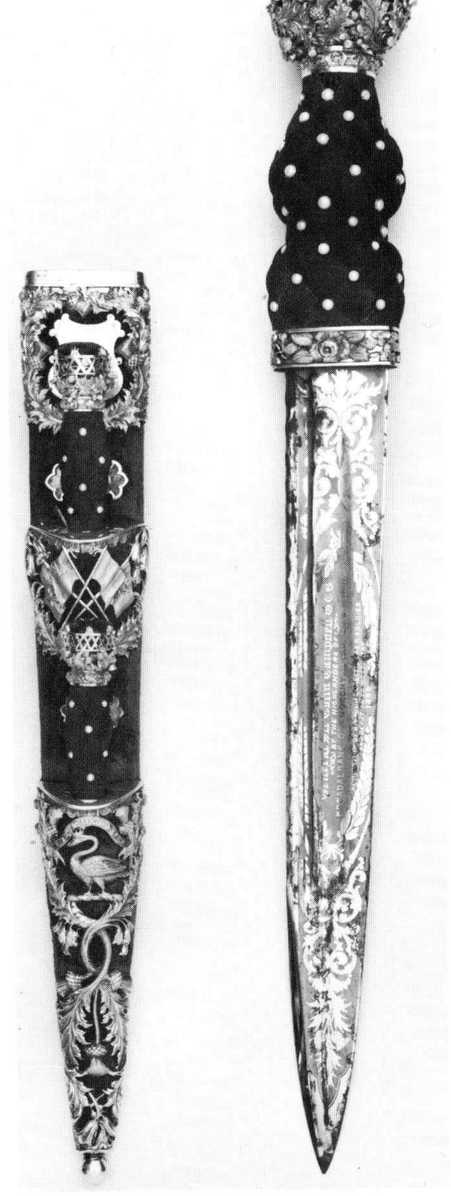

610

611

610. Silver-mounted presentation dirk
Edinburgh, 1881-1882
The carved wood hilts of the dirk and byknives are mounted in silver and set with cairngorm pommels. The etched blade inscribed 'PRESENTED TO GENERAL SIR COLIN CAMPBELL, G.C.B. BY THE HIGHLANDERS OF BREADALBANE, GLENORCHY AND NETHER LORNE, AS A MARK OF ADMIRATION OF HIS HIGH QUALITIES AS A SOLDIER AND DEVOTION TO HIS COUNTRY, 1856'. The hallmarks, later than the date of the inscription, suggest that the dirk has been refurbished. Fine quality, a little worn on the blade.
£800 — £1,200

611. Dirk of the 74th Highland Regiment
Length 17½ins. (44.5cm) Second half 19th century
An example in very fine condition with gilt-brass mounts and cairngorm pommels. The saw-backed blade etched with the Victorian cypher, and signed 'HENRY WILKINSON, PALL MALL, LONDON'.
£500 — £600

Photographs: Christie's

612 613

614 615

612. Italian hunting dirk
Length 18ins. (45.7cm) About 1750
Ivory grip and single-edged blade with bodkin tip. Complete with steel-mounted leather scabbard. Reasonable condition. The blade and scabbard worn.
£80 — £100

613. Genoese silver-mounted dirk
Length 16ins. (40.6cm)
About 1750-1760
The fullered blade heavily pitted.
£20 — £30

614. Italian silver-mounted dirk
Length 10ins. (25,4cm)
Mid-18th century
An example with a blade of diamond section. Poor condition.
£10 — £25

615. Italian dirk
Length 13¾ins. (33.7cm)
Mid-18th century
A better quality example with a writhen horn grip. The blade is chiselled at the forte with leaves.
£80 — £120

Photographs: Christie's

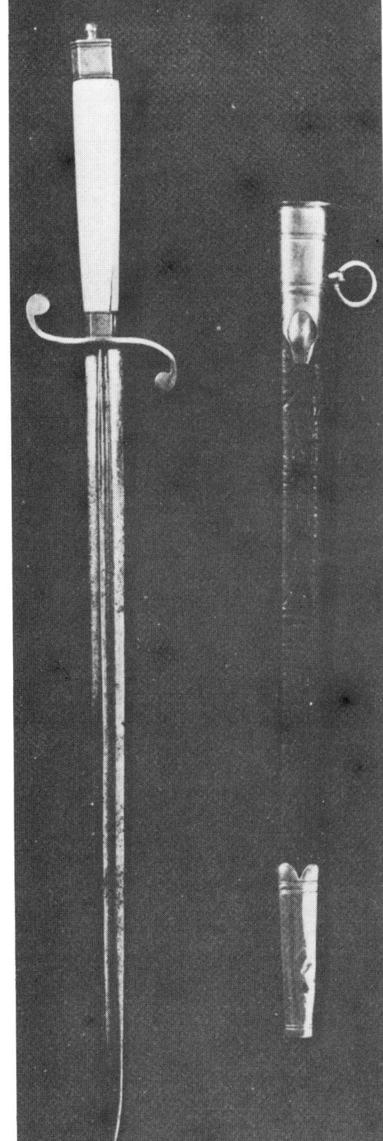

616

616. British naval dirk
About 1780-1820
Gilt-brass mounted hilt and tooled leather scabbard. Ivory grip and straight blade. Good quality and condition. National Maritime Museum (No. 109).
£150 — £300

617

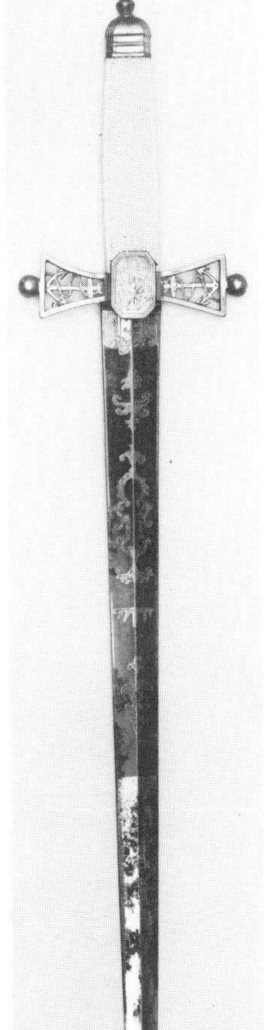

618

618. American naval dirk
Length 10¼ins. (26cm)
Early 19th century
A very good example with brass guard and scabbard (worn) and ivory grip. Etched, blued and gilt blade.
£300 — £350

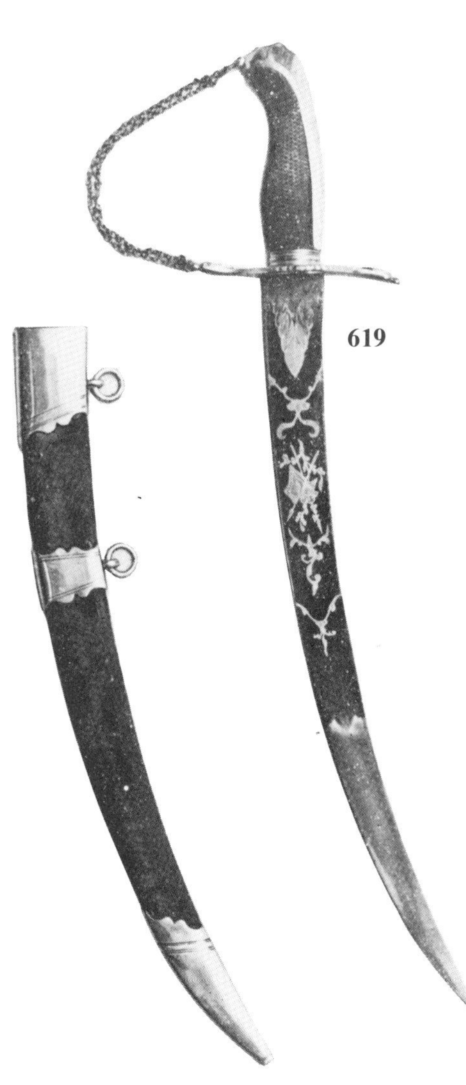

619

617. Dirk of Captain Robert Cuthbert
Length 21½ins. (54.6cm)
About 1800
Hilt of gilt-copper with chequered ivory grip. The blued and gilt two-edged blade is worn. The scabbard is missing but the mounts (not shown) are signed on the locket 'PROSSER, CHARING CROSS, LONDON'. A very attractive example. See 281 for the sword once belonging to this officer.
£400 — £500

619. British naval curved dirk
Early 19th century
Gilt-metal hilt with chequered ebony grip and chainlet. Blued and gilt single-edged blade. Fine quality and condition. National Maritime Museum (No. 18).
£400 — £500

Photographs: 617 Sotheby's; 618 Christie's

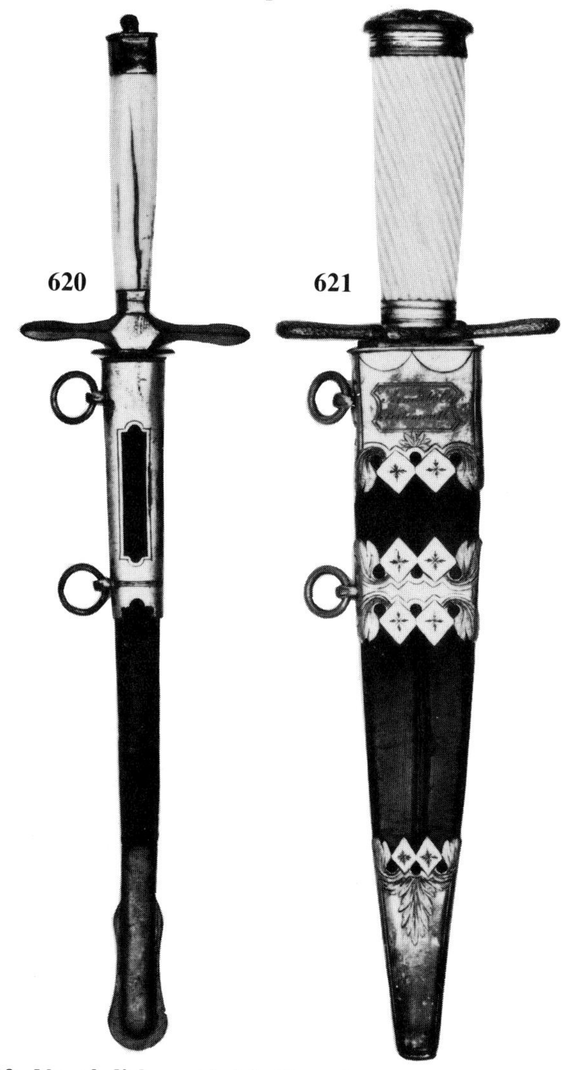
620 621

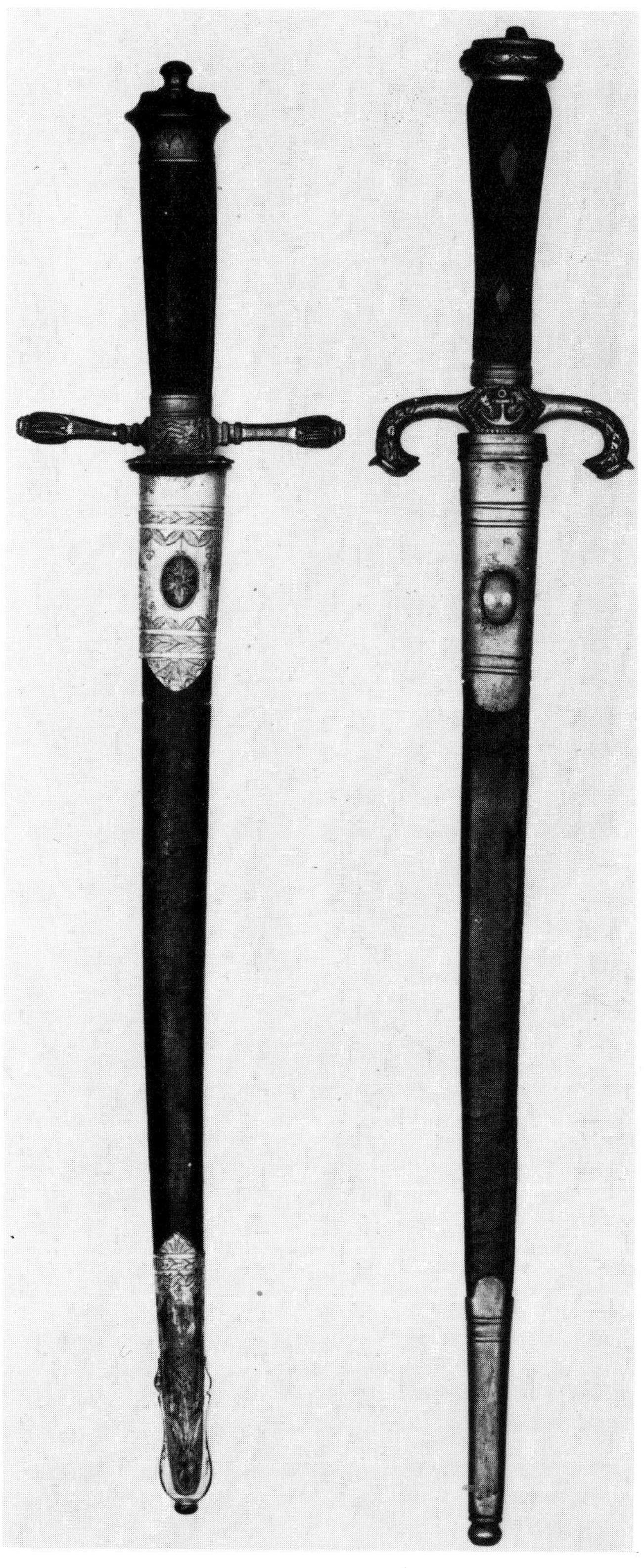
622 623

620. Naval dirk, probably French
Length 13⅛ins. (33.4cm) Late 18th century
Gilt-metal hilt and scabbard mounts; ivory grip. An example in reasonable condition. The leather on the scabbard has been replaced and the grip is cracked.
£80

621. British naval dirk
Length 13¼ins. (33.7cm) Early 19th century
This good robust example is inscribed on the gilt-copper scabbard mounts 'ARNOLD & CO., PORTSMOUTH'.
£200 — £250

622. French naval dirk
Length 19ins. (48.2cm) Early 19th century
Gilt-metal mounted hilt and leather scabbard. Chequered ebony grip. Reasonable condition.
£200

623. French brass-mounted naval dirk
Length 20ins. (50.8cm) Early 19th century
Another example in reasonable condition. The blade has traces of engraving at the forte.
£400 — £450

Photographs: Sotheby's

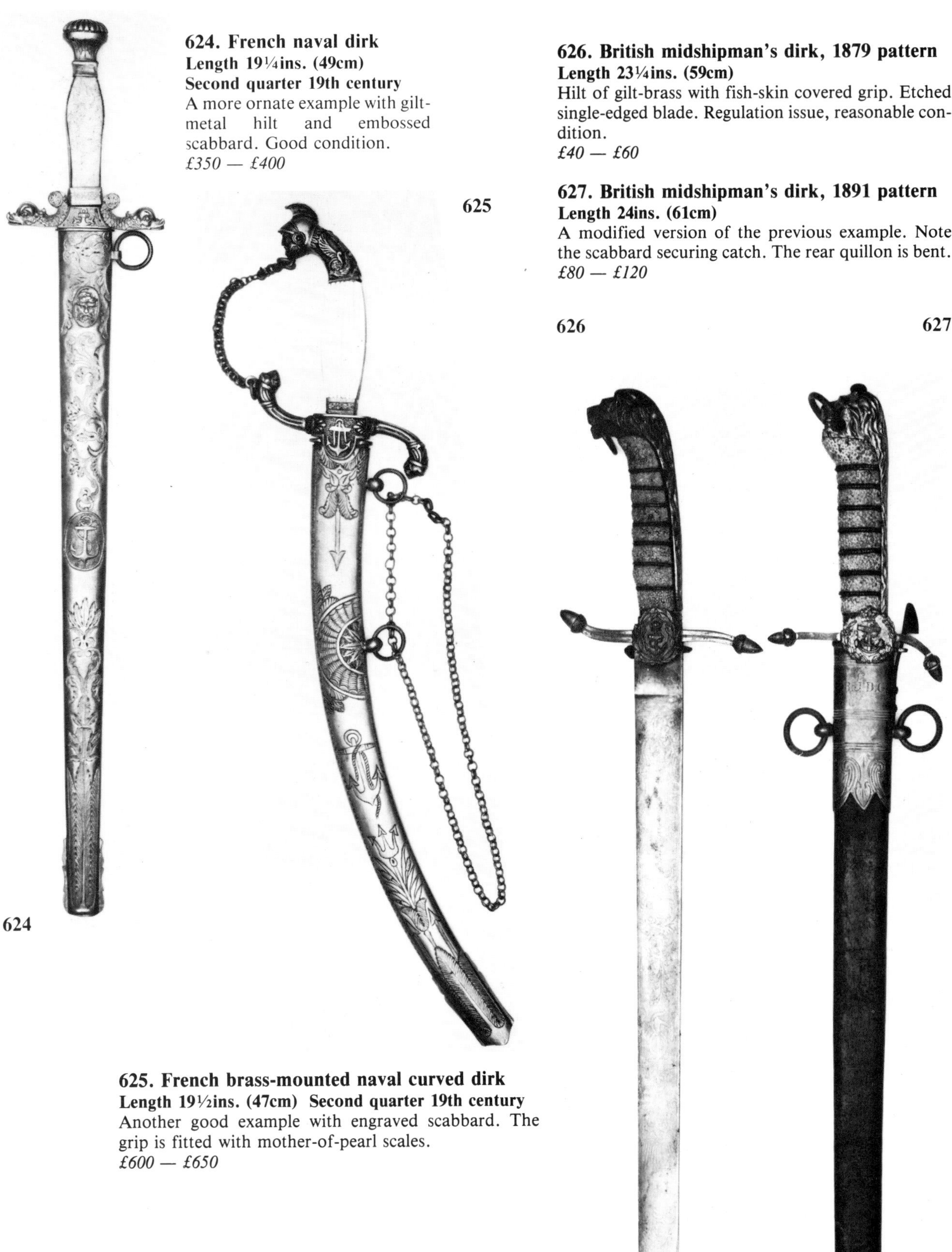

624

624. French naval dirk
Length 19¼ins. (49cm)
Second quarter 19th century
A more ornate example with gilt-metal hilt and embossed scabbard. Good condition.
£350 — £400

625

625. French brass-mounted naval curved dirk
Length 19½ins. (47cm) Second quarter 19th century
Another good example with engraved scabbard. The grip is fitted with mother-of-pearl scales.
£600 — £650

626

626. British midshipman's dirk, 1879 pattern
Length 23¼ins. (59cm)
Hilt of gilt-brass with fish-skin covered grip. Etched single-edged blade. Regulation issue, reasonable condition.
£40 — £60

627

627. British midshipman's dirk, 1891 pattern
Length 24ins. (61cm)
A modified version of the previous example. Note the scabbard securing catch. The rear quillon is bent.
£80 — £120

Photographs: Sotheby's

628

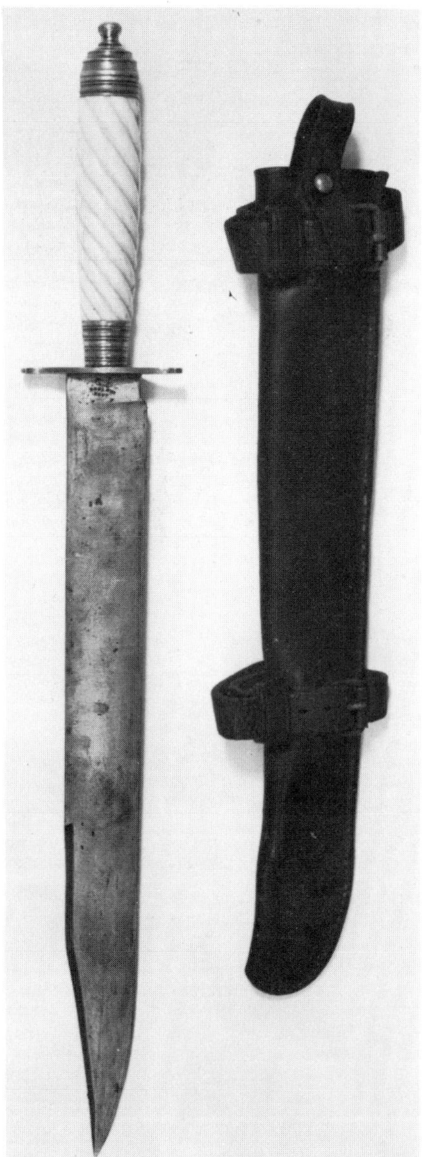

628. American Bowie knife
Length 18ins. (45.7cm) About 1847
Hilt of nickel silver with writhen ivory grip. Blade of characteristic form stamped 'ROSE, NEW YORK'. A rare example in good condition. The leather sheath is a replacement.
£600 — £1,000

629. English (Sheffield) Bowie knife made for American market
Length 14¼ins. (36.2cm) About 1850
Of robust form with nickel silver mounts and ivory grip. Blade inscribed 'CAST STEEL BOWIE KNIFE, SAMUEL C. WRAGG, No. 25, FURNACE MILL, SHEFFIELD'. A fine example in good condition.
£1,000 — £1,500

630. American Bowie knife
Length 12ins. (30.5cm) About 1850
The hilt of similar form to 629. Blade stamped 'ROSE, NEW YORK'. Rare, reasonable condition, sheath associated.
£300+

631. English (Sheffield) Bowie knife for American market
Length 12½ins. (31.7cm) Mid-19th century
Guard and pommel of German silver. The latter is embossed on one side with a horse and on the other with an alligator, the symbols of the backwood's rifleman. Horn grips. The blade stamped 'G. WOODHEAD, 86 HOWARD STREET, SHEFFIELD'. A fine example.
£500+

Photographs: Sotheby, Park-Bernet, LA

629

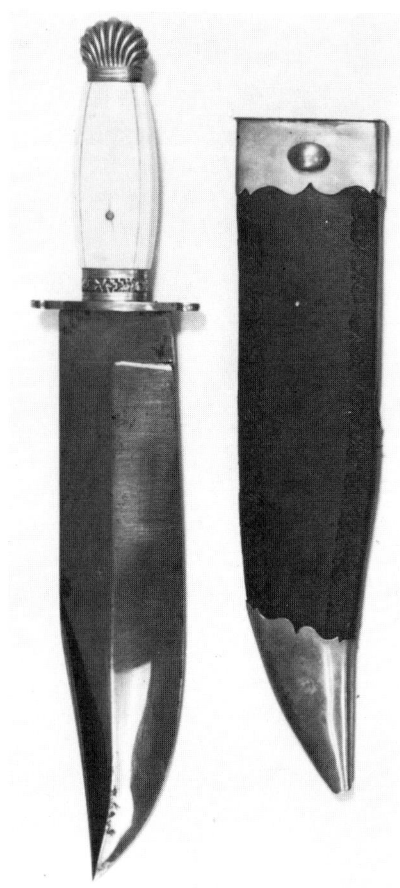

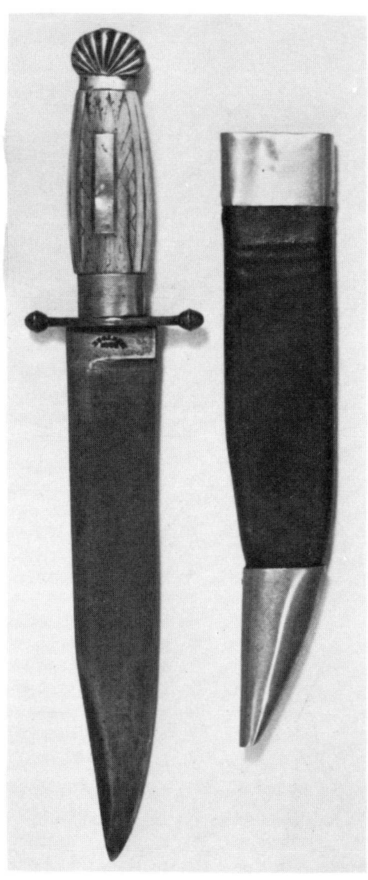

630

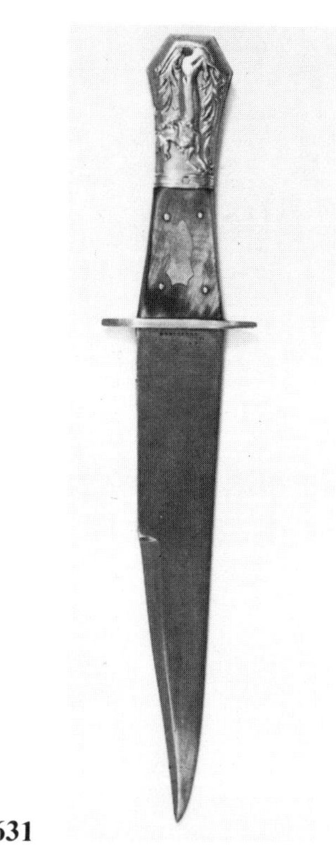

631

632. English (Sheffield) Bowie knife
Length 13½ins. (34.3cm) About 1860
Embossed German silver hilt. Blade etched with American slogans and stamped 'EDWARD BARNES & SONS, SHEFFIELD'. A good example, but worn on the blade and sheath.
£500+

633. English (Sheffield) Bowie knife
Length 13½ins. (34.3cm) Mid-19th century
Embossed German silver hilt. Blade inscribed 'HUNTER'S COMPANION, THE REAL OIO KNIFE', and 'SHIRLEY'S CELEBRATED OIO CUTLERY'. A rare example in good condition.
£500+

632 633

634

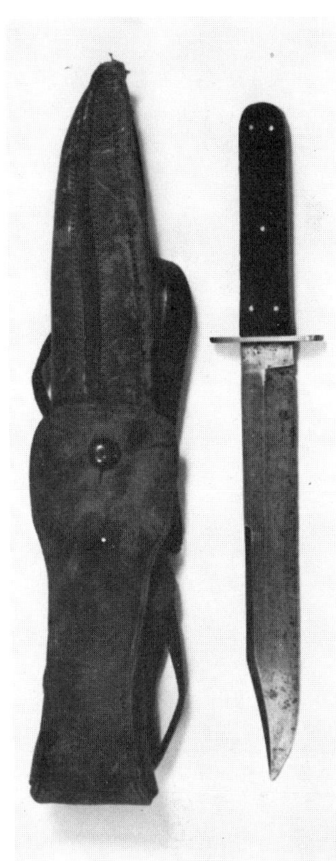

635

634. English (Sheffield) Bowie knife
Length 15¼ins. (38.8cm) About 1850
Hilt with nickel silver guard and pommel and stag-horn grip. Blade stamped 'G. WOSTENHOLM & SONS, WASHINGTON WORKS, SHEFFIELD' and with the company's trade mark 'I*XL'. Of good quality but worn.
£100 — £150

635. English (Sheffield) Bowie knife
Length 12¼ins. (31cm) About 1875
Hilt with silver guard and chequered ebony scales. Blade stamped 'NEEDHAM BROTHERS, SHEFFIELD'. Complete with sheath and outer case.
£150 — £180

Photographs: Sotheby, Parke-Bernet, LA

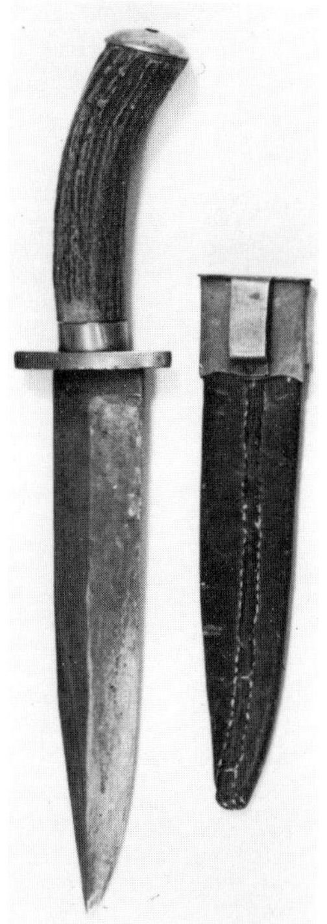

636

636. American brass-mounted Bowie knife
Length 12ins. (30.5cm)
Mid-19th century
Stag-horn grip. Blade stamped 'CHEVALIER'S CALIFORNIA KNIFE'. Good quality.
£100 — £120

637

637. Bowie knife
Length 13ins. (33cm)
About 1850
Tapered horn grip. The re-sharpened blade stamped 'MARSH BROS. & CO. CELEBRATED CUTLERY'. Reasonable condition.
£100 — £150

638

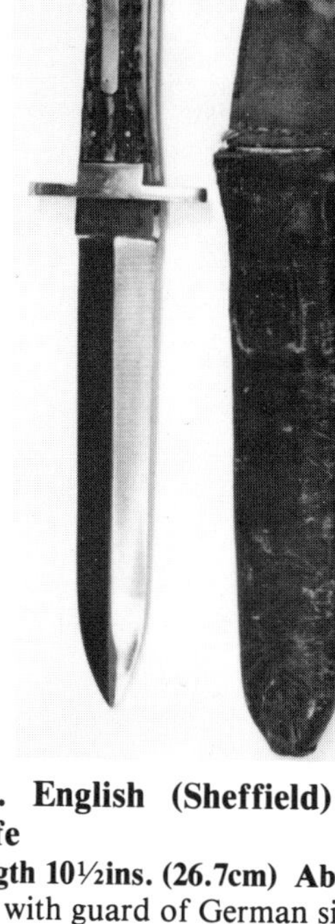

638. English (Sheffield) Bowie knife
Length 10½ins. (26.7cm) About 1860
Hilt with guard of German silver and stag-horn grips. The spear-pointed two-edged blade stamped 'ALEXANDER, SHEFFIELD'. Good quality and condition.
£100 — £120

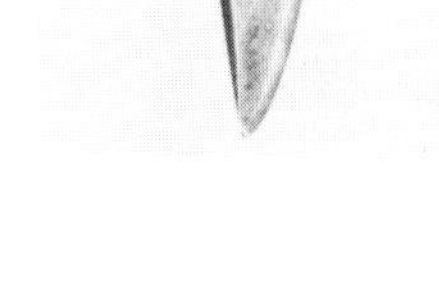

639

639. English (Sheffield) Bowie knife
Blade 9⅜ins. (23.8cm)
About 1860
The clip-pointed blade stamped 'G. WOSTENHOLM AND SON, WASHINGTON WORKS, SHEFFIELD' and 'I*XL'. Reasonable condition, associated sheath.
£80 — £100

640

640. Continental Bowie knife
Length 15ins. (38cm)
About 1880
Blued and gilt clip-pointed blade. The cloth-covered wooden sheath with engraved German silver mounts. Good quality and condition.
£120 — £150

641

641. East Indian silver-mounted Bowie knife for the European or American market
Length 12¾ins. (32.5cm)
About 1880
The worn blade stamped 'AUSTIN' and 'TRIGHINPOTY'. Good quality.
£100 — £120

Photographs:
Sotheby, Parke-Bernet, LA

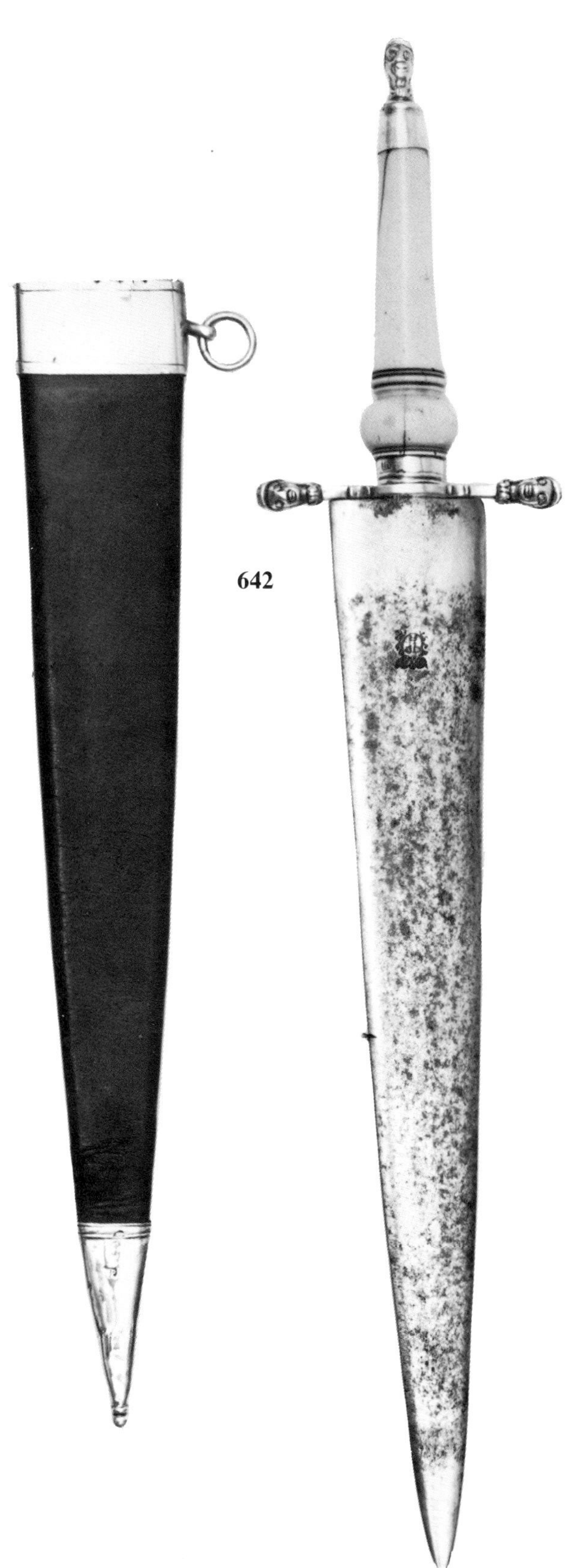
642

642. English silver-mounted plug bayonet
About 1680-1690
Silver hilt and scabbard mounts with indistinct hall-marks. Tapered ivory grip. Worn blade stamped with bladesmith's mark (a crowned head). Fine quality.
£600 — £800

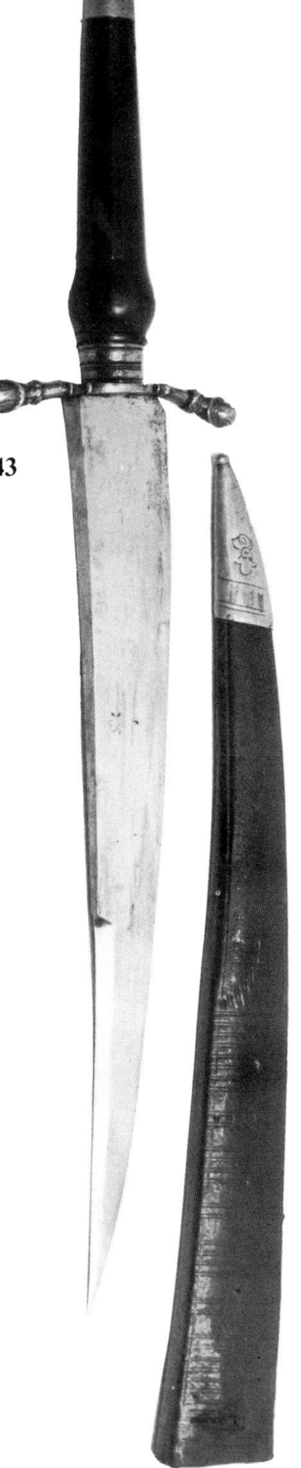
643

643. English brass-mounted plug bayonet
About 1685
The hilt with wooden grip. The blade struck with the mark of the London Cutlers' Company (a dagger). Good quality and condition.
£500 — £700

Photographs: Peter Dale Ltd.

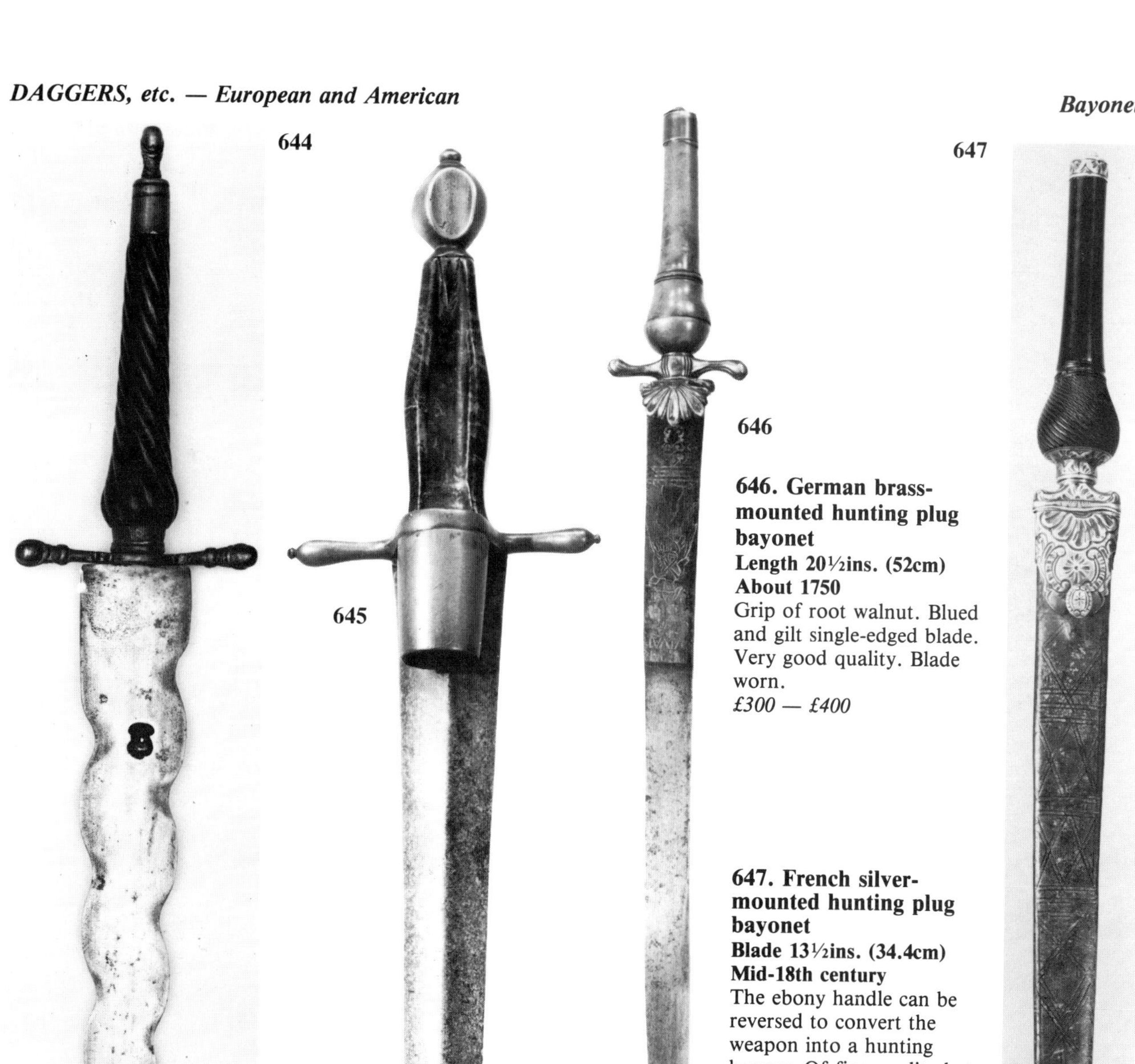

646. German brass-mounted hunting plug bayonet
Length 20½ins. (52cm)
About 1750
Grip of root walnut. Blued and gilt single-edged blade. Very good quality. Blade worn.
£300 — £400

647. French silver-mounted hunting plug bayonet
Blade 13½ins. (34.4cm)
Mid-18th century
The ebony handle can be reversed to convert the weapon into a hunting hanger. Of fine quality but a little worn. Chape missing.
£400 — £600

644. English plug bayonet
Length 17½ins. (44.5cm)
About 1680-1690
Brass guard and pommel. Wood grip. The flamboyant blade with the mark of the London Cutler's Company above the letter 'T'. A familiar but good example, worn on the blade.
£400 — £500

645. English socket bayonet of early form
Blade 14ins. (35.5cm)
About 1680-1700
Brass guard with socket. Grooved wooden grip and brass pommel. Rare, blade pitted.
£700 — £900

Photographs: 644 Sotheby's; 645-647 Christie's

649

650

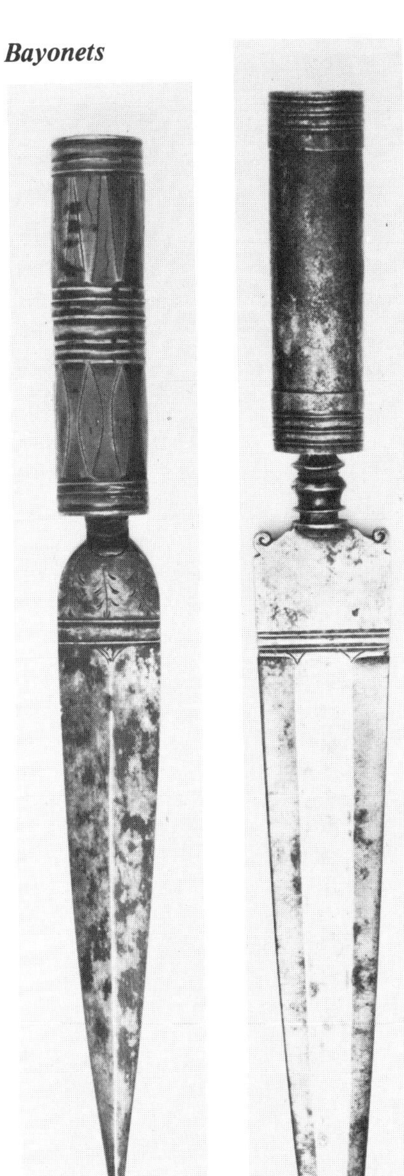

648

650. French all-steel sword bayonet
Length 27½ins. (69.8cm)
About 1750-1775
The colichemarde blade is blued and gilt, and etched with the royal arms of France and inscribed 'VIVE LE ROY'. Rare, good condition.
£700 — £800

651. British sword bayonet with detachable hilt
Blade 24ins. (61cm)
About 1798
Steel hilt of 1796 light cavalry pattern. A rare example but pitted on the guard and socket. National Army Museum (7303-16).
£500 — £600

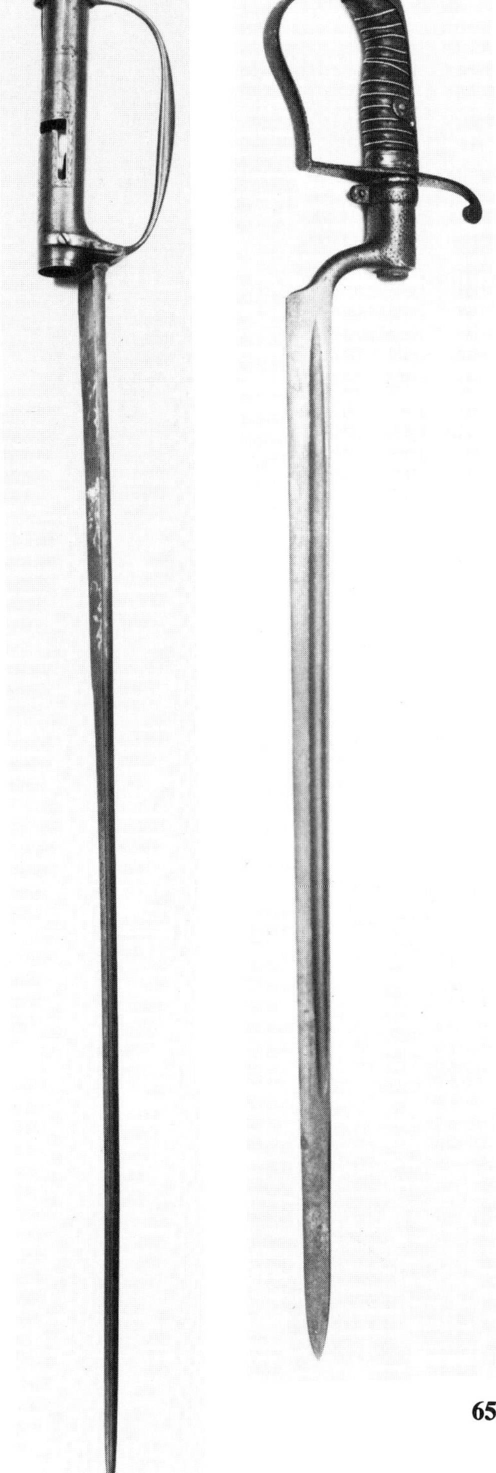

651

648. Italian hunting socket bayonet
Length 11¼ins. (28.5cm) 18th century
Socket of brass. Blade heavily worn.
£60 — £80

649. Italian hunting socket bayonet
Length 13½ins. (34.3cm) 18th century
All steel. Worn overall.
£60 — £80

Photographs: 648-650 Christie's

652 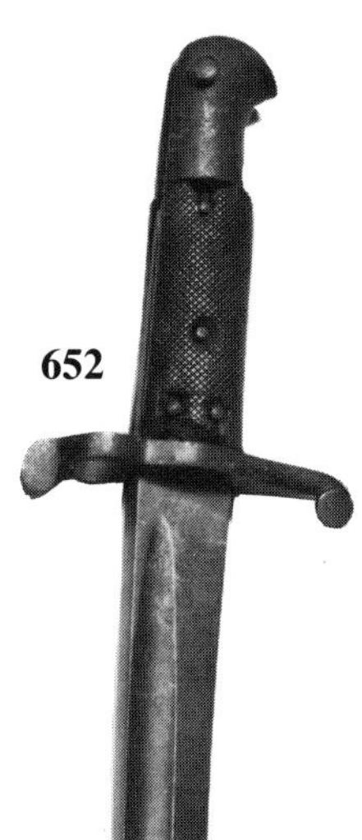

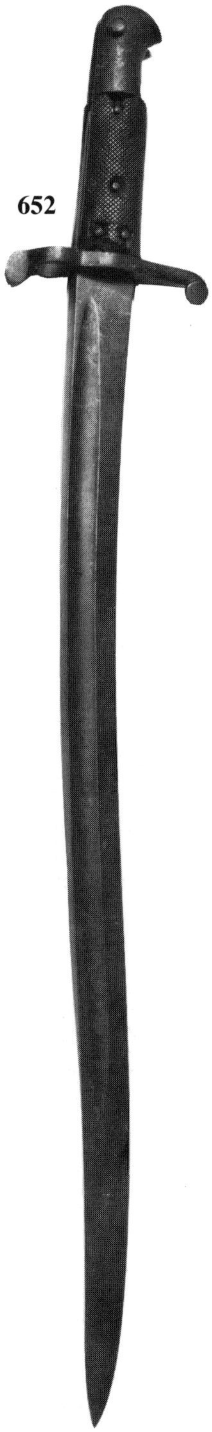

652. British Enfield Artillery bayonet, 1853 pattern
Length 28ins. (71.1cm)
Yataghan blade. Poor condition. The grips with pieces missing.
£10

653. British Lancaster sword bayonet
Length 28⅞ins. (73.3cm) About 1860
Brass hilt. The pipe-backed blade with spear point. Regulation issue. Reasonable condition.
£15 — £20

654. French Chassepot bayonet
Length 27½ins. (69.8cm) About 1870
A regulation example with brass hilt and yataghan blade.
£10

655. Danish bayonet, 1870 pattern
Length 27ins. (68.5cm)
Yataghan blade. Regulation issue.
£10

656. French Lebel bayonet, 1886 pattern
Length 25⅛ins. (63.7cm)
Hilt with white metal handle. The robust spike blade of + section. Reasonable condition.
£10

657. French Gras bayonet
Length 25⅜ins. (64.5cm) Dated 1886
Hilt with brass pommel and wooden grips. Worn.
£10

653 654 655 656 657

Photographs: Sotheby's

658. American trowel or spade bayonet, 1873 pattern
Quite rare. Worn overall. Weller and Dufty Ltd.
£20

662. British Lee Metford bayonet
Length 18ins. (45.7cm)
About 1900
In poor condition. Steel-mounted leather sheath.
£5

662

658

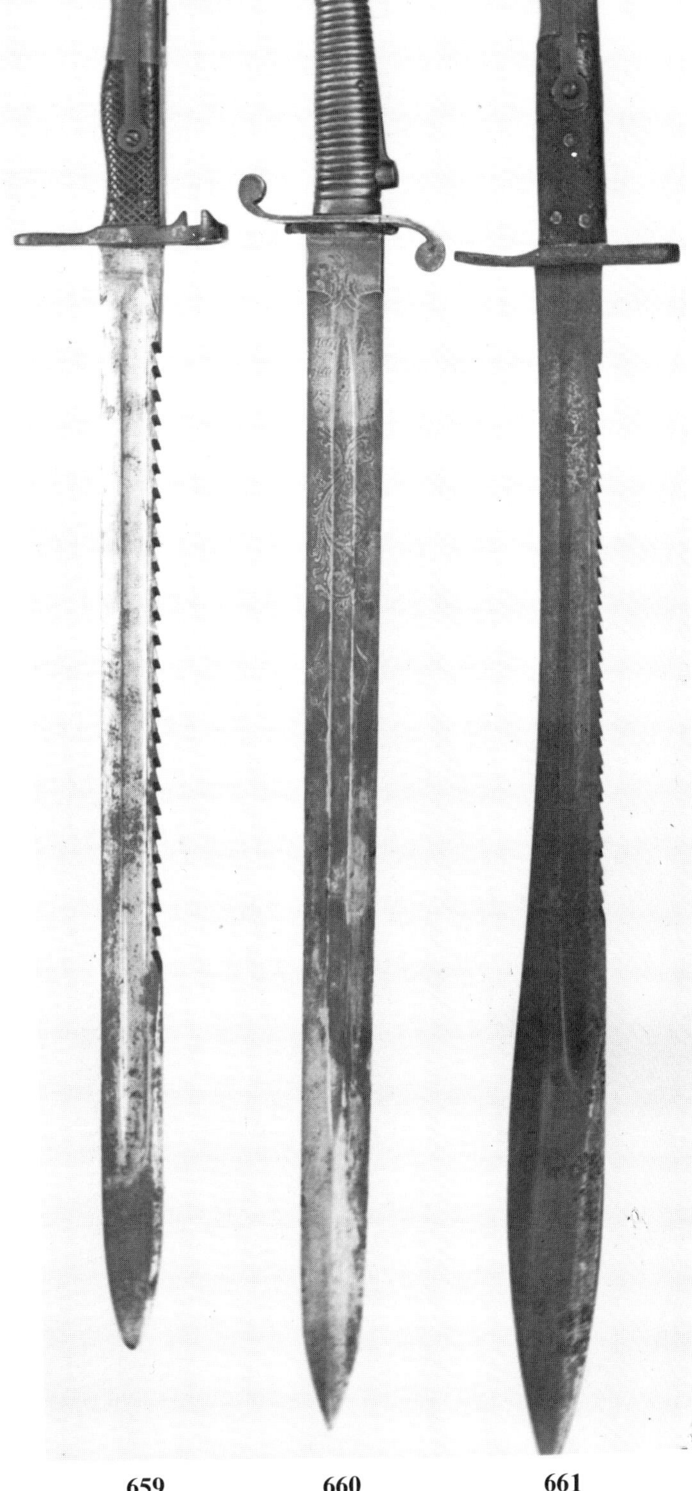

659 660 661

Photograph: 662 Sotheby's

659. Swiss Vetterli saw-backed bayonet, 1878 pattern
Reasonable condition. Weller and Dufty Ltd.
£20

660. British volunteer Brunswick rifle bayonet
Mid-19th century
Brass hilt. The blade etched 'REILLY, Oxford St., LONDON'. Worn, especially on the blade. Weller and Dufty Ltd.
£30 — £50

661. British Elcho sword bayonet for a Martini-Henri rifle, 1871 pattern
In poor condition. Weller and Dufty Ltd.
£10 — £15

663

663. German hunting set
16th century
Ebony handles fitted with engraved and gilded steel mounts. The blade of the serving knife is etched with a coat of arms adapted from that of Anne of Cleves (d.1557) but surrounded by a motto with the date 1559. Tooled leather scabbard inscribed 'I. O. VERBUM, DOMINI. MA'. Fine quality (see Christie's catalogue, 25 February 1976, lot 196).
£4,000

664

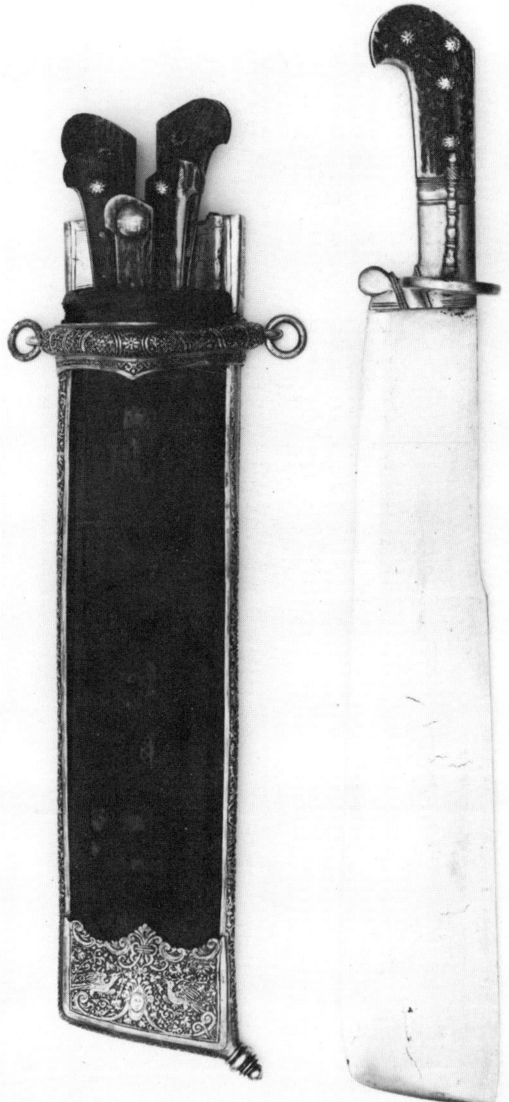

664. Saxon woodknife
Length 18¾ins. (47.6cm)
First quarter 17th century
Steel hilt faced with stag horn. The hilts of the dissecting knives and skewer file decorated *en suite*. Silver-mounted leather and velvet-covered wooden scabbard. Fine quality, a little worn on the scabbard. Also known as a *trousse de chasse*, and *waidpraxe*.
£10,000+

Photographs: 663 Christie's; 664 Sotheby's

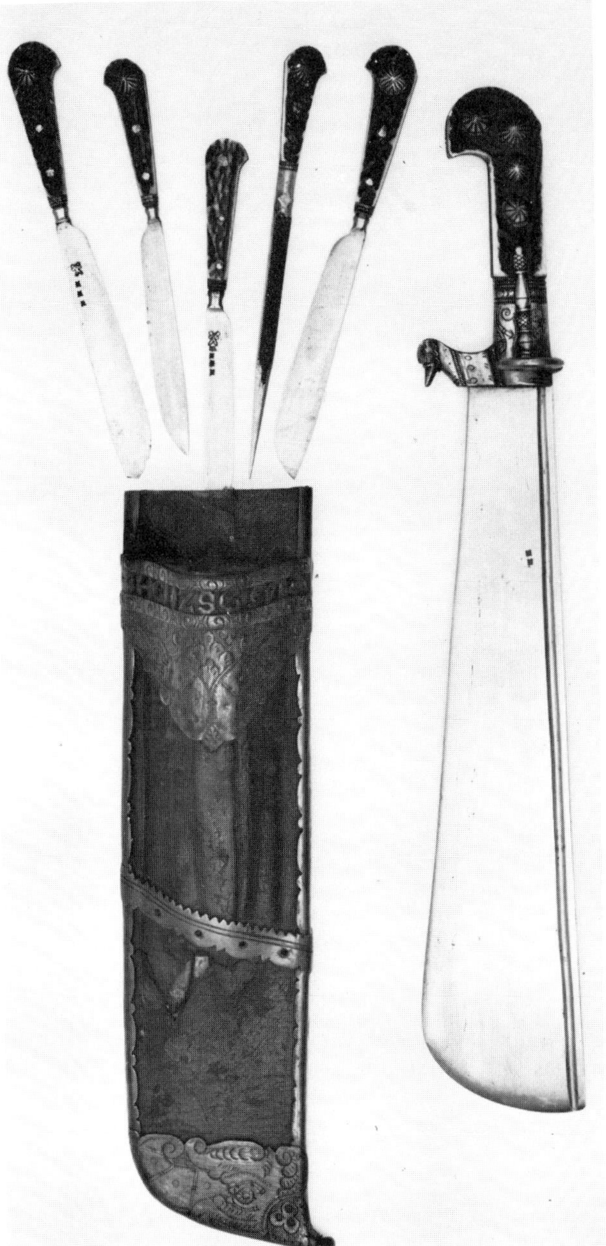

665

666

666. German woodknife with calendar blade
Blade 18½ins. (47cm) Dated 1676
Hilt of chiselled steel with stag horn grip. The etched blade signed 'FEC. IOH. AD. EHINGER' (Made by Johann Adam Ehinger [Regensburg]). A fine and rare example with some patches of wear on the blade.
£2,000 — £3,000

667. American buffalo hunter's bone saw and skinning knives
Saw blade 8ins. (20.3cm),
knife blades 5ins. (12.7cm)
About 1870
Handles faced with stag horn. The saw blade stamped 'RICHARDSON SPRING STEEL, NEWARK N.J. WARRANTED'. The knife blades signed 'TIFFANY & CO. MAKERS, NEW YORK'. In leather case. Quite rare and in very good condition.
£800 — £1,500

665. Saxon woodknife
Length 19ins. (48.2cm) Dated 1662
Similar in form to the preceding example but showing all the implements out of the iron-mounted scabbard. The locket with the initials 'H.G.H.Z.S.G.C.V.B.C' (Johann Georg Herzog Zu Sachsen Gulich Cleve und Berg Churfürst). A fine example which forms a garniture with sword 429.
£5,000 — £6,000

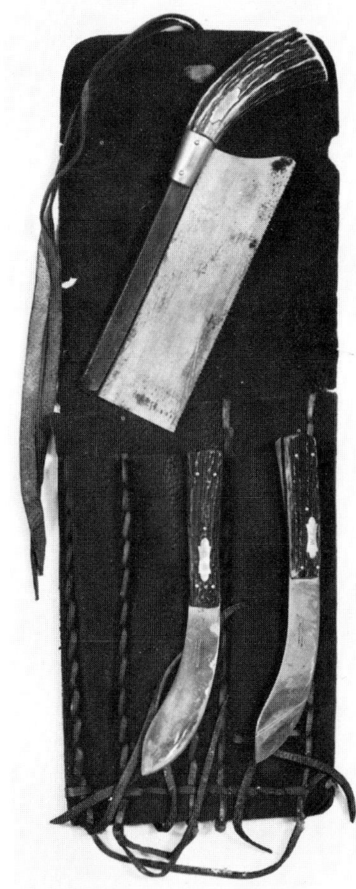

667

Photographs: 665 Sotheby's; 666 Christie's; 667 Sotheby, Parke-Bernet, LA

668. Caucasian silver and bone mounted kindjal
Length 20½ins. (52cm)
Dated A.H. 1220 (A.D. 1805)
The bone grips and scabbard mounts are inlaid with silver and gold and the silver mountings are embellished with niello and filigree. Inscribed 'MASH 'ALLAH AMAL MOHAMED' and dated. Fine quality.
£1,000+

668

669

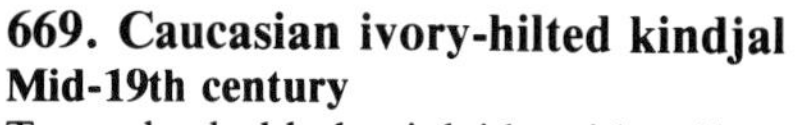

669. Caucasian ivory-hilted kindjal
Mid-19th century
Two-edged blade inlaid with silver. Chiselled steel-mounted leather-covered sheath. Good quality.
£150 — £300

670 **671** **672**

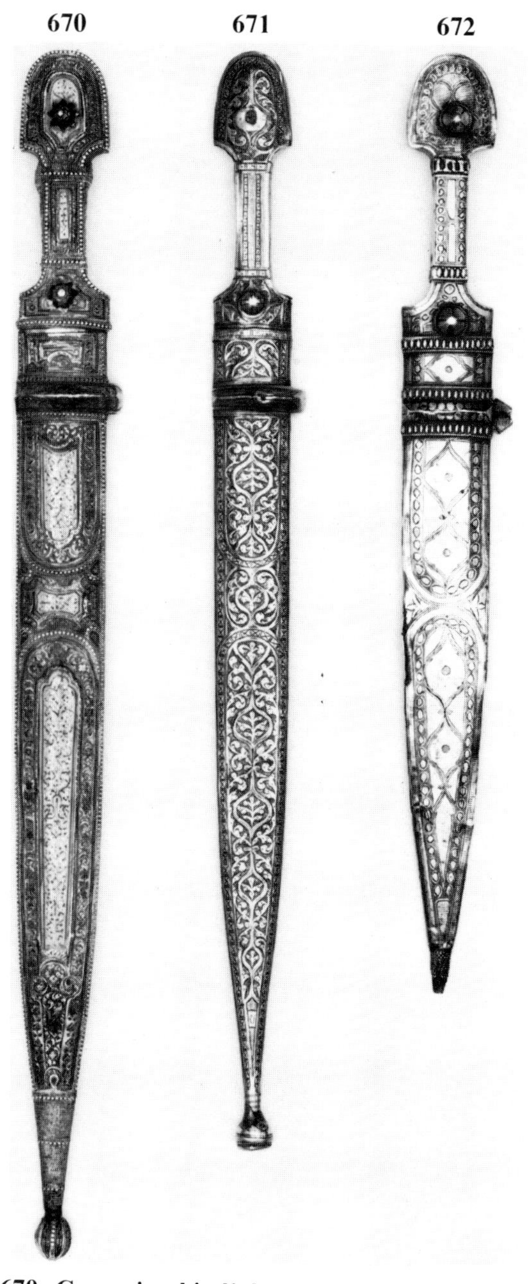

670. Caucasian kindjal
Late 19th century
A good example mounted in silver and embellished with niello.
£150 — £300

671. Caucasian kindjal
Late 19th century
Similar in quality to 670.
£150 — £300

672. Caucasian kindjal
Late 19th century
The sheath slightly dented.
£150 — £300

Photographs: 668 Christie's; 669-672 Sotheby's

673. Caucasian kindjal
Late 19th century
A silver-mounted example of good quality. Horn grips.
£200 — £400

674. Caucasian kindjal
Late 19th century
Hilt and sheath overlaid with silver and embellished with niello. Good quality.
£200 — £400

673 **674**

675

675. South Georgian kindjal
Mid-19th century
Silver-mounted hilt and silver locket embellished with niello. Broad blade. An example in reasonable condition. The steel chape is normal.
£150 — £300

676 **677**

676. Persian silver-mounted kindjal
Mid-19th century
Horn grips and leather-covered sheath. The silver mounts embossed with figural scenes.
£150 — £250

677. Turkish kindjal
Mid-19th century
Gilt-brass hilt and mounts. The two-edged blade inlaid with gold at the forte. Good quality and condition.
£150 — £250

Photographs: Sotheby's

678

679

680

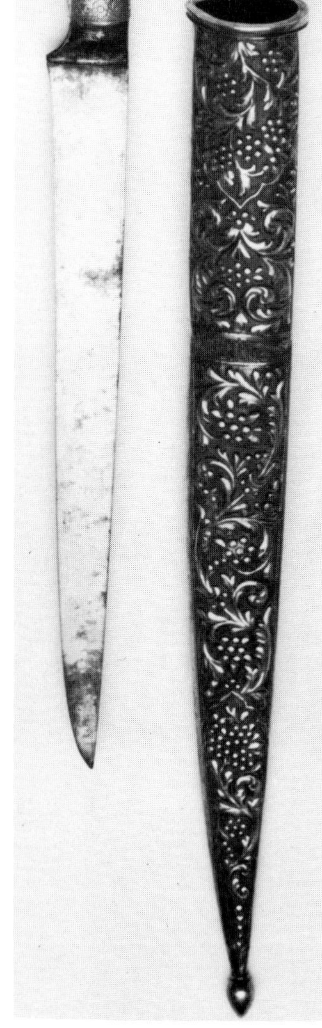

681

678. Persian ivory-hilted kard
18th century
The collar of the hilt, and the forte of the watered steel blade, decorated with Koranic inscriptions and the maker's or owner's name against a gilt ground. The silver scabbard is of Cossack (south-west Russian) workmanship of the second half of the 19th century and was made to fit the knife. Very good quality. The blade a little worn.
£300

679. Persian ivory-hilted kard
Late 18th century
Ivory hilt carved with legendary Babylonian scenes. The single-edged blade chiselled and gilt with Arabic calligraphy. Without scabbard. Very good quality and condition.
£450

680. Greek silver-mounted kard
19th century
Another very good example with engraved silver hilt and silver scabbard embossed with flowers and leaves. Plain blade.
£120 — £150

681. Turkish jade-hilted kard
Length 8½ins. (21.6cm) 19th century
Gold mounted mutton-fat jade hilt set with rubies. Watered steel blade damascened with gold. Fine quality. Scabbard not shown.
£600 — £800

Photographs: 678 Sotheby's; 679-680 Robert Hales Antiques Ltd.; 681 Christie's

682. Persian carved ivory-hilted jambiya
About 1780-1850
Gold damascened curved blade with prominent central rib. Good quality but worn.
£150 — £200

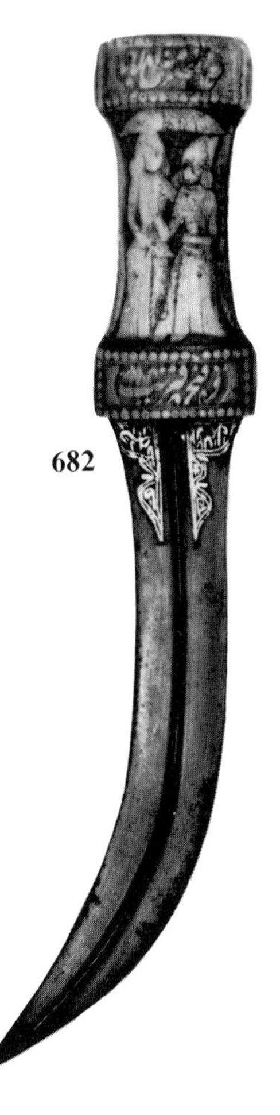

682

683. Persian carved ivory-hilted jambiya
Early 19th century
An attractive example with a watered-steel blade reinforced at the point.
£200 — £250

683

684. Persian gilt-copper jambiya
Length 18ins. (45.7cm)
Dated A.H. 1207 (A.D. 1792)
A fine piece decorated over the whole surface of the hilt and scabbard with a flower-and-leaf design. Curved blade of watered steel.
£1,000 — £2,000

684

685. Persian enamel decorated jambiya
Length 16½ins. (42cm)
Mid-19th century
Extensively and finely decorated with green, pink, blue and yellow enamel and inscribed 'YA MAHMUD'. The scabbard is associated although its design is very similar to that on the hilt. Very fine quality.
£4,000+

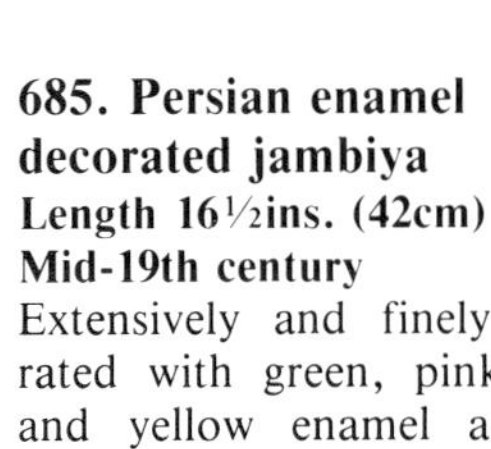

685

Photographs: 682 Sotheby's; 683-685 Christie's

686. Persian gilt-copper jambiya
Late 19th century
A good example. The slightly curved flamboyant blade with reinforced point.
£100 — £150

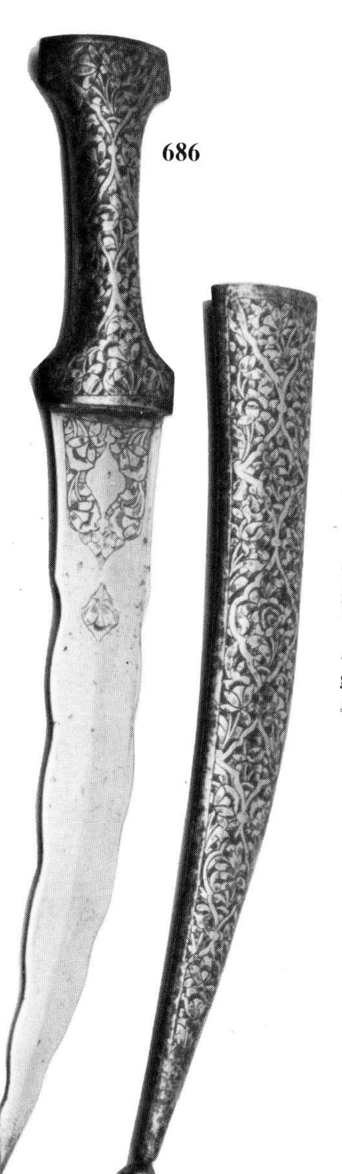

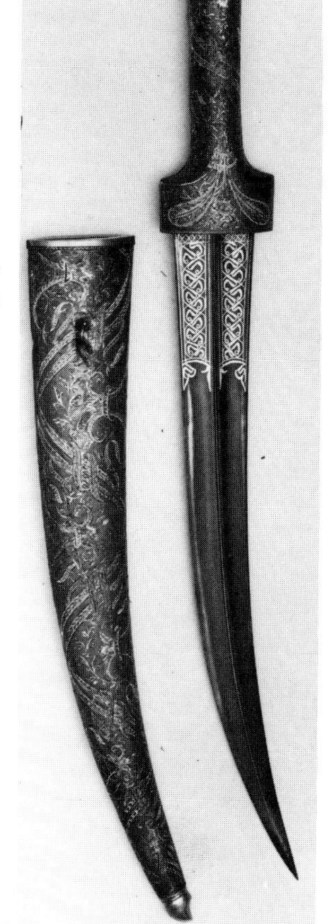

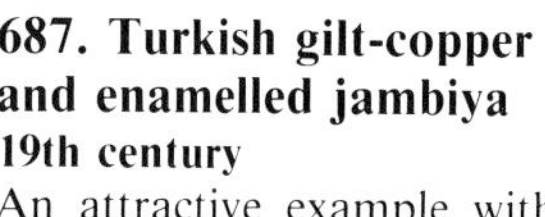
687. Turkish gilt-copper and enamelled jambiya
19th century
An attractive example with a gold inlaid watered-steel blade.
£600 — £800

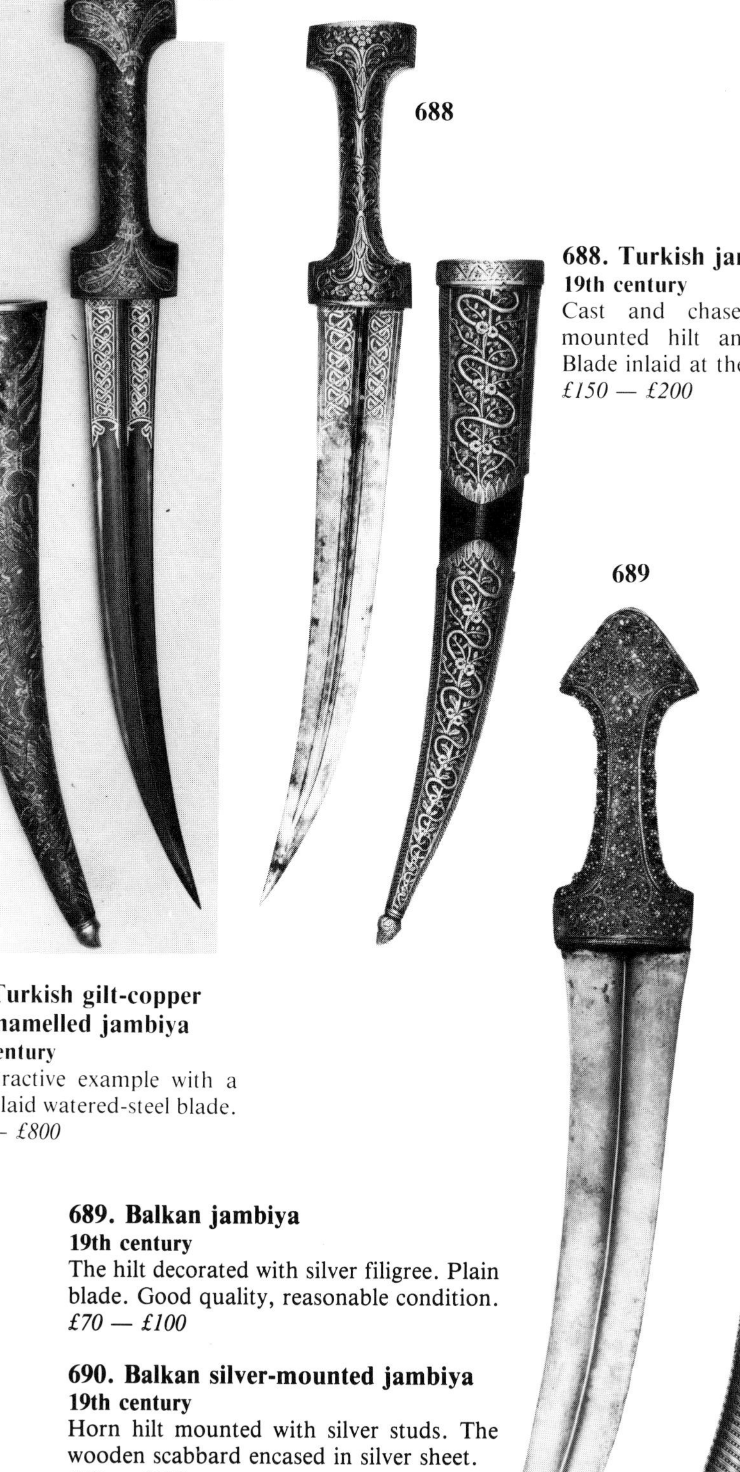

688. Turkish jambiya
19th century
Cast and chased gilt-metal mounted hilt and scabbard. Blade inlaid at the forte.
£150 — £200

689. Balkan jambiya
19th century
The hilt decorated with silver filigree. Plain blade. Good quality, reasonable condition.
£70 — £100

690. Balkan silver-mounted jambiya
19th century
Horn hilt mounted with silver studs. The wooden scabbard encased in silver sheet.
£70 — £100

Photographs: 686 Christie's; 687-690 Sotheby's

691. Turkish jambiya
Length 21ins. (53.3cm) 19th century
Walrus ivory-hilt. The silver-gilt scabbard is struck with a Turkish hallmark and a French assay mark. Blade reduced in size. A good quality piece but with worn gilding and a pitted blade.
£100 — £120

691

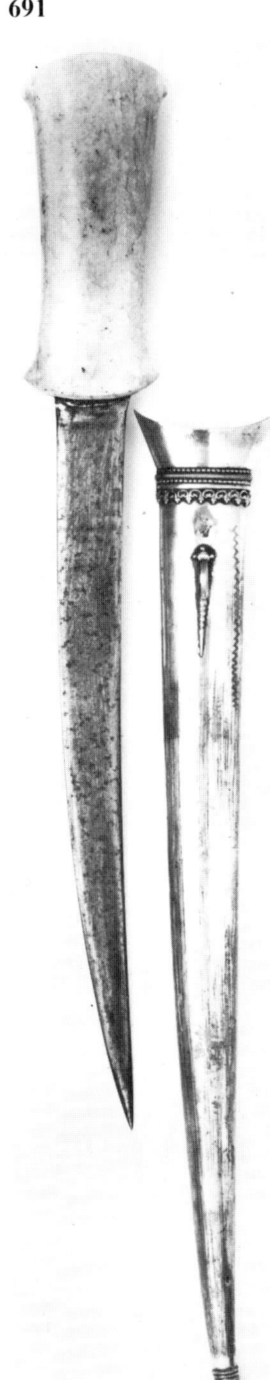

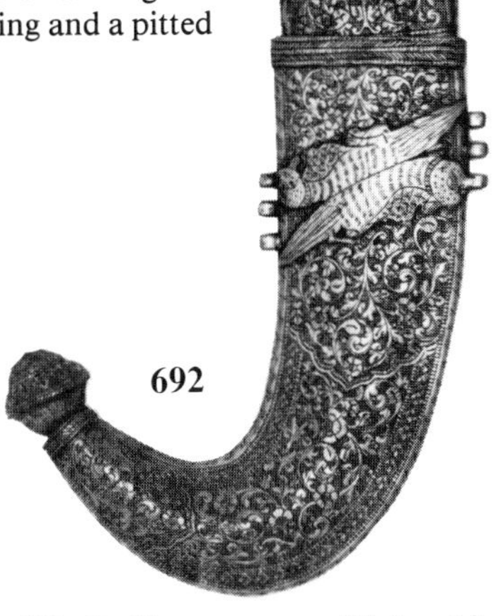

692

693

694

692. Indian copper-gilt jambiya
Second half 19th century
Decorated over the whole surface of the hilt and scabbard with floral designs.
£100 — £150

694. Moroccan jambiya
Length 16ins. (40.6cm)
Late 19th century
A typical example but of poor quality and in poor condition. It has a wood hilt with a brass pommel, and an engraved brass scabbard.
£15 — £20

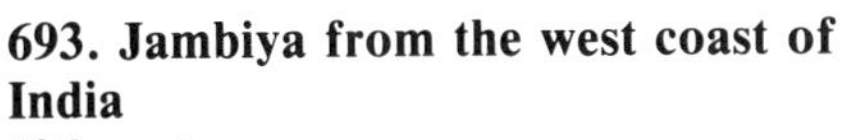

693. Jambiya from the west coast of India
19th century
Blade and iron hilt inlaid with gold. Reasonable condition.
£150

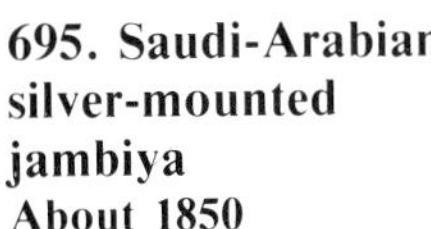

695. Saudi-Arabian silver-mounted jambiya
About 1850
Hilt and scabbard of wood encased in embossed silver and complete with belt fittings. A good example of a familiar and characteristic type.
£150 — £200

695

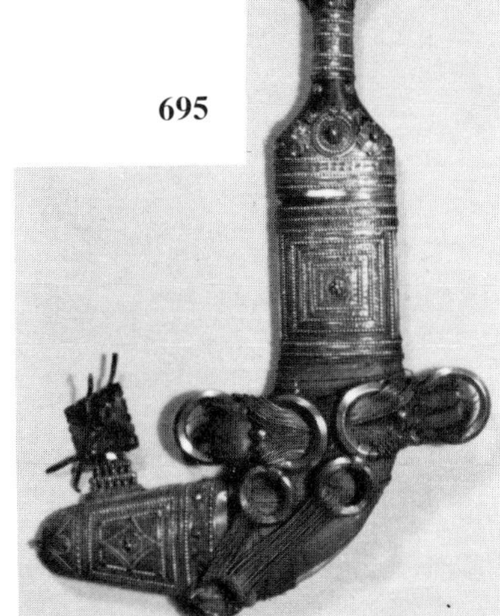

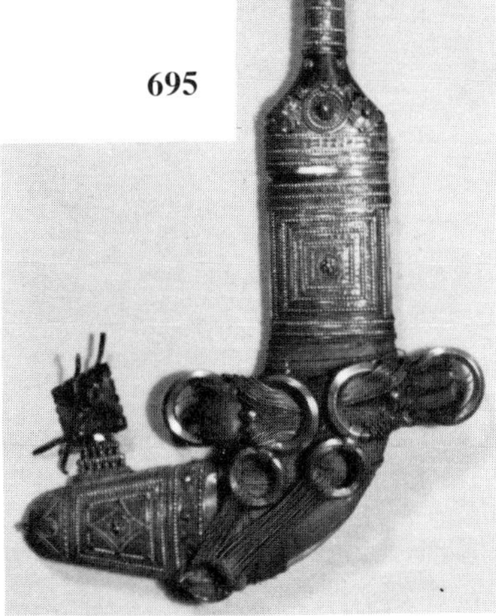

696

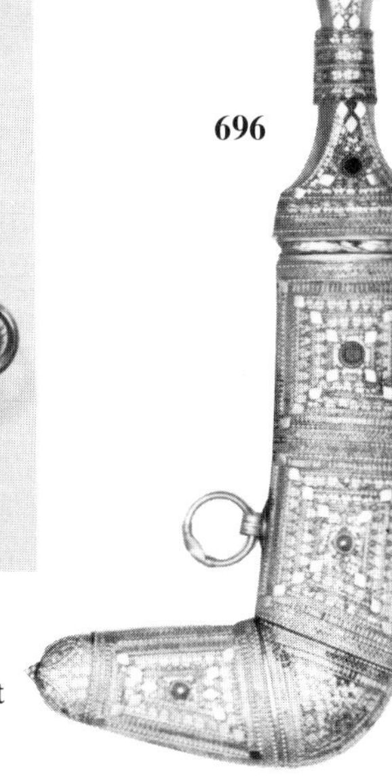

696. Saudi-Arabian gold-mounted jambiya
Early 20th century
Similar to 695 but of higher value because of the amount of gold overlaying the hilt and scabbard.
£300+

Photographs: 691-694 and 696 Sotheby's;
695 Michael C. German Ltd.

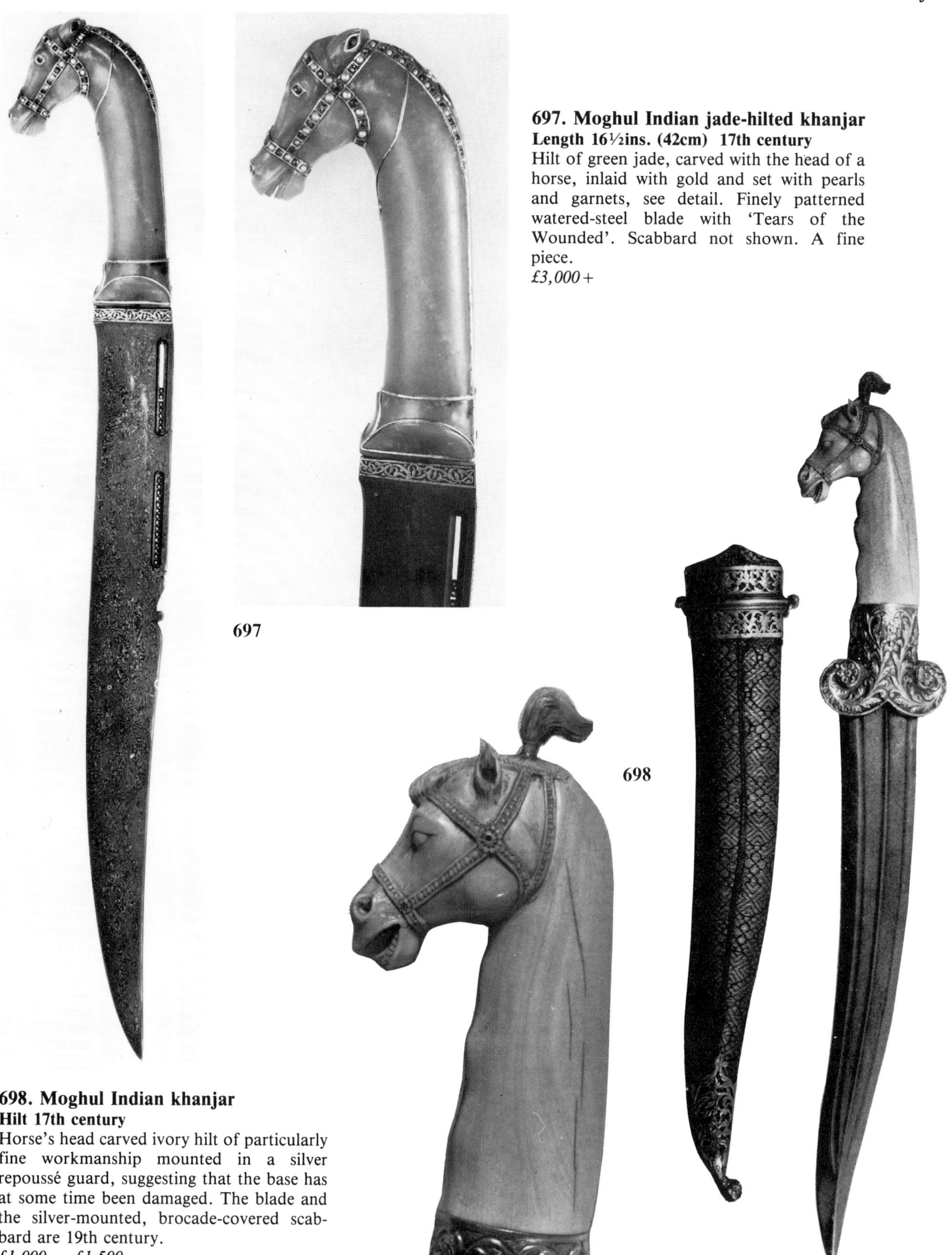
697

698

697. Moghul Indian jade-hilted khanjar
Length 16½ins. (42cm) 17th century
Hilt of green jade, carved with the head of a horse, inlaid with gold and set with pearls and garnets, see detail. Finely patterned watered-steel blade with 'Tears of the Wounded'. Scabbard not shown. A fine piece.
£3,000+

698. Moghul Indian khanjar
Hilt 17th century
Horse's head carved ivory hilt of particularly fine workmanship mounted in a silver repoussé guard, suggesting that the base has at some time been damaged. The blade and the silver-mounted, brocade-covered scabbard are 19th century.
£1,000 — £1,500

Photographs: 697 Christie's; 698 Michael C. German Ltd.

699 700

699. Indian gold and enamelled khanjar
Length 15½ins. (39.4cm) 18th century
Hilt and scabbard mounts of gold decorated with blue and green enamel and set with rubies. Watered-steel blade. Fine quality. The velvet covering on the scabbard a little worn.
£2,000+

700. Indian celadon jade hilted khanjar
Length 15¼ins. (38.7cm) 18th century
Hilt carved with lotus flowers and leaves. Velvet-covered scabbard with gold mounts set with rubies and emeralds. Fine quality and very good condition.
£1,000+

701. Indian enamelled khanjar
Length 17¼ins. (43.8cm) 18th century
Of very fine quality set with diamonds and rubies, with a watered steel blade and velvet-covered scabbard.
£3,000 — £4,000

701

702. Moghul Indian celadon jade hilted khanjar
Length 14ins. (35.5cm)
18th century
Bejewelled and gold set jade hilt designed with a pattern of flowers and foliage. The curved Persian blade of finely patterned watered steel with central rib and wide forte.
£1,500 — £2,000

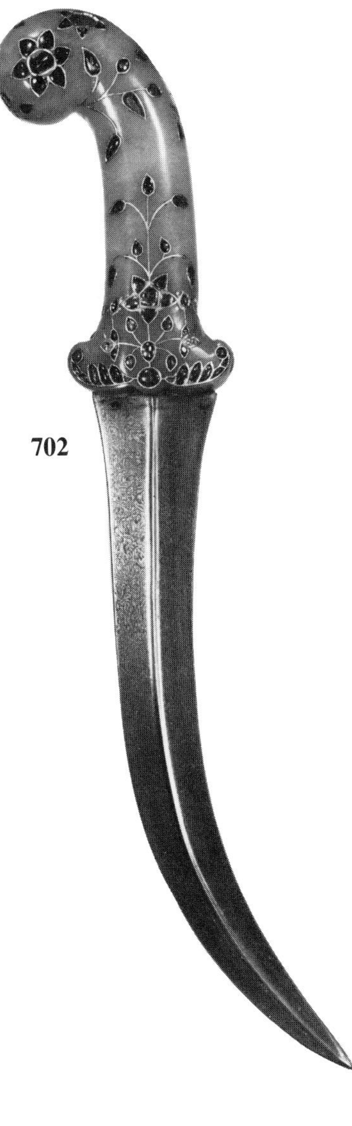

702

Photographs: Christie's

703

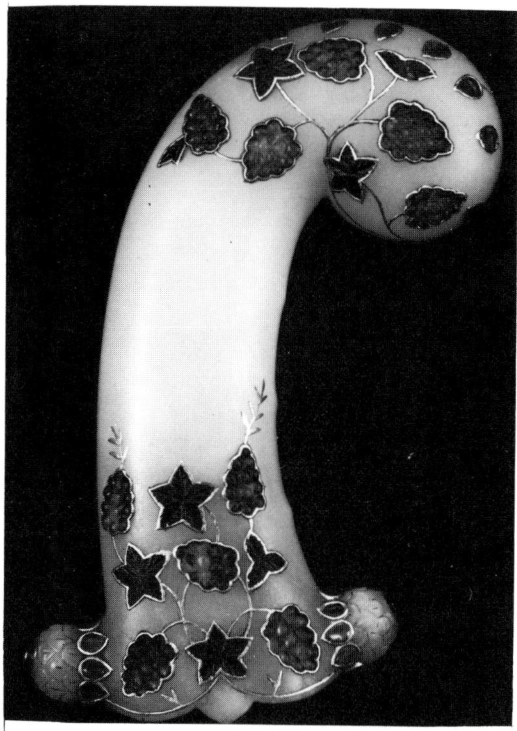

703. Moghul Indian jade khanjar hilt
Length 5¼ins. (13.3cm) 18th century
Of fine quality, the mutton-fat jade is embellished with rubies, emeralds and a darker jade in a gold setting.
£2,000+

704

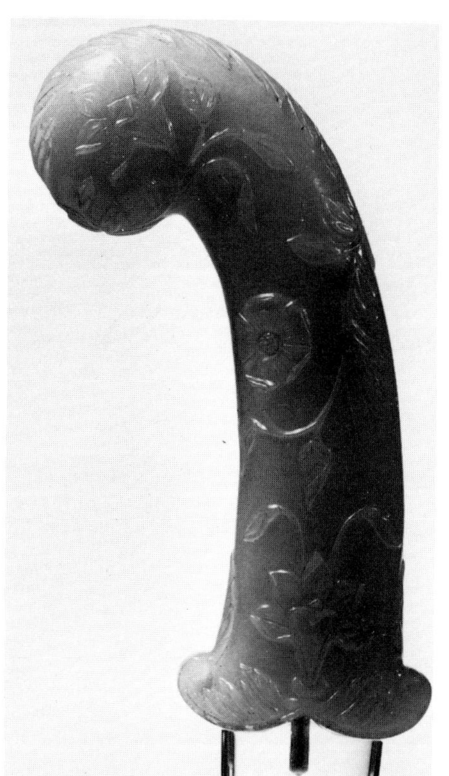

704. Moghul Indian polished jade khanjar hilt
Length 5¼ins. (13.3cm)
18th century
Finely carved with lotus flowers and leaves.
£600 — £800

705

706

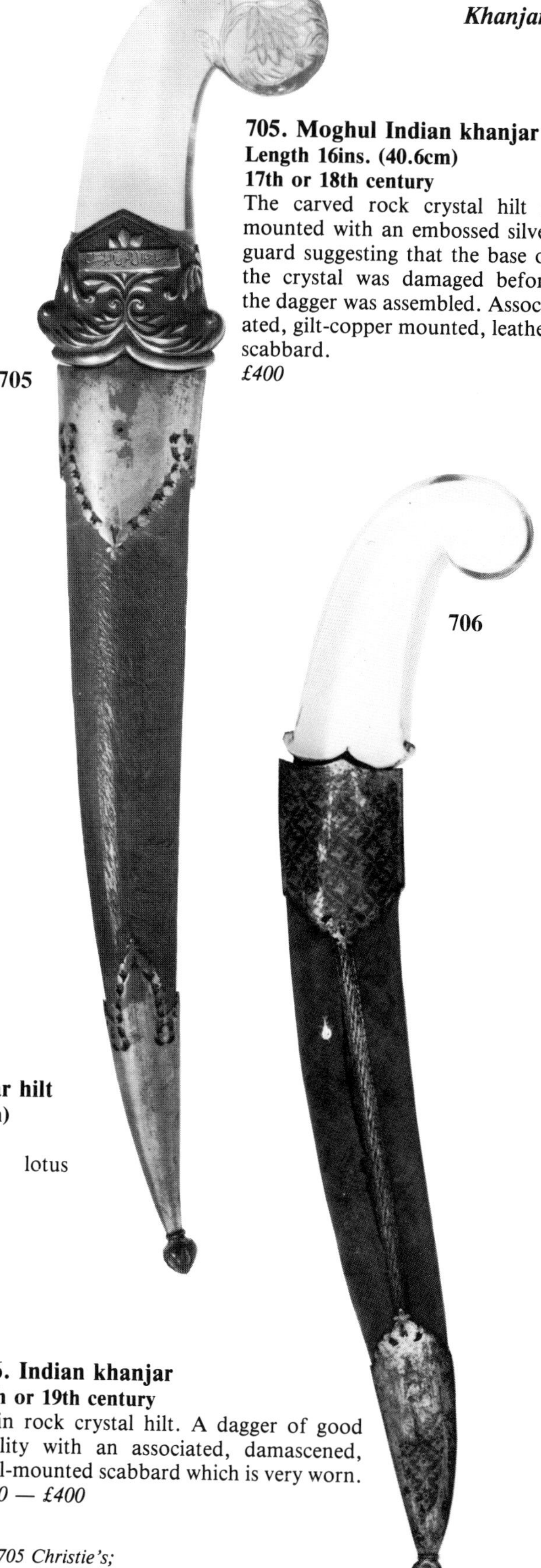

705. Moghul Indian khanjar
Length 16ins. (40.6cm)
17th or 18th century
The carved rock crystal hilt is mounted with an embossed silver guard suggesting that the base of the crystal was damaged before the dagger was assembled. Associated, gilt-copper mounted, leather scabbard.
£400

706. Indian khanjar
18th or 19th century
Plain rock crystal hilt. A dagger of good quality with an associated, damascened, steel-mounted scabbard which is very worn.
£300 — £400

Photographs: 703 and 705 Christie's; 704 Howard Ricketts Ltd.; 706 Sotheby's

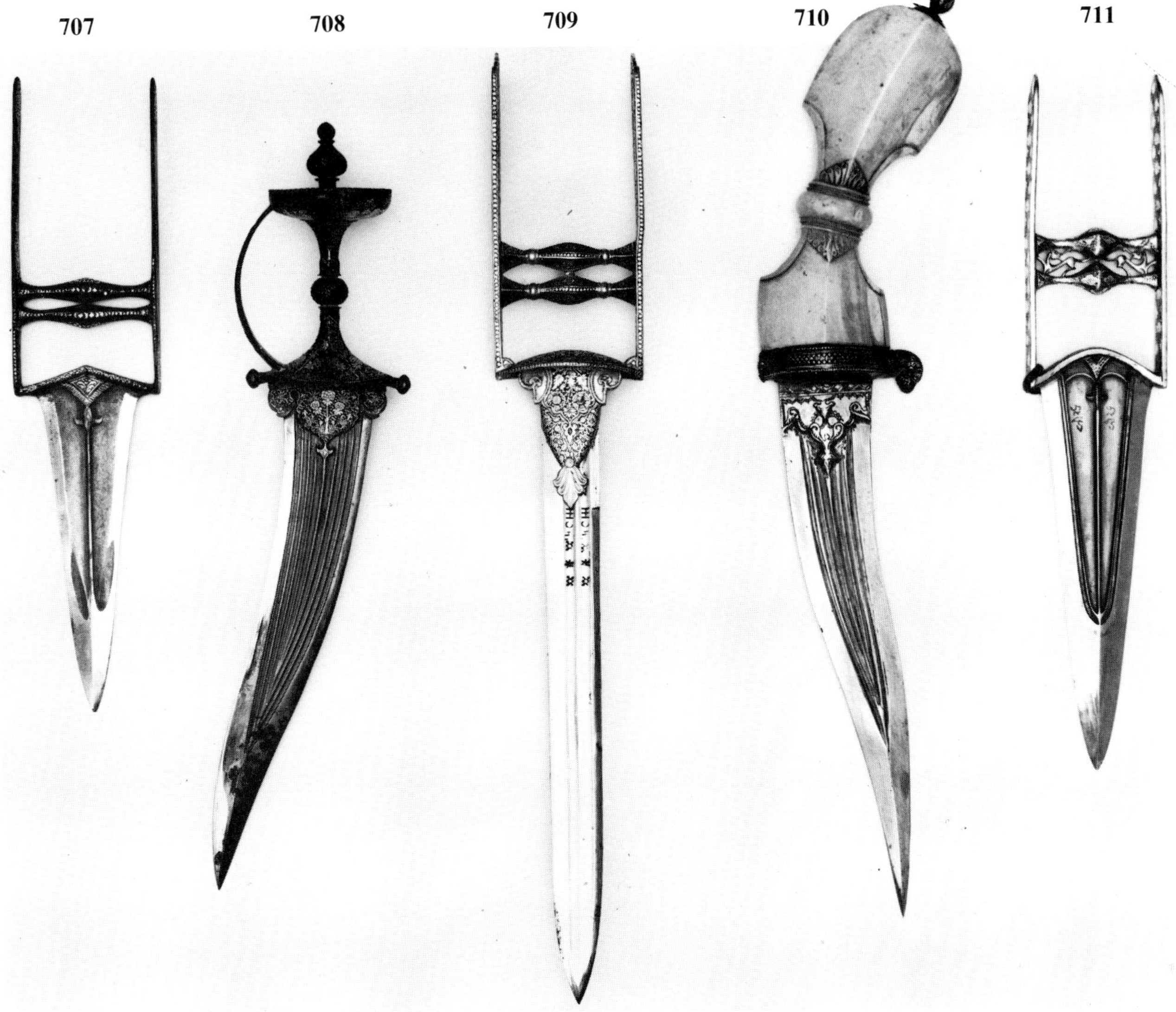

707. Indian katar
Length 13¾ins. (35cm) Late 18th/early 19th century
Gold damascened hilt of characteristic form. A reasonable to good quality example complete with scabbard, smaller knife and tweezers (not shown).
£150+

708. Indian (Deccan) khanjarli
Length 17ins. (43.2cm) 18th century
Iron hilt inlaid with flowers and leaves in two-colour gold. Fluted blade with reinforced point. Good quality but a little worn. Complete with scabbard.
£250 — £300

709. Indian katar with European blade
Length 20ins. (50.8cm) Late 18th century
Hilt attractively damascened in gold. The fullered blade has been cut down from a broadsword blade. Good condition. With scabbard.
£200 — £250

710. Indian (Deccan) khanjarli
Length 20ins. (50.8cm) 18th century
Carved girdled large ivory hilt with silver pommel and guard. An interesting dagger of good quality, complete with scabbard.
£200 — £250

711. Indian katar
Length 15⅜ins. (39cm) 19th century
Damascened hilt cast with animals at the grip. Robust blade with reinforced point. Reasonable quality. With scabbard.
£150 — £180

Photographs: Sotheby's

712

712. Persian peshkabz
Length 16½ins. (42cm)
Late 18th century
Hilt with walrus ivory grips. The watered-steel blade (see detail) with pronounced T-shaped rib on the back edge, chiselled and inlaid with gold at the forte. Embossed gold scabbard mounts with owner's insignia on the locket. A fine example of a familiar dagger. Highly valuable due to the weight of gold.
£2,000

713

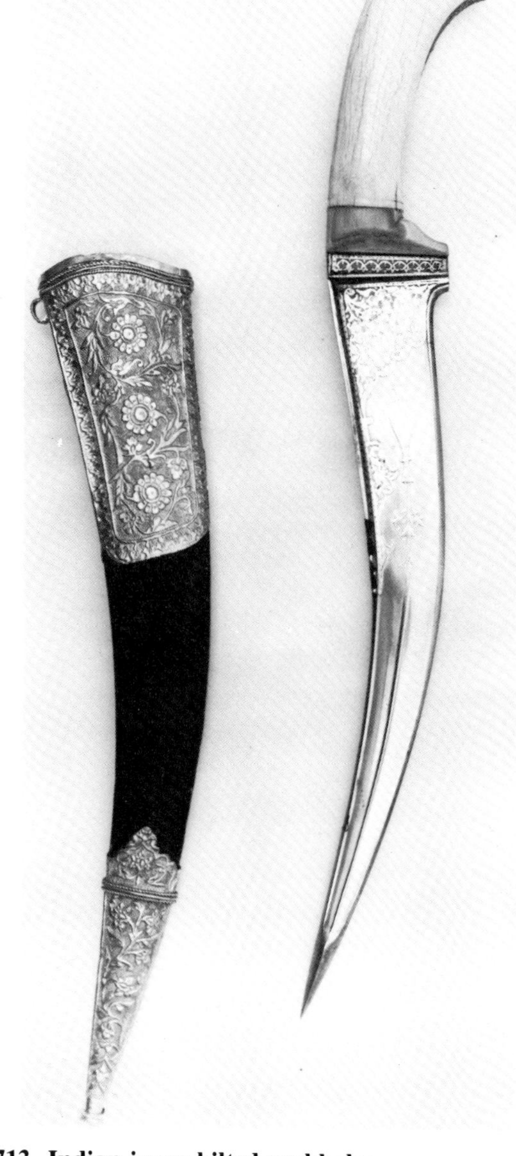

713. Indian ivory-hilted peshkabz
Length 17¾ins. (45cm)
Late 18th/early 19th century
Similar to 712 with finely embossed gold mounts on the leather-covered scabbard. Another fine example.
£1,000+

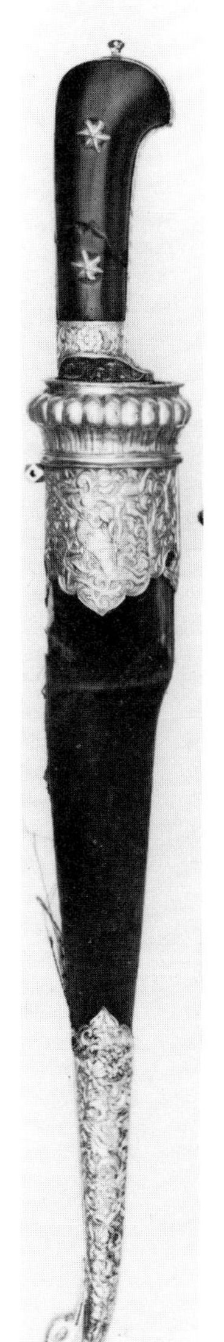

714

714. Indian peshkabz
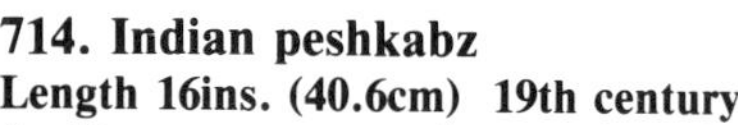
Length 16ins. (40.6cm) 19th century
A gilt-copper mounted example, with grips of amber, and watered-steel blade. A decorative dagger rather than one of high quality. One grip is cracked and the velvet covering on the scabbard is worn.
£100 — £150

Photographs: 712 Michael C. German Ltd.; 713 and 714 Sotheby's

715

715. North Indian Khyber knife
19th century
Hilt overlaid with mother-of-pearl and damascened at the shoulder. The single-edged blade worn. Reasonable quality.
£150 — £250

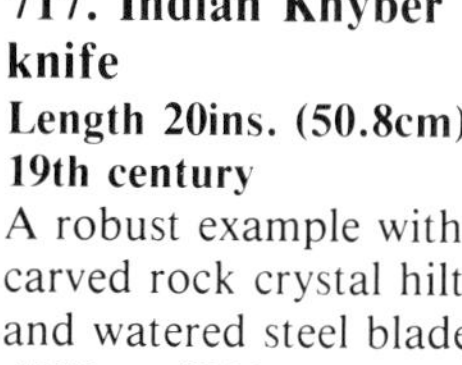

716

716. Indian Khyber knife
Length 18¼ins. (46.3cm)
19th century
A good plain example with rock crystal hilt. Some wear on the blade.
£200 — £300

717. Indian Khyber knife
Length 20ins. (50.8cm)
19th century
A robust example with carved rock crystal hilt and watered steel blade.
£200 — £300

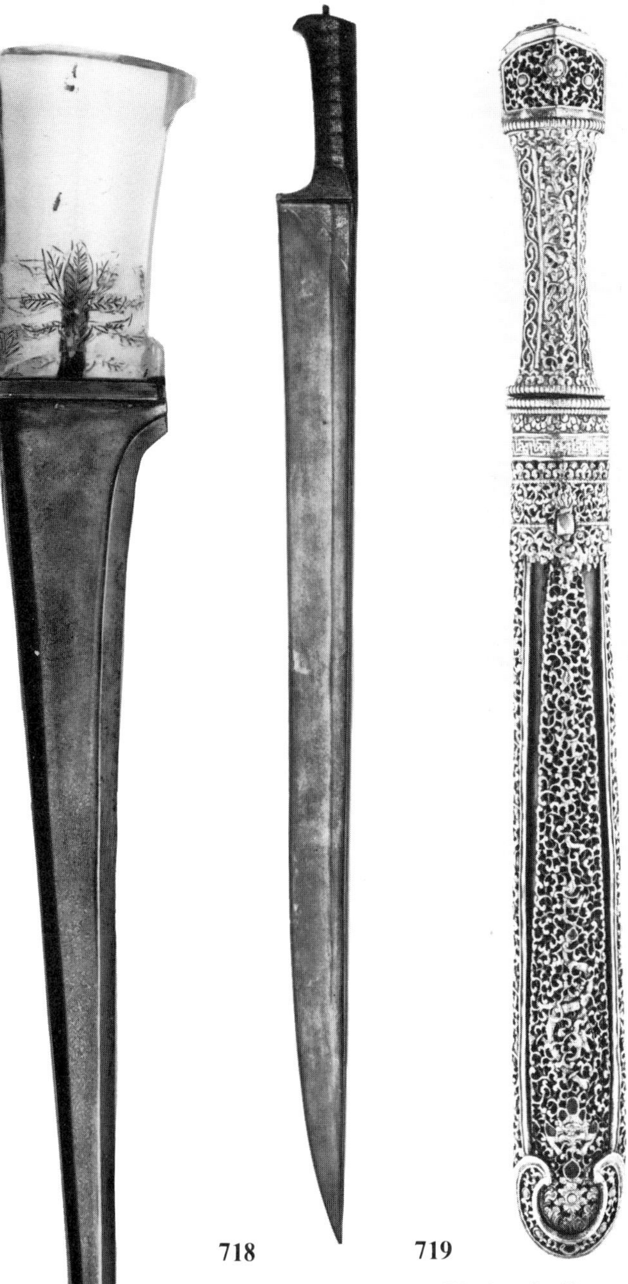

717

718

719

718. Afghan long Khyber knife
19th century
A typical example of the longer weapon used by tribesmen in the Khyber region. The gold damascened hilt and blade are worn. Reasonable quality.
£150 — £300

719. Tibetan silver-mounted dagger
Early 19th century
Hilt and leather-covered scabbard overlaid with pierced silver. The scabbard is also set with turquoise and has an applied gilt dragon on the central panel. Fine quality.
£220

Photographs: 715-718 Sotheby's; 719 Robert Hales Antiques Ltd.

720

720. Nepalese kukri
Length 18ins. (45.7cm) 19th century
A good example with an ivory hilt and an embossed silver-mounted leather scabbard fitted with a plaque of gold near the mouth. Complete with two small companion knives.
£80 — £120

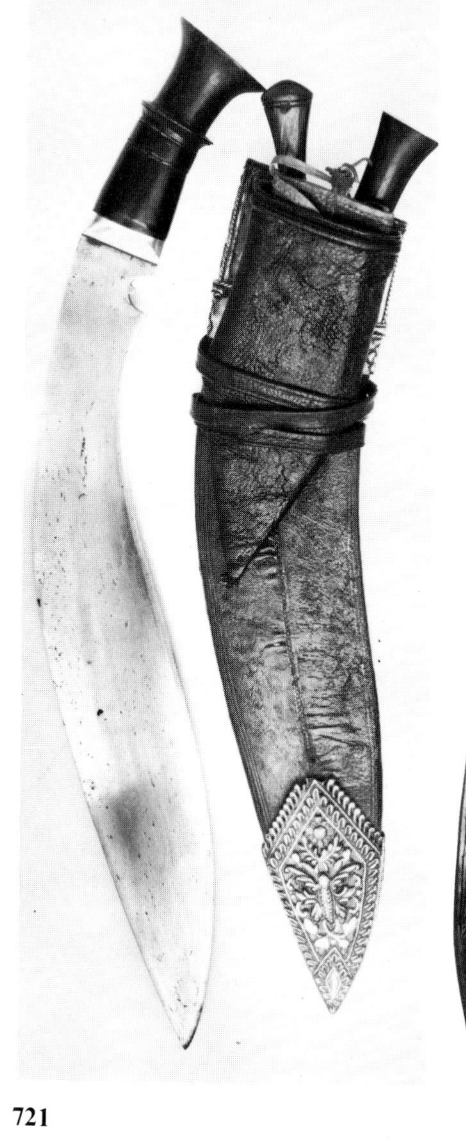

721

722

721. Nepalese Gurkha kukri
Length 18½ins. (47cm) 19th century
The knife is of characteristic form. The silver mounting on the scabbard adds value. It is shown in reverse with the two smaller knives in their pocket compartment. Reasonable quality. Blade pitted and cleaned.
£50 — £80

722. Nepalese Gurkha kukri
Length 18ins. (45.7cm) 19th century
An example of the plainest type, with horn hilt. Very poor condition (the black patches on the blade are rust) and without the protection of a scabbard.
£10 — £25

Photographs: 720 Robert Hale Antiques Ltd.; 721 and 722 Christie's

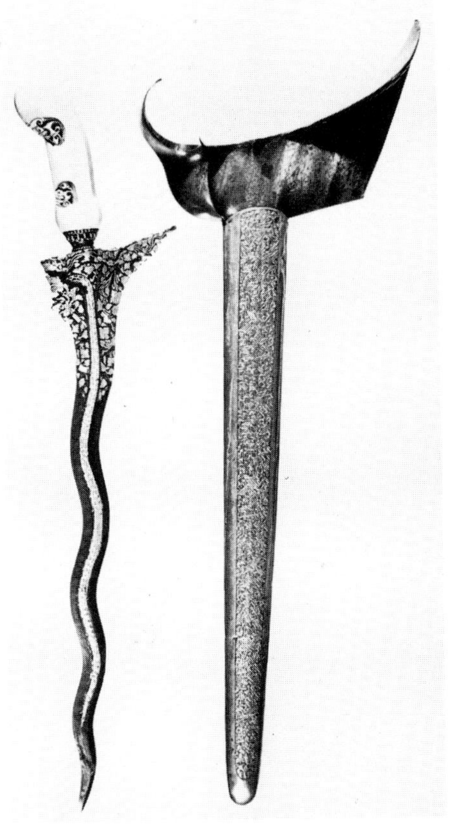

723

723. Javanese (Djogjakata) royal kris
18th century'
Ivory hilt. The gold-encrusted blade decorated with flowers and with the snake god Nagá. The winged wooden scabbard has a pierced silver sarong (central panel). Fine quality.
£1,500 — £1,800

Photographs: Robert Hales Antiques Ltd.

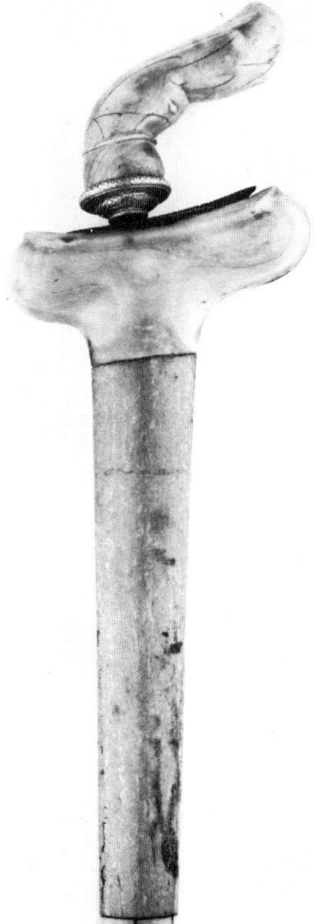

724

724. Kris, probably Malayan
18th or 19th century
The hilt and scabbard are of particular interest. The carved grip is of elephant ivory, the sampir (top part of the scabbard) of sperm whale tooth, the sarong (central panel) of walrus tusk, and the buntut (base panel) of bone.
£180 — £200

725 726

725. Indonesian (Celebes) kris
18th or 19th century
An example of very good quality with carved wood hilt and a finely patterned multi-layered blade of twenty-three waves.
£80

726. Small Javanese kris
18th or 19th century
Polychrome figurative hilt.
£75

Photographs: 727 Christie's;
728-731 Robert Hales Antiques Ltd.

727. Balinese gold-hilted kris
Length 25½ins. (64.8cm) 19th century
Gold hilt, in the form of a deity, set with precious stones. The scabbard, with tortoiseshell sarong (central panel) and ebony sampir (top panel), is associated. The 18th century blade is waved and figured. A fine familiar piece with the gold hilt adding to the value.
£300 — £500

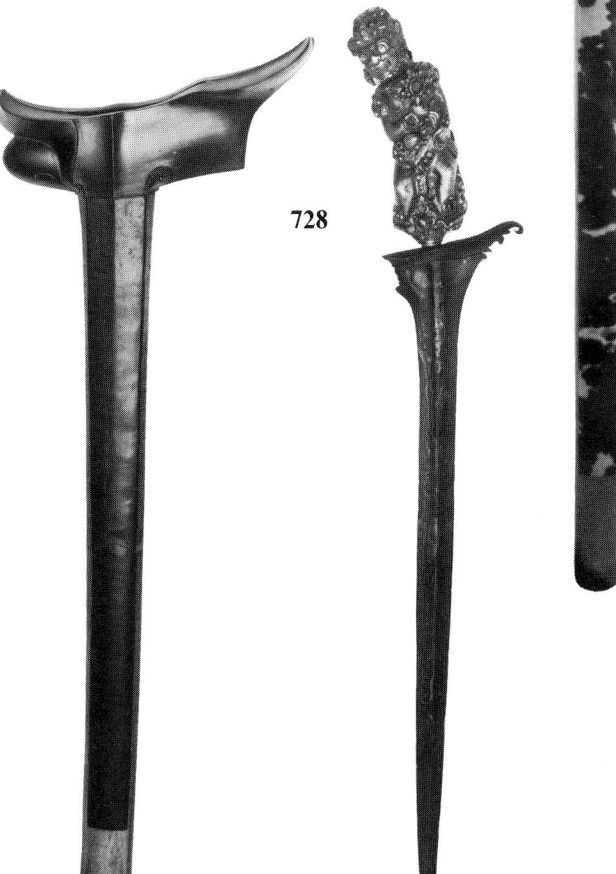

727

728

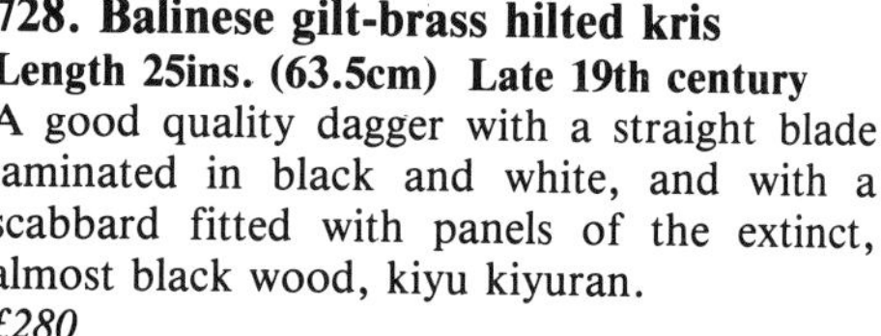

728. Balinese gilt-brass hilted kris
Length 25ins. (63.5cm) Late 19th century
A good quality dagger with a straight blade laminated in black and white, and with a scabbard fitted with panels of the extinct, almost black wood, kiyu kiyuran.
£280

729. Malayan carved ivory-hilted kris
19th century
Hilt in the form of a stylised human deity and blade finely laminated in contrasting metals.
£125

730. North Javanese (Tjeribon) kris
19th century
Finely carved wooden hilt in the form of a squatting figure. The patterned blade with regular waved outline. Good quality.
£150

731. North Javanese (Tjeribon) kris
19th century
Hilt carved in a similar manner to 730. Blade of poor quality.
£100

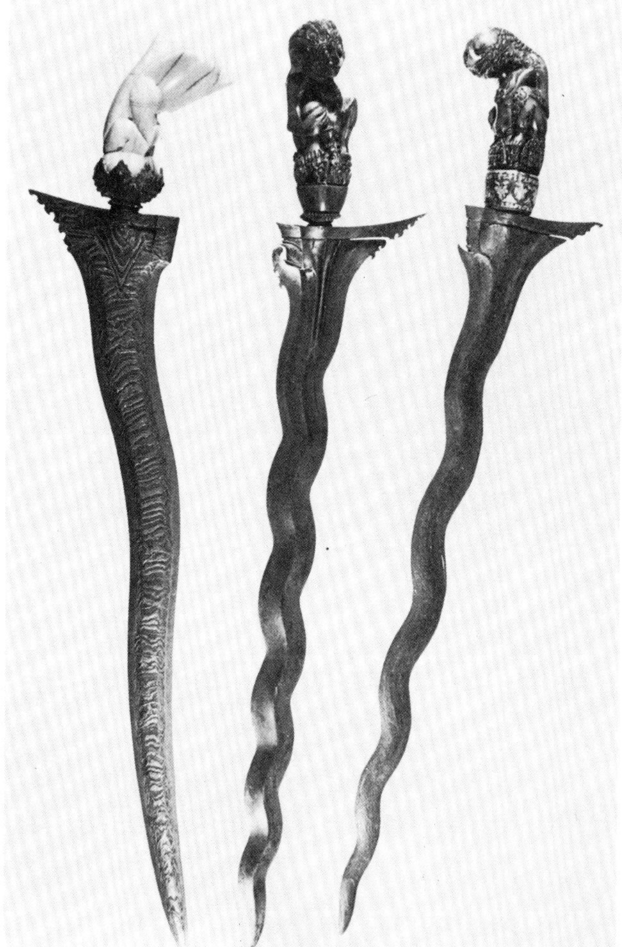

729 730 731

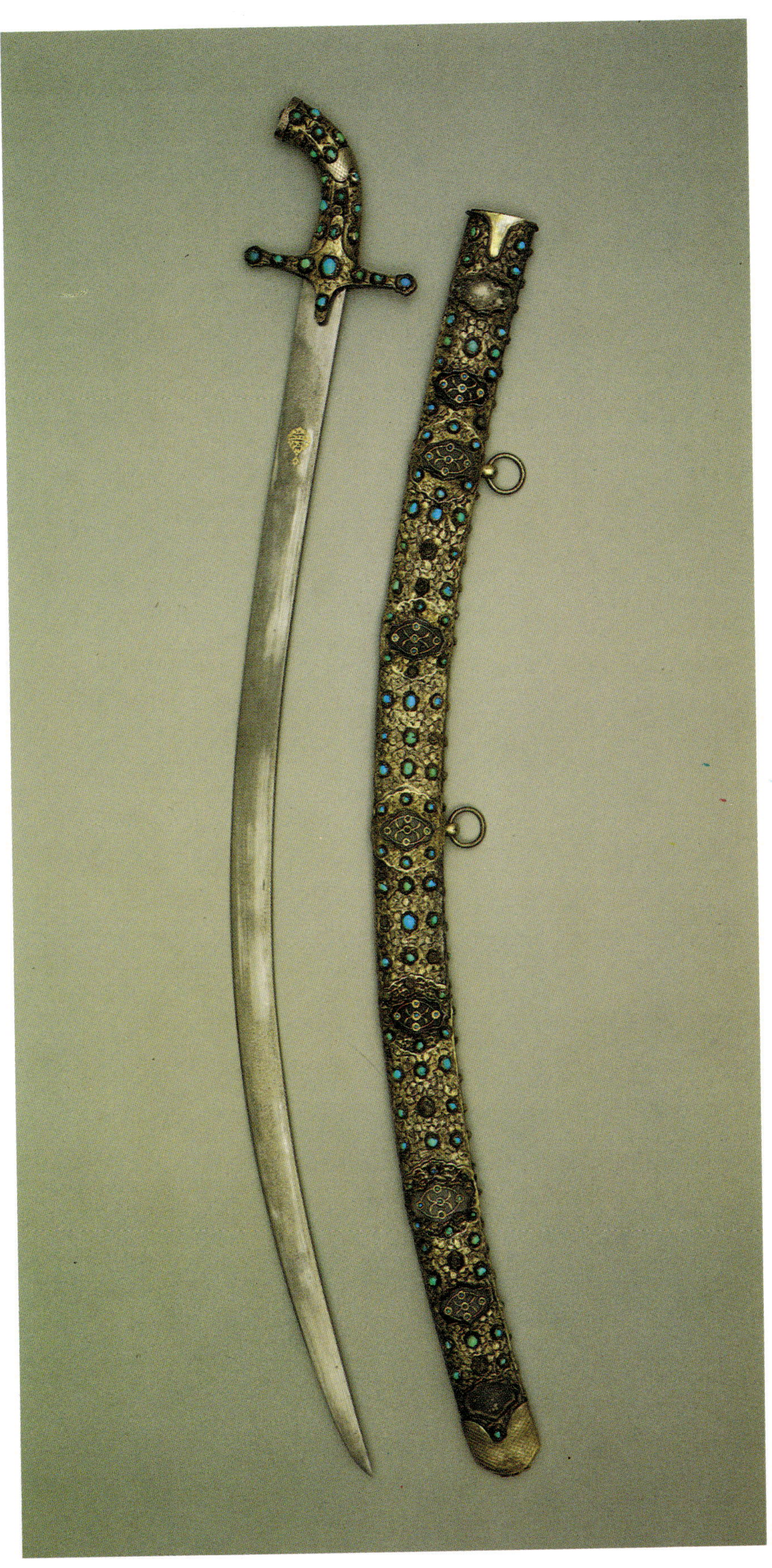

Colour Plate 8. *Turkish or Persian sabre, 16th or 17th century. For details see no. 498.*

732. Cingalese silver-mounted piha-kaetta
Length 12ins. (30.5cm)
18th century
A good example of characteristic form mounted in silver on the hilt, blade and scabbard.
£180

732

733

733. Cingalese silver-mounted piha-kaetta
Length 12½ins. (31.7cm)
18th or 19th century
An example in poorer condition than 732, and without the same amount of silver decoration. Complete with stylus.
£60 — £80

734. Malayan or Sumatran silver-mounted bade-bade
19th century
The hilt, and the wing on the silver-encased scabbard, are of horn carved in relief with foliage. Good quality. Blade worn.
£50 — £60

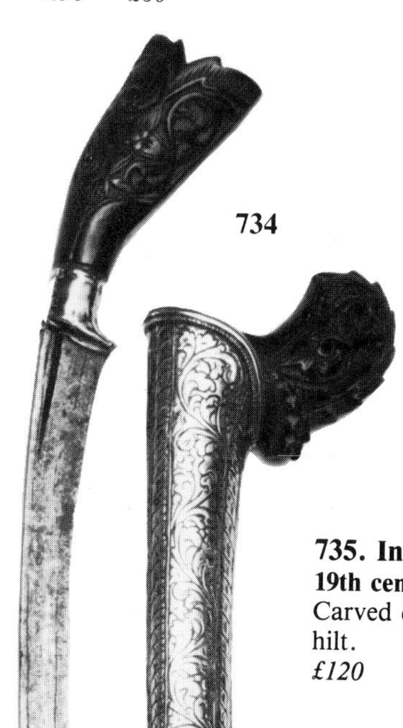

734

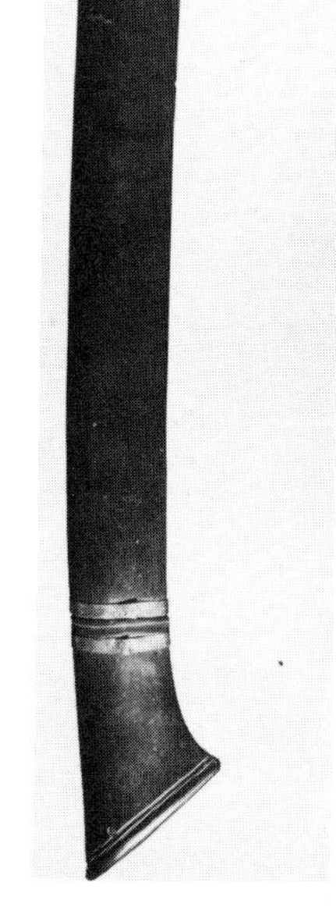

735

735. Indonesian klewang
19th century
Carved dragon's-head horn hilt.
£120

Photographs: 732, 734 and 735 Robert Hales Antiques Ltd.; 733 Christie's

736

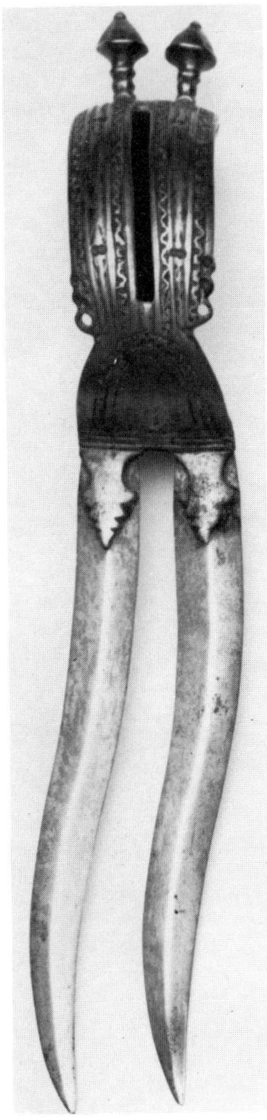

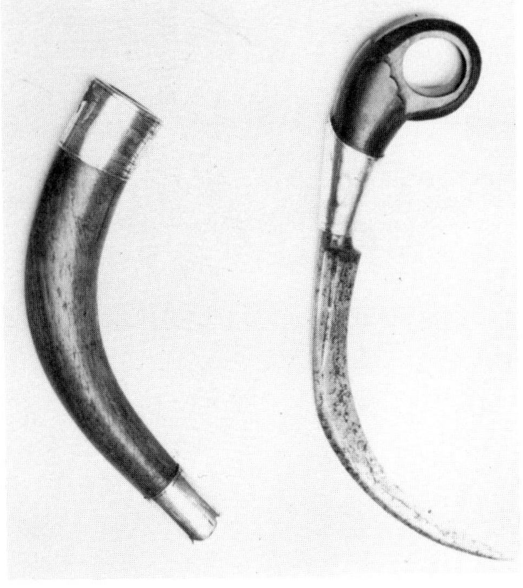

737

739

737. Sumatran korambi
19th century
This small but quite lethal weapon has a razor sharp blade and a horn hilt with finger loop.
£75

739. Indian dagger hilt
Length 5ins. (12.6cm)
16th century
Of gilded iron. The pommel button flanked by lions. Rare and of fine quality. Gilding worn.
£2,000 — £2,500

736. Indian all-steel bichwa
18th century
An interesting dagger with loop hilt and double-pronged blade. Good condition.
£70

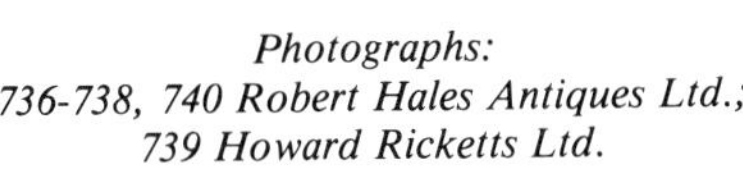

Photographs:
736-738, 740 Robert Hales Antiques Ltd.;
739 Howard Ricketts Ltd.

738

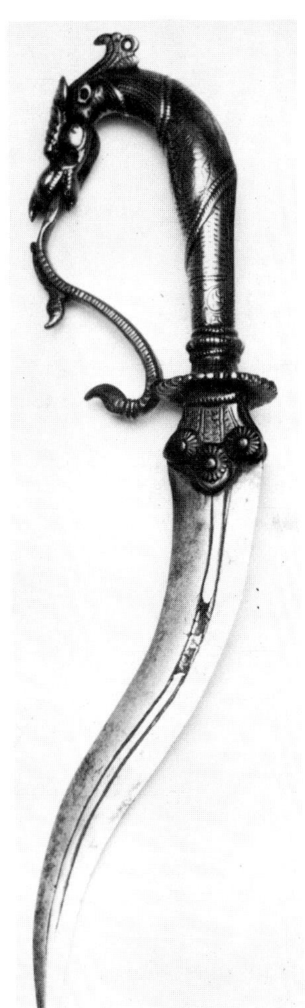

740

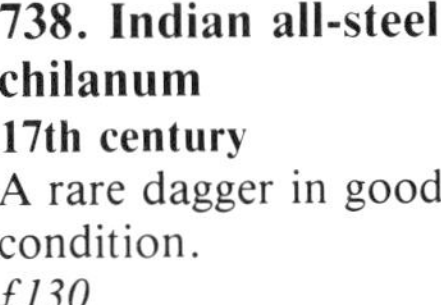

738. Indian all-steel chilanum
17th century
A rare dagger in good condition.
£130

740. South Indian (Mysore) brass-hilted dagger
18th century
A good example. The hilt cast in the form of a mythical lion.
£160

741

741. Japanese silver-mounted tanto
Blade 11⅛ins. (28.3cm)
19th century
A fine example with foliate decorated mounts and gilded black lacquer sheath. Blade signed 'UME TADA SADANORI'.
£2,000

Photographs: Christie's

742. Japanese silver-mounted tanto
Blade 11⅜ins. (28.8cm) 19th century
Similar in quality to 741. The mounts signed 'MOTOAKI'. 17th century blade.
£2,000 — £2,500

743. Japanese tanto
Blade 10⁵⁄₁₆ ins. (26.2cm)
Blade probably 14th century
An attractive example with gilt-copper mounts, ribbed red lacquer sheath, and fish-skin covered grip. Mounts inscribed 'JOSHIKU'. Blade signed 'RAI KUNITOSHI'.
£600 — £800

744. Japanese tanto with gilt-metal mounts
Blade 10ins. (25.3cm) 18th or 19th century
Another high quality example with delicately cast mounts and cord-bound grip. Blade inscribed 'SOSHU JU AKIHIRO'.
£1,000 — £1,500

742 743 744

3. STAFF WEAPONS

Halberds

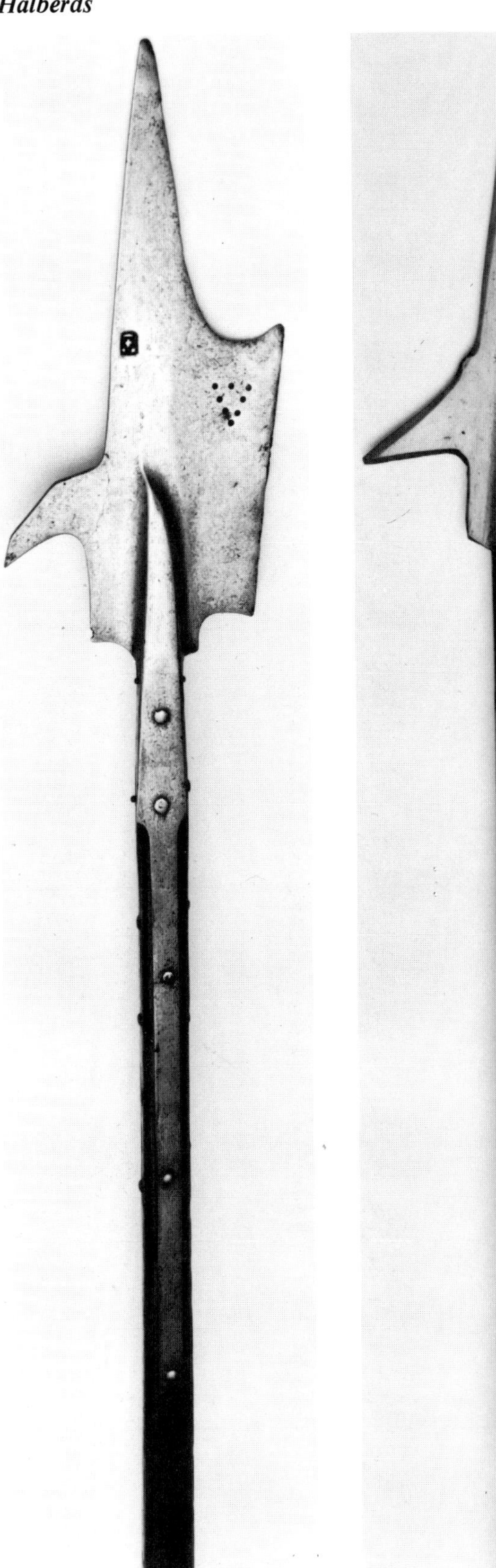

745

746

745. Halberd, probably Swiss
Length of head 20½ins. (52cm)
Second half 15th century
The head is secured to the haft by four straps and is struck with a mark (a crescent above a cross with two pellets in a rectangle). Rare.
£2,500 — £3,000

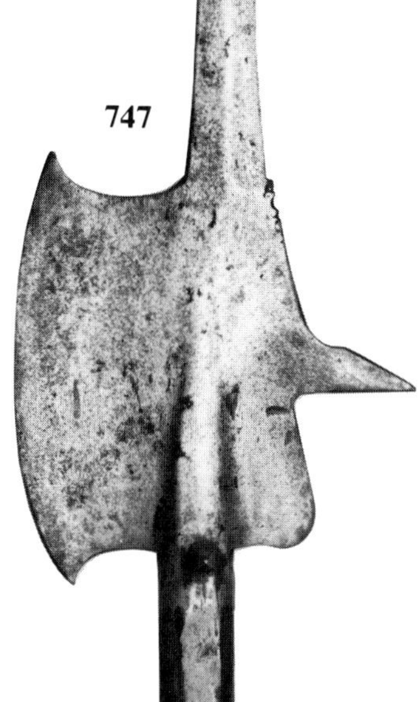

747

746. Swiss halberd
Length of head 14½ins. (36.8cm)
Probably 17th century
Of early (so-called Sempach) type, but probably one of a number known to have been made for the Zürich arsenal by Lamprecht Koller (Würenlos, Canton Aargau), between 1640 and 1681.
£800 — £1,000

747. Swiss (Solothurn) halberd
About 1450-1500
A rare, early example covered in surface dirt.
£2,000 — £2,500

Photographs: Christie's

748. German or Swiss halberd
Length of head 24½ins. (61cm)
Late 15th century
The head struck with three clover-leaf marks. Worn and on later haft.
£1,500 — £2,000

749. German or Swiss halberd
Length of head 15½ins. (39.3cm) About 1500
A good example in reasonable condition. The fluke struck with a mark (a crown).
£1,500

750. Halberd, possibly Austrian
Length of head 22ins. (55.8cm)
Early 16th century
Of similar quality and condition to 749. The head with maker's mark (the letter ?'T' with three pellets in a shield).
£1,500

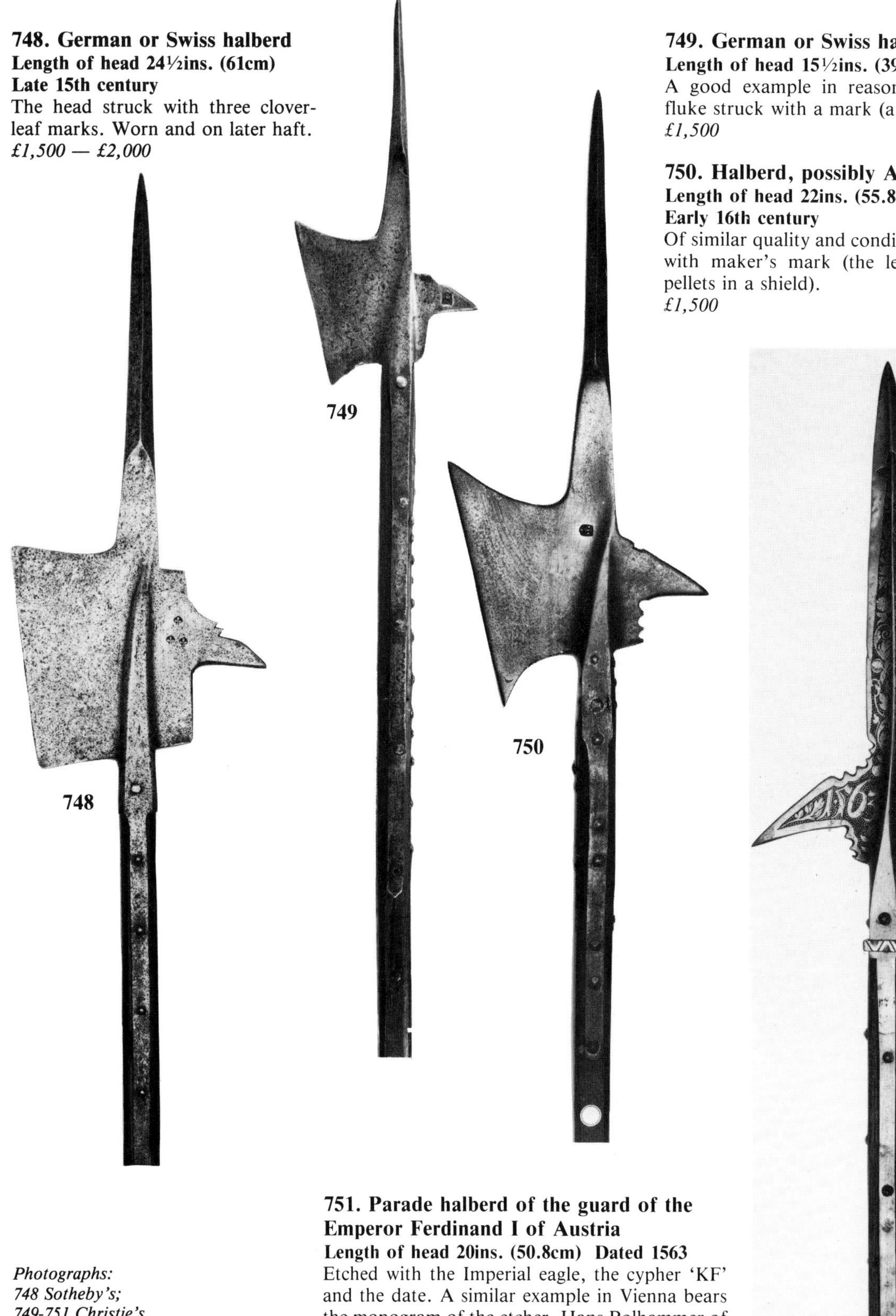

748

749

750

751. Parade halberd of the guard of the Emperor Ferdinand I of Austria
Length of head 20ins. (50.8cm) Dated 1563
Etched with the Imperial eagle, the cypher 'KF' and the date. A similar example in Vienna bears the monogram of the etcher, Hans Polhammer of Innsbruck. Fine quality.
£2,500 — £3,000

751

Photographs:
748 Sotheby's;
749-751 Christie's

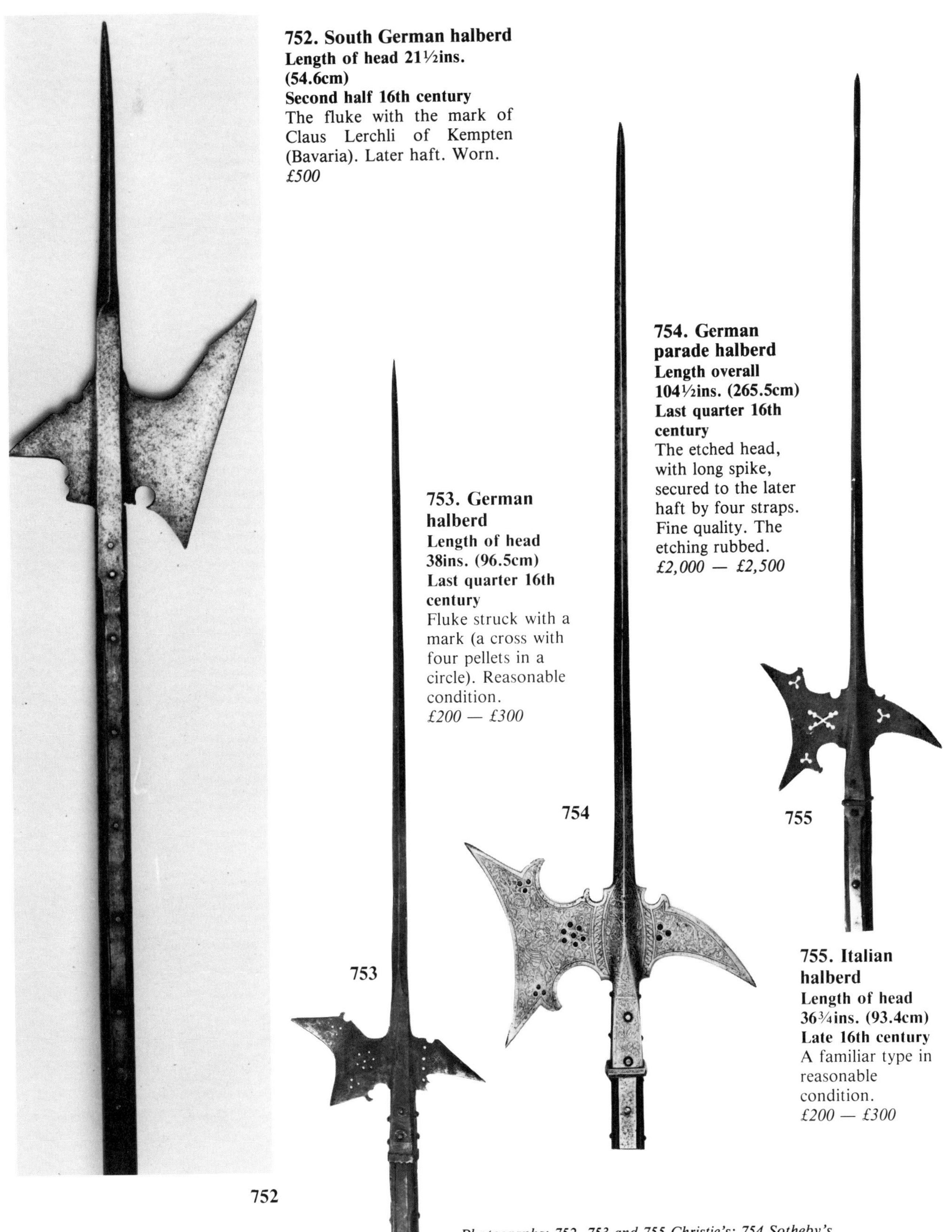

752. South German halberd
Length of head 21½ins. (54.6cm)
Second half 16th century
The fluke with the mark of Claus Lerchli of Kempten (Bavaria). Later haft. Worn.
£500

753. German halberd
Length of head 38ins. (96.5cm)
Last quarter 16th century
Fluke struck with a mark (a cross with four pellets in a circle). Reasonable condition.
£200 — £300

754. German parade halberd
Length overall 104½ins. (265.5cm)
Last quarter 16th century
The etched head, with long spike, secured to the later haft by four straps. Fine quality. The etching rubbed.
£2,000 — £2,500

755. Italian halberd
Length of head 36¾ins. (93.4cm)
Late 16th century
A familiar type in reasonable condition.
£200 — £300

Photographs: 752, 753 and 755 Christie's; 754 Sotheby's

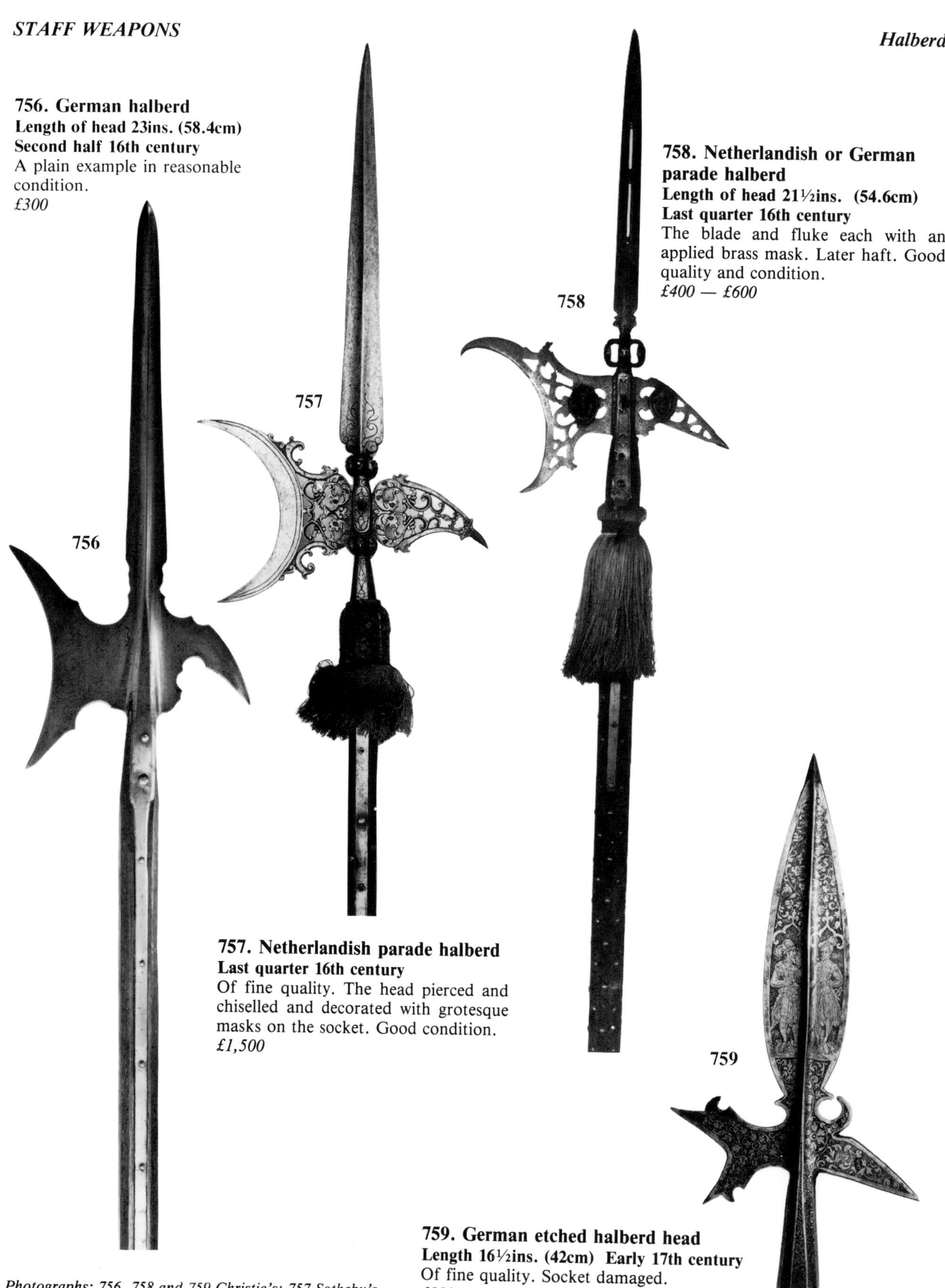

756. German halberd
Length of head 23ins. (58.4cm)
Second half 16th century
A plain example in reasonable condition.
£300

757. Netherlandish parade halberd
Last quarter 16th century
Of fine quality. The head pierced and chiselled and decorated with grotesque masks on the socket. Good condition.
£1,500

758. Netherlandish or German parade halberd
Length of head 21½ins. (54.6cm)
Last quarter 16th century
The blade and fluke each with an applied brass mask. Later haft. Good quality and condition.
£400 — £600

759. German etched halberd head
Length 16½ins. (42cm) Early 17th century
Of fine quality. Socket damaged.
£800

Photographs: 756, 758 and 759 Christie's; 757 Sotheby's

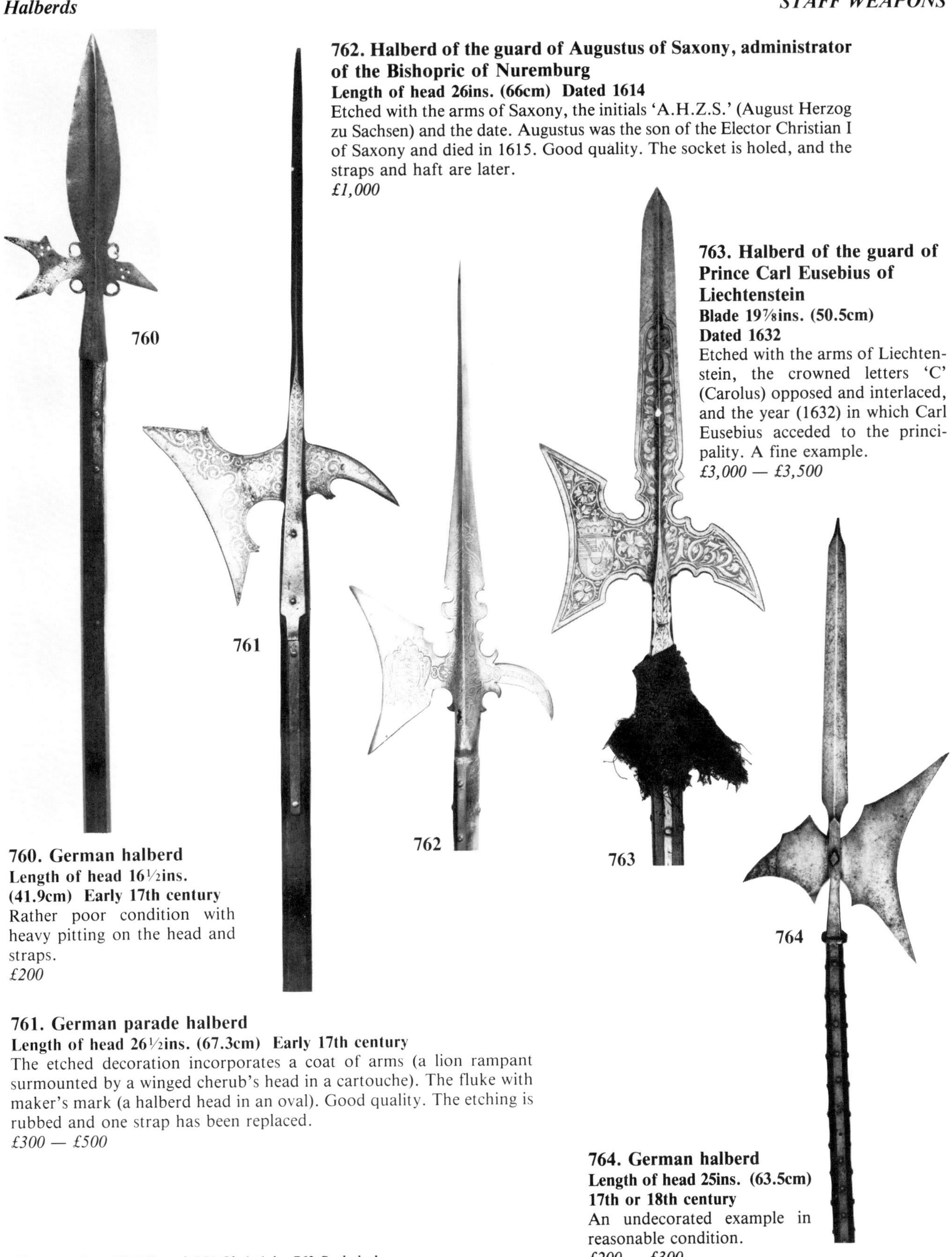

762. Halberd of the guard of Augustus of Saxony, administrator of the Bishopric of Nuremburg
Length of head 26ins. (66cm) Dated 1614
Etched with the arms of Saxony, the initials 'A.H.Z.S.' (August Herzog zu Sachsen) and the date. Augustus was the son of the Elector Christian I of Saxony and died in 1615. Good quality. The socket is holed, and the straps and haft are later.
£1,000

763. Halberd of the guard of Prince Carl Eusebius of Liechtenstein
Blade 19⅞ins. (50.5cm)
Dated 1632
Etched with the arms of Liechtenstein, the crowned letters 'C' (Carolus) opposed and interlaced, and the year (1632) in which Carl Eusebius acceded to the principality. A fine example.
£3,000 — £3,500

760. German halberd
Length of head 16½ins. (41.9cm) Early 17th century
Rather poor condition with heavy pitting on the head and straps.
£200

761. German parade halberd
Length of head 26½ins. (67.3cm) Early 17th century
The etched decoration incorporates a coat of arms (a lion rampant surmounted by a winged cherub's head in a cartouche). The fluke with maker's mark (a halberd head in an oval). Good quality. The etching is rubbed and one strap has been replaced.
£300 — £500

764. German halberd
Length of head 25ins. (63.5cm)
17th or 18th century
An undecorated example in reasonable condition.
£200 — £300

Photographs: 760-762 and 764 Christie's; 763 Sotheby's

765

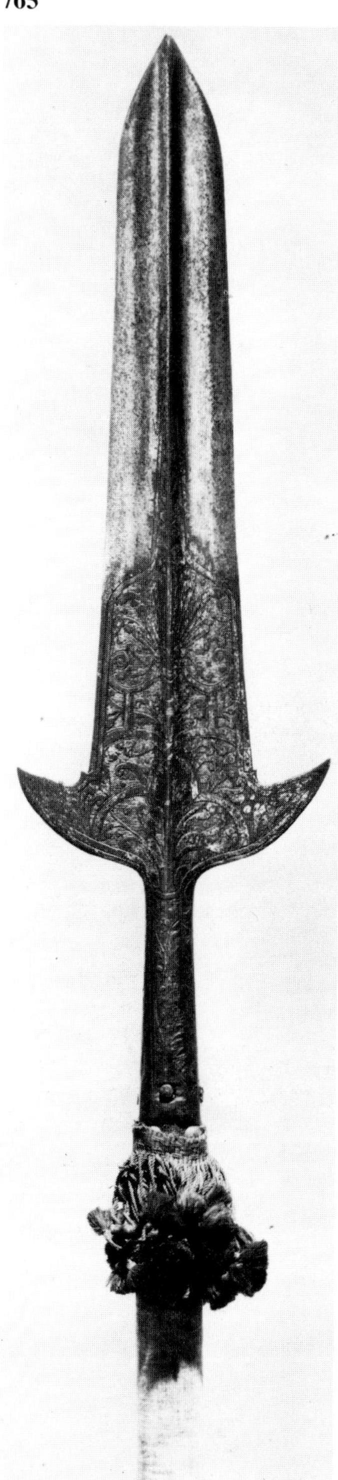

766. Parade partisan of the guard of Count Lodron, Archbishop of Salzburg
Length of head 27½ins. (69.8cm) Dated 1620
Finely etched head with the Archbishop's coat of arms and the date. Modern haft. The etching rubbed.
£1,500 — £2,000

768

766

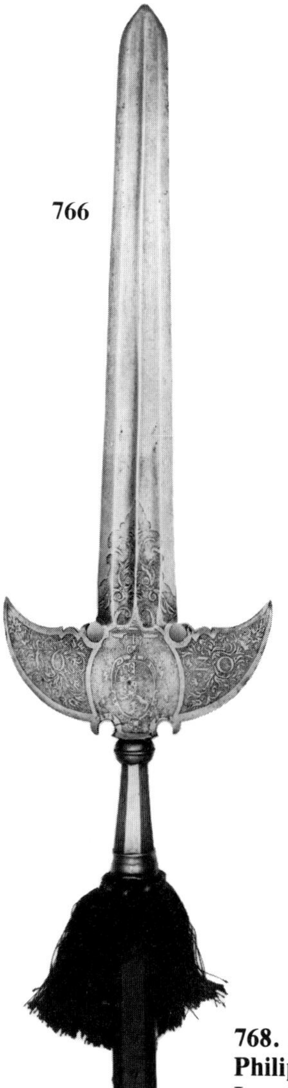

767

767. Partisan of the Polish guard of Noblemen of Augustus II, Elector of Saxony and King of Poland
Early 18th century
A fine example of a distinctive and well-known group.
£2,000 — £4,000

768. Parade partisan of the guard of Damian Hugo Philipp, Count Schönborn, Cardinal Bishop of Speyer
Length overall 97¼ins. (247cm) About 1720
Etched head with the Cardinal's coat of arms and the letters 'D.H.S.R.E.C. de S. S.R.I.P. ac E.S' (Damian Hugo Sanctæ Romanæ Ecclesiæ Cardinales de Schönborn, Sacrium Romanum Imperum Princeps atque Episcopus Spirensis (Damian Hugo, Cardinal of the Holy Roman Church, Prince of the Holy Roman Empire, Bishop of Schönborn and of Speyer). Good quality. Later haft.
£1,200 — £2,000

765. French partisan
17th century
Of very good quality with an etched and gilt head (worn). Later haft.
£1,000 — £1,200

Photographs: Sotheby's

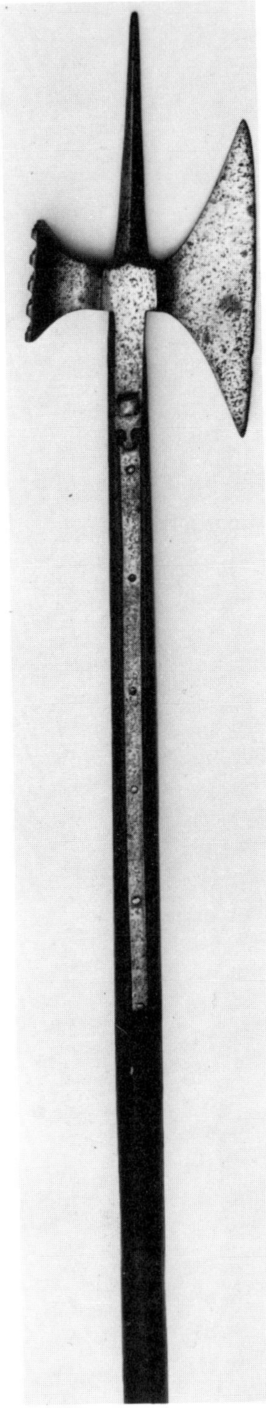

769. Poleaxe
Length of head 12½ins. (31.7cm)
Second half 15th century
Of robust form, but pitted and fitted to a later haft.
£800

770

770. Poleaxe, possibly French
Length of head 14ins. (35.5cm)
Last quarter 15th century
A fine example inlaid with brass and with a spike projecting from the face of the hammer. Modern haft.
£1,200 — £2,000

771

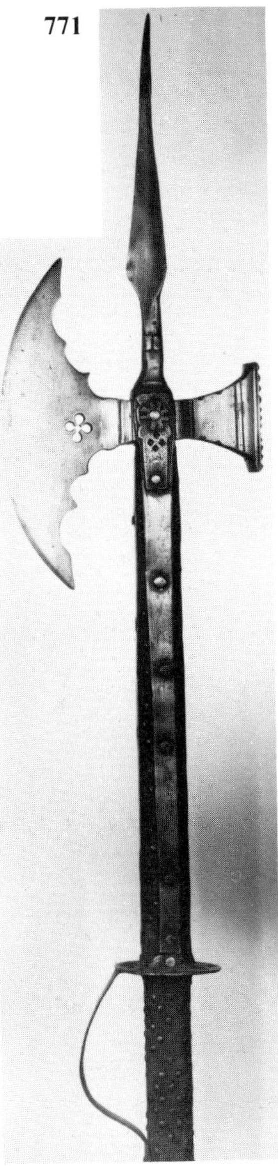

771. Italian poleaxe
Length of head 15ins. (38.1cm)
16th century
The studded haft fitted with a disc hand guard. Good quality and condition.
£800 — £1,000

769

772. Venetian etched parade poleaxe
Length overall 73⅜ins. (186.3cm)
16th century
A sturdy example with studded haft. Good condition.
£400 — £500

Photographs: 769-771 Christie's; 772 Sotheby's

772

773. Swiss pole hammer
Length of head 10½ins. (26.6cm)
Late 15th/early 16th century
Of robust form and in good condition. The beak with a maker's mark (a hammer in a shield).
£1,200 — £1,500

775. Swiss Lucerne hammer
Length of head 15ins. (38.1cm)
16th century
The beak struck with a mark (a flower head). Later haft. Good condition.
£1,000 — £1,500

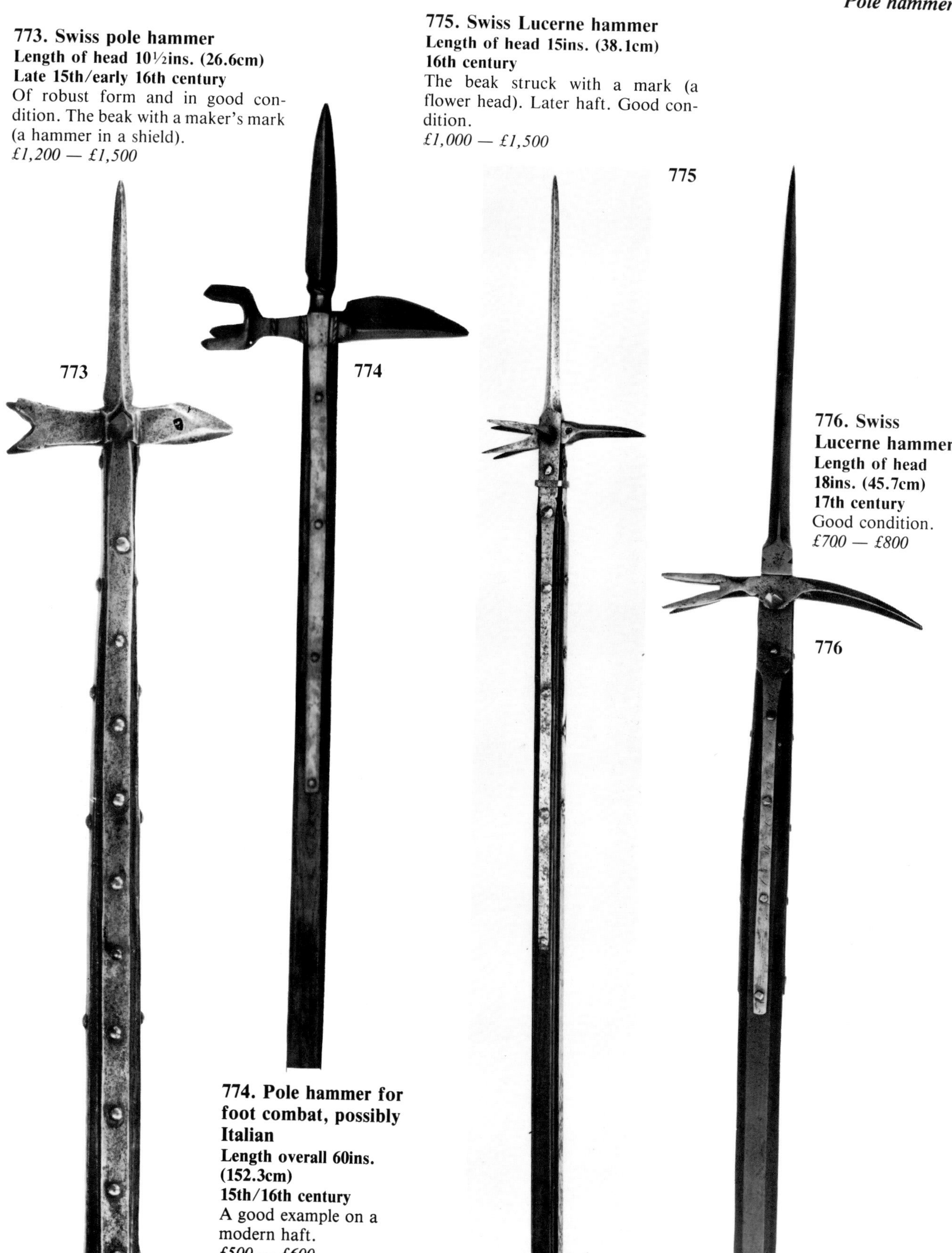

776. Swiss Lucerne hammer
Length of head 18ins. (45.7cm)
17th century
Good condition.
£700 — £800

774. Pole hammer for foot combat, possibly Italian
Length overall 60ins. (152.3cm)
15th/16th century
A good example on a modern haft.
£500 — £600

Photographs: 773, 774 and 776 Christie's; 775 Sotheby's

777. Bill, possibly English
Length of head 17½ins. (44.5cm)
15th or 16th century
The fluke struck with a mark (?the letter 'B'). An early example, heavily pitted and fitted to a later haft.
£350

778. English bill
Second half 16th century
A rare weapon, but heavily corroded. Tower of London Armouries (VII-1513).
£300 — £400

777

778

779

779. Italian etched bill
Length of head 28ins. (71.1cm) Late 15th century
The etched and formerly gilt head includes a coat of arms (a lion rampant on a field semé with mullets) in its design. Fine quality, now very worn and on a later haft.
£500 — £600

780. Bardiche, possibly east European
Length of head 23½ins. (59.7cm) 16th or 17th century
Quite rare. Worn.
£500 — £600

780

781

781. Gisarme
Length of head 24ins. (61cm)
16th or 17th century
A particularly rare form of hafted weapon struck with two marks on the blade. One mark appears to be a star or cross with a pellet in a circle. Very worn.
£300

Photographs: 777, 780 and 781 Christie's; 778 Crown Copyright; 779 Sotheby's

783. Venetian glaive
Length of head 35½ins. (90.2cm) Early 17th century
The worn head pierced with flower heads. Reasonable condition.
£500

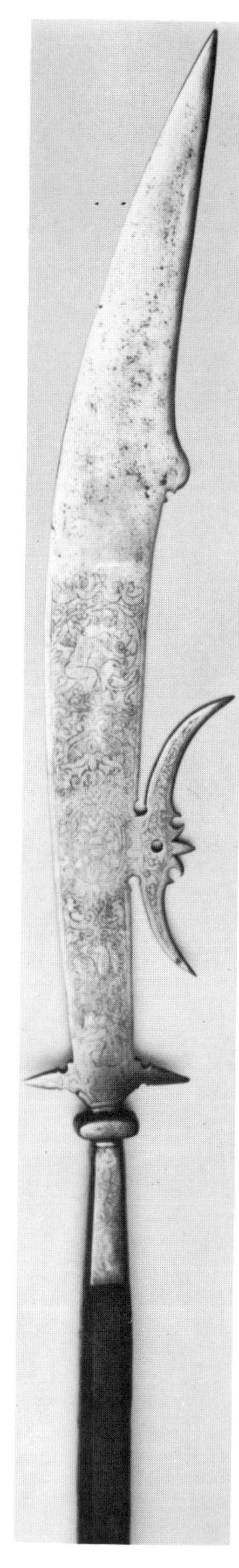

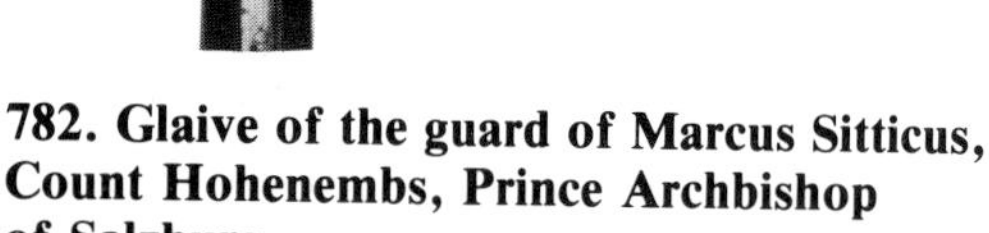

782. Glaive of the guard of Marcus Sitticus, Count Hohenembs, Prince Archbishop of Salzburg
Blade 21¾ins. (55.2cm) About 1615
A fine example with some wear on the blade. The haft restored. This particular form of weapon is also sometimes known as a *couse* and as a *couteau-de-breche.*
£1,200 — £2,000

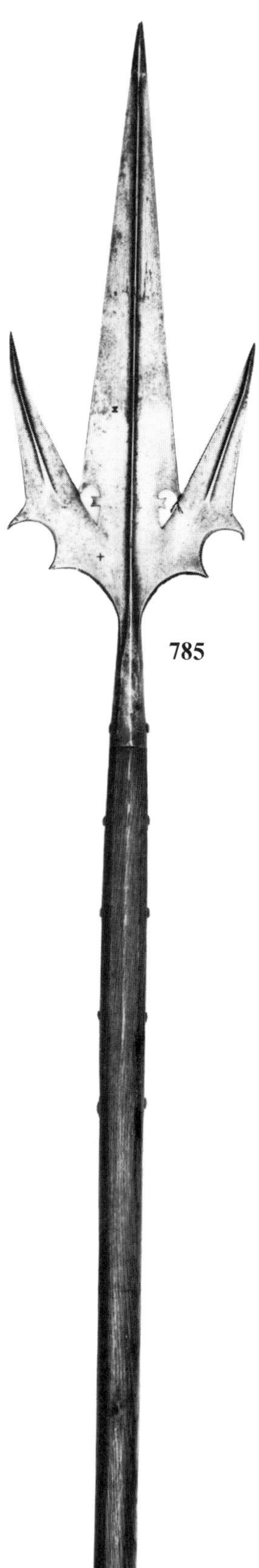

784. Glaive of Venetian type
Length of head 35ins. (88.8cm) 17th century
An example of good quality, etched with the Habsburg coat of arms. The blade is pitted and the etched decoration rubbed.
£600

785. Italian corseque
Length of head 24½ins. (62.2cm) Mid-16th century
The head struck with two marks (a tower and a cross). Modern haft. Quite rare, blade worn. Also known as *chauve-souris.*
£500 — £800

784

Photographs: 782 and 785 Sotheby's; 783 and 784 Christie's

Spears

786. North European boar-hunting spear
Second half 15th century
Of robust form with two side lugs. A good example fitted to an old but associated haft. Tower of London Armouries (VII-75).
£500 — £800

787. Italian boar-hunting spear
About 1530
A bolt, complete with stopping bar, secures the head to the modern haft. The tassel and straps are also modern. Tower of London Armouries (VII-1374).
£500 — £800

788

789

788. Swiss lugged spear head
Length 20¾ins. (52.7cm) 15th century
Pitted and worn.
£300

789. Swiss lugged spear
Length of head 19ins. (48.2cm) 16th century
A good example on a later haft. The blade struck with a mark (?ship's wheel in a shield).
£800 — £1,000

787

786

Photographs: 786 and 787 Crown Copyright; 788 and 789 Christie's

790. British cavalry lance
Length of head 16¼ins. (41.3cm)
19th century
A familiar weapon but rarely appearing for sale. Head stamped 'HYLAND'. Tower of London Armouries (unnumbered).
£150 — £200

790

791. German awl-pike (Ahlspiess)
Spike 32ins. (81.2cm)
15th century
Long spike fitted to a wooden haft. The straps bound with metal strip. Worn overall.
£300

791

792. Italian brandistock
17th century
The retractable blades are released from the steel haft by opening a safety catch and jerking the weapon forward. Rare.
£400 — £500

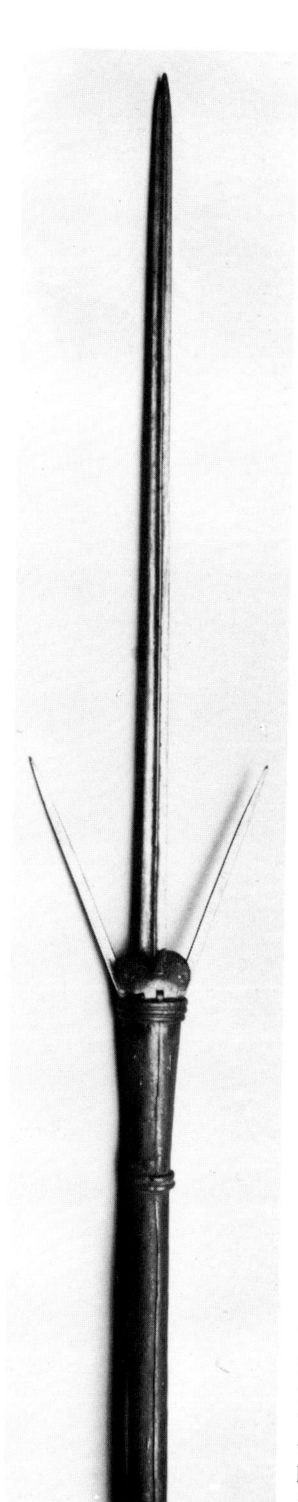

792

793

793. Italian brandistock
Length of head 31½ins. (80cm)
17th century
The retractable spike is released in the same way as those on 792. The steel haft is overlaid with leather. Rare but worn.
£700 — £800

794

794. Italian artilleryman's linstock
Length of head 17½ins.
(44.5cm) 17th century
The head with two serpentine match-cord holders. Very good condition.
£600 — £800

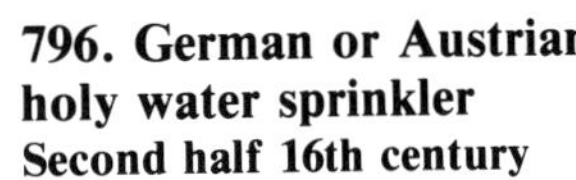

796. German or Austrian holy water sprinkler
Second half 16th century
A rare weapon in good condition. Tower of London Armouries (VII-1343).
£500

795

796

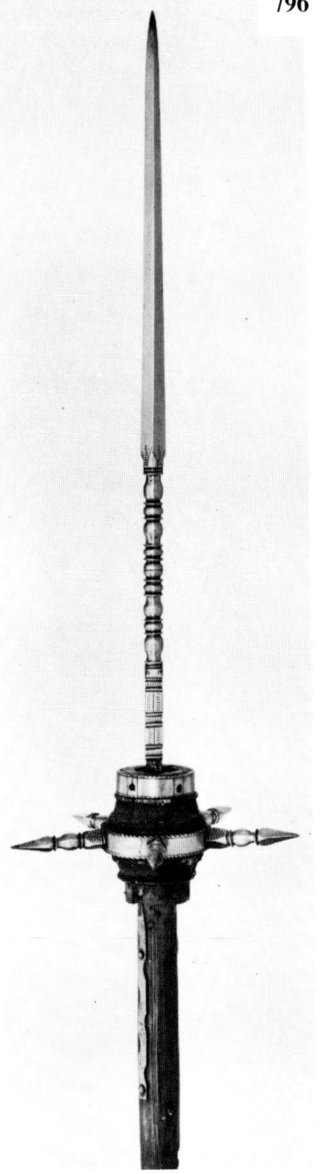

797

797. German combined mace and four-barrelled matchlock gun
Length 31ins. (79cm)
Last quarter 16th century
The four barrels are enclosed in the wooden head secured by three spiked bands. The muzzle cover is retained by a spring catch. The head and haft are inlaid with engraved stag horn. This rare weapon is variously known as a 'shooting club' or (the English form) as 'Henry VIII's walking staff'. Good condition. Some inlay restored.
£3,000+

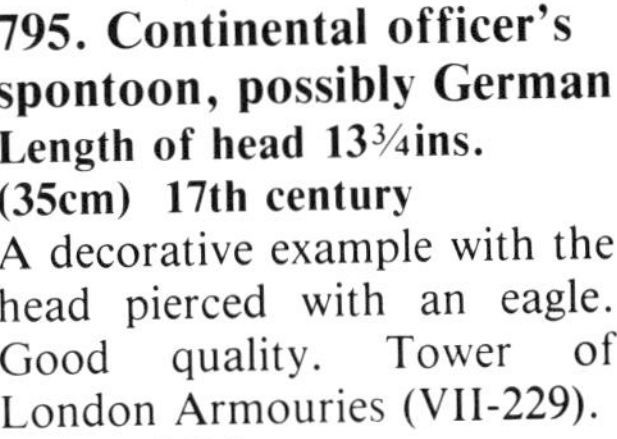

795. Continental officer's spontoon, possibly German
Length of head 13¾ins.
(35cm) 17th century
A decorative example with the head pierced with an eagle. Good quality. Tower of London Armouries (VII-229).
£80 — £150

Photographs: 794 Christie's; 795 and 796 Crown Copyright; 797 Sotheby's

798. Mace, probably German
Length 20ins. (50.8cm)
Second half 15th century
Of fine quality. The head with six flanges and the grip overlaid with leather.
£1,000 — £2,000

800. Italian mace
Length 25 3/16 ins. (64cm)
About 1530
The haft chiselled with scrolling foliage and with basketwork on the grip. Good quality.
£1,000 — £1,200

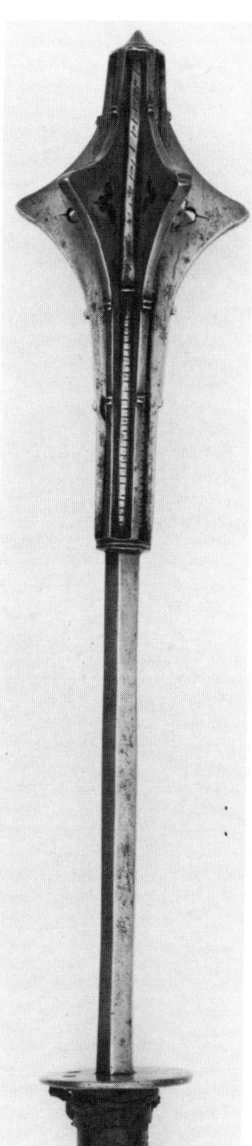

798

799

799. German mace
Length 18¾ins. (47.6cm)
About 1500
A good example with six-flanged head. The grip pierced for a wrist thong.
£1,000 — £2,000

800

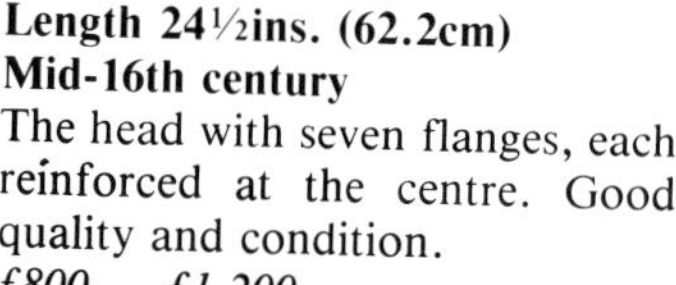

801. German mace
Length 24½ins. (62.2cm)
Mid-16th century
The head with seven flanges, each reinforced at the centre. Good quality and condition.
£800 — £1,200

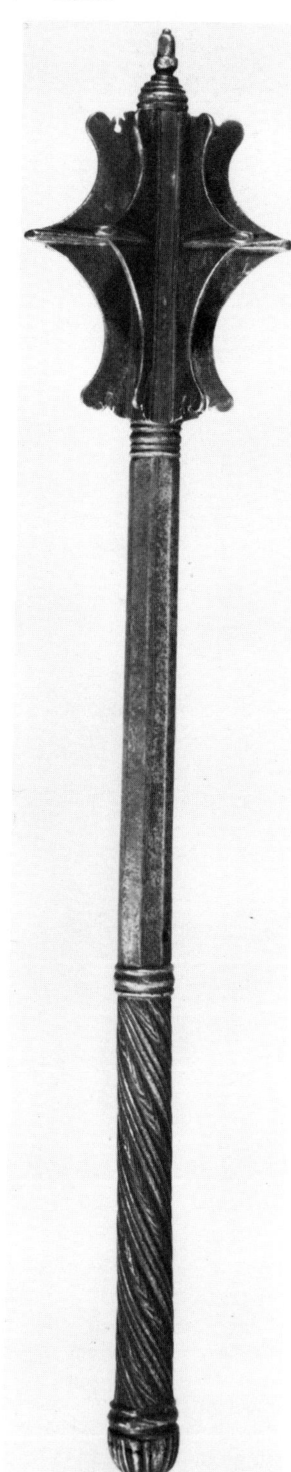

801

Photographs: 798 and 799, Sotheby's; 800 and 801 Christie's

802. Mace, possibly east German
Length 24½ins. (62.2cm)
16th century
Plain and in reasonable condition.
£750

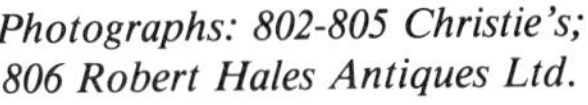
Photographs: 802-805 Christie's; 806 Robert Hales Antiques Ltd.

805

802

803. Polish mace
Length 24½ins. (62.2cm)
17th century
Spherical head of steel with six flanges reinforced in brass. Quite rare, reasonable condition.
£400 — £600

806

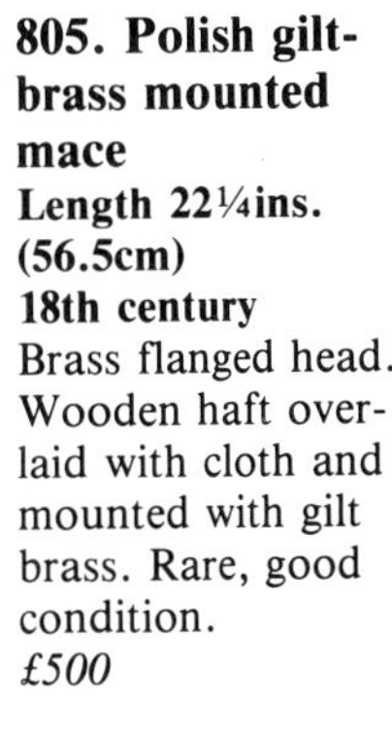

805. Polish gilt-brass mounted mace
Length 22¼ins. (56.5cm)
18th century
Brass flanged head. Wooden haft overlaid with cloth and mounted with gilt brass. Rare, good condition.
£500

804

803

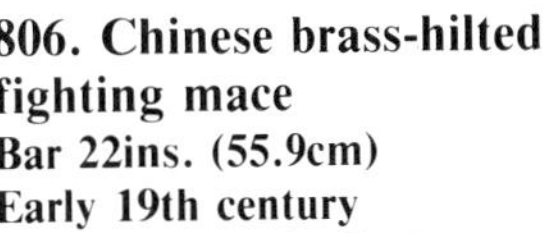

806. Chinese brass-hilted fighting mace
Bar 22ins. (55.9cm)
Early 19th century
The steel bar is finely cast in the form of a bamboo shoot and emerges from the mouth of a dragon's head located beneath the guard. Quite rare.
£180 — £200

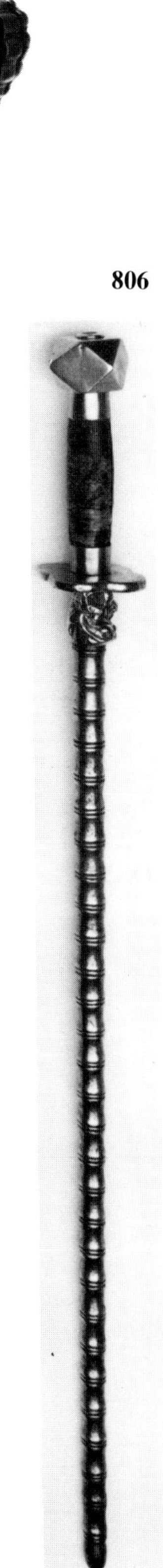

804. Polish silver-mounted mace
Length 21¼ins. (54cm)
Late 17th century
Six-flanged rock crystal head inlaid with silver. A fine quality piece but worn and with pieces missing.
£800 — £900

Colour Plate 9. *Hungarian silver-gilt mounted dress sabre, second quarter 18th century. For details see no. 481.* Howard Ricketts Ltd.

Below left: ***Colour Plate 10.*** *Persian royal shamshir, 17th century. For details see no. 499.* Howard Ricketts Ltd.

Below right: ***Colour Plate 11.*** *Indian silver-gilt and enamel hilted sword, 18th century. For details see no. 501.* Howard Ricketts Ltd.

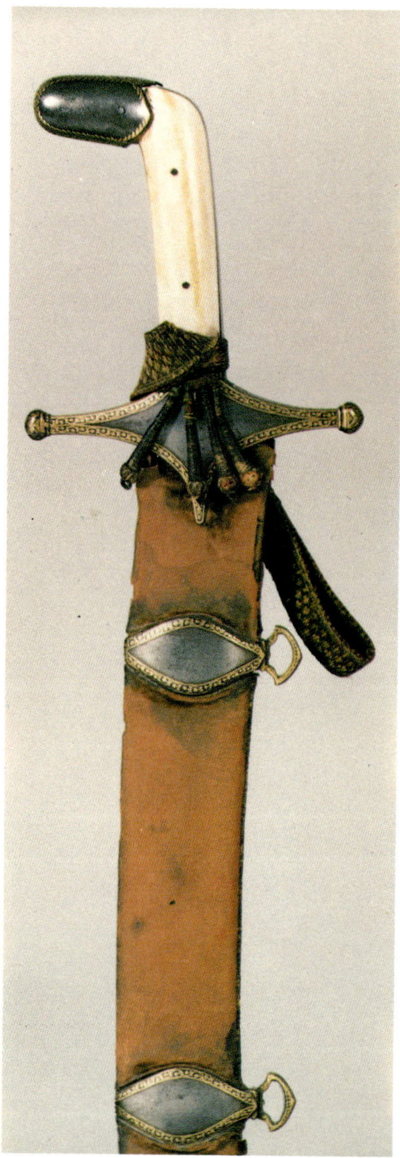

807

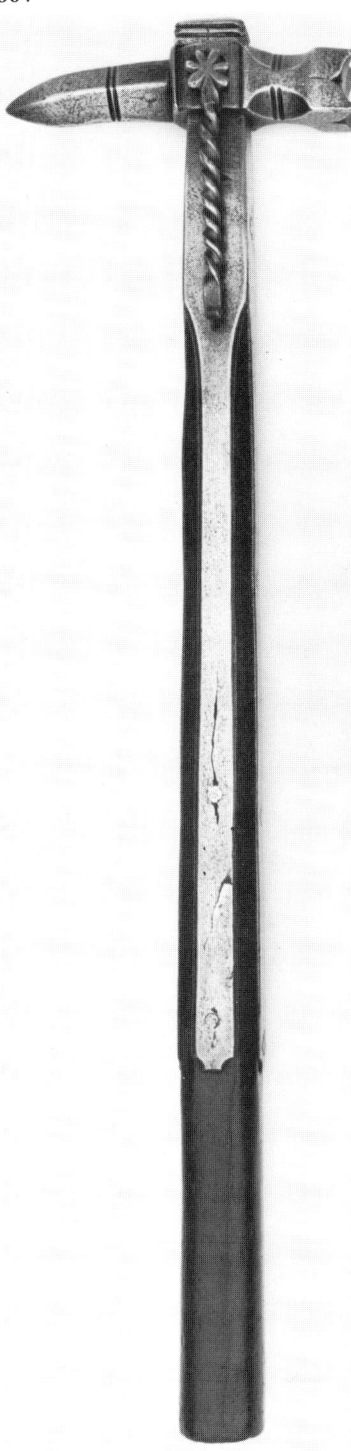

807. German horseman's war hammer
Length 20½ins. (52cm)
Second half 15th century
The head, with spirally twisted saddle hook, mounted on a wooden haft. A fine example in good condition.
£1,200 — £1,800

808

808. German horseman's war hammer
Length 24½ins. (62.2cm)
Second half 15th century
The head is inlaid with brass and probably originally had a spike mounted above. Later studded cloth-covered haft.
£1,000 — £1,500

810

809. German horseman's war hammer
Length 25ins. (63.5cm)
16th century
A good example.
£1,000 — £1,500

809

810. Saxon horseman's hammer
Length 21ins. (53.3cm) First half 17th century
A fine example with saddle hook and copper wire-bound blackened grip.
£3,000

Photographs: 807 and 810 Sotheby's; 808 and 809 Christie's

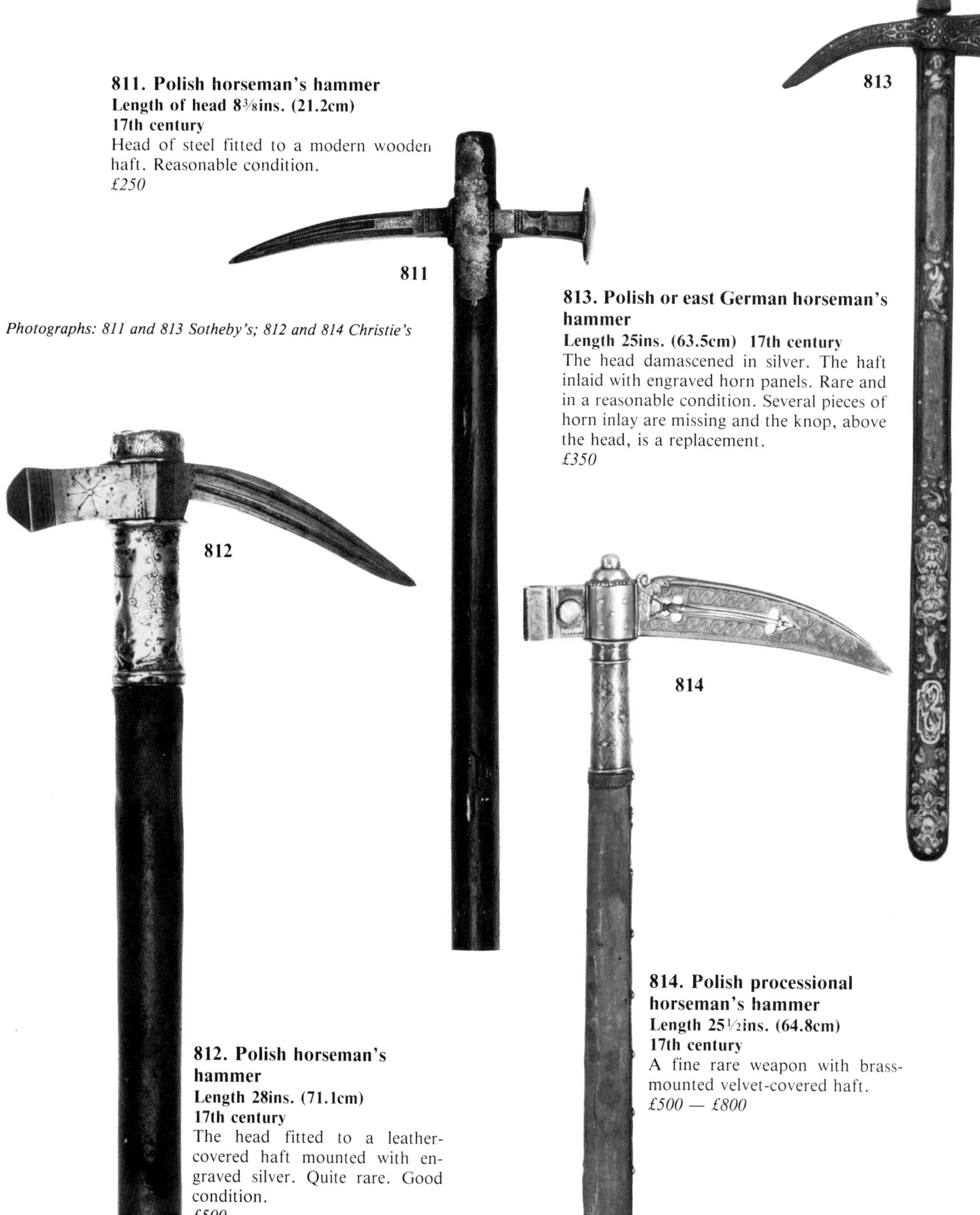

811. Polish horseman's hammer
Length of head 8⅜ins. (21.2cm)
17th century
Head of steel fitted to a modern wooden haft. Reasonable condition.
£250

Photographs: 811 and 813 Sotheby's; 812 and 814 Christie's

813. Polish or east German horseman's hammer
Length 25ins. (63.5cm) 17th century
The head damascened in silver. The haft inlaid with engraved horn panels. Rare and in a reasonable condition. Several pieces of horn inlay are missing and the knop, above the head, is a replacement.
£350

814. Polish processional horseman's hammer
Length 25½ins. (64.8cm)
17th century
A fine rare weapon with brass-mounted velvet-covered haft.
£500 — £800

812. Polish horseman's hammer
Length 28ins. (71.1cm)
17th century
The head fitted to a leather-covered haft mounted with engraved silver. Quite rare. Good condition.
£500

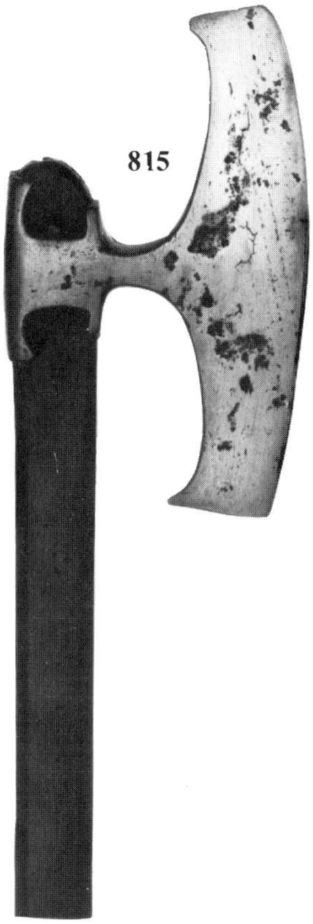

815

815. German fighting axe
Length of head 10½ins. (26.7cm)
14th century
Patches of wear on the plain blade. The haft later.
£450

816

816. North European fighting axe
Length of head 7¼ins. (18.4cm) 15th century
The pitted head struck with a crescent moon mark. Later haft.
£400

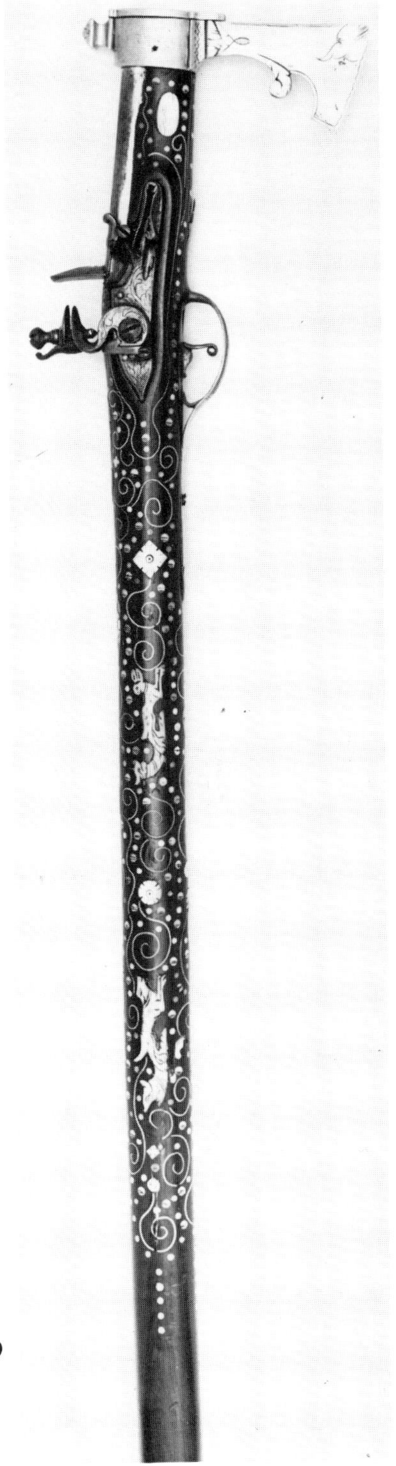

Photographs: 815-818 Christie's; 819 Sotheby's

818

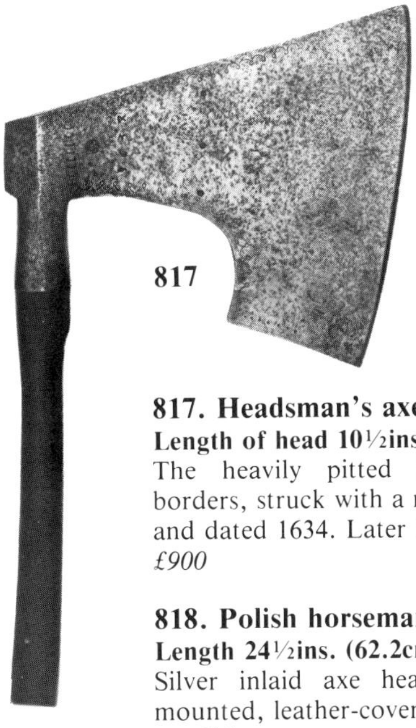

817

817. Headsman's axe, probably German
Length of head 10½ins. (26.7cm) Dated 1634
The heavily pitted blade with engraved borders, struck with a mark (a star in a circle) and dated 1634. Later haft.
£900

818. Polish horseman's axe
Length 24½ins. (62.2cm) 17th century
Silver inlaid axe head fitted to a brass-mounted, leather-covered wooden haft. Good condition.
£200 — £300

819

819. Silesian fokos (combined ceremonial axe and flintlock gun)
Length 50ins. (127cm)
Late 17th/early 18th century
Brass axe head with restored muzzle cover. The wooden haft inlaid with engraved horn and mother-of-pearl. Quite rare. Good condition.
£1,200 — £2,000

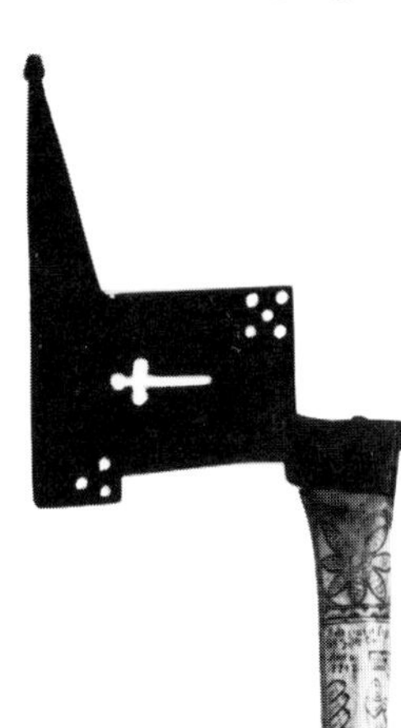

820

820. Saxon Miner's Guild processional axe
Length 32ins. (81.3cm) Dated 1717
A good example of a characteristic and familiar piece. The haft of engraved stag horn.
£300 — £400

821

821. Persian all-steel horseman's axe
Length 26ins. (71cm)
16th or 17th century
The blade damascened in gold. Fine quality.
£1,000

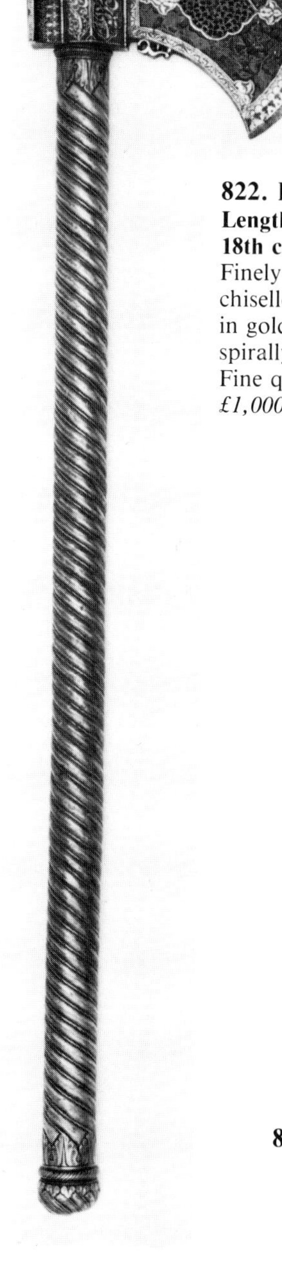

822

822. Indian tabar
Length 25⅝ins. (67.5cm)
18th century
Finely pierced and chiselled, and damascened in gold. The steel haft spirally turned and gilded. Fine quality.
£1,000 — £1,200

823

Photographs: 820 and 821 Christie's; 822 Sotheby's; 823 Robert Hale Antiques Ltd.

823. North Indian tabar
Length 26ins. (66cm)
18th century
Of plain form inscribed in Urdu on the block. Wood haft.
£95

Axes/Ankus

824. Central Indian armour-piercing horseman's war axe
Early 18th century
Curved reinforced blade of crow-bill form, surmounted by two crouching lions. The hammer in the form of a trumpeting elephant. Painted wooden haft with iron core. Good quality.
£175

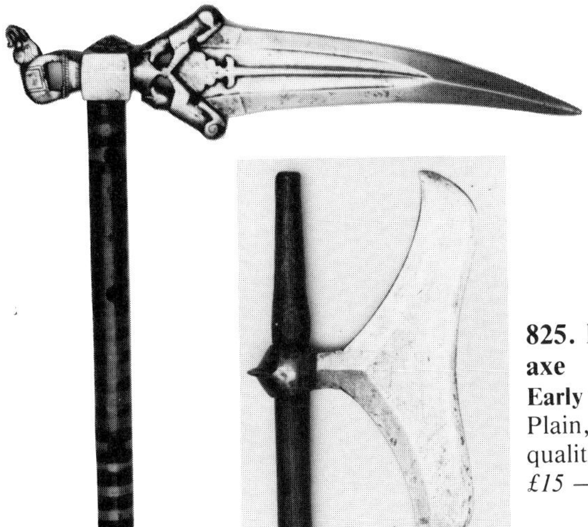

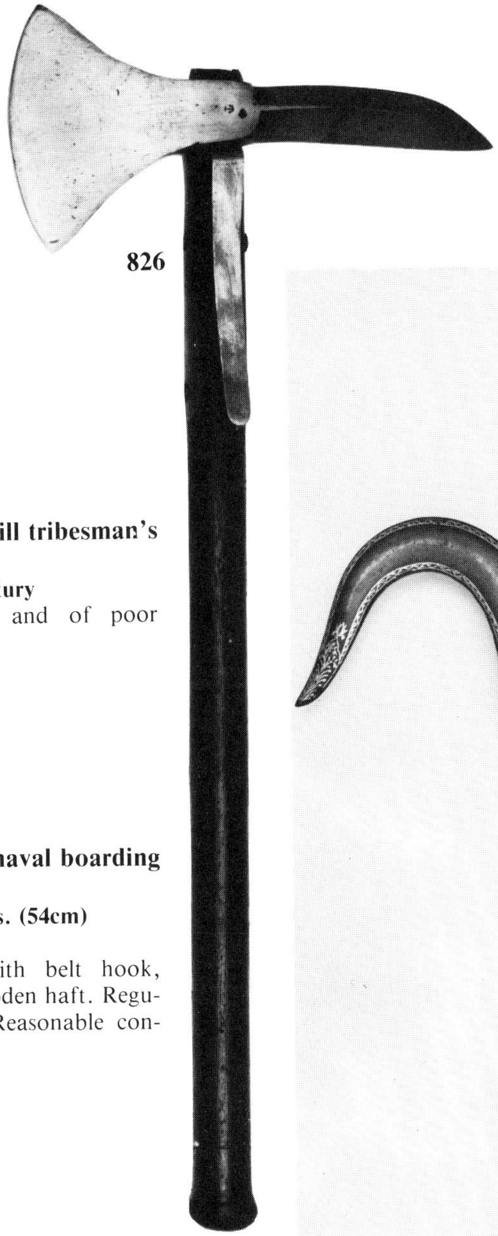

826

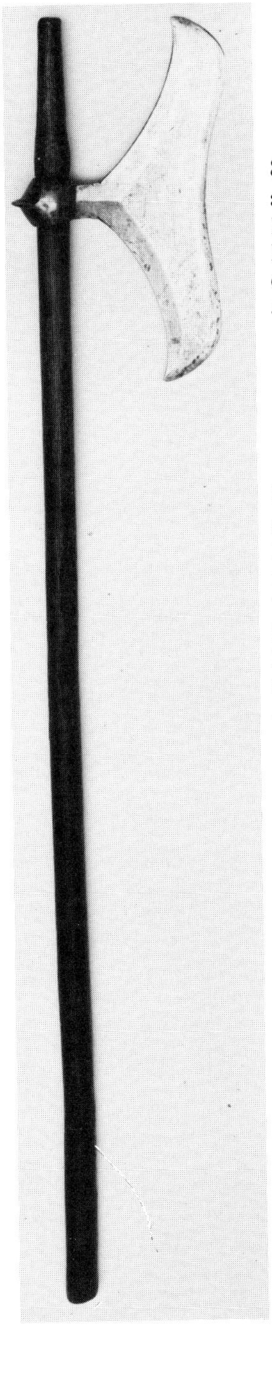

827

825. Indian hill tribesman's axe
Early 19th century
Plain, simple and of poor quality.
£15 — £25

826. French naval boarding axe
Length 21¼ins. (54cm)
19th century
The head, with belt hook, fitted to a wooden haft. Regulation issue. Reasonable condition.
£50 — £60

Photographs:
824-825 Robert Hales Antiques Ltd.;
826-827, Sotheby's

824

827. Indian jade-hafted ankus
Length 15¼ins. (38.7cm)
18th century
Gold damascened head and socket. The green jade haft mounted with a gold band set with rubies and diamonds. This fine quality example was reputedly owned by Tippoo Sultan, killed when British troops stormed Seringapatam in 1799.
£1,200 — £1,500

825

GLOSSARY

A.H. *Anno Hegirae* — in the year of the Hegira (A.D. 622). Mohammed's flight from Mecca to Medina marks the beginning of the Islamic calendar.

A LA MONTMORENCY. A curved single-edged blade with one shallow and one narrow fuller on each side, for example the blade on sword 264.

ANKUS. An Indian bladed instrument, often highly decorative, used for goading elephants.

ARMING SWORD. A military fighting sword in use from the late 15th century to the 17th century.

ARMS OF THE HILT. The two half-circular guards below the quillons (see Terminology). Until recently known as the *pas d'ane,* which probably originally meant one of the two shell guards found, for example on a small-sword or military-hilted sword (see Blair, 1962, v, and Norman, 15-17).

ASSOCIATED. Part of a weapon (pommel, grip, blade, etc.) which is not original.

AWL-PIKE (Ahlspiess). 15th and 16th century infantry thrusting spear with a long spike fitted to a haft. Often a disc guard is fitted at the base of the spike to protect the hand. Used also for foot combat in the lists.

BACK PLATE, BACK PIECE OR BACK STRAP. Metal plate on the back of the grip extending from the pommel to the guard. On military and naval swords, the back plate is usually integral with the pommel (see Terminology).

BACKSWORD. Military sword with a straight, single-edged blade. The other edge is blunted or has a back. The hilt is usually of the same design as a broadsword hilt.

BADE-BADE. Small single-edged knife used in the Malay archipelago. The sheath is usually characterised by a pronounced 'wing' near the opening.

BALLOCK-KNIFE/DAGGER. Phallic-like hilted weapon used in northern Europe, especially Flanders, England and Scotland, from the 14th to the early 17th century. In the 16th century known as a 'dudgeon dagger' because of its dudgeon (boxwood) hilt, and in the 19th century retermed a 'kidney dagger'.

BARDICHE. Distinct 16th and 17th century east European and Scandinavian infantry long-handled axe (see 780).

BASELARD. Knightly dagger with a distinctive hilt in the form of a capital letter I, and in use from the late 13th to the late 15th century. Originated probably in south Germany or Basel.

A Raja uses an ankus to goad his elephant during a hunting expedition. Indian (Bundi) about 1790. (Sotheby's.)

BASKET HILT. Sword hilt formed of bars and/or panels, which enclose the hand.

BASTARD SWORD. 15th and 16th century term for a hand-and-a-half sword.

BAYONET. A dagger for attaching to a gun barrel. The bayonet was named after the blade-producing centre of Bayonne in south-west France and was probably first used for hunting in the 16th and 17th centuries. By the last quarter of the 17th century most European armies had equipped their troops with bayonets so they could defend themselves after firing. The early plug bayonet had a tapered handle which fitted into the gun muzzle. This was soon replaced by the socket bayonet which fitted over the barrel enabling the gun to fire when the bayonet was attached.

BEAD-PATTERN HILT (also known as a five-ball hilt). A late 18th/early 19th century military and naval spadroon hilt of stirrup type, decorated with five regulated beads (or balls) on the knuckle guard and side ring. This hilt usually has a 'cushion' pommel and a grip of ivory or ebony. Bead-pattern hilted naval dirks are decorated in a similar way, but do not have a knuckle guard.

BICHWA, BICH'HWA (scorpion). Indian dagger with a looped hilt and a double curved blade. Some examples have a double-pronged blade (see 736). So named because the blade is said to resemble the sting of a scorpion.

BILBO HILT. Distinctive Spanish broadsword hilt with two large plate guards (shells) curved towards the pommel, as well as quillons, arms and knuckle guard. The name derives from the northern Spanish port of Bilbao.

BILL. Probably one of the earliest of all staff weapons. It was developed from the agricultural pruning hook and sickle, and was in use from the 11th-17th century.

BLUEING. Attractive dark blue effect achieved by heating steel and quenching when the required shade of colour is reached. Blueing is found on weapons of high quality, and was often used as a background to gold or silver decoration. It also helped to prevent rusting. Chemical blueing processes were introduced in the 19th century and some modern weapons such as shotguns, rifles and bayonets have their metal parts blued. Antique weapons can be reblued and this is not always easy to detect. Unless the weapon has a known provenance, hilts which have all their blueing should be regarded with caution. If, for example, parts of the metal show corrosion but the blueing is almost perfect, it is likely that the object has been chemically recoloured.

BOAT-SHELL HILT. Hilt on a small-sword and on some military swords (for example 184) which has a heart-shaped guard which splits on the upturned side to accommodate the forward quillon.

BOWIE KNIFE. A robust hunting and all-purpose knife named after the American frontiersman and Indian fighter Colonel James Bowie (1795-1836). The original knives were made in the southern states of America, but from the 1830s until the decline of the true Bowie, after about 1880, large quantities of big hunting knives (called Bowies) were exported from the steel-making centres of England (notably Sheffield) and the Continent (see Peterson, 1968, 70-5).

BRANDISTOCK. Staff weapon with one or more spikes concealed in the tubular haft and released by jerking the weapon forward (see 792 and 793).

BROADSWORD. Military sword with a straight, wide, two-edged blade.

BYKNIVES (Scottish *bykniffis*). The small companion knives accompanying a sword or dirk and decorated *en suite*.

CALENDAR SWORD. Sword with a blade etched with a perpetual calendar, often involving saints' days and signs of the zodiac.

CARRIER. A metal clip, with two chains linked to the scabbard lockets, which fitted over the waistband of the trousers when wearing a small-sword.

CASE OF SWORDS (or pair of swords). Two swords, flattened on one side of each hilt, which clip together and fit into a single scabbard and give the appearance of one. The rarest examples are cases of duelling rapiers. One rapier was held in the left hand for parrying.

CHAPE. Metal mount or cap fitting over the tip of the scabbard (see Terminology).

CINQUEDEA. Italian civilian short sword/dagger which developed during the second half of the 15th century (probably in northern Italy) and lasted until about 1520. The name derives from the Italian for five fingers (*cinque diti*) denoting the width of the blade below the quillons, although Florio's explanation (*New World of Words,* 1611) is that the term referred to a Venetian dagger with a blade five fingers long. Genuine cinquedeas are rarely found for sale.

CLAYMORE (Gaelic *claidheamh mòr* = great sword). The 16th century Highland hand-and-a-half sword, with the down-turned quillons ending in quatrefoil finials.

CLIPPED POINT. The concave curve on a blade from the back edge to the point. This is seen most clearly on certain Bowie knives and falchions. Sometimes the curve has a 'false edge' (i.e. is sharpened).

COLICHEMARDE. A small-sword blade with a strong wide forte narrowing abruptly a third of the way down from the hilt.

COMBINED WEAPON. Usually an edged weapon fitted with a gun mechanism or pistol.

CORSEQUE. A staff weapon with three-bladed head (see 785). Also known by the modern French term *chauve-souris*.

COUNTER GUARDS. The guards on a sword (particularly a rapier) consisting of side rings, arms of the hilt and inner guards, devised to counter, or prevent, an opponent's blade from wounding the hand.

COURT SWORD. A light dress sword of late small-sword form, usually with a knuckle guard, single quillon and single shell guard turned down towards the blade.

CROSS HILT OR CRUCIFORM HILT. The simplest and earliest form of hilt with a guard formed of a single bar (the cross or quillons). The cross can be straight or its two sides can be arched towards the blade.

CUP HILT. Spanish and Italian rapier hilt of the 17th and 18th centuries, comprising hemispherical cup guard, long quillons and knuckle guard. The cup hilt was the best designed guard for duelling as the cup adequately protected the swordsman's hand from an opponent's sword thrust.

CUTLASS. A regulation naval short sword with a straight or slightly curved blade.

CUTTOE. English 18th century hunting hanger of elegant form derived from the French *couteau-de-chasse*. In saleroom catalogues usually referred to as a 'hunting hanger'.

CYPHER. Interlaced initials forming a monogram. The one most frequently found on edged weapons is the royal cypher, for example, V.R. for Victoria Regina.

DAISHŌ ('large-small'). The two weapons, one large (*tachi* or *katana*) and one small (*tanto* or *wakizashi*), worn by the *samurai*.

DAMASCENING. The technique of inlaying precious metal into steel. Two forms exist. 'True' damascening has the design cut into the surface and gold or silver hammered securely into V-shaped grooves. 'False' or 'counterfeit' damascening has the precious metal laid on to a design drawn on a hatched surface. The second technique is more common but less permanent, as the design can be worn or rubbed away.

DHA. The national sword of Burma, with a curved single-edged blade and guardless hilt.

DIRK. A Scottish dagger which developed from the medieval ballock knife during the second half of the 17th century. Early hilts were made of heather root and the blades cut down from sword blades. The term is also given to certain Mediterranean knives, and to daggers carried by naval officers from the late 18th century onwards.

DISH HILT. The hilt on a duelling rapier with a saucer-shaped steel guard, long quillons and occasionally a knuckle guard. Introduced about 1625, it was the most effective guard for defending against the thrust before the appearance of the cup hilt.

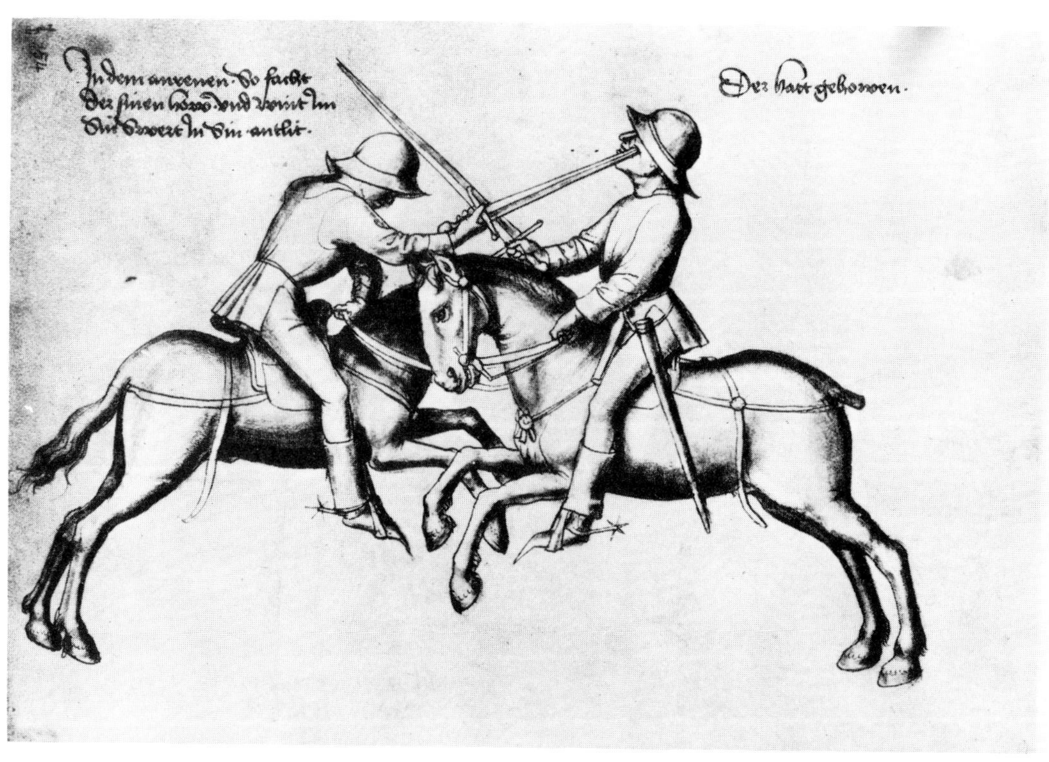

Horsemen using cross-hilted swords from Talhoffer's Fechtbuch aus dem Jahre 1467, *published by G. Hergsel, Prague, 1887.*

DOUBLE-EDGED BLADE. A blade sharpened along both edges. A two-edged blade.

DRESS SWORD. A sword worn on special occasions, such as military reviews, royal birthdays, etc. Not used on active service.

EAR DAGGER. A collectors' term for a dagger with a pommel formed of two splayed discs. Near Eastern in origin, it was produced in Spain and Venice from the 14th to the 16th century. Genuine examples are rare.

EARS. (1) The projections from the back plate on some military swords which support and secure, by riveting, the grip to the tang (see Terminology). (2) Double langets.

ECUSSON. The small triangular extension from the quillon block found on the medieval cross hilt. This fitted into a similarly shaped recess on the scabbard to prevent damp and rain ruining the blade.

ENCRUSTING. The process of securing precious metal (usually silver) on to iron to be chiselled or engraved. It differs from damascening in that it stands proud of the surface.

EN SUITE. 'The same way as . . .' Normally refers to one part of a weapon or object being decorated the same way as another part.

ESTOC. See Tuck.

EXCAVATED CONDITION. The condition of a weapon which has been dug up from the ground or river bed, and has lost most of its original finish and fittings.

FAIBLE. The part of a sword blade furthest from the hand, extending about two-thirds up from the point.

FALCHION. A short sword with a single-edged curved blade with a 'clipped point'. The much rarer medieval falchion has a broad chopper-like blade.

FALSE EDGE. Part of the back edge of a blade (about one-third from the point) which, instead of being blunt, is sharpened.

FERRARA, ANDREA. North Italian, 16th century, swordmaker from Ferrara whose name (in a variety of spellings) appears on sword blades of the 17th and 18th centuries. These later blades were almost certainly of German manufacture but marked with a name which indicated quality.

FERRULE. A woven wire band (often in the form of a Turk's head knot) or metal band or cap, placed at one or either end of the grip to secure the grip binding and help stabilise the grip (see Terminology).

FIRANGI, PHIRANGI ('foreign'). An Indian sword hilt (usually of khanda type) fitted with a European blade.

FIVE-BALL HILT. See bead-pattern hilt.

FLAMBOYANT BLADE. Blade with waved or undulating edges.

FORTE. The strongest part of the sword blade, extending about one-third of the way down from the hilt.

FORTY STEPS. See Kirk Nardaban.

FRESH. A trade term describing an object in very good condition.

FROG. A loop attachment for carrying a sword or bayonet from the belt. It is attached to the frog button (a metal lug) on the locket or sheath.

FULLER. A channel or groove on a sword or dagger blade which lightened, without weakening, the blade.

GARNITURE. A set of two or more objects made to match each other.

GISARME. A rare staff weapon with a large crescent-shaped axe blade (see 781).

GLAIVE. Staff weapon with a long knife-like blade socketed to a haft (782-4).

GOTHIC HILT. A modern term for the hilt of the 1822 pattern British infantry officer's sword, which has cast and pierced decoration resembling stone tracery on Gothic windows. The 'solid Gothic-hilt' (found on the 1827 naval pattern) has a similar guard but is not pierced.

GRIP. The part of the hilt which is held, known as the 'handle' until the 18th century.

GRIPS. A technical term to describe two scales or plaques of ivory, ebony, horn, stone, etc., which are riveted on either side of the tang and thus form the grip.

GUARDAPOLVO (dust guard). The plate or washer inside the cup-guard on a cup hilt rapier.

HAFT. The handle of wood or metal fitted with a metal head to form a staff weapon. Sometimes described as a shaft or pole.

HALBERD. A long staff weapon for foot soldiers, with an axe blade balanced by a fluke and with a spike above. Used from the end of the 14th century until the 16th century, and for processional purposes until the 18th century.

HALF-BASKET HILT. A sword hilt, formed of a series of bars and/or plates, which does not entirely enclose or protect the hand. The majority are constructed to defend the right side, or outside, of the hand.

HAMMER. (1) Pole hammer for use by infantry, or for foot combat in the lists.
(2) Horseman's war hammer. A knightly weapon with a hammer head balanced by a pick for piercing armour.

HAND-AND-A-HALF SWORD. A sword with a lengthened grip (in use from the mid-13th to 16th century) to enable the swordsman to use one or both hands if necessary. The grip is too short to take a second hand but, by overlapping on the pommel, a forceful blow could be struck. Known also as a bastard sword.

HANGER. (1) An all-purpose short sword with a short, straight or slightly curved, single-edged blade, which hung from a belt. The hanger was in use from the late medieval period until the 18th century, and was favoured by hunters, travellers and naval officers until regulation swords were introduced.
(2) A triangular shaped attachment for carrying a rapier. It was attached to the waist belt by a hook.

HILT. The upper part of a sword or dagger comprising pommel, grip and guard (see Terminology).

HOLBEIN DAGGER. See Swiss dagger.

HOLY WATER SPRINKLER. A club with a spiked head (see 796). The type known since the 17th century as 'Henry VIII's walking staff' (797) is a mace or club with four matchlock gun barrels enclosed in the head.

HOUNSLOW. A sword factory established at Hounslow in Middlesex by two German smiths, Henry Hoppie and Peter English, in 1629. It was particularly active during the 1630s and 40s producing the distinctive silver-encrusted hilted rapiers and hangers, and also 'Mortuary' hilted cavalry swords. The Hounslow factory apparently did not survive the English Civil War.

I.H.S. A sacred monogram standing for the first three letters of *Ihsus* (Greek for 'Jesus'). It is frequently found on 16th and 17th century sword blades.

INNER GUARDS. One or more bars on the inner side of the hilt intended to protect the inside of the hand, wrist and forearm from an opponent's blade (see Terminology).

JACOBITE SWORD BLADES. Blades found on Scottish basket-hilted swords etched with inscriptions and devices supporting James Stuart, the Old Pretender (1688-1766). The first group, known as Anti-Union blades, calls for the repeal of the Act of Union (1707) between the parliaments of Scotland and England, and proclaims for King James VIII. These can be dated up to the 1715 rebellion. The so-called 'Rhyming blades' can be dated to the time of the 45 rebellion and proclaim James III of Great Britain. The blades were almost certainly made in Germany and exported to Scotland. The Jacobite sentiments ended when the Scots were defeated at Culloden in 1746 (see Wallace, 25-26; illus. 27 and 28).

JAMBIYA. Arab dagger with curved two-edged blade. The form of the hilt varies but generally it is in the form of a capital letter I, with the pommel usually the same width as the guard.

JAPANNING. Blackening of sword hilts by a process of coating with black varnish which was heat dried and then often decorated with gold, etc. Japanning, as well as being decorative, prevented rusting.

KARABELA. A Polish sabre with stylised bird's-head grip fitted with two plaques of horn, ivory, etc., riveted to the tang. The quillons are straight with flattened or down-turned tips. No knuckle guard. Turkish in origin, the oldest karabelas in Poland were captured from the Turks at Vienna in 1683 (see J. Ostrowski with W. Bochnak 'Polish sabres: their origin and evolution' in Held, 1979).

KARD. A near-eastern dagger of Persian origin. Examples are usually of good quality with a stone or ivory hilt, and a watered-steel blade. The sheath is sometimes as long as the dagger.

KASKARA. A cross-hilted sword from the Sahara and the Sudan, often fitted with an earlier European blade. Most examples are from the 19th century and of poor quality.

KASTANE. The national sword of Ceylon.

KATANA. Japanese fighting sword carried, when not in use, by being thrust through the girdle.

KATAR. An Indian thrusting dagger with a hilt fitted with two side bars and two parallel bars for gripping. Some examples are fitted with a plate guard. Some have a blade which opens into three prongs when the grip is pressed; and others have a smaller katar which fits inside a larger one.

A portrait of Maharana Pratap Singh II of Mewar (1752-55), holding a tulwar and wearing a katar in his waistband. Indian (Mewar) dated 1753. (Sotheby's.)

KHANDA. Indian sword of distinctive form with a padded hilt with a plate guard and wide knuckle guard, and a spike extending from the pommel. Blades are of spatula form usually with reinforced edges.

KHANJAR. Persian and Indian dagger, often of fine quality, with an ivory, crystal or jade hilt of 'pistol' form, or carved with an animal's head. The blade has a gentle double curve.

KHANJARLI. Indian dagger of characteristic form with double-curved blade.

KHYBER KNIFE. North Indian or Afghan dagger/knife of distinct form. Blades have a rigid T-shaped rib down the straight back edge and a concave curved cutting edge.

KILIJ. Turkish sabre, one of the two major near-eastern types (the other being the shamshir) and the one correctly described as a 'scimitar'. The kilij and shamshir can be distinguished by their blades. The kilij blade is curved and blunted along the back edge for about two-thirds of its length from the hilt. At this point the blade noticeably widens and is sharpened (a 'false edge') and runs in a straight line to the point.

KINDJAL. Caucasian dagger with a straight two-edged blade. The hilt and scabbard are often decorated with silver and niello.

KIRK NARDABAN ('Forty Steps'). A pattern of rungs or vertebrae found on some of the finest near-eastern and Indian blades. The pattern is also sometimes described as 'Mohammed's Ladder' or 'the Ladder of the Prophet'.

KLEWANG. A commonly found south-east Asian single-edged knife/dagger. The pommel is usually turned to one side (see 735).

KNIGHTLY SWORD. A one-handed cross-hilted sword, part of a knight's equipment from the 12th to the 15th century.

KOFTGARI. Indian term for the technique of 'false' damascening. The area to be decorated is scratched with a file to act as a key for the silver and gold decoration which is pressed into the lines of the design. Hilts decorated with koftgari work are often worn and rubbed. These contrast strongly with fine examples of 'true' damascening which is found on 18th century swords exported to Europe.

KORA. The national sword of Nepal (see 544).

KORAMBI. A small Sumatran disembowelling or ripping dagger with a horn hilt with finger loop and a short razor-sharp, sickle-like, blade.

KRIS. Characteristic dagger/short sword of the Malay peninsula with carved wood, ivory or bone hilt, and laminated blade often with waved edges.

KUKRI. All-purpose knife of the Nepalese Gurkha.

Portrait of Nawab Sa'adat-Ullah Khan holding a khanda. Indian (Deccan) about 1720. (Sotheby's.).

LANCE. A horseman's spear. The long war and jousting lances of the medieval period and the later cavalry lances are rarely found at auction. The knight's lance was made of wood with a small steel head and fitted with a disc guard (vamplate). Some swelled before and behind the hand. The cavalry lance of the 19th century is light and has a leaf-shaped blade (see 790).

LANDSKNECHT. A German or Swiss mercenary of the late 15th and 16th century.

LANGETS. (1) Small shield-shaped or tongue-like metal extensions on each side of the hilt below the cross guard (see Terminology). Like the *écusson,* the langets fit into a similarly shaped recess on the scabbard or locket to prevent rain ruining the blade. Double langets are the metal plates extending down over the blade and upward on to the grip. These are most clearly seen on Eastern sabres and Mameluke-hilted swords.

(2) Strips of metal, forged with the head of a staff weapon, which secure the head to the haft. Usually termed 'straps' today (see Terminology).

LEFT-HAND DAGGER. Parrying dagger held in the left hand during rapier and dagger play. In use in northern Europe from about 1550 until the 1620s, the left-hand dagger continued to be used in Spain and Italy, with the cup-hilt rapier, until the 18th century.

LINSTOCK. Artilleryman's staff with a fork-like head with match cord attached for igniting cannon. Some examples (see 794) have spear heads in the centre of the U-shaped fork.

LLOYDS PATRIOTIC FUND SWORDS. Gilt-mounted swords awarded by the Patriotic Fund (established at Lloyds coffee house in the Strand, London, 20 July, 1803) to those who had shown courage in the war against France. The swords were divided into three main grades: swords to the value of £100 for commanders and captains; £50 swords for lieutenants; and swords of £30 for mates and midshipmen. A special £100 sword was also presented to those captains who had taken part in the Battle of Trafalgar, 1805.

Most of the Lloyds swords were awarded to naval officers, but thirteen were given to officers in the Royal Marines and four went to army officers. Most were made by Richard Teed of Lancaster Court in the Strand. The design of the sword was taken from the 1796 pattern light cavalry sabre, and is virtually the same for all grades. It is the scabbard which clearly indicates the difference in sword value.

A printed card, enclosed in the sword case, explained the symbolism found on the hilt. The guard, in the shape of Roman fasces, symbolises national unity. This produces Herculean effort, shown by the club of Hercules which forms the knuckle guard. These efforts aided by wisdom (denoted by the serpent entwining the club) eventually lead to victory, symbolised by the skin of the Nemean lion on the grip. See D. Spalding, 'Trafalgar Swords of Honour' in Held, 1973; and May & Annis, Vol. 1, pp. 58-62.

LOCKET. Metal mount at the top of the scabbard or sheath near the opening (see Terminology). A middle locket (or middle band) is a second metal mount near the centre of the scabbard.

LONDON, CITY OF, SWORDS OF HONOUR. Presentation swords (usually accompanied by the freedom of the City) awarded by the Corporation of the City of London to officers who distinguished themselves during wartime. The practice began in 1797 and the first swords were awarded to those who had distinguished themselves in the war against France. They were of two kinds — swords valued at one hundred and two hundred guineas. The City's practice of awarding outstanding war leaders with a sword and the freedom of the City has continued into the 20th century.

LOOP-GUARD HILT. Sword hilt with a guard branching off from the knuckle guard and curling round in a loop to join the rear quillon.

MACE. A club, probably one of the oldest weapons known. Today, the most familiar example is the horseman's mace, sometimes made entirely of steel, and with a flanged head.

MAIN-GAUCHE. See left-hand dagger.

MAMELUKE HILT. European sword hilt modelled on eastern hilts, particularly those found on the shamshir and kilij. They are named after the line of Egyptian Mameluke sultans, who were in power when Napoleon invaded Egypt in 1798. The practice of wearing such swords in the British army may have originated from the Egyptian Campaign of 1801, or from service in India.

ME FECIT (Latin). 'Made me'.

MOPLAH. Characteristic sword/knife of the Mohammedans of the Malibar coast of India (see 542).

MORTUARY HILT. The distinctive half-basket hilt found on English cavalry swords used during the English Civil War, and so named (by modern collectors) because many examples are chiselled, often crudely, with bearded heads believed to represent Charles I. The portrait likenesses probably antedate the King's death in 1649.

MOUNTS. Ornamental metal parts of a scabbard or sheath, for example, the locket and chape.

MOURNING SWORD. 18th century small-sword with blackened hilt, and worn with black mourning dress.

MOUTH. Opening of the scabbard or sheath. Also known as the 'throat'.

NIMCHA. Arab sword with curved blade.

NODACHI. Japanese long slung sword (tachi).

PALLASH, PALLASK. Polish and Continental horseman's sword with a single- or double-edged straight blade. The Polish pallash has an open, sabre-like hilt, while the Danish regulation cavalry pallask, for example, has a hilt of half-basket type.

PAPPENHEIMER HILT. A collectors' term for a particularly distinctive and popular rapier and sword hilt named after the Thirty Years War cavalry leader, Gottfried Heinrich, Graf von Pappenheim (1594-1632). Typical features are a swept hilt fitted with three side rings below the hand on each side. The top ring is linked to the middle ring and this in its turn is filled by a pierced steel plate. The quillons are recurved horizontally and end in fish-tail finials. The pommel is often fig-shaped.

PARTISAN. Staff weapon with a tall blade surmounting two crescent-shaped lugs. The early form of partisan (before 1500) had a tall, narrow, triangular, shaped head without the distinctive side lugs.

PAS D'ANE. See Arms of the hilt.

PATA. Indian horseman's gauntlet sword. The long two-edged blade is usually of European manufacture.

PATTERN. A design of weapon officially approved and introduced into service. It is usually known by its year of adoption and by the arm of the service which used it; for example, Light Cavalry sword, 1796 pattern.

PESHKABZ. Indian and Persian dagger, similar to the Khyber knife, but usually with a gentle double-curved blade reinforced along the cutting edge and at the point.

PIHA-KAETTA. Characteristic knife of Ceylon, with carved wood handle, and mounted on the hilt and blade with silver.

PIKE. Very long spear (up to 22ft. long, 6.70m), used by disciplined foot soldiers (pikemen) formed into ranks to protect the halbardiers and musketeers from cavalry attack. The shorter 'half-pike' was used as a leading staff in the 16th and 17th centuries and the 'boarding pike' (about 6ft., 1.83m) was used until the 19th century. Pikes rarely appear for sale, although examples can be found in the major armouries.

PILLOW SWORD. Modern term describing a very light, small-hilted sword, worn as an alternative to the small-sword in the mid-17th century. The term derives from the belief that the sword was hung from the bed head in case of attack at night.

It is more probable that the contemporary term was 'scarf sword', which described a light sword worn hanging from the shoulder or waist sash (see Norman, 184). The typical features are short, rather stumpy quillons, fitted occasionally with a side ring.

PIPE-BACKED BLADE. Sword blade with a solid cylindrical rib running down the back edge for about two-thirds of its length. It was first used on the British Infantry Officer's sword, 1822 pattern, and later on the Naval Officer's sword, 1827 pattern. It was replaced by Wilkinson blades.

PITTING. Small holes on the surface of metal caused by rust. The rust can be removed but its destructive effects remain.

POLE ARMS. Alternative term for staff or hafted weapons.

POLEAXE. Long handled fighting axe for foot combat. A knight's weapon, the poleaxe had an axe-bladed head balanced by a hammer and with a spike above.

POLE HAMMER. Long handled weapon for foot combat with a pronged hammer head balanced by a fluke and with side lugs and spike above. Used also for knightly combat in the lists.

POMMEL. Shaped knob at the top of a sword or dagger hilt. It holds down the parts of the hilt and balances the sword blade (see Terminology).

Pole hammer combat from Talhoffer's Fechtbuch aus dem Jahre 1467, *published by G. Hergsel, Prague, 1887.*

PRESENTATION SWORDS. Swords awarded, from medieval times, for allegiance, friendship, service or valour. The practice was revived during the American War of Independence (1775-83) and during the Napoleonic Wars in Europe (1791-1815), and has continued down to today. Many swords are of the highest quality and were made by the finest craftsmen of the time. Often the presentation piece was based on a sword currently in fashion (such as the small-sword) which lent itself to a demonstration of artistic expertise. Alternatively, the sword was a more ornate version of a specific pattern of military or naval sword. In contrast, unadorned versions of specific types of swords were inscribed and presented as marks of respect to company leaders or members. Presentation swords are invariably inscribed with the name of the presenting body or person, the recipient's name, and the action or service for which the sword was given. This gives the weapon a provenance, which is often untraceable in other weapons.

PRISTINE. Term to describe an object in near perfect condition; as new.

PULOUAR. Indian sword of tulwar type with a curved blade and quillons arched towards the blade.

QUILLON BLOCK. The widened and reinforced centre of the cross bar (quillons) which is pierced to enable the tang of the blade to pass through (see Terminology).

QUILLON DAGGER. Modern term for a cross-hilted dagger. The most common of all dagger hilts, in use from the medieval period onwards.

QUILLONS. The cross guard on a sword hilt (see Terminology).

RAM DAO. North Indian and Nepalese sacrificial temple sword. Used for decapitating animals, particularly buffalo.

RAPIER. Civilian duelling sword, with long straight blade, used in northern Europe throughout the 16th and until the mid-17th century, and in Spain and parts of Italy until the 18th century. The origins of the rapier are not precisely known. The French term *epée rapière,* which gave the sword its name, is found first in a French document of 1474, but this term appears to have derived from the Spanish for robe or costume sword, *espada ropera,* used in The Peninsula in the 15th century (see Blair, 1962, 6-7; and Norman, 19-21). Certainly, by 1532 in England, *la rapière* was being defined as 'the Spannyshe sword', which lends support to the theory that the civilian duelling weapon of the 16th-17th century developed from the long, narrow-bladed sword worn in Spain in the late middle ages.

The rapier is probably the best known of all European edged weapons and one of the most sought after by collectors. It was a sword worn not only for offence but also as an accompaniment to male dress. Rapiers could denote wealth and status and many were decorated by the leading craftsmen of the time. Othmar Wetter in Dresden, Daniel Sadeler in Munich and Claude Sauvigny of Tours, are just three of the most renowned masters of the late 16th century, who could turn a rough piece of metal into a work of art. Blades were manufactured in towns close to sources of iron ore, such as Toledo, Milan and Solingen.

Rapier and dagger play from the late 16th century Traité d'escrime dédié au Roi Henri III *by G.A. Lovino of Milan. Facsimile edition, Bibliothèque Nationale, Paris, n.d.*

REGULATION SWORDS. Swords authorised for use by those in command of the armed forces. From the 18th century onwards, regulation swords are usually known by the date a specific pattern of sword was adopted for service.

REINFORCED POINT. The point of a blade enlarged and strengthened for piercing.

RICASSO. The unsharpened section of a blade immediately below the quillons, devised to allow the forefinger to cross the quillons and grip the blade without being cut on a sharp edge. This method of holding the sword enabled greater force to be given to a blow and more direction to be given to a thrust. Known from early times, the ricasso became common on medieval swords from the 14th century onwards, and is a particularly marked feature on the rapier (see Terminology).

RIDING SWORD. 16th and 17th century horseman's sword. The form of the hilt is often the same as on the rapier but the 'cut-and-thrust' blade is more robust.

ROMPEPUNTAS. The rim of the cup on a cup-hilt rapier which is turned outwards and towards the blade, and which was intended to trap momentarily the point of an opponent's blade.

RONDEL DAGGER. 14th-16th century knightly dagger with disc-shape metal guard, and often with a pommel of similar form.

RUNKELL, J.J. John Justus Runkell, a German, who was the chief importer of Solingen blades into England from about 1780 until 1808.

RUNNING WOLF MARK. A trade mark of the bladesmiths of Passau and Solingen.

RUSSETING (browning). The result of applying a corrosive solution to metal to produce a brown patination and so prevent rusting.

SABRE. Sword of eastern origin, with an elegantly curved single-edged blade. Usually a horseman's or light cavalry weapon.

SAIF. Arab sabre.

SAW-BACK BLADE. A blade cut with teeth down the back edge to enable the sword to be used as a saw.

SCABBARD. Protective cover for a sword blade usually made of wood and covered with leather, cloth, etc. Leather scabbards, without the wooden lining, are found on 18th century spadroons; and metal scabbards are found accompanying many regulation swords from the late 18th century onwards. The term is also often used to describe the sheath of a dagger or knife.

SCARF SWORD. See pillow sword.

SCHIAVONA. Distinctive basket-hilted sword carried by the *schiavoni*.

SCHIAVONI. Slavonic (Dalmatian) mercenaries in the service of the Venetian Republic.

SCIMITAR. Strictly speaking a kilij, although the term is often loosely applied to describe a near eastern, curve-bladed sword.

SCRAMASAX. North European all-purpose knife/short sword, in use from the 8th to the 14th century.

SHAGREEN. The skin of shark and ray fish ground flat and used on grips and scabbards.

SHAKUDO. A Japanese black alloy of copper and gold.

SHAMSHIR. The most elegant of the eastern sabres with a long, curved, single-edged blade. Persian in origin, the shamshir was also made in India, Turkey and other parts of the Near East.

Mounted warriors fighting with shamshirs, from an 18th century Persian epic manuscript. (Sotheby's.)

SHASHQUA. Cossack sabre decorated with silver and niello mountings on the hilt and scabbard. Military shashquas are less ornate being mounted in brass or gilt metal.

SHEATH. Protective covering for a knife or dagger and made in the same way as a scabbard, being lined with wood and overlaid with leather or cloth. Examples are found solely of leather and also of metal.

SHELL OR SHELL GUARD. A steel plate or plates fitted to the hilt to protect the hand and often shaped or fluted like a scallop shell. The original term probably meant a 'single shell guard' of the type found on hunting hangers.

SIDE RING. The ring guard extending outwardly at right angles from the quillon or quillon block. In the case of 'double side rings', the lower smaller ring guard extends from the arms of the hilt (see Terminology). Side rings are also known as 'ports.'

SINCLAIR SABRE. A 19th century term (still used by collectors) to describe a distinctive half-basket hilted German infantry sabre (see 346) of the type imported into Norway in the late 16th century. It was mistakenly believed that this sabre was the type of sword carried by Col. George Sinclair and his band of Scottish mercenaries on their fatal expedition to Scandinavia in 1612 (see Blair, 1962, 10).

SINGLE-EDGED BLADE. A sword or knife blade with one sharpened edge.

SKEAN DHU (Gaelic *sgian-dubh* — black knife). A small knife worn by Scotsmen in their stockings.

SLOTTED HILT. Hilt of the second half of the 18th century, with a wide metal guard and knuckle guard pierced and cut with longitudinal or crescent-shaped slots or holes. This hilt is invariably found on hangers.

SMALL-SWORD. The lighter, more manageable, sword which succeeded the rapier in the middle years of the 17th century, and which has remained in use as a court and dress sword. The small-sword, worn by men of rank as an accompaniment to male dress, evolved from a more scientific study of the art of fence in 17th century France. The design of the hilt is simple compared to the rapier, and the basic form of knuckle guard, arms, shell guards and one or two quillons essentially remained the same from about 1650 until the late 18th century.

SPADROON. An 18th century term describing a military or naval sword with a narrow, straight blade (usually single-edged) which could be used for both cutting and thrusting.

SPONTOON. A small variety of partisan, used as a leading staff by officers and later by sergeants from the late 17th to the 19th century.

STAFF WEAPON. A term to describe the many types of weapons which are fitted with a staff, pole or haft. The long-handled variety were known as staves until the 17th century.

STILETTO. A 17th century Italian dagger with a short robust blade designed for stabbing. Many examples have the hilts made of turned steel.

SWEPT HILT. A collectors' term describing a rapier hilt which has one or more branches extending from the knuckle guard and curving down and round to join the rear quillon, side ring or rear arm of the hilt.

SWISS DAGGER. Distinctive 16th century dagger of late baselard form, used in Switzerland and Germany and notable for its sheath, which was overlaid in gilt metal or silver and cast and chased with figurative scenes in relief. Often termed 'Holbein daggers' by collectors after the German artist Hans Holbein the Younger (1497/8-1543) who produced designs for sheaths, although other artists, such as Urs Graf and Heinrich Aldegrave, also did so. Genuine examples are extremely rare.

SWORD-BREAKERS. A modern term to describe devices, usually in the form of holes, struts or comb-like teeth, found on the blades of left-hand daggers for catching an opponent's blade in order to counter-attack. It is unlikely that rapier blades would have been broken by such devices.

Duelling with a small-sword from Angelo's The School of Fencing, *London, 1787.*

Two-hand sword fighting from Talhoffer's Fechtbuch aus dem Jahre 1467, *published by G. Hergsel, Prague, 1887.*

SWORD KNOT. A wrist cord or thong attached to a sword hilt to prevent the sword being lost during action, or when riding. On some military swords of the late 18th century onwards, a ring is fitted, or a slot is cut, at the top of the knuckle guard for attaching the cord.

SWORD-RAPIER. A modern term to describe a sword with a rapier-type hilt fitted with a robust, tapered blade used for both cutting and thrusting, and which could be used in the field.

TABAR. Indian horseman's battle axe.

TACHI. Japanese sword slung from a girdle.

TANG. The narrow continuation of the blade which is fitted with quillons, grip and pommel, and thus forms the core for the hilt. Tangs on medieval swords are clearly seen because the grip is usually missing (see Terminology).

TANTO. Japanese dagger about 10-14ins. long, carried by being thrust through the girdle.

THROAT. Entrance of a scabbard or sheath. Sometimes termed the 'mouth' (see Terminology).

THUMB RING. A metal loop, on the inner side of the hilt, linked to the quillon block and inner ring guard which gives purchase to the thumb when holding the sword and when delivering a blow.

TIRED. Trade term describing an object which is not in the best condition. The metal or wooden parts may be worn and the decoration, such as etching, gilding, etc., rubbed.

TRANSITIONAL SWORD. A modern term describing certain rapiers and small-swords made from about 1640-80. Usually the sword has a small-sword hilt and a long, fullered blade of flattened oval or hexagonal section, rather than a hollow ground blade.

TUCK (estoc). Sword with a long, rigid blade of hollow triangular, square or diamond section designed solely for thrusting.

TULWAR. Indian sabre of characteristic form with a flattened disc pommel and short quillons. Certain types of tulwar have extra guards fitted to the hilt. The most familiar of all Indian swords and the one which appears for sale in a wide variety of conditions and quality.

TURK'S HEAD. Turban-like ornamental knot of stranded wire used to secure the wire-binding at either end of the grip. See also Ferrule.

TWO-HAND SWORD. Sword with a lengthened grip to be wielded with two hands. The war sword of the 14th and 15th century was beautifully balanced; but in the 16th century two-hand swords became very long and unwieldy.

UNDRESS SWORD. A sword used on active service or general use, rather than one used for reviews, levées, etc.

WAKIZASHI. Japanese short sword.

WALLOON-HILT. A collectors' term to describe a 17th century north European military hilt with a knuckle guard, in-filled side rings on each side, and a thumb ring.

WATERED STEEL. Patterns produced by etching with acid blades which have been made from forging and reforging different qualities, hardnesses or different colours of steel.

WOODKNIFE. Large cleaver-like huntsman's knife, usually accompanied by dissecting and skinning implements and all fitting into a single sheath. Also known as a *trousse de chasse* and as *waidpraxe*.

YATAGHAN. Turkish sword of characteristic form with a distinctive double-curved blade, and a pommel formed of a twin or splayed ear design.

SELECT BIBLIOGRAPHY

Annis, P.G.W., *Naval swords: British and American naval edged weapons, 1660-1815,* London, 1970.

Ariès, C., *Armes blanches militaires françaises,* Paris 1966 (in progress).

Arms and Armour Society, *The Art of the Armourer,* Victoria and Albert Museum, 19th April-5th May, 1963.

Aylward, J.D., *The Small-sword in England, its history, its forms, its makers, and its masters,* London, 1945, revised 1960.

Bartocci, A. and Salvatici, L., *Armamento Individuale dell'esercito Piemontese e Italiano 1814-1914, Cavalleria Artigheria a Cavallo Treno di Provianda,* Florence, 1978.

Blackmore, H.L., *Hunting Weapons,* London, 1971.

Blair, C., *European and American Arms,* London, 1962, revised 1964.

Blair, C. *Three presentation swords in the Victoria and Albert Museum, and a group of English enamels,* Victoria and Albert Museum Brochure 1, London, 1972.

Boccia, L.G. and Coelho, E.J., *Armi bianche Italiane,* Milan, 1972.

Castle, E., *Schools and masters of Fence from the Middle Ages to the eighteenth century,* London, 1885, reprinted 1910, facsimile edition, York, Pennsylvania, 1969.

Davidson, H.R.E., *The Sword in Anglo-Saxon England,* London, 1962.

Dean, B., *The Metropolitan Museum of Art: Catalogue of European Daggers,* New York, 1929.

Dean, B., *The Metropolitan Museum of Art: Catalogue of European Court and Hunting Swords,* New York, 1929.

Dufty, A.R. and Borg, A.C.N., *European swords and daggers in the Tower of London,* London, 1974.

Elgood, R. (ed.), *Islamic Arms and Armour,* London, 1979.

German, M.C., *A guide to Oriental daggers and swords,* London, 1967, privately published.

Hayward, J.F., *Victoria and Albert Museum Swords and Daggers,* London, 1951, revised 1963.

Held, R. (ed.), *Arms and Armor Annual, Vol. 1,* Northfield, Illinois, 1973.

Held, R. (ed.), *Art, Arms and Armour, an international anthology, Vol. 1 1979-80,* Chiasso, Switzerland, 1979.

Hoffmeyer, A.D., *Middelalderens Tveæggede Svaerd,* Copenhagen, 1954.

Holmes, M.R., *Arms and Armour in Tudor and Stuart London,* The London Museum, 1970.

Kienbusch, C.O. von, *The Kretzchmar von Kienbusch Collection of Armor and Arms,* Princeton, N.J., 1963.

Laking, Sir Guy F., *Wallace Collection Catalogues: Oriental Arms and Armour,* London, 1914, revised edition 1964.

Laking, Sir Guy F., *A Record of European armour and arms through seven centuries,* 5 vols., London, 1920-2.

Mann, Sir James, *Wallace Collection Catalogues: European Arms and Armour, Vol. II, Arms,* London, 1962.

May, W.E. and Annis, P.G.W., *National Maritime Museum, Greenwich, Swords for Sea Service,* 2 vols., London, 1970.

Mollo, E., *Russian Military Swords, 1801-1917,* London, 1969.

Neumann, G.C., *Swords and Blades of the American Revolution,* Newton Abbot, 1973.

Nielsen, K.S., *Danske Blankvåben,* Copenhagen, 1978.

Norman, A.V.B., *The Rapier and Small-sword, 1460-1820,* London, 1980.

North, A., *An Introduction to European Swords,* H.M.S.O., 1982.

Oakeshott, R.E., *The Archaeology of Weapons: Arms and Armour from Prehistory to the Age of Chivalry,* London, 1960.

Oakeshott, R.E., *The Sword in the Age of Chivalry,* London, 1964.

Oakeshott, R.E., *European Weapons and Armour. From the Renaissance to the Industrial Revolution,* London, 1980.

Peterson, H.L., *The American Sword, 1775-1945,* New Hope, Pa., 1945, revised edition, published Philadelphia 1965, includes *American silver-mounted swords, 1700-1815.*

Peterson, H.L., *Daggers and Fighting Knives of the Western World, from the Stone Age till 1900,* London, 1968.

Rawson, P.S., *The Indian Sword,* London, 1968.

Robinson, B.W., *The Arts of the Japanese Sword,* London, 1961, second edition 1970.

Robson, B., *Swords of the British Army, the Regulation Patterns 1788-1914,* London, 1975.

Schneider, H., *Schweizer Waffenschmiede vom 15. bis 20. Jahrhundert,* Bern, 1976.

Seitz, H., *Kungl. Armémuseums Handböcker Svärdet och Värjan som armévapen,* Stockholm, 1955.

Seitz, H., *Blankwaffen I, Geschichte und Typenentwicklung im europäischen Kulturbereich von der prahistorischen Zeit bis zum Ende des 16. Jahrhunderts,* Brunswick, 1965; *Vol. II vom 16. bis 19. Jahrhundert,* Brunswick, 1968.

Stephens, F.J., *The Collector's Pictorial Book of Bayonets,* London, 1976.

Stone, G.C., *A Glossary of the Construction, Decoration and Use of Arms and Armor in all countries and in all times, together with some closely related subjects,* Portland, Maine, 1934.

Valentine, E., *Rapiers. An illustrated reference guide to the rapiers of the 16th and 17th centuries with their companions,* London, 1968.

Wallace, J., *Scottish Swords and Dirks. An illustrated reference guide to Scottish edged weapons,* Harrisburg, Pa., 1970.

INDEX

Numbers in medium type refer to page numbers. Numbers in bold type refer to the numbered illustrations in the book.